David Aucsmith (Ed.)

Information Hiding

Second International Workshop, IH'98
Portland, Oregon, USA, April 14-17, 1998
Proceedings

Springer

Series Editors

Gerhard Goos, Karlsruhe University, Germany
Juris Hartmanis, Cornell University, NY, USA
Jan van Leeuwen, Utrecht University, The Netherlands

Volume Editor

David Aucsmith
Intel Corporation
JF3-373
Hillsboro, OR 97124-5961, USA
E-mail: awk@intel.com

Cataloging-in-Publication data applied for

Die Deutsche Bibliothek - CIP-Einheitsaufnahme

Information hiding : second international workshop ; proceedings / IH '98,
Portland, Oregon, USA, April 14 - 17, 1998. David Aucsmith (ed.). - Berlin ;
Heidelberg ; New York ; Barcelona ; Hong Kong ; London ; Milan ; Paris ;
Singapore ; Tokyo : Springer, 1998
  (Lecture notes in computer science ; Vol. 1525)
  ISBN 3-540-65386-4

CR Subject Classification (1998): E.3, K.6.5, D.4.6, E.4, C.2, J.1, K.4.1,
K.5.1, H.4.3, H.3.4

ISSN 0302-9743
ISBN 3-540-65386-4 Springer-Verlag Berlin Heidelberg New York

© Springer-Verlag Berlin Heidelberg 1998
Printed in Germany

Typesetting: Camera-ready by author
SPIN 10692859   06/3142 – 5 4 3 2 1 0   Printed on acid-free paper

Preface

The mid-1990s saw an exciting convergence of a number of different information protection technologies, whose theme was the hiding (as opposed to encryption) of information. Copyright marking schemes are about hiding either copyright notices or individual serial numbers imperceptibly in digital audio and video, as a component in intellectual property protection systems; anonymous communication is another area of rapid growth, with people designing systems for electronic cash, digital elections, and privacy in mobile communications; security researchers are also interested in 'stray' communication channels, such as those which arise via shared resources in operating systems or the physical leakage of information through radio frequency emissions; and finally, many workers in these fields drew inspiration from 'classical' hidden communication methods such as steganography and spread-spectrum radio.

The first international workshop on this new emergent discipline of information hiding was organised by Ross Anderson and held at the Isaac Newton Institute, Cambridge, from the 30th May to the 1st June 1996, and was judged by attendees to be a successful and significant event. In addition to a number of research papers, we had invited talks from David Kahn on the history of steganography and from Gus Simmons on the history of subliminal channels. We also had a number of discussion sessions, culminating in a series of votes on common terms and definitions. These papers and talks, together with minutes of the discussion, can be found in the proceedings, which are published in this series as Volume 1174.

Delegates were unanimous in their wish to have further conferences on this topic, and so the second workshop was held in Portland, Oregon, in April 1998 under my chairmanship. I was well supported by a program committee consisting of Ross Anderson (Cambridge), Steve Low (Melbourne), Ira Moskowitz (US Navy Labs), Andreas Pfitzmann (Dresden), Jean-Jacques Quisquater (Louvain), and Michael Waidner (IBM), who helped select 25 papers from 41 submissions. The standard was extremely high.

These papers cover a wider range of topics than was the case in 1996, and show how this young field is growing. Papers describe the application of copyright marks to protect banknotes, software, and circuit designs, as well as new ways of hiding data in images; how to provide anonymity in applications from file systems to biometrics; how to hide information in everything from audio and video conferencing traffic to the stray RF emanations from personal computers; some significant improvements in the art of image marking; the use for the first time of techniques such as game theory in analysing systems; and a number of practical papers showing how existing marking and hiding systems can be attacked.

The papers in this volume must stand for themselves. However, we can see three directions of growth, all of them encouraging. Firstly, the range of applications in which information hiding techniques are being used is increasing. Secondly, we are starting to understand some of the earliest applications (such as hiding copyright marks in digital images) more deeply. And thirdly, as people find interesting new ways to break some of the first-generation schemes, we are starting to see the rapid coevolution of attack and defence, which has pushed forward the state of the art in such fields as cryptography, computer security, and electronic warfare.

The future of information hiding looks extremely promising.

Finally, I would like to thank Fabien Petitcolas of Cambridge for his invaluable assistance in helping me edit these proceedings, Gary Graunke at Intel for handling the administrative arrangements for the conference, and Intel Corporation for its sponsorship of this event.

October 1998   David Aucsmith
                                                    Program Chair
                                            Intel Architecture Labs
                                                 Portland, Oregon

Table of Contents

Steganography

Other Applications

Copyright Marking

Attacks

Theory

Information Hiding to Foil the Casual Counterfeiter

Daniel Gruhl and Walter Bender

Massachusetts Institute of Technology Media Laboratory

Abstract. Security documents (currency, treasury bills, stocks, bonds, birth certificates, etc.) provide an interesting problem space for investigating information hiding. Recent advances in the quality of consumer printers and scanners have allowed the application of traditional information hiding techniques to printed materials. This paper explores how some of those techniques might be used to address the problem of counterfeiting as the capability of home printers to produce "exact" copies improves.

1   Introduction

The appearance of commercial color photocopiers in the 1970's presented treasury departments around the world with a problem. No longer were special equipment and expertise required to produce passable reproductions of most currencies. Anyone with access to a copy store was a potential counterfeiter. Steps had to be taken to limit the possibility of a counterfeiting explosion.

The U.S. Treasury Department took a multi-pronged approach to deal with this problem [11,12,13]. First, they tried to make the bills themselves more difficult to copy. A combination of features were introduced, such as very fine engraving designed to alias noticeably when undersampled, watermarks, embedded plastic strips, and more recently, special inks that change color when light strikes them at different angles. The treasury sought to make it extremely difficult to produce reasonable copies of bills using color photocopiers.

While this approach is an effective deterrent, and in the end may be the right approach to the prevention of counterfeiting, there remains a problem. The U.S. government honors at face value any bill it has ever printed. Therefore, bills printed prior to the 1970's are still good. Thus, counterfeits of older bills might still be accepted, and those bills do not have as many security features as the new bills do. This is not as much of a problem as it might first appear, since paper money only has an active life of on average 18 months [11]. Until old bills leave common circulation, however, there is still a problem.

Two steps are being taken as intermediate measures. First, many modern color photocopiers have a circuit that tries to detect when a bill is being photocopied, and refuses to do so. This circuit seems to use a simple feature recognition on the image being copied to try to determine if it is a bill. It is, however, easy to defeat this system. One must speculate that this device is meant primarily to "protect people from themselves", forcing them to think about what they are doing when they first attempt to counterfeit a bill.

A second measure has been articulated by Representative Michael Castle, Republican of Delaware and chairman of the House of Representatives Subcommittee

David Aucsmith (Ed.): Information Hiding 1998, LNCS 1525, pp. 1-15, 1998.
© Springer-Verlag Berlin Heidelberg 1998

on Domestic and International Monetary Policy. Representative Castle has said that "practical and realistic" measures to tag scanners and printers must be considered, in order to identify the source of the counterfeit notes [14]. If copiers were to encode their serial number in continuous-tone images, possibly through modifications to the dithering algorithm, treasury agents would be able to identify which machine was used in the creation of a bogus bill. It would then be possible to "stake out" the photocopier in question and apprehend the culprits the next time they create some counterfeit cash.

The difficulty that treasury departments have been encountering in recent years is the proliferation of very good, very inexpensive color scanning and printing technology for personal computers [14]. A 720×720 color ink-jet printer lists for $200–$300, and a 300 DPI flatbed scanner for $75. Using these devices, it is possible to create color reproductions that exceed the quality of modern color copiers costing $20 000–$45 000.

The Problem

The problem addressed in this paper is how to find a way to bring the same kind of technologies that exist in modern color copiers to the realm of ink-jet printers. The second modification mentioned above, how can a serial number be hidden in an image, is a standard information-hiding problem. The first problem, can an encoding be placed in an image such that the printer can detect it and refuse to print it, is more challenging.

The problem space this presents differs from traditional information-hiding problems. Typically for images, an assumption is made that the image quality might be largely degraded in a signal-to-noise ratio sense (through perceptual coding such as JPEG [Joint Photographic Experts Group]), that arbitrary resampling might be done (through scaling), and that cropping is a possibility. Most commercial systems assume that the image presented to the decoder is not rotated, and often it must not have been translated. Further, there is often an assumption that the image will be in a similar color/luminance space to the original (RGB vs. CMYK for example).

For the money problem, an almost reverse set of circumstances prevails. The image quality sent to the printer is usually excellent. No one is going to make a bill that looks only a little like a real one, and then try to spend it. The size of the reproduction is fixed. Again, trying to spend a bill twice or half-normal size is unlikely to be successful. On the other hand, if someone can print the bill out at a 45 degree angle and defeat the system, it is likely that the will. The same applies to arbitrary translation. It is unlikely, however, that someone will radically crop a bill, as again this adversely impacts the chance of passing it successfully.

Additionally, since the typical consumer ink-jet printer has five to seven fixed colors to use (four to six inks and white from the paper) the image is dithered, trading spatial resolution for color depth. This process results in nonlinear modifications to the image in transferring it to paper. When the image is scanned in again, more nonlinear modifications are introduced, since the scanner acquires an RGB representation of what is scanned, usually at still another resolution, rotation, and translation.

A consideration for any encoding method intended to be embedded in a printer is how the printer "sees" what it is printing. This is usually a small number of lines at a time. A single pass for an ink-jet printer is typically 0.25"×8.5". Any processing should require only image data from one pass at a time.

Lastly, since such a method might be embedded in a $200–$300 consumer product, the encoder cannot be as expensive as one being placed in a $20000–$45000 color photocopier. Thus the method needs to be computationally inexpensive.

Paper Overview

The rest of this paper addresses potential solutions to the problems addressed above. Much of the work described in this paper is based upon a statistical method of data hiding, Patchwork [9]. This method is detailed in Section 2. In Section 3, Patch Track, a method of encoding a tracking number in an image is discussed. Section 4, Tartan Threads, deals with the more difficult problem of having a printer detect when it should refuse to print a document. This method employs direct-sequence spread spectrum (DSSS). In Section 5, experimental results are presented. The paper concludes with some observations of how these applications of information hiding differ from the more traditional ones and what the future might hold for these techniques.

2   Patchwork

Patchwork is a statistical method that will allow the detection of a single, specific bit in an image. Patchwork imperceptibly embeds in a host image a specific statistic, one that has a Gaussian distribution. This is usually interpreted as a watermark, in the sense "Is IBM's watermark in this image, yes or no?" By a single, specific bit, it is meant that the algorithm, when given a certain password, can tell if an encoding using that password has been embedded in the image. There are actually two possible encodings that can be made for a given password, a positive one and a negative one. For each encoding, it is also possible to assign a "confidence", or a measure of how certain it is that the image has been encoded with a particular bit, in a positive or negative sense. Patchwork is independent of the contents of the host image. It shows reasonably high resistance to most nongeometric image modifications.

The Patchwork algorithm [9,10] is detailed here. The following simplifying assumptions are made for the analysis presented here (these assumptions are not limiting, as is shown later): Patchwork is operating in a 256 level, linearly quantized system starting at 0; all brightness levels are equally likely; all samples are independent of all other samples.

The Patchwork algorithm proceeds as follows: take any two points, A and B, chosen at random in an image. Let a equal the brightness at point A and b the brightness at point B. Now, let

$$S = a - b \qquad (1)$$

The *expected* value of S is 0, i.e., the average value of S after repeating this procedure a large number of times is *expected* to be 0.

Although the *expected* value is 0, this does not reveal much about what S will be for a specific case. This is because the variance is quite high for this procedure. The

Standard Deviations Away	Certainty	n
0	50.00%	0
1	84.13%	679
2	97.87%	2713
3	99.87%	6104

Table 1. Degree of certainty of encoding given deviation from that expected in a Gaussian distribution (d = 2)

variance of S, σ_S is a measure of how tightly samples of S will cluster around the expected value of 0. To compute this, make the following observation: Since $S = a - b$ and a and b are assumed independent, σ_S^2 can be computed as follows (this, and all other probability equations are from Drake[12]):

$$\sigma_S^2 = \sigma_a^2 + \sigma_b^2 \tag{2}$$

where σ_a^2 for a uniform S is:

$$\sigma_a^2 \approx 5418 \tag{3}$$

Now, $\sigma_a^2 = \sigma_b^2$ since a and b are samples from the same set, taken with replacement. Thus:

$$\sigma_S^2 = 2 \times \sigma_a^2 \approx 2 \times \frac{(255 - 0)^2}{12} \approx 10836 \tag{4}$$

which yields a standard deviation $\sigma_S \approx 104$. This means that more than half the time, S will be greater than 43 or less than −43. Assuming a Gaussian clustering, a single iteration does not tell much. However, this is not the case if the procedure is performed many times.

Repeat this procedure n times, letting a_i and b_i be the values a and b take on during the ith iteration, S_i. Now let S_n be defined as:

$$S_n = \sum_{i=1}^{n} S_i = \sum_{i=1}^{n} a_i - b_i \tag{5}$$

The *expected* value of S_n is:

$$S_n = n \times S = n \times 0 = 0 \tag{6}$$

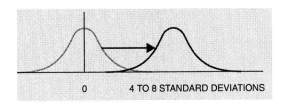

0   4 TO 8 STANDARD DEVIATIONS

Fig. 1.   As δ or n increases, the distribution of S_n' shifts further to the right.

This makes intuitive sense, since the number of times a_i is greater than b_i should be offset by the number of times the reverse is true. Now the variance is:

$$\sigma_{S_n}^2 = n \times \sigma_S^2 \qquad (7)$$

And the standard deviation is:

$$\sigma_{S_n} = \sqrt{n} \times \sigma \approx \sqrt{n} \times 104 \qquad (8)$$

Now, compute S_{10000} for a picture, and if it varies by more than a few standard deviations, it is fairly certain that this did not happen by chance. In fact, since as will be shown later S_n' for large n has a Gaussian distribution, a deviation of even a few σ_Ss indicates to a high degree of certainty the presence of encoding (see Table 1).

The Patchwork method artificially modifies S for a given picture, such that S_n' is many deviations away from expected. To encode a picture, we:
1. Use a specific key for a known pseudo-random number generator to choose (a_i, b_i). This is important, because the encoder needs to visit the same points during decoding.
2. Raise the brightness in the patch a_i by an amount δ, typically in the range of 1 to 5 parts in 256.
3. Lower the brightness in b_i by this same amount δ (the amounts do not have to be the same, as long as they are in opposite directions).
4. Repeat this for n steps (n typically ~10 000).
    Now, when decoded, S_n' will be:

$$S_n' = \sum_{i=1}^{n} (a_i + \delta) - (b_i - \delta) \qquad (9)$$

or:

$$S_n' = 2\delta n + \sum_{i=1}^{n} (a_i - b_i) \qquad (10)$$

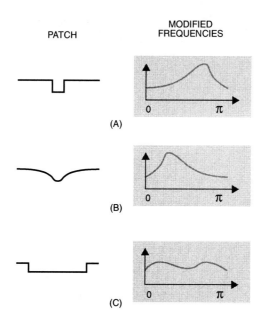

PATCH

MODIFIED
FREQUENCIES

(A)

(B)

(C)

Fig. 2. The contour of a patch largely determines which frequencies will be modified by the application of Patchwork.

So each step of the way an expectation of $2 \times \delta$ is accumulated. Thus after n repetitions, S'_n is expected to be:

$$\frac{2\delta n}{\sigma_{S'_n}} \approx 0{,}028\delta\sqrt{n} \tag{11}$$

As n or δ increases, the distribution of S'_n shifts over to the right (Figure 1 and Table 1). In Figure 1, as δ or n increases, the distribution of S_n shifts further to the right. If shifted far enough, any point that is likely to fall into one distribution is highly unlikely to be near the center of the other distribution.

While this basic method works well by itself, a number of modifications have been made to improve performance including:

1. Treating *patches* of several points rather than single points. This has the effect of shifting the noise introduced by Patchwork into the lower spatial frequencies, where it is less likely to be removed by lossy compression and typical Finite Impulse Response (FIR) filters. Additionally, it makes alignment easier.

2. Making Patchwork more robust by using a combination with either affine coding (described later) or some heuristic based upon feature recognition (e.g., alignment using the interocular line of a face). Patchwork decoding is sensitive to affine transformations of the host image. If the points in the picture visited during encoding are offset by translation, rotation, or scaling before decoding, the code is lost.

RECTILINEAR   HEXAGONAL   RANDOM

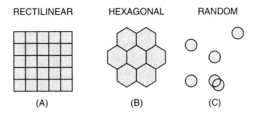

(A)   (B)   (C)

Fig. 3.   Patch placement affects patch visibility.

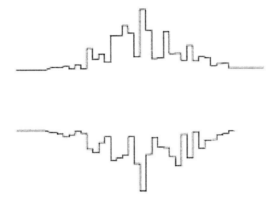

Fig. 4.   Random cone-shaped patch used with Patch Track method. The depth across the patch is chosen at random, but constrained to a cone of radius 15 and depth 10 for most of the experiments.

3. When decoding large patches, sampling all the points around the center point.
4. Using a visibility mask to avoid putting patches where they would be noticeable.
5. Superimposing a random mask on top of a cone-shaped patch to mask visibility (see Figure 4).

Patch Shape

The shape of the patches deserves some comment. Figure 2 shows three possible one-dimensional patch shapes, and next to them a very approximate spectrum of what a line with these patches dropped onto it pseudo-randomly would look like. In Figure 2A, the patch is very small, with sharp edges. This results in the majority of the energy of the patch being concentrated in the high frequency portion of the image spectrum. This makes the distortion hard to see, but also makes it a likely candidate for removal by lossy compressors and for the non-linear transforms introduced by dithering. If one goes to the other extreme, as in Figure 2B, the majority of the information is contained in the low-frequency spectrum. The last choice, Figure 2C, shows a wide, sharp-edged patch, which tends to distribute the energy around the entire frequency spectrum.

The optimal choice of patch shape is dependent upon the expected image modifications. If JPEG encoding or dithering is likely, then a patch that places its energy in

Fig. 5.   Patch Track on a one-dollar bill

the low frequencies is preferable. If contrast enhancement is to be done, placing energy in higher frequencies would be better. If the potential image modifications are unknown, then spreading the patch energy across the spectrum would make sense.

The arrangement of patches has an impact on patch visibility. For illustration, three possibilities are considered (Figure 3). The simplest method is shown in Figure 3A, a simple rectilinear lattice. While simple, this arrangement is often a poor choice if a high n is to be used. As the grid is filled in, continuous edges of gradient are formed. The human visual system (HVS) is very sensitive to such edges. A second choice, Figure 3B, breaks this symmetry by using hexagons for the patch shape. A preferred solution, shown in Figure 3C, is a completely random placement of patches. An intelligent selection of patch shape in both the horizontal and vertical dimensions will enhance the effectiveness of patchwork for a given picture.

Variance

In order to evaluate the likelihood that a bill is encoded, some idea of the variance of S_n is needed. In currency all luminance values are not equally likely. In U.S. currency there tend to be many white or black regions and few mid-tone regions.

While the variance differs for each sample, for decoding purposes it helps to choose a typical variance rather then recomputing the variance for each bill examined. S_n was calculated for 10000 seeds, using 10000 patch pairs and a 3×3 decoding area on both a one-dollar bill and a five-pound note. In both cases the full bill was examined by the decoder, rather than just a small patch. The variance of these S_n was then computed.

The variance of the dollar bill is $77\,621$. The variance of the pound note is $79\,105$. Allowing for the consideration of nine times as many points, it was found that these notes have a variance about 60% higher than an assumption of uniform variance would suggest. This can be corrected by simply encoding with 60% more depth.

Summary

There are several limitations inherent to the Patchwork technique. The first is the extremely low embedded data rate it yields, usually a one-bit signature per image. This limits its usefulness to low bit-rate applications such as the digital watermark. Second, it is necessary to *register* where the pixels in the image lie. While a number of methods have been investigated, it is still somewhat difficult to decode the image in the presence of severe affine transformations. These disadvantages aside, without the key for the pseudo-random number generator, it is extremely difficult to remove the Patchwork coding without degrading the picture beyond recognition.

The Patchwork method is subject to cryptographic attack if it is used to encode a large number of identically sized images using the same key. If the images are averaged together, the *patches* will show up as lighter or darker than average regions. This weakness is a common one in cryptography, and points to the truism that for a static key as the amount of traffic increases, it becomes easier to "crack" the encryption. One solution is to use multiple pseudo-random patterns for the patches. Even the use of just two keys, while increasing decoding time, will make Patchwork much more robust to attack. Another solution is to use the same pattern, but to reverse the polarity of the patches. Both solutions deter cryptographic attack by averaging.

3   Patch Track

If an image is printed on a particular printer, is it possible to figure out which printer was used given only a printed sample? This problem is addressed in color copiers by using a dither pattern that encodes the copier's serial number. This is not as practical for ink jet-type printers, where the dithering is usually done in software on a host computer, or on a plug-in card such as a Postscript processing module.

In seeking an alternative method, there are several constraints: such a method needs to be able to encode on the order of 32 bits in the target image to hold a serial number. The encoding needs to not impact image quality adversely. For analysis purposes, it should be possible to "find" these bits using a flatbed scanner of typical consumer resolution (600 DPI or less). And lastly, the encoding should be one that does not require extensive computational resources, since ultimately the goal would be to embed such an encoding method in the printer itself. (Perhaps the algorithm should be executable on a Microchip PIC16C84 microprocessor or similar chip). A simple modification of an existing information hiding technique, Patchwork meets these requirements.

Tracking bits are encoded in an image using a sequence of these positive and negative watermarks to encode the ones and zeros. For example, the "password" for the first bit might be "IBM0", the second bit "IBM1", etc. Since when using the Patchwork method, the embedded watermarks corresponding to different passwords

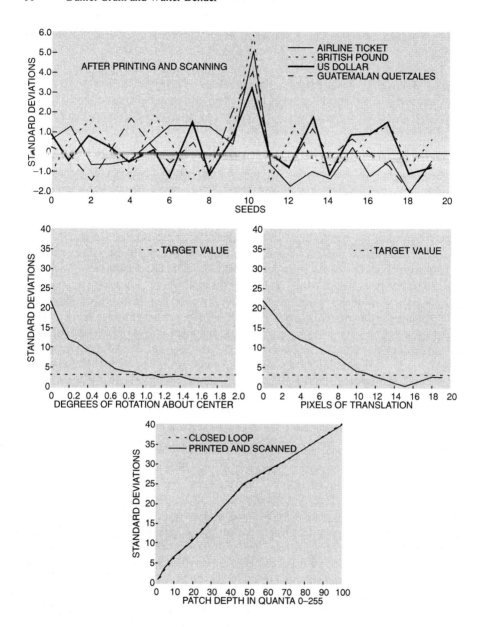

Fig. 6. Patch Track results. A variety of documents, encoded with a password of 10 are decoded after printing and scanning with various passwords (top), decoded after rotation (middle, left), decoded after translation (middle, right), and encoded at various pixel depths (bottom). Note that printing and scanning had almost no impact on data recovery.

are nearly orthogonal, many bits can usually be encoded in an image before either visibly degrading the image quality, or interfering with the ease of data recovery.

This method can serve a dual role. Traditional watermarking is used to identify whether an image has been encoded with a particular mark at all. Image tracking tries to encode a tracking number in an image, but the decoder is just trying to recover the bits with high accuracy, not identify if the image has been encoded in the first place.

In Patch Track, the first bit can serve as a "marker", by encoding that bit to a much higher level of certainty. This is important because if a bit is only encoded to the 99% certainty level, there will be on average one false positive for every hundred images or orientations examined. For a watermarking application used on the Internet, the marker bit realistically needs to have an encoding level that returns one false positive in 100000 (99.999%) or better, or a method will be swamped with false positives.

If this lead marking bit is detected, it is known that the image has watermarks in the particular orientation being tested. The rest of the bits which define the tracking number can be encoded in a much "lighter" (less certain and less degrading to the image) fashion, since there is no question of whether there are bits in the image, only if those bits are positive or negative.

Encoding Algorithm

The serial number tracking algorithm presented here is an asymmetric algorithm. The encoding is easy to place in a document, but at the expense of being difficult to recover, due to potential variations in orientation of the encoded document. This is a reasonable assumption if the encoding is going to be embedded in nearly every document printed while the decoding is done only in the few cases where a crime has been committed. Thus, no special effort is taken to make the Patch Track data easy to find, since it is assumed that many orientations can be searched on a counterfeit bill to identify the printer used.

However, in order to detect features placed in a bill using the Patchwork algorithm, it has been experimentally determined that they need to be on the order of a tenth of an inch in size. This allows for the drop in effective resolution because of dithering, as well as slight misalignments when the bill is scanned.

Since the bill is 2.5 inches across on the short side, this suggests using patch zones that are around 0.88 inches, guaranteeing that at least three of them will fall completely on the bill. Each of these regions, then, will need to hold about 12 bits (See Figure 5).

Taken together, these constraints equate to encoding an image in area approximately 760×760 pixels of printer resolution, using patches around 90 pixels in size. One bit in each region will have to be strongly encoded, and the rest weakly. Strong encoding corresponds to about 10000 patches, and weak encoding to about 2000 patches. An encoding depth of 20 out of 256 is used with a simple visibility mask. The encoding is done using the random cone method.

Decoding

The decoding process is more computationally intensive. There is first a grid search of the image in a variety of rotations. Once a target region has been located, a gradient search may be done to find the exact alignment of the system. The "weak" bits (that

Fig. 7.   The region of the bill used in the Tartan Thread experiment

is, the tracking numbers) are then decoded, and the alignment of the system tells where other blocks might be found. If desired, the overlap of several copies of the same encoded regions may allow multiple copies of the region to contribute to the decoding process.

4   Tartan Threads

The second half of the counterfeiting problem involves preventing bills from being printed in the first place. The ink-jet printer only "seeing" a print line a quarter inch wide complicates this problem. This limits the size of the features that the printer can examine when determining whether or not to print.

As a result, the approach considered here involves inserting a chosen feature in the document to be printed which can later be detected, even when looking at a region as small as a single print line.

Approach

The approach we have tried involves the scattering of "threads" of encoding through-out the image. These "threads" can be created by any of a number of spread spectrum techniques, including Patchwork. The particular technique chosen depends on the medium. For detecting a code using a simple piece of hardware, a simple encoding method is needed. Given the constraints of this problem, traditional linear Direct Sequence Spread Spectrum (DSSS) [4, 5] seems to be a good choice.

A "thread" might be arranged as a grid of long, narrow regions. The thread itself is broken up into several regions, typically between one and two hundred of them. Within each region some algorithm is used to hide a "bit". Since these regions are very small, it is assumed that the accuracy of these bits will be suspect. It is important that the method chosen makes it equally likely that an unencoded region returns a positive or negative encoding. So, to encode a "thread", a pattern of positive and negative encodings is chosen. The regions of the thread are then encoded with those bits.

To check if a certain region is encoded, one decodes each region of the suspect thread. This decoded bit stream is then compared to the encoded bit stream, and a

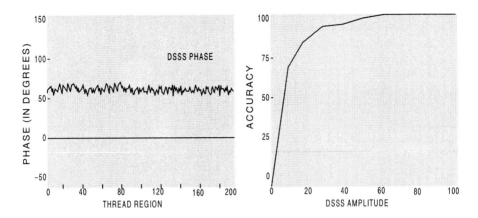

Fig. 8. Tartan Thread results: phase for each 200 thread elements (left) and error rate versus encoding amplitude (right)

binomial probability distribution function can be calculated to check for the likelihood of encoding.

5   Experiments

For all of the trials done, the printer was an Epson Color Stylus 800™ operating at 720×720 DPI, with Microweave enabled. The images were translated from Postscript to Epson printer control language by Ghostscript, version 5.04. They were dithered by the Floyd-Steinberg algorithm operating in a CMYK color space model. Printing was done on Epson photo-quality ink-jet paper to achieve the highest possible resolution.

For scanning, an HP ScanJet 4C™ flatbed scanner was used, operating at a variety of resolutions (all less then 300 DPI). Images were acquired directly into Adobe PhotoShop™ operating in RGB mode for saving to 24 bit TIFF files.

The limiting factor for most of these techniques was the available memory on the analysis machines. Operating on a 2000×3000 full color image stored in high precision format requires ~138 megabytes of RAM, per copy of the image being stored. Continued work in this area necessitates either moving to disk-based memory methods, or as was done for this paper, working with smaller then maximum resolution images. Our standard image size for these experiments was around 1000×450 for encoding and two to three times that for scanning and decoding (printed at 100 dpi and scanned at 100–300 dpi).

Patch Track Results

Tests were performed using a U.S. five-dollar bill, a British five pound bank note, a Guatemalan one hundred quetzales bank note, and an airline ticket. The encoded area is spread throughout each document. Each document is printed and then scanned. A random cone-shaped patch of maximum depth 10 (out of 256) and radius 15/100 of an inch was used in the experiments. To test the Patch Track method, the bill is "decoded" with a number of different password values, using a 3×3 decoding block. The encoding was done with the password of 10.

As can be seen in Figure 6 (top), Patch Track returns a significant result for the encoded password value (10) and a much smaller response for the other values in variety of documents, include currencies from several nations and an airline ticket. In interpreting these results, it is important to remember that the σ calculated has a Gaussian distribution, therefore the target value of 4 represents a degree of certainty that exceeds 99.98%. As can be seen in Figure 6 (bottom), the encoding can be increased to any desired value without much difficulty by varying either the patch depth or number of patches.

Also shown in Figure 6 are examples of the impact of affine transformations on the Patch Track method. A Barbados five-dollar bank note was subject to rotation and translation during the scanning process. The one degree of rotation resistance is equivalent to misalignment of up to a 12th of an inch, an easily achieved target. The shape of the translation data reflects the shape of the cone-shaped patches used in the experiment.

Tartan Thread Results

Tests were performed using a "weathered" U.S. one-dollar bill. For this test, the encoding was restricted to the densely printed region (See Figure 7) of the bill. All of the thread-area phases were encoded to 90 degrees. After encoding, the bill was printed. This print out was then scanned in. This scanned image was used for decoding. Each thread area was decoded and the phase of its carrier was found. The results are shown in Figure 8.

While there is an obvious phase alignment error, it is clear that most of the thread areas decode to within a very tight tolerance of each other. Several bits per area could be sent with a tolerance this tight. Assuming all phases are equally likely, a clustering this tight (±10 degrees out of 360) will occur less then 1 in 10^{251} times. There is little likelihood of unintentional triggering.

Discussion

Information hiding of this type presents a challenge, mainly because the size of the target data space (i.e., the region the printer sees at any one time) is so small. With current technologies the data space does not exceed 180 pixels in width. When considering the aliasing effects caused by scanning and resampling, this effective data space drops to 90 pixels. To be able to compensate for possible misalignments, the necessary redundancy drops the data space to 45 pixels. The shortest dimension on a dollar bill is approximately 2.5 inches. Quartering results in length of around 450 pixels. Thus, the largest data space that could be reasonably hoped for on a dollar bill is about 20 250 pixels. This is less then a third of the pixels in a 320×240 image found on a typical web page. Furthermore, since the typical print head is using only four to six inks, it has at most a "4 bit" image depth. In practice, dithering reduces the spatial resolution even further.

Another bottleneck to consider is with the scanner. A 300 DPI scanner has uniquely distinguish features at 150 DPI. This means that a 2.5"×0.25" area will give the potential counterfeiter less then 20 000 pixels to start with. Once this is reduced by dithering and aliasing, the data space is comparable to a 40×50 thumbnail. This is simply too small an area to hope to do the kind of robust, effective information hiding one would like.

These are transitory problems. As scanning and printing resolutions continue to increase, there will soon be adequate data space to do more interesting experiments.

6   Conclusions

The problem space of security documents (high-value certificates such as airline tickets, stock certificates, etc.) presents an intermediate step between the geometrically constrained world of today's commercial watermarking techniques and that of translation, rotation, and cropping independent information hiding.

Fixed scale allows the migration of many traditional time-domain spread-spectrum techniques into a "2D" environment. Exploiting the "printer/scanner" data path presents the opportunity to explore the highly non-linear and relatively poorly understood "transmission medium." It also takes information hiding "out of the computer" and allows its application to tangible media (i.e., physical objects).

7   References

1. E. Adelson, *Digital Signal Encoding and Decoding Apparatus*, U.S. Patent No. 4,939,515 (1990).
2. D. L. Hecht, "Embedded Data Glyph Technology for Hardcopy Digital Documents," *SPIE* **2171** (1995).
3. K. Matsui and K. Tanaka, "Video-Steganography: How to Secretly Embed a Signature in a Picture," *IMA Intellectual Property Project Proceedings* (1994).
4. R. C. Dixon, *Spread Spectrum Systems*, John Wiley & Sons, Inc., New York (1976).
5. S. K. Marvin, *Spread Spectrum Handbook*, McGraw-Hill, Inc., New York (1985).
6. G. B. Rhoads, *Method and apparatus responsive to a code signal conveyed through a graphic image*, U.S. Patent No. 5,710,834 (1995).
7. I. Cox, J. Kilian, T. Leighton, and T. Shamoon, "Secure Spread Spectrum Watermarking for Multimedia," *NECI Technical Report* 95-10, NEC Research Institute, Princeton, NJ (1995).
8. A. V. Drake, *Fundamentals of Applied Probability*, McGraw-Hill, Inc., New York (1967).
9. W. Bender, D. Gruhl, N. Morimoto, and A. Lu, "Techniques for Datahiding," *IBM Systems Journal* **35** 3&4 (1996).
10. W. Bender, D. Gruhl, and N. Morimoto, *Method and Apparatus for Data Hiding in Images*, U.S. Patent No. 5,689,587 (1996).
11. "Fundamental Facts About Money," *Federal Reserve Bank of Atlanta*, http://www.frbatlanta.org/publica/brochure/fundfac/money.htm (1997).
12. "Genuine or Counterfeit?," *Federal Reserve Bank of Atlanta*, http://www.frbatlanta.org/publica/brochure/counter/counterf.htm (1997).
13. "Currency Page," *The Department of the Treasury*, http://www.treas.gov/whatsnew/newcur/currency.html (1997).
14. "Ink-jet counterfeiting on the rise," *Reuters*, http://www.zdnet.com/zdnn/content/reut/0401/302907.html (April 1, 1998).

8   Acknowledgments

This work was sponsored in part by the MIT Media Laboratory's News in the Future research consortium and IBM. The authors would like to thank Fernando Paiz and Raymond Hwang for their help in conducting the characterization experiments.

Fingerprinting Digital Circuits on Programmable Hardware

John Lach[1], William H. Mangione-Smith[1], Miodrag Potkonjak[2]

University of California, Los Angeles
[1] Department of Electrical Engineering
56-125B Engineering IV
Los Angeles, CA 90095
{jlach, billms}@icsl.ucla.edu
[2] Department of Computer Science
4532K Boelter Hall
Los Angeles, CA 90095
miodrag@cs.ucla.edu

Abstract. Advanced CAD tools and high-density VLSI technologies have combined to create a new market for reusable digital designs. The economic viability of the new core-based design paradigm is pending on the development of techniques for intellectual property protection. A design watermark is a permanent identification code that is difficult to detect and remove, is an integral part of the design, and has only nominal impact on performances and cost of design. Field Programmable Gate Arrays (FPGAs) present a particularly interesting set of problems and opportunities, because of their flexibility. We propose the first technique that leverages the unique characteristics of FPGAs to protect commercial investment in intellectual property through fingerprinting. A hidden encrypted message is embedded into the physical layout of a digital circuit when it is mapped into the FPGA. This message uniquely identifies both the circuit origin and original circuit recipient, yet is difficult to detect and/or remove. While this approach imposes additional constraints on the back-end CAD tools for circuit place and route, experiments involving a number of industrial-strength designs indicate that the performance impact is minimal.

1 Introduction

We introduce a fingerprinting technique that applies cryptographically encoded marks to Field Programmable Gate Array (FPGA) digital designs in order to support identification of the design origin and the original recipient (i.e. customer of record). The approach is shown to be capable of encoding long messages and to be secure against malicious collusion. Nonetheless, the technique is efficient and requires low overhead in terms of hardware area and circuit performance.

1.1 Motivation

It is generally agreed that the most significant problem facing digital IC designers today is system complexity. The process of large system implementation has followed

David Aucsmith (Ed.): Information Hiding 1998, LNCS 1525, pp. 16-31, 1998.
© Springer-Verlag Berlin Heidelberg 1998

an evolutionary path from multiple ICs, through single ICs, and now into portions of ICs. For example, twenty years ago a 32-bit processor would require several ICs, ten years ago a single IC was necessary, and today a 32-bit RISC core requires approximately 25% of the StrongARM 110 device developed by Digital Semiconductor in collaboration with ARM Limited [1-3]. Fortunately, complex systems tend to be assembled using smaller components in order to reduce complexity as well as to take advantage of localized data and control flows. This trend toward partitioning enables design reuse, which is essential to reducing development cost and risk while also shortening design time. While systems designers have employed design reuse for years, what is new is that the boundaries for component partitions have moved inside of the IC packages.

A number of design houses have appeared that provide a wide range of modules, such as parameterized memory systems, I/O channels, ALUs and complete processor cores. These reusable modules are collectively known as Intellectual Property (IP), as they represent the commercial investment of the originating company but do not have a natural physical manifestation.

Direct theft is a concern of IP vendors. It may be possible for customers, or a third party, to sell an IP block as their own without even reverse engineering the design. Because IP blocks are designed to be modular and integrated with other system components, the thief does not need to understand either the architecture or implementation.

This paper presents a deterrent to such direct misappropriation. The essential idea involves embedding a digital mark, which uniquely identifies the design origin and recipient, in an IP block. This mark (origin signature + recipient fingerprint) allows the IP owner to not only verify the physical layout as their property but to identify the source of misappropriation, in a way that is likely to be much more compelling than the existing option of verifying the design against a registered database. This capability is achieved with very low overhead and effort and is secure against multiparty collusion.

Any effective fingerprinting scheme should achieve the following goals:
1. The mark must be difficult to remove.
2. It must be difficult to add a mark after releasing the IP to a customer.
3. The mark should be transparent.
4. The mark should have low area and timing overhead and little design effort.

The benefits of properties 1 and 2 are readily apparent and can be achieved by integrating the mark into the design. It then becomes more difficult to detect and remove, as there is no clear distinction between the mark and parts necessary to the design, thus making it more difficult to add another mark. Any attempts to remove the mark or add another incur a much greater risk of changing the design function.

Property 3 is important to provide IP protection across a wide community of developers and is the key to extending the benefits of IP protection to those who do not employ fingerprinting. By masking the presence of a mark, we discourage all forms of theft. Ayres and Levitt compared the impact of obtrusive and unobtrusive theft-preventive measures for automobiles [4]. They provide compelling evidence that unobtrusive tracking measures are significantly more effective at reducing theft than measures that are apparent to the thief, because of the deterring impact of uncertainty. We believe that a parallel exists between measures such as fingerprinting and more apparent techniques such as conventional design encryption.

Property 4 requires that the overhead in terms of area, timing, and design effort needed to mark the design is not excessive.

1.2   Motivational Example

Our fingerprinting approach builds upon two existing techniques: an FPGA watermarking technique that hides a mark [5] and an FPGA design tiling and partitioning technique that greatly reduces the cost of generating many different circuit instances which are functionally equivalent [6].

FPGAs are programmable logic devices that are composed of an array of configurable logic blocks (CLBs) which are connected via a programmable network. A device is configured with a bitstream generated by CAD tools specifying the functionality of the CLBs and the routing of the network. While the concepts developed here can be applied to a wide range of FPGA architectures, all of the discussion and experimental work will be conducted in the context of the Xilinx XC4000 architecture [7]. CLBs in an XC4000 each contain two flip-flops and two 16x1 lookup tables (LUTs). A hierarchical and segmented network is used to connect CLBs in order to form a specific circuit configuration.

A secure and transparent mark can be placed in an FPGA design using a previously developed FPGA watermarking technique [5]. Consider the case of PREP Benchmark #4 [8], a large state machine, which can be mapped into a block of 27 CLBs. This mapping results in 3 unused CLBs, or $3 \times 32 = 96$ unused LUT bits. Each unused LUT bit is used to encode one bit of the mark. Figure 1 shows the layout of the original design as produced by the standard Xilinx backend tools, while Fig. 2 shows the layout for the same design after applying the mark constraints to the three unused CLBs and re-mapping the design. The marked CLBs are incorporated into the design with unused network connections and neighboring CLB inputs, further hiding the mark.

Tiling [6] is then used to efficiently support fingerprinting. Consider the Boolean function $Y = (A \wedge B) \wedge (C \vee D)$, which might be implemented in a tile containing four CLBs as shown in Fig. 3.I. This configuration contains one spare CLB, and its LUT can hold a mark indicating the owner's signature and recipient's fingerprint. Each recipient could receive this original configuration with a unique fingerprint. Using the same base configuration for a different recipient, and therefore a different fingerprint, would facilitate simple comparison collusion (e.g. XOR), as the only difference between the designs would be the fingerprint. Note however that each implementation in Fig. 3.I–IV is interchangeable with the original, as the interface between the tile and the surrounding areas of the design is fixed and the function remains unchanged. The timing of the circuit may vary, however, due to the changes in routing. With several different instances of the same design, comparison collusion would highlight functional differences, thus disguising the differences between the various recipients' fingerprints.

If a design had four tiles the size of the instance in Fig. 3 (i.e. the design is a 2×2 array of tiles; each tile is a 2×2 array of CLBs), the total number of CLBs in the design would be 16. Assuming each CLB has a total of 32 LUT bits and each tile has one CLB free, 128 LUT bits would be available to encode a mark. Each tile has four instances, making the total number of design instances $4^4 = 256$. A non-tiled design would have $\binom{16}{4} = 1820$ possible instances, but each instance requires a complete execution of the backend CAD software which may require X amount of design effort. Each tile instance only requires X/4 amount of effort, but each instance can be used in $4^3 = 64$ different design instances. Therefore, the effective effort required to generate each tile instance is X/(4×64), and each instance of the total tiled design requires X/64 amount of effort.

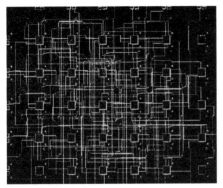

Fig. 1. Original layout of PREP benchmark #4

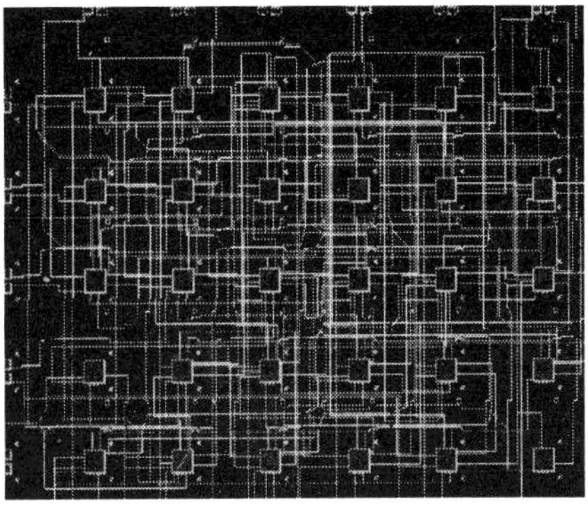

Fig. 2. Marked layout of PREP benchmark #4 with a 96-bit mark

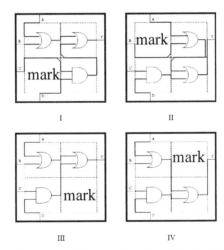

Fig. 3. Four instances of the same function with fixed interfaces

1.3   Limitations

The standard digital design flow follows these steps: behavioral hardware description language (HDL), synthesis to register transfer language (RTL), technology mapping, and finally physical layout involving place and route. Marks can be applied to any level of this design flow and, if developed properly, will propagate to later stages. However, because a mark is nonfunctional, it may be removed by reverse engineering a design to a stage in the flow before the mark has been applied. Fortunately, most FPGA vendors will not reveal the specification of their configuration streams, specifically to complicate the task of reverse engineering and thus protect the investment of their customers. For example, the Xilinx XC4000 devices follow a form of Pareto's rule: the first 80% of the configuration information can be determined relatively easily by inspection, the next 16% is much more difficult, etc. The complexity is enhanced by an irregular pattern that is not consistent between rows or columns, as a result of the hierarchical interconnect network. Xilinx does not take any specific actions to make their configurations difficult to reverse engineer. However, they do believe that it is difficult to do in general, and they promise their customers that they will keep the bitstream specification confidential in order to raise the bar for reverse engineering [9].

1.4   Contributions

This paper presents the first fingerprinting method for protecting reusable digital circuit IP, even after the IP has been delivered in commercial products. By manipulating hardware resources, we are able to encode relatively long messages in a manner that is difficult to observe by a third party, resists tampering and collusion, and has little impact on circuit performance or size. This capability provides three main benefits:
1. It reduces the risk that a circuit will be stolen, i.e. used illegally without payment or transferred to a third party.
2. It identifies not only the origin of the design, but also the origin of the misappropriation.
3. It can be used to identify the backend tool chain used to develop a design, and thus be part of the royalty mechanism used for CAD tools.

1.5   Paper Organization

The remainder of the paper is organized in the following way. Section 2 discusses work related to this fingerprinting approach, and section 3 details the approach itself. Section 4 evaluates the approach through experimentation, and the work is summarized in section 5.

2   Related Work

Related work can be divided into three main areas: digital watermarking, fingerprinting, and reverse engineering.

Ad-hoc techniques for marking text and image documents have been manually practiced for many centuries [10]. Recently, techniques for hiding signature data in image, video, and audio signals have received a great deal of attention. A spectrum of steganographic techniques for protection of digital images has been proposed [11-13]. While many of the initial techniques for marking images were not able to provide proper proof of ownership [14], several recent techniques provide protection against all known attacks [15].

Although protection of digital audio signals emerged as a more difficult task, at least three different techniques have been proposed [12, 16, 17]. The protection of video streams using steganography has been demonstrated by several European and US research teams [18-20].

Recently, a set of techniques has been proposed for protection of digital circuit IP through watermarking at the behavioral level using superimposition of additional constraints in conjunction to those specified by the user [21]. In this paper, we propose the first fingerprinting technique for FPGA designs. The majority of intellectual property is already programmable components, and all economic and historical trends indicate that the importance of these components will continue to rise. Finally, note that addressing the design at a lower level of abstraction has one additional advantage. All designs are significantly larger at lower levels of abstraction, enabling marks that are more difficult to detect and remove.

There has been a number of fingerprinting efforts reported in data hiding and cryptographic literature [22-24]. A spectrum of protocols has been established which greatly enhance the protection of both buyers and merchants of digital artifacts. All of these techniques are targeting protection of still artifacts, such as image and audio streams. To the best of our knowledge, this work is the first effort that addresses IP protection using fingerprinting.

While Xilinx and other FPGA vendors make some efforts to complicate the task of reverse engineering, it certainly is possible to crack the configuration specification with a concerted effort. NeoCAD Inc. was able to accomplish this for the Xilinx XC4000 series devices through a directed investigation of the output produced by the Xilinx backend tools. Given this information, it should be relatively straightforward to produce a Xilinx netlist file and then use commercial tools to move back up the design flow. Another line of attack involves removing the packaging material and successive layers and using image processing inspection to produce a circuit representation of the CLB. This approach has been used to produce a complete layout of a 386 microprocessor in approximately 2 weeks [25].

As a consequence of the proven success of reverse engineering, we believe that hiding the mark is necessary but not sufficient. Any effective fingerprinting scheme should make the mark appear to be part of the functional digital circuit to whatever extent is possible.

3   Approach

The watermarking technique is the general approach of inserting marks in unused CLB LUTs as introduced in the motivational example above. Results [5] indicate that the area and timing overhead required for inserting large marks in a design is low and that the approach is secure against most attacks.

Directly applying the watermarking technique to fingerprinting (i.e. replace the design origin signature with the recipient's fingerprint for each copy) is susceptible to collusion. Performing a simple comparison between the two bitstreams would reveal that the only differences were due to the individual fingerprints. Removing the differences would yield a fully functional yet unmarked circuit.

This vulnerability can be avoided by taking advantage of the flexible nature of FPGAs to create differences among functional components of the designs. By moving the location of the fingerprint for each instance of the design (i.e. reserve different CLBs for the fingerprint), the functional components will also have a different layout. Therefore, all comparisons that are done yield functional differences, and any attempt to remove the differences would yield a useless circuit.

However, generating an entire layout for each instance of the design would require a trip through the place-and-route tools for the entire circuit. Tiling requires that only a small portion of the design be changed. The algorithm divides a design into a set of tiles that possess the same characteristics as the example in Fig. 3. That is, each tile has specific functionality and a locked interface to the rest of the design. Several instances of each tile can be generated, and each instance can replace another without affecting the rest of the circuit (except timing) due to the locked interface. The various tile instances can then be matched to create one instance of the entire design. This reduces the total number of instances that need to be generated, and vastly reduces the effort and memory required to produce each instance.

The design tiling algorithm was originally developed in an eye toward fault-tolerance, but with the same goal of effort and memory reduction [6]. For fault-tolerance, different instances of each tile reserve different CLBs as unused. In the face of a CLB fault, the appropriate instance can be activated without affecting the rest of the circuit. The same result could be achieved by storing a great many instances of the entire design, leaving various CLBs free in each instance, but the effort to place and route each instance and the memory required to store each instance makes this approach impractical.

Much in the same way that tiling for fault-tolerance reduces the effort required to generate the various fault-tolerant instances and the memory to store them, tiling also makes fingerprinting more efficient and practical.

3.1   Watermark Preparation, Embedding, and Validation

We use cryptography tools to generate a set of FPGA physical designs (configurations) which correspond to the signature of the author of the design. The application of cryptographic techniques ensures also cryptographically strong hiding and low correlation of the added features.

The first step of the signature preparation and embedding process is encoding of the authorship signature as a 7-bit ASCII string. The signature string is given to the fingerprinting system for embedding in the circuit and is later produced by the verification program. The string is first compressed using a cryptographic hash function. The output is processed using public-key encoding. Finally, to produce a message that corresponds to the initial signature, we use a stream cipher. Note, in such a way, we generate a signature of arbitrary length.

Specifically, we use for the signature preparation the cryptographic hash function MD5, the public-key cryptosystem RSA, and the stream cipher RC4 [26, 27], on which many of today's state-of-the-art cryptographic commercial programs are based.

The next step in signature preparation involves adding error-correction coding (ECC). By introducing ECC into the signature, we combat the malicious third party that manages to identify a part of a signature and attempts to modify or remove it. A fundamental tradeoff exists between the number of bits allocated to the signature and ECC, and the sum must not exceed an estimate of the available bits free for encoding. We propose using a fault-tolerant encoding scheme that is similar to that used for marking file system structures on disk drives: the system decides upon a level of ECC protection based on the available free space and writes these settings into the available space. Using this approach, each design can have an appropriate amount of ECC while still guaranteeing that a generic verification system will be able to retrieve the signature.

The final step in signature preparation involves interleaving multiple ECC blocks. Consider the case where all signature information is encoded in the 16×1 LUTs of a Xilinx XC4000 device. It is possible that a malicious third party would be able to identify a particular LUT that is non-essential to the device function and change its programming. If sixteen consecutive ECC blocks are interleaved, one bit at a time, over a set of LUTs, then each LUT will only contain one bit from any ECC. This interleaving guarantees that the validation software can successfully retrieve the signature in the face of any single point fault, i.e. a LUT that has been tampered with.

Validation involves retrieving the signature embedded in the configuration. The essential element to validating any signature is retrieving the FPGA configuration. This step is straightforward for FPGAs based on static memory, as they are loaded over an external bus that can be monitored. It may not be possible to retrieve the configuration for technologies based on anti-fuse or flash-memory, though the issue remains open given recent successful efforts at reverse engineering. For this reason, we have focused our technique on static memory devices.

When the owners of an IP block believes their property has been misappropriated, they must deliver the configuration in question to an unbiased validation team. The IP vendor produces a seed that they claim was used to produce the block. With the seed and signature, the validation team reverses the signature preparation and embedding process: identify the CLBs used for hiding the signature based on the specific tile instances of the suspected instance of the complete design, reverse the block interleaving, apply the ECC if necessary, decrypt the message using a known key, and finally print out the resulting signature. If the signature matches that claimed by the IP vendor, then the source of the misappropriation has been established.

Essentially, the owners must demonstrate that encoded constraints match their encrypted signature. Therefore, they must provide the validation team with their original and encrypted signatures. The encrypted signature can be verified to match the constraints in the realized design, but this procedure assumes that the third party (validation team) will not reveal the signature to others later. We plan to address zero-knowledge proofs for signatures (where this restriction is removed) in future efforts.

3.2   Fingerprinting

After each instance for each tile is generated, the instances are prepared for marking. Every unused CLB is incorporated into the design with unused network connections and neighboring CLB inputs, and timing statistics are generated for each instance.

Depending on the timing specifications of the design, some instances may be discarded. The remaining instances are collected in a database. For example, MCNC benchmark c499 can be divided into 6 tiles, each with 8 instances, creating the possibility for $8^6 = 262,144$ different instances of the total design.

When a copy of the design in needed, an instance for each tile is extracted from the database and the recipient's fingerprint is inserted in the unused CLBs.

A group of people colluding may be able to find that they have instance matches among some of their tiles, thus allowing for tile comparison collusion, but it extremely unlikely that matches will be found among all (or even a large portion) of the tiles. Furthermore, the tile structure and boundaries are not generally apparent to the colluders, as they are not an inherent property of the FPGA configuration. Therefore, the colluding recipients may be able to remove a portion of their fingerprints, but the majority of the fingerprints will remain intact. The key to this approach is efficiently introducing wide variation among the functional parts of the designs, so that collusion cannot be used to separate common functional components from unique fingerprints.

The pseudo-code in Fig. 4 summarizes the approach.

```
1.  create initial non-fingerprinted design;
2.  extract timing and area information;
3.  while (!complete) {
4.     partition design into tiles;
5.     if (!(mark size && collusion protection)) break;
6.     for (i=1;i<=# of tiles;i++) {
7.        for (j=1;j<=# of tile instances;j++) {
8.           create tile instance(i,j);
9.           if (instance meets timing criteria) {
10.             incorporate unused CLBs into design;
11.             store instance;
12. } } } }
13. for (i=1;i<=# of recipients;i++) {
14.    prepare mark(i);
15.    select tile instances from database;
16.    insert mark in unused LUTs;
17. }
```

Fig. 4. Pseudo-code for fingerprinting approach

Lines 1 and 2 initialize the process by establishing the physical layout for the non-fingerprinted design, on which all area and timing overhead is based. Lines 3–12 perform the tiling technique, creating a database of tile instances. The variables for this section are mark size, collusion protection (level of security based on presumed number of collaborators), and timing requirements. Mark size and collusion protection affect the tiling approach, while the timing requirements define the instance yield (i.e. individual tile instances are accepted contingent upon their meeting the timing requirements). Lines 13–17 are executed for each distributed instance of the design. Line 14 derives the unique recipient fingerprint with asymmetric fingerprinting techniques [23, 24].

3.3   Tiling Optimization

The tiling technique performed in lines 3–12 involves selecting a tile size x that best balances the security of the fingerprint and the design effort required for the finger-printing process. The selection of x is based on a set of given constants and user de-fined variables, including the desired emphasis on either security or effort.

The constants are the FPGA device size d and the CLB utilization (a = # unused CLBs/# total CLBs). The variables defined by the user are the timing specifications (which impact instance yield y, the percent of tile instances that meet the timing speci-fications), a collusion set size n, and the maximum percentage of the mark that can be removed while leaving enough of the fingerprint intact for unique recipient identifi-cation b. These five criteria lead to preliminary calculations: the number of tiles in the design $t = d/x$, the number of free CLBs per tile $f = \lfloor x \cdot a \rfloor \approx x \cdot a$, the number of instances per tile $i = \begin{pmatrix} x \\ f \end{pmatrix}$, the number of instances per tile that meet the timing constraints $j = i \cdot y$, and the design effort required for the fingerprinting technique $e = t \cdot x \cdot i = d \cdot i$. Design effort refers to the number of complete passes through the CAD tools (i.e. configurations of the entire design) that are required.

The above information can be used to calculate the odds that n people could collude to remove their fingerprints in one tile:

$$c_1 = 1 - \frac{j!}{(j-n)! \, j^n} \tag{1}$$

Odds to remove fingerprint from one tile.

Equation (1) assumes that the only way to remove a fingerprint from a tile is to find two matching tile instances, thus making the recipient fingerprint the only difference between two tiles. A simple XOR comparison between the two tiles would remove the two fingerprints, thus creating an instance which can be distributed to all participating colluders. The owner's signature remains in all tiles, however.

The process of removing the fingerprint from one tile can be repeated until a certain portion of the complete design has been cleaned. A binomial calculation indicates the odds that b% of the fingerprint can be removed:

$$c_\% = \sum_{k=b \cdot t}^{t} \begin{pmatrix} t \\ k \end{pmatrix} \cdot c_1^k \left(1 - c_1\right)^{t-k} \tag{2}$$

Chance to remove fingerprint from b% of the tiles.

The security of the fingerprint improves with a larger tile size x as a result of the greater number of instances: $\begin{pmatrix} d \\ f \cdot t \end{pmatrix} > \begin{pmatrix} x \\ f \end{pmatrix} \cdot t$. However, as mentioned above, larger tile sizes require more effort e to generate. The product of security and design effort yields:

$$c_{\%} \cdot e = d \cdot i \cdot \sum_{k=b \cdot d/x}^{d/x} \binom{d/x}{k} \cdot \left(1 - \frac{(i \cdot y)!}{(i \cdot y - n)!(i \cdot y)^n}\right)^k \cdot \left(\frac{(i \cdot y)!}{(i \cdot y - n)!(i \cdot y)^n}\right)^{(d/x)-k} \qquad (3)$$

Design effort times odds to remove fingerprint from b% of the tiles

This equation reveals that there is a critical value for x which balances the tradeoff between security and design effort. Certain applications may put a stronger emphasis on one or the other. For today's FPGA applications, design effort is one of the prime limiting factors. FPGA mapping is extremely time consuming, thus forcing an emphasis on limiting design effort. Also, today's applications see configuration bitstreams being distributed directly to approved recipients, thus requiring any collusion effort to bring n number of people together. Any one person would have a difficult time collecting a larger number of distributed instances of the design.

Conversely, trends in FPGA technology and applications may put a reduced emphasis on design effort and a greater emphasis on security. FPGA CAD tools continue to improve and workstations on which the software runs are improving tremendously. Therefore, in the future, design effort won't be as onerous. Also, one forseable application of FPGA designs includes distributing designs over the internet, either directly to recipients or available as a form of hardware application. In either situation, one person could gain access to a great many instances of the design, either by eavesdropping on a network line or downloading numerous instances of the application, each time receiving a different fingerprint. Then n becomes not the number of people colluding but the number of instances that are being compared, possibly by one person. This possibility raises the importance of fingerprint security.

4   Experimental Results

To evaluate the area and timing overhead of the approach, we conducted an experiment on nine MCNC designs. For design effort and fingerprint security, the following constants were assumed: device size $d = 400$ CLBs, number of unused CLBs/number of total CLBs $a = 0.1$, and instance yield $y = 0.9$.

The overhead of the proposed approach comes in the form of area (physical resources), timing, and design effort. Area overhead is inevitable, as previously unused LUTs are used to encode the mark. Table 1 shows the area of the designs before and after the application of the fingerprinting approach. A number of factors complicate the task of calculating the physical resource overhead. The place-and-route tools will indicate the number of CLBs that are used for a particular placement. However, these utilized CLBs rarely are packed into a minimal area. Unused CLBs introduce flexibility into the place-and-route step that may be essential for completion or good performance. For example, the initial c880 design possesses a concave region that contains 42 utilized CLBs but also 10 unutilized CLBs (19%). Therefore, we will report overhead in terms of the area used by the fingerprinted design minus the total area of the original design, including unused CLBs such as the 19% measure above. The average, median and worst-case area overheads were 5.4%, 5.3%, and 9.8% respectively. The size of the mark (signature + fingerprint) that can be encoded is dependent on this overhead. If a larger mark is desired, extra CLBs can be added thus increasing overhead.

Design	Original # of CLBs	Final # of CLBs	Final – Original / Original
9sym	46	49	.065
c499	94	96	.021
c880	110	115	.045
duke2	93	100	.075
rd84	27	28	.037
planet1	95	100	.053
styr	78	81	.038
s9234	195	206	.056
Sand	82	90	.098

Table 1. Variation of resources used among instances for each tile

Timing overhead may arise due to the constraints on physical component placement as defined by the size and location of the mark. A LUT dedicated to the mark may impede placement of circuit components and lengthen the critical path. As the mark size grows relative to the design size, more constraints are made on the placement of the design, thus increasing the possibility for performance degradation.

Timing overhead is show in Fig. 5. For each design, the instance yield (i.e. number of tile instances that meet the timing specifications / total number of tile instances) is shown as the timing specifications (measured as percent increase over the original, non-fingerprinted design timing) grow more lenient. The results reveal that a 20% increase in timing yields approximately 90% of total tile instances as acceptable. Relatively small changes in a circuit netlist or routing constraints can often result in a dramatically different placement and a corresponding change in speed. It appears that the impact of fingerprinting on performance is below this characteristic variance.

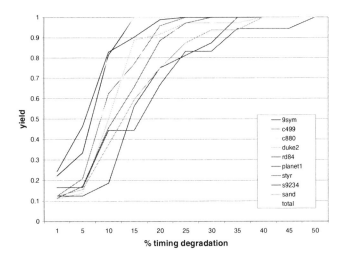

Fig. 5 Instance yield vs. timing specifications

As the equations in section 3.3 indicate, effort e increases with tile size x. Design effort may often be the limiting factor in tile size selection, despite the fact that security increases with tile size. By examining the chance that an increasing number of colluders have to break one tile (1) and all tiles – (2) with b = 100% – by direct comparison collusion with varied tile sizes, it is clear that larger tile sizes drastically reduce the chance that any portion of the fingerprint may be removed. Even for a tile size of 40 and 200 people colluding, there is only one chance in approximately 5 million that the entire fingerprint could be removed. It therefore is important to compare the tradeoff between design effort and fingerprint security in a proper manner. Figure 6 is a direct multiplication comparison (3). Other comparisons may be more relevant based on the application and design setting. As mentioned above, current applications do not require as much security, as a large number of design instances aren't easily available to a group of colluders. Also, current design settings place a strong emphasis on design effort, as modern FPGA mapping technology is time consuming. Therefore, a different comparison (e.g. security $\times$ effort^2) may present a more useful measure of current needs. As mentioned above, future applications may require a different comparison, perhaps placing a greater emphasis on fingerprint security and a smaller emphasis on effort. Figure 6, however, reveals that for a large number of colluders and direct multiplication comparison, it is better to have a larger tile size.

Figure 7 shows the same data as Fig. 6, but it instead plots various collusion sizes against tile size and focuses in on a smaller, more reasonable number of colluders. The minimum value for each plot is the critical value denoting the optimal tile size for the particular collusion group size. It is easy to see here, that the best tile size actually is a mid-sized tile for a small collusion group (e.g. $n = 2 \Rightarrow$ best $x = 40$; $n = 10 \Rightarrow$ best $x = 80$), and the specific optimum tile size increases for larger collusion groups.

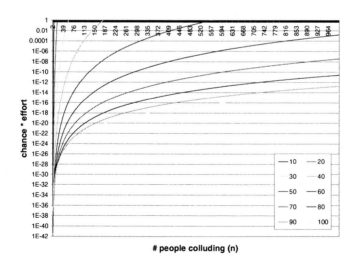

Fig. 6. Chance to break all tiles $\times$ design effort

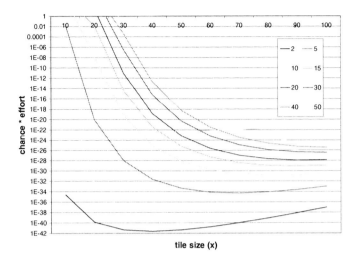

Fig. 7. Tile size critical value

Figure 8 displays the chance that a growing number of colluders have to remove a certain percentage of the fingerprint for a tile size x of 40. Even for a small tile size such as 40, it remains extremely unlikely that a colluding group could remove even a small portion of the fingerprint. The chance that 15 colluders would be able to remove 30% of the fingerprint by comparison collusion is one chance in approximately 4 million.

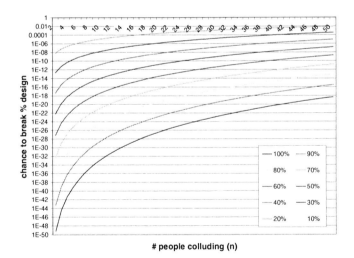

Fig. 8. Chance to break % of fingerprint (tile size = 40)

Figure 9 directly multiplies security by design effort for each tile size revealing that the optimal tile size for a growing number of colluders is predominantly mid-sized tiles because the fingerprint security remains extremely high for mid-sized tiles while requiring significantly less design effort.

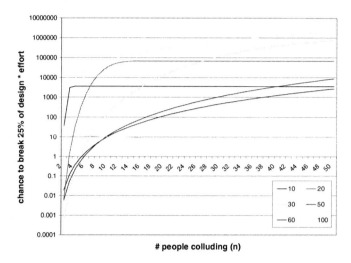

Fig. 9. Chance to break 25% of fingerprint × effort

5   Conclusion

As digital IC design complexity increases, forcing an increase in design reuse and third party macro distribution, intellectual property protection will become more important. The fingerprinting approach presented here creates such protection for FPGA intellectual property by inserting a unique marker identifying both the origin and recipient of a design. The fingerprinting process produces an extremely secure mark (chance of removing a fingerprint is always less than one in a million) but requires little extra design effort. Although the mark is applied to the physical layout of the design by imposing constraints on the backend CAD tools, experiments reveal that the area and timing overhead is extremely low.

Acknowledgements

The authors would like to thank Gang Qu for his assistance. This work was supported by the Defense Advanced Research Projects Agency of the United States of America, under contract DAB763-95-C-0102 and subcontract QS5200 from Sanders, a Lockheed Martin company.

References

[1] J. Turley, "ARM Grabs Embedded Speed Lead," *Microprocessor Report*, vol. 10, 1996.
[2] J. Montanaro et al., "A 160MHz 32b 0.5W CMOS RISC Microprocessor," *Proc. of International Solid-State Circuits Conference*, 1996.

[3] S. Furber, *ARM System Architecture*, Menlo Park: Addison-Wesley, 1996, p. 329.

[4] I. Ayres and S. D. Levitt, "Measuring Positive Externalities from Unobservable Victim Precaution: An Empirical Analysis of Lojack," *The Economics Review*, 1997.

[5] J. Lach, W. H. Mangione-Smith, and M. Potkonjak, "Signature Hiding Techniques for FPGA Intellectual Property Protection," submitted to *ICCAD '98*, 1998.

[6] J. Lach, W. H. Mangione-Smith, and M. Potkonjak, "Low Overhead Fault-Tolerant FPGA Systems," *IEEE Transactions on VLSI*, vol. 6, 1998.

[7] Xilinx, *The Programmable Logic Data Book*, San Jose, CA, 1996.

[8] Programmable Electronic Performance Group, "PREP Benchmark Suite #1, Version 1.3," Los Altos, CA, 1994.

[9] S. Trimberger, Personal Communication, Xilinx Corporation, 1997.

[10] H. Berghel and L. O'Gorman, "Protecting Ownership Rights Through Digital Watermarking," *IEEE Computer*, 1996, pp. 101-103.

[11] J. Brassil and L. O'Gorman, "Watermarking Document Images with Bounding Box Expansion," *First International Workshop on Information Hiding*, Cambridge, U.K., 1996.

[12] I. J. Cox et al., "Secure Spread Spectrum Watermarking for Images, Audio and Video," *International Conference on Image Processing*, 1996.

[13] J. Smith and B. Comiskey, "Modulation and Information Hiding in Images," *First International Workshop on Information Hiding*, Cambridge, U.K., 1996.

[14] S. Craver et al., "Can Invisible Watermarks Resolve Rightful Ownership?" *The International Society for Optical Engineering*, 1997.

[15] A. H. Tewfik and M. Swanson, "Data Hiding for Multimedia Personalization, Interaction, and Protection," *IEEE Signal Processing Magazine*, 1997, pp. 41-44.

[16] W. Bender et al., "Techniques for Data Hiding," *IBM Systems Journal*, vol. 35, 1996, pp. 313-336.

[17] L. Boney et al., "Digital Watermarks for Audio Signals," *International Conference on Multimedia Computing and Systems*, 1996.

[18] G. A. Spanos and T. B. Maples, "Performance Study of a Selective Encryption Scheme for the Security of Networked, Real-Time Video," *International Conference on Computer Communications and Networks*, 1995.

[19] F. Hartung and B. Girod, "Copyright Protection in Video Delivery Networks by Watermarking of Pre-Compressed Video," *ECMAST '97*, 1997.

[20] F. Hartung and F. Girod, "Watermarking of MPEG-2 Encoded Video Without Decoding and Re-Encoding," *Multimedia Computing and Networking*, 1997.

[21] I. Hong and M. Potkonjak, "Behavioral Synthesis Techniques for Intellectual Property Protection," unpublished manuscript, 1997.

[22] D. Boneh and J. Shaw, "Collusion-Secure Fingerprinting for Digital Data," *CRYPTO '95*, 1995.

[23] I. Biehl and B. Meyer, "Protocols for Collusion-Secure Asymmetric Fingerprinting," *STACS '97, 14th Annual Symposium on Theoretical Aspects of Computer Science*, 1997.

[24] B. Pfitzmann and M. Waidner, "Anonymous Fingerprinting," International Conference on the Theory and Application of Cryptographic Techniques, 1997.

[25] R. Anderson and M. Kuhn, "Tamper Resistance - A Cautionary Note," *USENIX Electronic Commerce Workshop*, 1996.

[26] B. Schneier, Applied Cryptography: Protocols, Algorithms, and Source Code in C. New York: John Wiley & Sons, 1996.

[27] A. J. Menezes, P. C. V. Oorschot, and S. A. Vanstone, *Handbook of Applied Cryptography*, CRC Press, 1996.

Steganography in a Video Conferencing System[*]

Andreas Westfeld[1] and Gritta Wolf[2]

[1] Institute for Theoretical Computer Science
[2] Institute for Operating Systems, Databases and Computer Networks

Dresden University of Technology
D-01062 Dresden, Germany
{westfeld, g.wolf}@inf.tu-dresden.de

Abstract. We describe a steganographic system which embeds secret messages into a video stream. We examine the signal path which typically includes discrete cosine transformation (DCT) based, lossy compression. Result is the technical realisation of a steganographic algorithm whose security is established by indeterminism within the signal path.

1 Introduction

The escalation of communication via computer network has been linked to the increasing use of computer aided steganography [5,6]. Steganographic methods usually hide ciphered messages in other, harmless-looking data in such a way that a third person can not detect or even prove this process. Examples for information hiding exist for digital image files, audio files, and in background sounds of phone calls [2]. There are more than 20 programs on the Internet (for examples see the list below).

- S-Tools by Andy Brown embeds data as least significant bits in audio files (.wav) or as least significant bits of the RGB color values in graphic files (.bmp). A third method hides data in free sectors of diskettes. Several symmetric encryption methods (DES, IDEA, ...) are offered for additional encryption of the secret data [9].
- Jsteg by Derek Upham embeds data in JFIF images. It overwrites the least significant bits of the coefficients [8,10].
- Hide and Seek by Colin Maroney hides data (encrypted with IDEA) in GIF files [11].
- PGE (Pretty Good Envelope) by Roche-Crypt packs data in GIF or JPEG files. The use of an additional secure encryption method is recommended [12].
- Mandelsteg by Henry Hastur calculates a GIF fractal from a file. The resulting images are very similar. Differences can only be seen when comparing their color values [13].

[*] This work is sponsored by the German Federal Ministry of Education, Science, Research and Technology (BMBF).

David Aucsmith (Ed.): Information Hiding 1998, LNCS 1525, pp. 32–47, 1998.

- Stego by John Walker transforms any file to a nonsensical text by means of a free choosable dictionary.
- Texto by Kevin Maher transfers files into poetic English sentences (comparable with stego, which produces nonsensical texts) [14].

Data camouflage is also used for compatible enlargement of norms, such as stereophony, color TV, videotext, traffic control system (TCS), and radio data system (RDS) at FM radio.

This paper does not deal with watermarking systems at all [1].

2   Video Conferencing Systems

Video conferences use compression algorithms to ensure an acceptable quality even on low data rate systems like ISDN. Usually, compression methods are lossy which means that the reconstructed image is not identical with the original.

The video conference used for the implementation of the steganographic system presented in this paper works on the H.261 standard. This is the most common standard for compression in video conferences and is recommended by the *Comité Consultatif International Télégraphique et Téléphonique*[1] (CCITT) [3]. In Fig. 4, we can see the points for embedding and extracting within the H.261 information flow.

Compression and data embedding have contrary goals. For data embedding we need a carrier that allows the possibility of unnoticeable modifications. Signal noise and irrelevance are common examples for it. Compression methods try to remove signal noise and irrelevance. The better a signal is compressed, the less possibilities for data embedding we have. In section 5 we investigate a typical signal path for data embedding.

3   Discrete Cosine Transformation

The steganographic algorithm described in section 6 embeds data in transformed blocks. Therefore we describe the transformation process used in this video conferencing system.

A suitable transformation is a means to separate essential information (visible for the human eye) from marginal parts (invisible for the human eye) of the image. The subsequent quantization removes the insignificant parts of the image. The transformation employed has to be invertible in order to regain the essential parts of the image.

Many digital video conferencing systems, for instance based on the standards H.261, M-JPEG, MPEG, use the two-dimensional discrete cosine transformation (DCT). It transformes an image of 8×8 pixels with $8 \cdot 8 = 64$ brightness values $F(0,0) \ldots F(7,7)$ into 64 values (so-called DCT coefficients) $f(0,0) \ldots f(7,7)$ (see Equation 1). The transformation causes no significant loss (rounding errors

---

[1] the former CCITT is now the International Telecommunication Union (ITU)

only). The retransformed image results from back transformation of the DCT coefficients (see Equation 2). It can also be understood as linear combination of the DCT coefficients (see Equation 3 and Fig. 2) with the DCT base images $B_{k,n}$ (see Fig. 1).

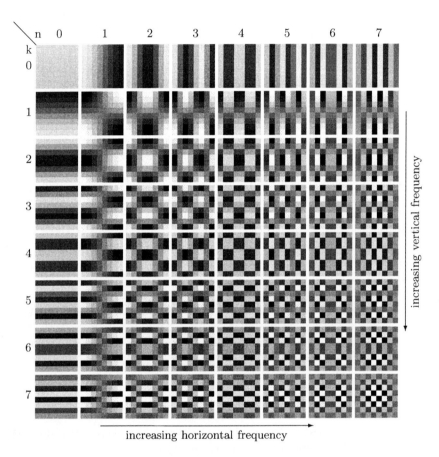

Fig. 1. DCT base images $B_{k,n}$

$$f(k,n) = \frac{C(k)}{2}\frac{C(n)}{2}\sum_{x=0}^{7}\sum_{y=0}^{7}F(x,y)\cos\left(\frac{\pi(2x+1)k}{16}\right)\cos\left(\frac{\pi(2y+1)n}{16}\right) \quad (1)$$

$$F(x,y) = \sum_{k=0}^{7}\sum_{n=0}^{7}\frac{C(k)}{2}\frac{C(n)}{2}f(k,n)\cos\left(\frac{\pi(2x+1)k}{16}\right)\cos\left(\frac{\pi(2y+1)n}{16}\right) \quad (2)$$

$$F(x,y) = \sum_{k=0}^{7}\sum_{n=0}^{7}f(k,n)B_{k,n}(x,y) \quad (3)$$

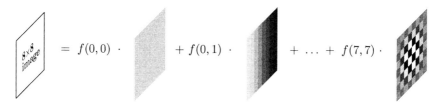

Fig. 2. Presentation of an 8×8 image by 64 base image parts

with

$$C(z) = \begin{cases} \frac{1}{2}\sqrt{2} & \text{for } z = 0 \\ 1 & \text{else} \end{cases}$$

4   An Example

In order to illustrate the DCT, we transform a dot over the i. Fig. 3 shows it strongly enlarged. As presented in Fig. 3 b) the dot over the i has a grating of 64 brightness values. Let's look at its transformed matrix:

$$\begin{bmatrix} 50 & -4 & -84 & -2 & -31 & -2 & -12 & -1 \\ -4 & 0 & 0 & 0 & 0 & 0 & 0 & 0 \\ -84 & 0 & -29 & 2 & 15 & 0 & 10 & 0 \\ -2 & 0 & 2 & 0 & 1 & 0 & 0 & 0 \\ -31 & 0 & 15 & 1 & 28 & -1 & 10 & -1 \\ -2 & 0 & 0 & 0 & -1 & 0 & -2 & 0 \\ -12 & 0 & 10 & 0 & 10 & -2 & 0 & -1 \\ -1 & 0 & 0 & 0 & -1 & 0 & -1 & 0 \end{bmatrix}$$

The quantization causes an accumulation of zeros by applying a step function (dividing and rounding) to the DCT coefficients:

$$\begin{bmatrix} 2 & 0 & -8 & 0 & -3 & 0 & -1 & 0 \\ 0 & 0 & 0 & 0 & 0 & 0 & 0 & 0 \\ -8 & 0 & -2 & 0 & 1 & 0 & 1 & 0 \\ 0 & 0 & 0 & 0 & 0 & 0 & 0 & 0 \\ -3 & 0 & 1 & 0 & 2 & 0 & 1 & 0 \\ 0 & 0 & 0 & 0 & 0 & 0 & 0 & 0 \\ -1 & 0 & 1 & 0 & 1 & 0 & 0 & 0 \\ 0 & 0 & 0 & 0 & 0 & 0 & 0 & 0 \end{bmatrix}$$

The example demonstrates that only 15 coefficients different from zero are left of the initial 64 brightness values. The coefficients are arranged in linear ordering and then are run and level coded. The new created sequence will be Huffman-coded. [3] and [4] enclose a description of run and level and Huffman coding. The significant fact is that they are **loss-free codings**. Fig. 3 c) shows the result of the back transformation.

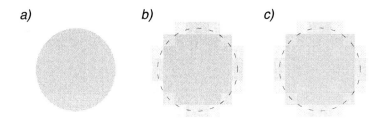

Fig. 3. "Dot over the i": a) original, b) rastered c) after decompression

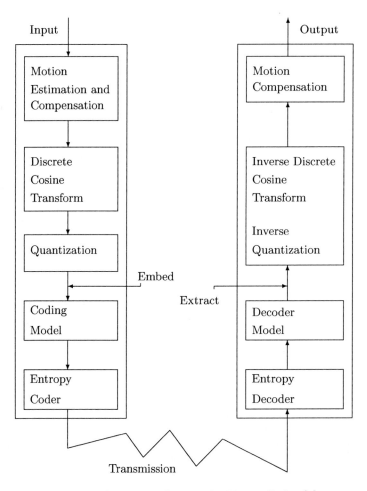

Fig. 4. Information flow in the H.261 Codec [4]

5 Signal Path

A precise knowledge of the signal path is important in order to be able to estimate the safety of a steganographic technique. From the camera to the coded sequence of pictures, the signal path is subject to losses by transformations as well as to influences and to disturbances. In the following, some transformation points on the path are designated, and in parentheses, the altered quantity.

The appearance of the original is influenced by the lighting conditions. The image of the original is preprocessed optically by the lens of the camera. Additionally, attitude aperture setting (depth of focus), the focuses (part of high video frequencies), the focal length (detail, video depth) and the quality of the lens (distortion) contribute essentially. Through dispersion, the focuses are dependent on the color of light. The light is usually transformed into an electrical signal in the camera by a charge coupled device (CCD). The tiny CCDs are characterized through their high sensitivity to light. The light in front of the about 380 000 photosensitive points is filtered by many colored, narrow, vertical stripes. Each three adjacent sensors, receiving respectively red, green, and blue filtered light, make one pixel. The horizontal distance of the three sensors is only a partial pixel distance and thus, is neglected. A CCD has a temporal inertness (the reader possibly observed the "tracing" in the case of a camera pan shot) and is operated with a specific sampling frequency. Afterwards, the altered and rastered image is available in the form of an electrical signal. In this form, it runs through a circuit which contains semiconductors (temperature dependence, noise), and it is changed into a NTSC or PAL signal. The signal path now leads to the computer over a coaxial cable (spectral phase shift, attenuation) from the camera. On the videocard in the computer the picture is locked, digitized and transmitted to the device driver.[2] A data structure in the RGB format results, which contains the image which is now even more coarsely rastered than in the NTSC or PAL signal. With the last step on the signal path, we exceeded the boundary to determinism (see Fig. 5). All further processing steps are digital and deterministic. With the transformation and quantization, desirable rounding errors occur. A loss-free entropy coding compresses the data between quantization and transfer.

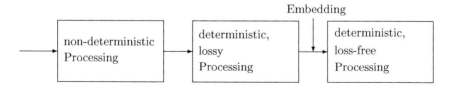

Fig. 5. Sections of the signal path

---

[2] Often only the interface of the device driver is documented. The programmer is unable to separate the activities of the videocard and those of the device driver.

The signal path can be divided into three parts. Non-deterministic processing means that resulting output signals differ from each other with high probability in the case of identical input signals.

An example is the noise of the semiconductor devices mentioned already. The noise level is dependent of the considered bandwidth. The image incorporated by the camera is filed in the PAL signal line by line from top to bottom, 15 625 lines per second (for 25 full frames). The voltage within a line varies during horizontal color change, with vertical from line to line. Therefore, upright brightness modifications are put in the signal at a bandwidth a maximum of 8 kHz (one line is white, one line is black, alternating). Up to 800 image elements per line can be placed in comparison to this, which corresponds to a bandwidth of 6 MHz. The bandwidth for horizontal video frequencies – and therefore the noise level – is up to 800 times as large as the bandwidth for vertical video frequencies.

Two scan lines are aligned by means of the horizontal synchronization pulse which is included in the CCVS signal. Line interlacing divides a full frame into two half frames. If one numbers the lines of a full frame from top to bottom, the first frame contains all odd lines and the second frame all even lines. Therefore, two straight adjacent lines of the full frame are $\frac{1}{50}$ frame separated from each other. Since the half frames are also registered at the frame rate, the screen content can already have changed.

Here follows an example with numbers. The about 380 000 sensors of a CCD might be placed in format 720 by 540. Three adjacent sensors will be summarized as one image point (RGB), although the sensors have a distance of $\frac{1}{720}$ line length. This horizontal distance is, referring to the smallest H.261 format (176 by 144), $\frac{1}{4}$ pixel distance. Table 1 shows, that already a horizontal displacement of the image content of $\frac{1}{10}$ pixels allows considerable modifications of the frequency spectrum.

We developed a little program which creates Table 1 when base images are generated with horizontal dephasing and transformed. The dephasing results if term $2y + 1$ is replaced by $2y + 1.2$ in Equation 1. Through consideration of Fig. 1, it is obvious that a horizontal "dephasing" of the base images $B_{k,0}$ brings no change. Under exclusion of the coefficients $f(0,0)$ (base brightness) and $f(k,n)$ (appropriate for the base image), the coefficient $f(k',n')$ with the largest absolute value was always searched in the transformed matrix. The values in brackets are not to be traced back to displacement and can be explained by truncated values during computation. In the line for $B_{0,1}$, the coefficient with the strongest differing amount probably is $f(0,0)$. Since this coefficient is excluded from consideration, the smaller next appears. Otherwise, for $n > 0$, the following pattern is valid:

$$\begin{matrix} k' = k \\ n' = n - 1 \end{matrix} \quad \text{and} \quad \frac{\Delta f(k',n')}{f(k,n)} \approx n \cdot 3\%$$

Column $f_{\min}$ contains the minimum amount for the coefficient $f(k,n)$ from that coefficient $f(k',n')$ currently changes by 1. Since the coefficients are integer, a modification less than 1 is not possible.

Table 1. Relative change of DCT coefficients $f(k', n')$ while horizontal dephasing of base images $B_{k,n}$ by $\frac{1}{10}$ pixel

k	n	k'	n'	$\frac{\Delta f(k',n')}{f(k,n)}$	$f_{\min}$
0	0	–	–	(0.00) %	(∞)
0	1	0	2	1.51 %	67
0	2	0	1	6.75 %	15
0	3	0	2	9.19 %	11
0	4	0	3	12.27 %	9
0	5	0	4	15.16 %	7
0	6	0	5	18.90 %	6
0	7	0	6	24.60 %	5
1	0	3	0	(0.27) %	(369)
1	1	1	0	3.61 %	28
1	2	1	1	6.79 %	15
1	3	1	2	9.28 %	11
1	4	1	3	12.28 %	9
1	5	1	4	15.13 %	7
1	6	1	5	18.98 %	6
1	7	1	6	24.55 %	5
2	0	6	0	(0.13) %	(780)
2	1	2	0	3.58 %	28
2	2	2	1	6.75 %	15
2	3	2	2	9.29 %	11
2	4	2	3	12.18 %	9
2	5	2	4	15.19 %	7
2	6	2	5	18.82 %	6
2	7	2	6	24.62 %	5
3	0	7	0	(0.14) %	(737)
3	1	3	0	3.61 %	28
3	2	3	1	6.79 %	15
3	3	3	2	9.28 %	11
3	4	3	3	12.30 %	9
3	5	3	4	15.16 %	7
3	6	3	5	18.98 %	6
3	7	3	6	24.55 %	5
4	0	3	6	(0.00) %	(∞)
4	1	4	0	3.57 %	29
4	2	4	1	6.75 %	15
4	3	4	2	9.19 %	11
4	4	4	3	12.29 %	9
4	5	4	4	15.16 %	7
4	6	4	5	18.90 %	6
4	7	4	6	24.60 %	5
5	0	1	0	(0.14) %	(736)
5	1	5	0	3.62 %	28
5	2	5	1	6.80 %	15
5	3	5	2	9.28 %	11
5	4	5	3	12.30 %	9
5	5	5	4	15.16 %	7
5	6	5	5	18.98 %	6
5	7	5	6	24.55 %	5
6	0	2	0	(0.26) %	(390)
6	1	6	0	3.59 %	28
6	2	6	1	6.76 %	15
6	3	6	2	9.29 %	11
6	4	6	3	12.20 %	9
6	5	6	4	15.21 %	7
6	6	6	5	18.82 %	6
6	7	6	6	24.67 %	5
7	0	3	0	(0.14) %	(736)
7	1	7	0	3.62 %	28
7	2	7	1	6.80 %	15
7	3	7	2	9.28 %	11
7	4	7	3	12.30 %	9
7	5	7	4	15.16 %	7
7	6	7	5	18.98 %	6
7	7	7	6	24.60 %	5

6   Algorithm

In this section we will discuss the image (dot over the i) of section 4 again. This time, we want to show an unverifiable modification, unverifiable in the sense of the calculated example in section 5. When embedding something, we have to change the carrier signal. The heart of a steganographic algorithm is a process that changes the signal. In our case it changes DCT coefficients. Although the changes cause an imperceptible horizontal dislocation of the image, the algorithm does not influence so-called motion vectors, at least not in a direct way. A motion compensation step (see Fig. 4) is not necessary for the implementation of this steganographic videoconferencing system. An attacker could get more precise image data by interpolating consecutive frames of an unchanging picture which he could match against the actual frame. This would reduce the space for embedding. However, delta frame coding in case of still images makes life easier for steganographers. An unchanging picture in front of the camera comes only once as a key frame. Hence, it is transmitted and used for steganography only once. It is very unlikely that the difference (or delta) frames of a still image contain a big coefficient (see $f_{\min}$ in Table 1) making them suitable for steganographic processing.

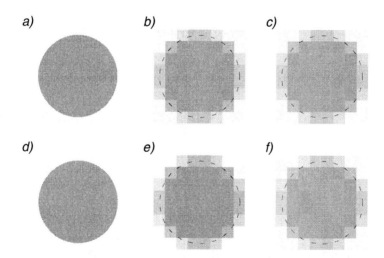

Fig. 6. "Dot over the i" and horizontal shifting: a) original, b) after decompression (unchanged), c) after decompression (changed by algorithm), d) by $\frac{1}{15}$ pixel shifted original, e) moved image after grating, f) moved image after decompression

The contrast of the original image has been increased (see Fig. 6 a)). As a result, the absolute value of one of the DCT coefficients according to Table 1 is large enough to allow a modification. (Refer to coefficient $f(0, 2)$ in the example.)

The following matrix includes the 64 brightness values of the original image with higher contrast.

$$\begin{bmatrix} 20 & 20 & 53 & 79 & 80 & 56 & 21 & 20 \\ 20 & 82 & 110 & 110 & 110 & 110 & 86 & 22 \\ 53 & 110 & 110 & 110 & 110 & 110 & 110 & 59 \\ 79 & 110 & 110 & 110 & 110 & 110 & 110 & 85 \\ 80 & 110 & 110 & 110 & 110 & 110 & 110 & 86 \\ 56 & 110 & 110 & 110 & 110 & 110 & 110 & 62 \\ 21 & 86 & 110 & 110 & 110 & 110 & 91 & 23 \\ 20 & 22 & 59 & 85 & 86 & 62 & 23 & 20 \end{bmatrix}$$

The following left matrix includes the DCT coefficients after quantization. The bold highlighted coefficient $f(0,2)$ allows a modification of 6.75 %, which means $16 \cdot 0.0675 = 1.08$. The right matrix shows this modification for $f(0,1)$.

$$\begin{bmatrix} 4 & 0 & -\mathbf{16} & 0 & -6 & 0 & -2 & 0 \\ 0 & 0 & 0 & 0 & 0 & 0 & 0 & 0 \\ -16 & 0 & -5 & 0 & 3 & 0 & 2 & 0 \\ 0 & 0 & 0 & 0 & 0 & 0 & 0 & 0 \\ -6 & 0 & 2 & 0 & 5 & 0 & 2 & 0 \\ 0 & 0 & 0 & 0 & 0 & 0 & 0 & 0 \\ -2 & 0 & 2 & 0 & 2 & 0 & 0 & 0 \\ 0 & 0 & 0 & 0 & 0 & 0 & 0 & 0 \end{bmatrix} \begin{bmatrix} 4 & -\mathbf{1} & -16 & 0 & -6 & 0 & -2 & 0 \\ 0 & 0 & 0 & 0 & 0 & 0 & 0 & 0 \\ -16 & 0 & -5 & 0 & 3 & 0 & 2 & 0 \\ 0 & 0 & 0 & 0 & 0 & 0 & 0 & 0 \\ -6 & 0 & 2 & 0 & 5 & 0 & 2 & 0 \\ 0 & 0 & 0 & 0 & 0 & 0 & 0 & 0 \\ -2 & 0 & 2 & 0 & 2 & 0 & 0 & 0 \\ 0 & 0 & 0 & 0 & 0 & 0 & 0 & 0 \end{bmatrix}$$

After recovery, the following matrixes of brightness values result, presented in Fig. 6 b) and c), too. The modification leads to a slight shifting to the right.

$$\begin{bmatrix} 26 & 26 & 53 & 76 & 76 & 53 & 26 & 26 \\ 26 & 83 & 105 & 104 & 104 & 105 & 83 & 26 \\ 54 & 107 & 103 & 104 & 104 & 103 & 107 & 54 \\ 73 & 105 & 106 & 104 & 104 & 106 & 105 & 73 \\ 73 & 105 & 106 & 104 & 104 & 106 & 105 & 73 \\ 54 & 107 & 103 & 104 & 104 & 103 & 107 & 54 \\ 26 & 83 & 105 & 104 & 104 & 105 & 83 & 26 \\ 26 & 26 & 53 & 76 & 76 & 53 & 26 & 26 \end{bmatrix} \begin{bmatrix} 26 & 26 & 52 & 76 & 77 & 55 & 26 & 26 \\ 26 & 81 & 104 & 104 & 105 & 107 & 85 & 26 \\ 52 & 105 & 102 & 103 & 104 & 105 & 109 & 57 \\ 71 & 103 & 104 & 103 & 104 & 107 & 108 & 75 \\ 71 & 103 & 104 & 103 & 104 & 107 & 108 & 75 \\ 52 & 105 & 102 & 103 & 104 & 105 & 109 & 57 \\ 26 & 81 & 104 & 104 & 105 & 107 & 85 & 26 \\ 26 & 26 & 52 & 76 & 77 & 55 & 26 & 26 \end{bmatrix}$$

The "natural" shifting as a comparison: Fig. 6 d) shows the original, shifted by $\frac{1}{15}$ pixel. The coefficients presented in the right following matrix result from transformation and quantization of the left following matrix (see also Fig. 6 e). The shifting of the original image would have caused a more intensive modification of the coefficient.

$$
\begin{bmatrix}
20 & 20 & 50 & 78 & 81 & 58 & 22 & 20 \\
20 & 76 & 110 & 110 & 110 & 110 & 91 & 23 \\
47 & 110 & 110 & 110 & 110 & 110 & 110 & 65 \\
73 & 110 & 110 & 110 & 110 & 110 & 110 & 91 \\
74 & 110 & 110 & 110 & 110 & 110 & 110 & 92 \\
50 & 110 & 110 & 110 & 110 & 110 & 110 & 68 \\
20 & 82 & 110 & 110 & 110 & 110 & 95 & 25 \\
20 & 21 & 56 & 84 & 87 & 64 & 24 & 20
\end{bmatrix}
\begin{bmatrix}
4 & -2 & -16 & 0 & -6 & 0 & -2 & 0 \\
0 & 0 & 0 & 0 & 0 & 0 & 0 & 0 \\
-16 & 0 & -5 & 1 & 3 & 0 & 2 & 0 \\
0 & 0 & 0 & 0 & 0 & 0 & 0 & 0 \\
-6 & 0 & 2 & 0 & 5 & 0 & 2 & 0 \\
0 & 0 & 0 & 0 & 0 & 0 & 0 & 0 \\
-2 & 0 & 2 & 0 & 2 & 0 & 0 & 0 \\
0 & 0 & 0 & 0 & 0 & 0 & 0 & 0
\end{bmatrix}
$$

Finally, Fig. 6 f) shows the following, recovered matrix.

$$
\begin{bmatrix}
26 & 26 & 48 & 73 & 79 & 59 & 26 & 26 \\
26 & 79 & 102 & 103 & 106 & 109 & 87 & 26 \\
49 & 103 & 102 & 103 & 104 & 104 & 110 & 60 \\
67 & 102 & 107 & 105 & 103 & 105 & 108 & 80 \\
67 & 102 & 107 & 105 & 103 & 105 & 108 & 80 \\
49 & 103 & 102 & 103 & 104 & 104 & 110 & 60 \\
26 & 79 & 102 & 103 & 106 & 109 & 87 & 26 \\
26 & 26 & 48 & 73 & 79 & 59 & 26 & 26
\end{bmatrix}
$$

As the example shows, early, non-deterministic effects at the beginning of the signal path can be reproduced in a later part (see Fig. 5).

7 Implementation

The implemented steganographic function "Embedding" (see the model in [7]) exploits the effect described in section 6: the frequency spectrum changes considerably already at minor changings of the phasing of the image.

At first, we distinguish between "suitable" and "unsuitable" blocks of DCT coefficients. Blocks are "suitable" if they include a coefficient which is larger than its minimum amount f_{min} (see Table 1). In the source code, all minimum amounts are represented by delta[]. All other blocks are "unsuitable" and will be transmitted without steganographic modification.

```
/*
    To be classified as "suitable", a block must contain one
    coefficient greater or equal to its correspondent value
    in the following matrix.
*/
unsigned int delta[64]={
    -1,-1,-1,-1,-1,-1,-1,-1,        /* -1 means infinity */
    -1,28,28,28,29,28,28,28,
    15,15,15,15,15,15,15,15,
    11,11,11,11,11,11,11,11,
     9, 9, 9, 9, 9, 9, 9, 9,
     7, 7, 7, 7, 7, 7, 7, 7,
```

```
    6, 6, 6, 6, 6, 6, 6, 6,
    5, 5, 5, 5, 5, 5, 5, 5
};

/*
    stego_in(p) is the steganographic function "embedding".
    The parameter p points to a matrix of 64 coefficients.
*/

void stego_in(int *p)
{
    int i, most_suitable, sum_of_block, is_stego, *steg_ptr;

    sum_of_block = 0; /* for sum (mod 2) */
    is_stego = 0;        /* 1 means "suitable" block */
    for (i=1; i<64; i++) {  /* skip DC coefficient p[0] */
        if (p[i]) {    /* consider non-zero coefficients */
            sum_of_block += abs(p[i]);    /* sum up */
            /* coefficient large enough? */
            if (abs(p[i]) >= delta[i]) {
                is_stego = 1;         /* "suitable" block */
                /* more suitable? then keep the pointer */
                if (abs(p[i])-delta[i] >= most_suitable) {
                    steg_ptr = &p[i-8]; /* this is f(k',n') */
                    most_suitable = abs(p[i]) - delta[i];
                }
            }
        }
    }
}
...
```

For a block classified as suitable, its further treatment depends on the modulo-2 sum of its coefficients (a kind of parity). If the parity is equal to the next bit for embedding, the block will be transmitted unchanged. If the parity is not equal, it has to be changed.

```
...
    if (is_stego)   /* suitable block? */
        /* compare the modulo-2 sum with the next bit to embed */
        if ((sum_of_block&1) != get_bit_to_embed()) {
            /* decrement abs(*steg_ptr), the coefficient */
            if (*steg_ptr > 0)
                (*steg_ptr)--;
            else if (*steg_ptr < 0)
                (*steg_ptr)++;
```

```
        else /* 0 ==> 1 */
            *steg_ptr = 1;
    }
}
```

Let $f(k, n)$ be the coefficient of a suitable block which, corresponding to Table 1, allows the maximum modification. In this case, the absolute value of the coefficient $f(k, n - 1)$ will be decreased by 1 or if it is zero, set to 1. This way, a coefficient of a block is changed by 1 and its parity flips.

All changed blocks are transmitted as well as those, where no change was necessary. The whole scenario is shown in Fig. 7. The recipient receives suitable and unsuitable blocks which are separated by the same criteria as at the sender. It has to be remarked that changed suitable blocks (suitable blocks with flipped parity) will always stay suitable blocks because the coefficient $f(k, n)$ has not been changed, but fulfills the criterion "suitable".

The recipient can extract the embedded data through reading out the parity bits of the suitable blocks sequentially. The recipient system uses all blocks for image reconstruction. The steganographic algorithm presented here acts like a quantization with a higher divisor. It increases the compression rate so that the introduced error looks natural. A lower quantizer should equalize the effect of the algorithm.

```
void stego_out(int *p) /* steganographic function "Extraction" */
{
    int i, sum_of_block, is_stego;

    sum_of_block = 0;      /* for mod-2 sum */
    is_stego = 0;        /* 1 means "suitable" block */
    for (i=1; i<64; i++) {
        if (p[i]) {      /* consider non-zero coefficients */
            sum_of_block += abs(p[i]); /* sum up */
            /* coefficient large enough? */
            if (abs(p[i]) >= delta[i])
                is_stego=1;     /* YES! suitable block! */
        }
    }
    if (is_stego) put_embedded_bit(sum_of_block & 1);
}
```

In Fig. 8 we show the surface of the application. ivsd is the daemon which receives conference calls. Per mouse click it is possible to open a window to call other daemons (single- or multicast-addresses). After establishing the video conference connection, the user of the conference *with* steganographic enhancement has two additional windows: one for the input of text (the secret message to hide) and one for displaying the embedded messages of the communicating partner.

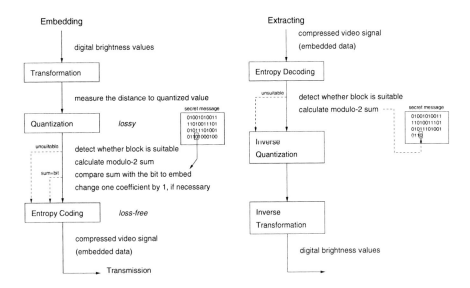

Fig. 7. Embedding and Extracting

The application is comparable to a combination of a video conference and the Unix standard command `talk`[3].

8   Conclusion

Through compression, as used with videoconferencing, the least significant bits gain importance, so every bit of the compressed signal contributes a significant part to the picture. The detection of a random replacement of these bits is possible as shown for Jsteg in [8]. However, it is possible to change parts of the carrier, making it impossible to detect these changes without direct comparison to the unchanged carrier, which should never leave the security domain. We use special features of the input devices, such as a camera or scanner. The analysis of the input devices shows free spaces permitting embedded data. If steganographic techniques simulate peculiarities of a camera, the changes do not raise any suspicion for a possible attacker. For this reason, we scrutinised the picture reception closely.

Our algorithm reproduces these effects artificially; the signal changes imperceptibly. A direct comparison with the original allows differentiation, but this still does not enable the observer to discern between the original and the altered signals. Furthermore, the sender merely transmits the changed frames. In this manner, a secret message can be embedded. The slight horizontal dephasing is unnoticeable.

---

[3] `talk` is a communication program for terminals.

Fig. 8. User interface of the implemented application

Algorithms are only trustworthy, when they are open to public scrutiny. For this it is necessary to separate the algorithm from the secrets. The simplest possibility is the generation of pseudo random bits. Both the sender and the receiver need the same key and procedure to generate these bits and use them as a pseudo one-time pad. Because the distribution of these bits has the same random uniformity as bits extracted from any video conference, the attacker can not discern between a normal video conference and one in which secret data has been embedded after encryption.

In an ISDN videoconferencing system it is possible to embed a GSM telephone conversation (up to 8 kBit/s). This depends upon the texture of the picture, because it is impossible to embed data in black frames.

References

1. Ingemar J. Cox, Joe Kilian, Tom Leighton, Tatal Shamoon, A Secure, Robust Watermark for Multimedia, In: Proceedings: Information Hiding. Workshop, Cambridge, U.K., May/June, 1996, LNCS 1174.
2. Elke Franz, Anja Jerichow, Steffen Möller, Andreas Pfitzmann, Ingo Stierand: Computer Based Steganography. In: Proceedings: Information Hiding. Workshop, Cambridge, U.K., May/June, 1996, LNCS 1174.
3. CCITT Recommendation H.261, Video Codec For Audiovisual Services At $p \times 64$ kbit/s, Genf, 1990
4. Andy C. Hung, PVRG-P64 Codec 1.1, Stanford University, 1993
5. Neil F. Johnson, Steganography, George Mason University, 1996
6. Marit Köhntopp, Steganographie als Verschlüsselungstechnik, iX 4/1996
7. Birgit Pfitzmann: Information Hiding Terminology. In: Proceedings: Information Hiding. Workshop, Cambridge, U.K., May/June, 1996, LNCS.
8. Robert Tinsley, Steganography and JPEG Compression, Final Year Project Report, University of Warwick, 1996
9. ftp://idea.sec.dsi.unimi.it/pub/security/crypt/code/s-tools4.zip
10. ftp://ftp.funet.fi/pub/crypt/steganography/
11. http://www.rugeley.demon.co.uk/security/hdsk50.zip
12. http://www.rugeley.demon.co.uk/security/
13. ftp://ftp.funet.fi/pub/crypt/mirrors/idea.sec.dsi.unimi.it/
        cypherpunks/steganography/MandelSteg1.0.tar.gz
14. http://ftp.giga.or.at/pub/hacker/stego/texto_os2.zip

Reliable Blind Information Hiding for Images [*]

Lisa M. Marvel[1], Charles G. Boncelet, Jr.[2], and Charles T. Retter[1]

[1] U.S. Army Research Laboratory, APG, MD 21005, USA
[2] University of Delaware, Newark, DE 19716, USA

Abstract. In this paper we present a new method for reliable blind image steganography that can hide and recover a message of substantial length within digital imagery while maintaining the original image size and dynamic range. Image processing, error-control coding, and spread spectrum techniques are utilized to conceal hidden data and the performance of the technique is illustrated. The message embedded by this method can be in the form of text, imagery, or any other digital signal. Applications for such a data-hiding scheme include in-band captioning, hidden communication, image tamperproofing, authentication, embedded control, and revision tracking.

1   Introduction

Digital steganography, or information hiding, schemes can be characterized by utilizing the theories of communication [17]. The parameters of information hiding such as the amount of data bits that can be hidden, the perceptibility of the message, and its robustness to removal can be related to the characteristics of communication systems: capacity, signal-to-noise ratio (SNR), and jamming margin. The notion of capacity in data hiding indicates the total number of bits hidden and successfully recovered by the stegosystem. The SNR serves as a measure of detectability. In this context, the message we are trying to conceal – the embedded signal – represents the information-bearing signal, and the cover image is viewed as noise. Contrary to typical communication scenarios where a high SNR is desired, a very low SNR for a stegosystem corresponds to lower perceptibility and therefore greater success when concealing the embedded signal. The measure of jamming resistance can be used to describe a level of robustness to removal or destruction of the embedded signal, intentional or accidental.

It is not possible to simultaneously maximize robustness, imperceptiveness, and capacity. Therefore, an acceptable balance of these items must be dictated by the application. For example, an information-hiding scheme may forgo robustness in favor of capacity and low perceptibility, whereas a watermarking scheme, which may not require large capacity or even low perceptibility, would certainly

---

[*] Prepared through collaborative participation in the Advanced Telecommunication/Information Distribution Research Program (ATIRP) Consortium sponsored by the U.S. Army Research Laboratory under Cooperative Agreement DAAL01-96-2-0002.

David Aucsmith (Ed.): Information Hiding 1998, LNCS 1525, pp. 48–61, 1998.
© Springer-Verlag Berlin Heidelberg 1998

support increased robustness. Finally, steganography used as a method of hidden communication would adopt the utmost imperceptiveness while sacrificing robustness and possibly capacity.

The prevalence of multimedia data in today's communication exposes a new avenue for hidden communication using digital steganography. Steganography, where the occurrence of communication is concealed, differs from cryptography in which communication is evident but the content of that communication is camouflaged. To be useful, a steganographic system must provide a method to *embed data invisibly*, allow the data to be *readily extracted*, promote a high information rate or *capacity*, and incorporate a certain amount of *robustness* to removal [1, 4].

With more of today's communications occurring electronically, there have been advancements in using digital signals as vehicles for steganographic communication. These signals, which are typically audio, video, or still imagery, are defined as cover signals. Schemes where the original cover signal is needed to reveal the hidden information are known as *cover escrow*. They can be useful in traitor tracing schemes such as those described in [12]. In this scenario, copies of the cover signal are disseminated with the assignee's identification embedded within, resulting in a modified cover signal. If illegal copies of the signal are acquired, the source of the copy is established by subtracting the original cover data from the modified signal, thereby exposing the offender's identity. However, in many applications it is not practical to require the possession of the unaltered cover signal in order to extract the hidden information. More pragmatic methods, known as blind or oblivious schemes, allow direct extraction of the embedded data from the modified signal without knowledge of the original cover. Blind strategies are predominant among steganography of the present day.

A block diagram of a blind system is depicted in Fig. 1 [11]. A message is embedded in a digital image by the stegosystem encoder, which uses a key or password. The resulting stegoimage is transmitted in some fashion over a channel to an intended recipient, where it is processed by the stegosystem decoder using the same key. During transmission, the stegoimage may be monitored by unintended viewers who will notice only the transmittal of the innocuous image without discovering the existence of the hidden message.

Our method, which we call Spread Spectrum Image Steganography (SSIS), is a data-hiding/hidden-communication steganographic method that uses digital imagery as a cover signal. SSIS provides the ability to hide and recover, error free, a significant quantity of information bits within digital images, avoiding detection by an observer. Furthermore, SSIS is a blind scheme because the original image is not needed to extract the hidden information. The proposed recipient need only possess a key in order to reveal the hidden message. The very existence of the hidden information is virtually undetectable.

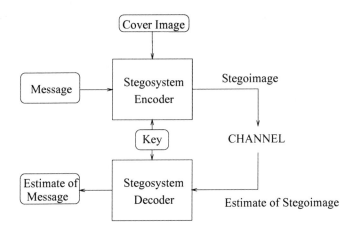

Fig. 1. Overview of steganographic system.

2   Existing Methods

During the past few years, there has been a surge of research in the area of digital image steganography. A majority of the work in the area has been performed on invisible digital watermarking. The thrust of this work can be attributed to the desire for copyright protection, spurred by the widespread use of imagery on the Internet, and the ease in which a perfect reproduction is obtained. Invisible watermarking is a form of steganography. The objective of digital watermarking is to embed a signature within a digital image to signify origin or ownership for the purpose of copyright protection. This signature is typically short in length or bits. Once added, a watermark must be robust to removal, and reliably detected even after typical image transformations such as rotation, translation, cropping, and quantization.

One method of data hiding entails the manipulation of the least significant bit (LSB) plane, from direct replacement of the cover LSBs with message bits to some type of logical or arithmetic combination between the two. Several examples of LSB schemes can be found in [21], [22], and [9]. LSB manipulation programs have also been written for a variety of image formats and can be found in [10]. LSB methods typically achieve both high capacity and low perceptibility. However, because the fact that the data are hidden in the least significant bit may be known, LSB methods are vulnerable to extraction by unauthorized parties.

There are, of course, many approaches that are cover escrow schemes, where it is necessary to possess the original cover signal in order to retrieve the hidden information. Examples of such schemes can be found in [4], [13], and [19].

Several procedures for data hiding in multimedia can be found in [1]. One of these, entitled Patchwork, alters the statistics of the cover image. First, pairs of image regions are selected using a pseudorandom number generator. Once a pair is selected, the pixel intensities within one region are increased by a constant value while the pixels of the second region are correspondingly decreased by the same value. The modification is typically small and not perceptible, but is not restricted to the LSB. A texture mapping method that copies areas of random textures from one area of the image to another is also described. Simple autocorrelation of the signal is used to expose the hidden information.

Smith and Comiskey presented several spread spectrum data-hiding methods in [17]. These techniques utilize the message data to modulate a carrier signal, which is then combined with the cover image in sections of nonoverlapping blocks. The message is extracted via cross correlation between the stegoimage and the regenerated carrier; hence, cover image escrow is not necessary. A thresholding operation is then performed on the resulting cross correlation to determine the binary value of the embedded data bits. Ideally, the modulated carrier signals should be orthogonal to the cover image and to each other for reliable message extraction. Some of the hidden data may be lost if the phase of the modulated carrier is recovered in error.

A data-hiding scheme using the statistical properties of dithered imagery is proposed by Tanaka et al. [20]. With this method, the dot patterns of the ordered dither pixels are controlled by the information bits to be concealed. This system accommodates two kilobytes of hidden information for a bilevel 256×256 image, yielding a capacity of data or information-hiding ratio of 1 information bit to 4 cover image bits. An information-hiding ratio of 1:6 is obtain for trilevel images of the same size. The method has high capacity but is restricted to dithered images and is not resistant to errors in the stegoimage.

Davern and Scott presented an approach to image steganography utilizing fractal image compression operations [5]. An information bit is embedded into the stegoimage by transforming one similar block into an approximation for another. The data are decoded using a visual key that specifies the position of the range and domain regions containing the message. Unfortunately, the amount of data that can be hidden using the method is small and susceptible to bit errors. Additionally, the search for similar blocks in the encoder, and the decoder comparison process, are both computationally expensive operations.

Recent research performed by Swanson, Zhu, and Tewfik [18] utilizes an approach of perceptual masking to exploit characteristics of the human visual system (HVS) for data hiding. Perceptual masking refers to any situation where information in certain regions of an image is occluded by perceptually more prominent information in another part of the scene [3]. This masking is performed in either the spatial or frequency domain using techniques similar to [4] and [17] without cover image escrow. The capacity of this system is naturally cover-image-dependent and not quantified.

3   SSIS

Techniques of spread spectrum communication, error-control coding, and image processing are combined to accomplish SSIS. The fundamental concept of SSIS is the embedding of the hidden information within noise, which is then added to the digital image. This noise is typical of the noise inherent in the image acquisition process and, if kept at low levels, is not perceptible to the human eye nor is it susceptible to detection by computer analysis without access to the original image. We do not assume that the cover image and the additive noise are orthogonal. In order for SSIS to be a blind steganography scheme, a version of the original image must be acquired from the stegoimage to recover an estimate of the embedded signal. To accomplish this, image restoration techniques are used. Finally, because the noise is of low power and the restoration process is not perfect, the estimation of the embedded signal is poor, resulting in a high embedded signal bit error rate (BER). To compensate, a low-rate error-correcting code is incorporated. This conglomeration of communication and image processing techniques provides a method of reliable blind image steganography.

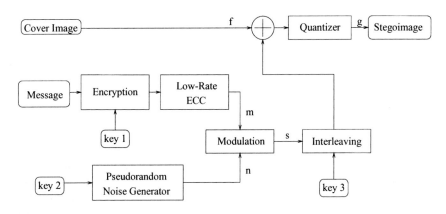

Fig. 2. SSIS encoder.

The major processes of the stegosystem encoder are portrayed in Fig. 2. Within the system, the message is optionally encrypted with key1 and then encoded via a low-rate error-correcting code, producing the encoded message, m. The sender enters key 2 into a wideband pseudorandom noise generator, generating a spreading sequence, n. Subsequently, the modulation scheme is used to spread the narrowband spectrum of m with the spreading sequence, thereby composing the embedded signal, s, which is then input into an interleaver and spatial spreader using key 3. This signal is now added with the cover image f to produce the stegoimage g, which is appropriately quantized to preserve the initial dynamic range of the cover image. The stegoimage is then transmitted in some manner to the recipient. At the receiver the stegoimage is received and the recipient, who maintains the same keys as the sender, uses the stegosystem decoder, shown in Fig. 3, to extract the hidden information. The decoder uses image restoration techniques to produce an estimate of the original cover image, $\hat{f}$, from the received stegoimage $\hat{g}$. The difference between $\hat{g}$ and $\hat{f}$ is fed into a keyed deinterleaver to construct an estimate of the embedded signal, $\hat{s}$. With key 2, the spreading sequence, n, is regenerated and the encoded message is then demodulated, and an estimate of the encoded message, $\hat{m}$, is constructed. The estimate of the message is then decoded via the low-rate error-control decoder, optionally decrypted using key 1 and revealed to the recipient.

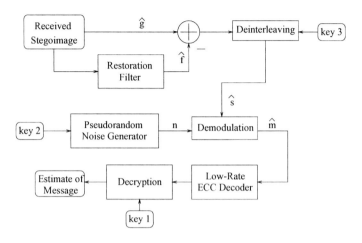

Fig. 3. SSIS decoder.

Wideband thermal noise, inherent to imagery of natural scenes captured by photoelectronic systems, can be modeled as additive white Gaussian noise (AWGN) [7]. SSIS uses this inherent noise to hide the hidden information within the digital image. In other types of coherent imaging, the noise can be modeled as speckle noise [7], which is produced by coherent radiation from the microwave to visible regions of the spectrum. We postulate that the concepts of SSIS can be extended to imagery with other noise characteristics than those modeled by AWGN. The additional noise that conceals the hidden message is a natural phenomenon of the image and, therefore, if kept at typical levels, is unsuspecting to the casual observer or computer analysis. Subsequently, even if the methodology of this system is known to eavesdroppers, they will be unable to decipher the hidden information without possession of the appropriate keys.

3.1   Spread Spectrum

Spread spectrum communication is the process of spreading the bandwidth of a narrowband signal across a wide band of frequencies. This can be accomplished by modulating the narrowband waveform with a wideband waveform, such as white noise. After spreading, the energy of the narrowband signal in any one frequency band is low and therefore difficult to detect. SSIS uses this concept to embed a message, which is a binary signal, within very low power white Gaussian noise for image steganography. The resulting signal, perceived as noise, is then added to the cover image to produce the stegoimage. Since the power of the embedded signal is low compared to the power of the cover image, the SNR is also low, thereby indicating lower perceptibility and providing low probability of detection by an observer. Subsequently, an observer will be unable to visually distinguish the original image from the stegoimage with the embedded signal.

To construct the embedded signal, we incorporate the concept of a stored reference spread spectrum communications system [16] to provide low probability of detection, either by computer or the HVS. The stored reference principle requires independent generation of identical pseudorandom wideband waveforms at both the transmitter and receiver. This can easily be accomplished by a private or public key [15] and identical pseudorandom waveform generators. Our initial system incorporated a simple sign modulation system similar to the technique of Hartung and Girod presented in [6]. However in order to obtain an increase in detection performance, a nonlinear modulation scheme was developed for SSIS to spread the spectrum of the narrowband message signal, m.

For each message bit, m_i, we need to produce two modulation values from a Gaussian distribution. One of these values will be selected based on the value of m_i, and added to a cover image pixels. In order to better distinguish between these two possible values during decoding, we want them to have the maximum Euclidean distance. To do this, consider the transformation from the cumulative distribution function of a Gaussian random variable to a uniform random variable shown in Fig. 4. Because the Gaussian cumulative distribution is a strictly increasing function, maximizing the distance between two Gaussian random variables corresponds to maximizing the distance between two uniform random variables. By selecting two uniform random variables under this criteria, we can then map the values into Gaussian random variables while maintaining the maximum distance property. Therefore we sought a transformation from one uniform random variable, u, to another, u', that maximizes their minimum distance. The transformation from u to u' must produce a uniformly distributed random variable for proper mapping.

This is accomplished by first generating the uniformly distributed random sequence, u. A second sequence, u' is generated by applying the nonlinear transformation of equation (1) to u. Both u and u' are transformed into Gaussian random variable using the inverse cumulative distribution function for a Gaussian random variable, Φ^{-1}. The embedded signal is formed by selecting signals from these two sequences arbitrated by the message bits, m_i, as shown in (2). A scale factor which dictates the power of the embedded signal is applied to the embedded signal, s, which is then added to the cover image. The result, after quantizing to grayscale values, is the stegoimage.

$$u'_i = \begin{cases} u_i + .5 & u_i < .5 \\ u_i - .5 & u_i \geq .5 \end{cases} \tag{1}$$

$$s_i = \begin{cases} \Phi^{-1}(u_i) & m_i = 0 \\ \Phi^{-1}(u'_i) & m_i = 1 \end{cases} \tag{2}$$

At the decoder, the stegoimage is obtained and image processing techniques are used to estimate the embedded signal without knowledge of the original cover

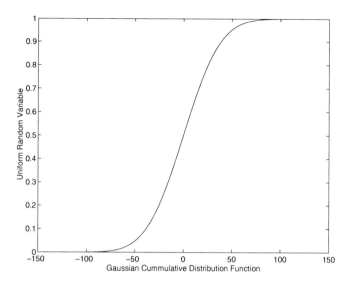

Fig. 4. Transformation from uniform random to Gaussian cumulative distribution function, $\mu = 0$, $\sigma^2 = 30$

in order to avoid the need for cover image escrow. By exercising image restoration techniques, an estimate of the embedded signal can be obtained by subtracting a version of the restored image from the stegoimage. Since the pixels of a digital image are highly correlated among neighboring pixels in natural scenes, filtering operations can be used to restore the original image. The problem of noise estimation now becomes an image restoration problem where the objective is to eliminate additive random noise in the received stegoimage. The restored image can be obtained with a variety of image processing filters, such as mean or median filters, or wavelet shrinkage techniques. However, favorable performance was obtained experimentally with adaptive Wiener filtering techniques.

3.2   Image Processing

The adaptive Wiener filter, a space-variant filter utilizing regional statistics of the image, is used by SSIS as image restoration to reduce the amount of additive random noise in the stegoimage. Assuming that a small local region of the original image $f(n_1, n_2)$ is stationary, the space-variant Wiener filter within this local region is given by (3), where σ_f^2 is the original image power estimated from the local region statistics of the stegoimage and σ_s^2 is the AWGN power known at the receiver from the regenerated sequence, n. This filter is invoked within SSIS using the algorithm developed by Lee [8]. The resultant restored image is scaled according to the relation of σ_f^2 and σ_s^2. If σ_s^2 is much greater than the contrast of the degraded image, the contrast is assumed to be primarily due to the signal

s and is significantly attenuated. Conversely, in the case that the estimated σ_f^2 is greater than σ_s^2, the local contrast is credited to the original image and little processing is done.

$$H(\omega_1, \omega_2) = \frac{\sigma_f^2}{\sigma_f^2 + \sigma_s^2} \tag{3}$$

Once obtained from the image restoration stage, the estimate of the embedded signal, $\hat{s}$, is then compared with an identical copy of the pseudorandom wideband waveform used at the encoder. The generation of the identical pseudorandom wideband waveforms is accomplished by the possession of a common key, which is used as a seed for duplicate random number generators known only to the sender and receiver. The typical spread spectrum challenge of synchronization of these waveforms is obviously alleviated in this system because the beginning of the stegoimage is easily identified.

Even though the image restoration yielded good performance, the estimate of such a low power signal, necessary to provide the degree of perceptibility essential for a steganographic system, is rather poor. Therefore, in order to compensate for the suboptimal performance of the noise estimation process, we have incorporated the use of error-control coding. The probability of error encountered during the estimation process is referred to as the embedded signal BER in succeeding sections.

3.3   Error-Control Coding

The use of low-rate error-control coding by SSIS compensates for the suboptimal estimation of the embedded signal and combats distortion, which may be encountered during the transmission process. The despread message signal may have a substantial number of bit errors, indicated by a high BER. When a large number of errors are expected to occur in a block of data, a low-rate error-correcting code must be used to correct them. The use of low-rate error-correcting codes within the SSIS system allows the hidden message to be recovered without error when the transmission channel is noiseless, thus compensating for the noise estimation process. When the transmission channel is expected to be noisy, the appropriate low-rate error-correcting code can be selected to provide desired performance.

Any error-correcting code that is capable of correcting for the high signal estimation BER can be used within SSIS. For proof of concept, binary expansions of Reed-Solomon codes [14] are used by SSIS for error correction. These codes can correct many binary errors if a decoder that corrects bits instead of Reed-Solomon code symbols is used. The decoders described in [14] are based on a simple idea of Bossert and Hergert [2]: if we have a large number of low-weight parity checks, then the number of failing parity checks tends to be proportional to the number of errors. Using this idea, we can change whichever bits reduce the number of failing parity checks until no checks fail. This algorithm works very well with binary expansions of low-rate Reed-Solomon codes because they have a large number of low-weight parity checks. With some other improvements described in [14], these decoders can correct far more binary errors than conventional Reed-Solomon decoders for the same codes. For example, the (2040,32) decoder corrects most error patterns with fewer than 763 bit errors, while a conventional Reed-Solomon decoder would be limited to 125 symbol errors, which is typically about 165 bit errors. The rate of this (2040,32) code is similar to that of a (64,1) repetition code, but because it has a much longer block length, its decoded error rate drops much more quickly as the fraction of errors per block is reduced. Even better error correction is possible with these codes if a maximum-likelihood decoder is used. However this type of coder is practical only codes with small block length.

The interleaving stage is incorporated into our system to distribute bursts of bit errors among the encoded data blocks. This is necessary because the error-correcting code has an upper bound the number of bit errors it can correct within a block. The interleaver is used to distributed errors among the blocks in a more uniform manner so that the average number of bit errors is approximately equal for all blocks. The inclusion of a key for the interleaver provides an additional level of security.

4   SSIS Performance

We use two images to demonstrate the performance of SSIS. The original 512×512 grayscale pixel images, which contain 262 kilobytes, appear in Fig. 5 entitled Allison and Sunflower. We presume the hidden message will be compressed in order to maximize capacity. Therefore, assuming that the compression method is intolerant of errors, as is the case with Huffman and arithmetic coding, we strive for total error-free recovery of the hidden data.

As an example, we have hidden messages within the images of Fig. 5 using the spreading sequence n with a variance equal to 10. The steganographic SNR, the ratio of embedded signal power to cover image power, for these two image is -31 and -34 dB, respectively. The Allison image with low SNR embedded signal has an embedded message capacity of 500 bytes where a (2040,32) code is used to compensate for the BER of 0.29. For the Sunflower image, with low SNR, the embedded signal BER is 0.20, requiring the use of a (155,25) maximum likelihood decoder resulting in a capacity near 5 kilobytes of hidden information.

By increasing the SNR, the performance of embedded signal estimation is improved at the cost of some perceptibility. To demonstrate, a higher power AWGN signal with variance 30 is used to embed information into the images with higher SNR, yielding SNR values of -27 and -29 dB, respectively. These images show only slight degradation, which is not readily apparent to a human observer. For the Allison image with high SNR, the (889,35) code is utilized to provide a hiding capacity of 1.2 kilobytes of information. The Sunflower image with higher SNR has a capacity near 5 kilobytes using a (155,25) maximum likelihood decoder to compensate for the signal estimation BER of 0.15.

In order to provide more insight into the presented methodology, a comparison between the original image pixels and the stegoimage pixels is presented

Allison original image

Sunflower original image

Allison with embedded signal,
low SNR.

Sunflower with embedded signal, low
SNR.

Allison with embedded signal, higher
SNR.

Sunflower with embedded signal,
higher SNR.

Fig. 5. Example of SSIS performance.

in Fig. 6. Here a single row of pixels has been extracted from both the original Allison image and the corresponding stegoimage with high SNR. It is evident that slight discrepancies between the two exist. However these discrepancies are slight and undetectable by human observer. Furthermore, without possession of the original image, the embedded signal is undetectable by computer analysis. The text hidden in the images is from an ASCII file containing the Treaty of Paris containing 12 kilobytes, 4.5 kilobytes compressed.

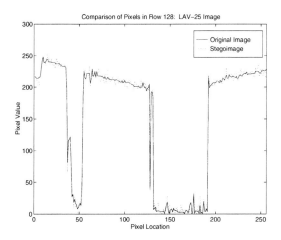

Fig. 6. Comparison of original image pixels to stegoimage pixels.

Additional protection can be provided for scenarios where additional errors are expected from the transmission process, such as in wireless environments, by using lower rate codes than those dictated by the signal estimation BER.

5   Conclusions

We have presented a novel steganographic methodology that uses error-control coding, image processing, and spread spectrum techniques correspondingly named SSIS. This process provides a method for concealing a digital signal within a cover image without increasing the size of the image. Additionally, the original image is not needed to extract the message hidden by the SSIS system. A level of security is provided by the necessity that both sender and receiver possess the same public or private keys. Furthermore, the embedded signal power is insignificant compared to that of the cover image, providing low probability of detection and thereby leaving an observer unaware of the hidden data.

Future research will be pursued to improve the performance of the embedded signal estimation. This will provide a lower embedded signal BER and thereby permit the use of higher rate error-control codes. The incorporation of higher rate codes will correspondingly increase the capacity of the system.

References

[1] W. Bender, D. Gruhl, N. Morimoto, and A. Lu. Techniques for data hiding. *IBM Systems Journal*, 35(3 & 4), 1996.

[2] M. Bossert and F. Hergert. Hard- and soft-decision decoding beyond the half minimum distance - an algorithm for linear codes. *IEEE Transactions on Information Theory*, 32(5):709–714, Sep 1986.

[3] I.J. Cox, J. Kilian, T. Leighton, and T. Shamoon. Secure spread spectrum watermarking for multimedia. Technical Report 95–128, NEC Research Institute, Technical Report, August 1995.

[4] I.J. Cox, J. Kilian, T. Leighton, and T. Shamoon. Secure spread spectrum watermarking for images, audio and video. *Proceedings of the IEEE International Conference on Image Processing, Lausanne, Switzerland*, III:243–246, September 1996.

[5] P. Davern and M. Scott. Fractal based image steganography. In R. Anderson, editor, *Information Hiding, First International Workshop*, volume 1174 of *Lecture Notes in Computer Science*, pages 279–294. Springer-Verlag, Berlin, 1996.

[6] F. Hartung and B. Girod. Fast public-key watermarking of compressed video. *Proceedings of the IEEE International Conference on Image Processing, Santa Barbara, CA*, October 1997.

[7] A.K. Jain. *Fundamentals of Digital Image Processing*. Prentice-Hall, Inc., Englewood Cliffs, NJ, 1989.

[8] J.S. Lee. Digital image enhancement and noise filtering by use of local statistics. *IEEE Transactions on Pattern Analysis and Machine Intelligence*, 2:165–168, March 1980.

[9] R. Machado. Stego, 1997. http://www.fqa.com/romana/romanasoft/stego.html.

[10] E. Milbrandt. http://members/iquest.net/mrmil/stego.html, October 1997. Steganography Info and Archive.

[11] B. Pfitzmann. Information hiding terminology. In R. Anderson, editor, *Information Hiding, First International Workshop*, volume 1174 of *Lecture Notes in Computer Science*, pages 347–350. Springer-Verlag, Berlin, 1996.

[12] B. Pfitzmann. Trials of traced traitors. In R. Anderson, editor, *Information Hiding, First International Workshop*, volume 1174 of *Lecture Notes in Computer Science*, pages 49–64. Springer-Verlag, Berlin, 1996.

[13] C.I. Podilchuk and W. Zeng. Digital image watermarking using visual models. In B.E. Rogowitz and T.N. Pappas, editors, *Human Vision and Electronic Imaging II*, volume 3016, pages 100–111. SPIE, Feb 1997.

[14] C.T. Retter. Decoding binary expansions of low-rate Reed-Solomon codes far beyond the BCH bound. *Proceedings of the 1995 IEEE International Symposium on Information Theory, Whistler, British Columbia*, page 276, Sep 1995.

[15] B. Schneier. *Applied Cryptography - Protocols, Algorithms, and Source Code in C*. John Wiley and Sons, Inc., New York, NY, 1996.

[16] M.K. Simon, J.K. Omura, R.A. Scholtz, and B. K. Levitt. *Spread Sprectrum Communications, Volume I*. Computer Science Press, Rockville, Maryland, 1985.

[17] J.R. Smith and B.O. Comisky. Modulation and information hiding in images. In R. Anderson, editor, *Information Hiding, First International Workshop*, volume 1174 of *Lecture Notes in Computer Science*, pages 207–226. Springer-Verlag, Berlin, 1996.

[18] M.D. Swanson, B. Zhu, and A.H. Tewfik. Robust data hiding for images. *Proceedings of the IEEE Digital Signal Processing Workshop, Loen, Norway*, pages 37–40, September 1996.

[19] M.D. Swanson, B. Zhu, and A.H. Tewfik. Transparent robust image watermarking. *Proceedings of the IEEE International Conference on Image Processing, Lausanne, Switzerland*, III:211–214, September 1996.

[20] K. Tanaka, Y. Nakamura, and K. Matsui. Embedding secret information into a dithered multi-level image. *Proceedings of the IEEE Military Communications Conference, Monterey, CA*, pages 216–220, 1990.

[21] R. van Schyndel, A. Tirkel, and C. Osborne. A digital watermark. *Proceedings of the IEEE International Conference on Image Processing*, 2:86–90, 1994.

[22] R.B. Wolfgang and E.J. Delp. A watermark for digital images. *Proceedings of the IEEE International Conference on Image Processing, Lausanne, Switzerland*, III:219–222, September 1996.

Cerebral Cryptography

Yvo G. Desmedt[1]*, Shuang Hou[2]*, and Jean-Jacques Quisquater[3]

[1] EE & CS, and the Center of Cryptography, Computer and Network Security
University of Wisconsin – Milwaukee, PO Box 784, WI 53201, USA, and
Dept. of Mathematics, Royal Holloway, University of London, UK
desmedt@uwm.edu
http://www.uwm.edu/~desmedt/
[2] Department of EE & CS, University of Wisconsin, Milwaukee
P.O. Box 784, WI 53201 Milwaukee, U.S.A.
hou@cs.uwm.edu
[3] Dept of Electrical Eng. (DICE) UCL Crypto Group, Place du Levant
3 Université Catholique de Louvain B-1348 Louvain-la-Neuve Belgium
Quisquater@dice.ucl.ac.be

Abstract. In this paper we present a new "hiding" scheme. Our method uses pictures and secret sharing. The approach is completely different from the one suggested by Kurak-McHugh. We use two pictures as in visual cryptography and each picture corresponds to a secret share of the message. Our scheme differs from visual cryptography. First, while visual cryptography is a cryptosystem, our scheme is both a cryptosystem as well as a hiding system. Our images are not random, but correspond to real photographs randomly altered. This modification of the original image is quite invisible to the naked eye. Secondly, our decryption method does not use the subtractive properties of light. The decryption is done by our brain using the perceived 3-D properties of the human visual system. A 3-D viewer is the only decryption hardware needed.

1 Introduction

In 1994 the concept of visual cryptography was presented in the unclassified world by Naor and Shamir [8]. Visual cryptography is a perfectly secure encryption scheme in which both the ciphertext and the key are pixels, with 1 bit depth, printed on transparencies. One can also view the ciphertext and the key as shares of the messages. The decryption is done by stacking the key transparency on top of the ciphertext transparency.

Biham [1] recently made transparencies for visual cryptography in which *a part* of each share forms a 1 bit deep real picture.

Our research has several goals, which we now motivate:

- Random transparencies and 1 bit deep pictures are very unusual. They are therefore suspect to censors. In some circumstances the user of a cryptoscheme wants to avoid censors (or in a more modern context, key escrow, e.g., [7,5,3]), as explained in [4, Chapter 16].

---

* A part of this research has been supported by NSF Grant NCR-9106327.

David Aucsmith (Ed.): Information Hiding 1998, LNCS 1525, pp. 62–72, 1998.
© Springer-Verlag Berlin Heidelberg 1998

– Many hiding techniques have the disadvantage that once their hiding method is known, anyone can find the hidden text. We therefore want to guarantee that knowledge of the techniques does not allow a censor to find the hidden text.
– In some countries electronic computer equipment (and other high tech equipment) is suspect. As in visual cryptography, the recipient should be able to decrypt the plaintext without using digital computer equipment. We also note that modern digital computers are insecure. Goldberg and Wagner just found that at least 10 digits out of 64 bits keys in GSM system were actually zeroes. GSM is the world's most widely used encryption system for cellular phones [16]. Not only is it dangerous to trust software, trusting complicated hardware is also not recommended.

It seems that the idea of using secret sharing [2,9] as in visual cryptography offers the highest form of security to protect the privacy. If the picture is sent via two different paths, the same censor needs to control both paths to breach the privacy. However, the problem with visual cryptography is that it is likely that *both* images will be censored (independently) since they are suspect. Visual cryptography is therefore unreliable in a context with censors. Our goal is to address these problems.

We note that our schemes also have cryptographic relevance, since:

– our decryption method is more stable than visual cryptography. In visual cryptography the receiver has to "synchronize" both transparencies. This makes the scheme very vulnerable to errors. So the transparencies must be transported very carefully.
– we use a completely different decryption method than the one used in visual cryptography.

The paper is organized as follows. First we introduce our model in section 2. In section 3 we present the main idea. In section 4 we discuss two schemes that satisfy our goals. We finally conclude and introduce open problems in section 5.

2   Model

Before we present our schemes we introduce the model on which our cryptosystems have been built.

There are 2 agents (or in general n) that transport some secret message from one country to another country. Each agent carries one (or in general m) pictures, in which the secret message is embedded. They can not use computers.

There are human censors at each custom office who checks each passenger's baggage. They cannot use a computer, either. We allow for two types of censors. Some that only censor suspicious pictures (then 2 pictures are sufficient). The other type of censor will randomly destroy pictures (then we need n agents).

There is also some counterintelligence who may intercept one suspect picture. They have unrestricted computer power, but we assume they never obtain 2 pictures.

Our goal is that at least 2 agents can enter the other country successfully and finally meet each other. They put their shares together and they can decrypt the message without using any computer.

Our model has the following security properties:

– Unconditional privacy, i.e., the conterintelligece has infinite computer power.
– A censor can only use human computation.

Note: Modern cryptography has three levels of computation powers, i.e.,

– infinite computer power
– quantum computer power
– polynomial time (Turing machine) computer power.

We have extended this to include human computation power.

In this paper, we use "embedded message" to refer to the plaintext, "cover" to represent the original image which is used to encrypt the plaintext and "stego-" to refer to the modified image which is transported by agents.

3   The Main Idea

Our goal is to use shares of the embedded message that are high quality real life pictures. We therefore start from a *single* high quality picture as the cover image after we get the message to be sent. We then want to produce two stego-images of high quality, if one composes these, one obtains the embedded message.

We have tried several methods to make visual cryptography work with such high quality real life pictures. In the many approaches we tried, the pictures had to be altered dramatically before our visual system was able to see the embedded picture. These alterations were obvious to a censor and therefore unacceptable. We concluded that we should approach the problem differently. We choose to modify the decryption method.

In visual cryptography it is the translucent properties of light that allow decryption. In our approach, we use the depth perception property of our human visual systems and the decryption is done by the human 3-D visual system including our two eyes and mainly our brain. We call cryptosystems based on such a decryption method "cerebral cryptosystems."

As in our failed attempts, we start from a real life picture and use it to create two pictures. However, this time we use a 3-D viewer [17] to see the embedded pictures. The main challenge was to guarantee at the same time perfect secrecy and make the alterations to the original picture invisible to the naked eye.

The cryptographic schemes we present in this paper are aimed to provide picturesque shares as well as perfect security. Both shares originate from a regular picture. Each share separately looks just as a regular picture. Moreover, one picture only does *not* reveal any information about the secret. Putting two pictures side by side and using a 3-D viewer one can see the embedded message coming out of the background.

4   Schemes

To transform a single picture into two that have some 3-D features we use one aspect of the depth perception property of our human eyes. Before we give the full description of our scheme, we need to explain a little bit about this property on which our scheme is based.

4.1   Depth Perception

We observe the distance of objects due to the perception property of our human visual systems [12]. There are two aspects of this property. One is that two eyes catch two different views. The other is that things get smaller if they are far away. We now discuss one simple method of generating *stereograms* based on the first aspect.

When looking at a 3-D object, our two eyes catch two different images. In Fig. 1 we give an illustration.

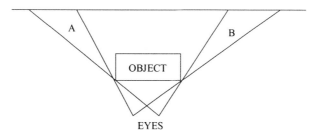

Two eyes (or photographic equipment) placed at
a horizontal distance from each other perceive a
different world as explained.

Fig. 1. A simple illustration of different views seen by two eyes.

Suppose there is an object in front of our eyes, we cannot see areas behind the object. Besides, the left eye can see area A while the right eye cannot. The right eye can see area B while the left eye cannot.

We start with two copies of a single picture. We then drop some pixels at area A in the first copy and drop some pixels at area B in the second copy. When we put the modified copies side by side and look at them through a 3-D viewer we can see the area between A and B sticking out of the background and therefore we get a perception of the distance. For later reference, we call this method *dropping pixel method*. Evidently, when the original picture is just an all white picture, the 3-D version will have no 3-dimensional aspect. So, we need enough variation (i.e., a large high frequency component) in the picture (or in the part of the picture) we use.

4.2   Basic Idea

For convenience, we will refer to our scheme as a 2-out-of-2 secret sharing scheme.

The basic idea of our 2-out-of-2 secret sharing scheme is to generate the share s_1 based on random coin flips b and the second share s_2 based on $b \oplus S$, where S is the secret we want to hide and $\oplus$ is the exclusive-or. It is clear from the properties of the *one-time pad* [15,14] that such schemes guarantee perfect secrecy.

4.3   A 3-D Bar Code Scheme

Our first algorithm is a direct implementation of the dropping pixel method, in which we drop entire vertical lines. Therefore, it requires the secret to be vertical lines only, as in bar codes. Following is the description of this algorithm.

The setting

a cover picture P which is any regular picture with enough variation.

an embedded picture S which is a one bit depth picture with only vertical lines. The total size of the bar code is identical to the size of the embedded picture P.

parameter N: determines among how many columns one will drop one column.

pattern $A_0 = 1000\ldots000$ **(N bits)**   represents N columns and bit "1" represents dropping. So this pattern indicates to drop the first column among the N columns currently considered.

pattern $A_1 = 0000\ldots000$ **(N bits)**   which says not to drop any column among the N columns.

Procedure:

- generate the first share s_1 as follows: For every N adjacent columns, flip a coin b. Modify the N corresponding columns of picture P accordingly to pattern A_b. I.e., randomly choose dropping the 1st column of the N columns or not dropping the column.
- Generate the second share s_2: For every N adjacent columns, compute $b' = b \oplus S$. Modify the N corresponding columns of picture P accordingly to pattern $A_{b'}$. In other words, if there are no lines in the corresponding area in the embedded picture then choose the same pattern as s_1 (copy s_1). If there is a line in the embedded picture then choose the opposite pattern as in s_1.

Looking at the shares s_1 and s_2 through the 3-D glasses, we can clearly see the edges bumping up and down which represent lines in the embedded picture. One set of pictures is provided with $N = 10$ (Fig. 3).

Due to the perfectness of the scheme, we cannot control whether a "bar" goes up or down. Indeed it depends whether area A (Sect. 4.1) or area B comes first, which is random.

4.4   A More General Scheme

Since bar code messages are not user friendly, we now try to increase the bandwidth. We tested whether we could use above process on a single row and repeat it independently for the next row. First of all, we found that if we process the images independently row by row and drop only one pixel at a time instead of dropping the whole column, we are not able to see the bumping edges. Secondly, the quality of pictures is damaged since we do not have the same amount of pixels dropped for each row. The last problem prevents us from proceeding with m rows at a time (where m is smaller than the total number of rows in the picture). In other words, to drop m pixels, instead of the full column.

It seems that only bar code pictures can be encoded, preventing us to send more readable characters, such as the English alphabet. However, a new idea allows us to solve this problem. We now present a solution to the aforementioned problem maintaining the picturesque quality of the two shares. We partition the pictures into rectangular blocks (submatrices in a block matrix). This allows us to encode more complex characters than bar codes. *In each block we drop in* both shares *the same number of pixels*. As in the previous method we use two patterns, however, both patterns contain the same number of 1's.

We pointed out in Section 4.3 that we cannot control whether a block goes up or down. This implies that (when we decode) the encoded character will not be seen as going up or down as one entity, but the blocks that make that character will go up or down. So, to decrypt, we need to mentally reconstruct which letter corresponds to a bunch of blocks going up and down randomly. If letters are not too close, this seems not to be a problem.

We now give the details.

Parameters:

block of size $M \times N$: N represents # of columns in a block, M represents # of rows in a block

pattern B_0, 100...000 (N bits)   represents an $M \times N$ block and bit "1" represents dropping a column. So, in this pattern, we drop the M pixels in the first column in the $M \times N$ block.

pattern B_1, 000...001 (N bits)   also represents an $M \times N$ block. In this pattern, we drop the M pixels in the last column in the $M \times N$ block.

The setting:

a cover picture P   which is any regular picture with enough variation.

an embedded message S   which is a one bit depth black and white picture, using blocks to represent the secret content.   For example, letter H might be represented by 7 blocks as illustrated in Fig. 2.

Procedure:

– Generate the first share as follows: For every $M \times N$ adjacent pixels (a block) flip a coin b. Modify picture P accordingly to pattern B_b.

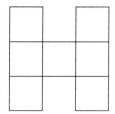

Fig. 2. Letter H in blocks.

– Generate the second share: For every $M \times N$ adjacent pixels (a block) compute $b' = b \oplus S$. Modify picture P accordingly to pattern $B_{b'}$. In other words if the corresponding block in S is not a secret block, then choose the same pattern as in s_1, if the block is a secret block, then choose the opposite pattern as in s_1.

We provide one set of 512×512 pictures with block size 40×20 (Fig. 4). Letter H is hidden in the hair area of the picture. Looking at s_1 and s_2 through the 3-D viewer, we can see 7 blocks bumping up and down randomly from the background which reconstruct letter H. Some training is required to see that it is a letter H because some parts of the letter go up and other parts go down and this is totally random. The block size can be as small as 10×10 in a 512×512 picture and letters can still be seen clearly.

We also use this example to demonstrate that our encryption method is quite different from visual cryptography. If one attempts to use the visual decryption method of visual cryptography to decrypt a cerebral encryption, one fails. To demonstrate this, we recommend to print two shares on transparencies and stack them up as in visual cryptography. By doing so, one can not see the embedded picture. However, it is easy to decrypt it with a 3-D viewer.

4.5   2-out-of-n Schemes

To generalize our previous 2-out-of-2 to 2-out-of-n, we use the secret sharing scheme discussed in [13] and use $\lceil \log_2(n) \rceil$ different pictures as cover pictures.

The 2-out-of-n secret sharing scheme in [13] is based on $\lceil \log_2(n) \rceil$ many 2-out-of-2 sharing schemes executed independently. So if k is the secret key, one has $k = r_0^i \oplus r_1^i$, where $1 \leq i \leq \lceil \log_2(n) \rceil$. When numbering the participants from 0 to $n-1$, participant j receives share r_0^i if the ith bit of the binary representation of the integer j is 0, else r_1^i.

So, in our context, one uses $\lceil \log_2(n) \rceil$ images as covers. For practical purposes they are different. For each of the $\lceil \log_2(n) \rceil$ picture one creates shares R_0^i and R_1^i as in our previous 2-out-of-2 cerebral cryptosystem. A participant j receives the image share R_0^j when the ith bit of the binary representation of j is 0, else receive R_1^i.

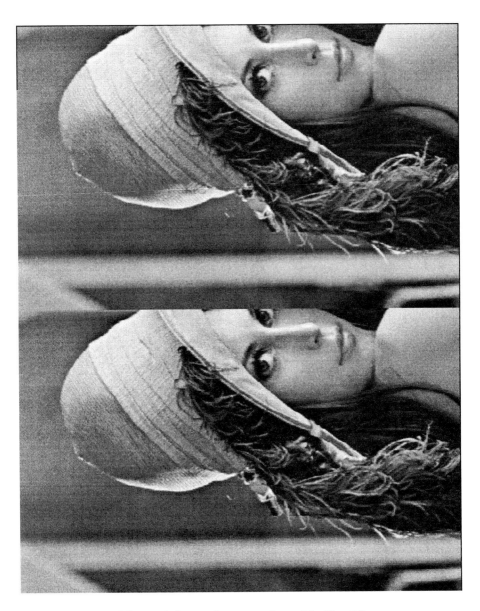

Fig. 3. A bar code encryption with $N = 10$.

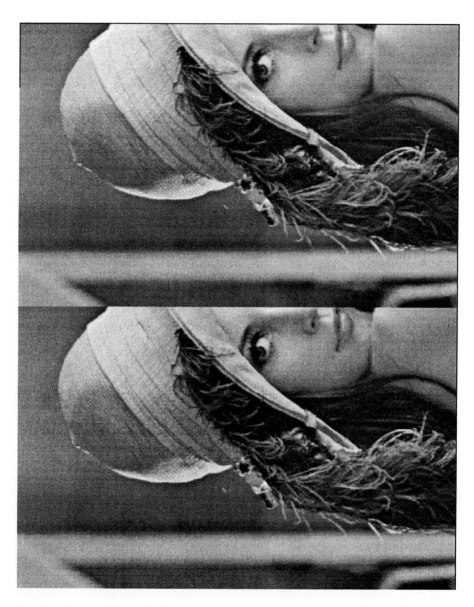

Fig. 4. An encryption of H, using our more general cerebral cryptoscheme with block size 40×20. Look at the hair area.

5   Conclusions and Open Problems

We have modified visual cryptography into a hiding technique. Our shares are innocent pictures that have been randomized in a subtle way. We have also demonstrated that our technique is different from visual cryptography and is therefore also of interest to the cryptographic community. Since the decryption is done by the brain, we called our method "cerebral cryptography."

Our method does not require transparencies. Our pictures can be printed on photographic paper, or normal paper using a laser printer and copied on transparencies.

Our decryption method is much more stable than the one in visual cryptography.

We want to point out that few people may not be able to see the embedded picture.

Visual cryptography as well as cerebral cryptography do not need a digital computer to decrypt the ciphertext, however they *do* require one to encrypt the plaintext. This introduces three open questions:

- can a cryptographic scheme be developed that does not need a digital computer or electronic hardware to encrypt plaintext, and
- can a scheme be developed that does not rely on digital computers (or electronic equipment) for encryption as well as for decryption.
- can this technique be extended to allow authentication, watermarking, etc.

Acknowledgments

We would like to thank V. Binga for the 3D machine, thank Bob Blakley for discussions on visual cryptography and thank Kieran G. Larkin for discussions at the workshop.

References

1. Biham, E.: September 21–26, 1997. Lecture given at Daghstuhl, Germany
2. Blakley, G. R.: Safeguarding cryptographic keys. In *Proc. Nat. Computer Conf. AFIPS Conf. Proc. (1979)* pp. 313–317
3. A proposed federal information processing standard for an escrowed encryption standard (EES). Federal Register July 30, 1993
4. Kahn, D.: *The Codebreakers.* Sphere Books Limited London, Great Britain
5. Kilian, J., Leighton, T.: Failsafe key escrow, revisited. In *Advances in Cryptology – Crypto '95, Proceedings (Lecture Notes in Computer Science 963) (1995)* D. Coppersmith, Ed. Springer-Verlag pp. 208–221
6. Kurak, C., McHugh, J.: A cautionary note on image downgrading. In *Proceedings of the 8th Computer Security Applications Conference (December 1992)*
7. Micali, S.: Fair public-key cryptosystems. In *Advances in Cryptology – Crypto '92, Proceedings (Lecture Notes in Computer Science 740) (1993)* E. F. Brickell, Ed. Springer-Verlag pp. 113–138

8. Naor, M., Shamir, A.: Visual cryptography. In *Advances in Cryptology – Eurocrypt '94, Proceedings (Lecture Notes in Computer Science 950) (May 9–12, 1995)* A. D. Santis, Ed. Springer-Verlag pp. 1–12

9. Shamir, A.: How to share a secret. *Commun. ACM* **22** *(1979)* 612–613

10. Simmons, G. J.: An introduction to shared secret and/or shared control schemes and their application. In *Contemporary Cryptology, G. J. Simmons, Ed. IEEE Press New York 1992* pp. 441–497

11. Stinson, D. R.: *Cryptography: Theory and Practice.* CRC Boca Raton 1995

12. MacMahan, Horace: *Stereogram book of contours, illustrating selected landforms.* Hubbard Press 1972.

13. Desmedt, Y. and G. Di Crescenzo and Burmester, M. : Multiplicative non-abelian sharing schemes and their application to threshold cryptography. In *Advances in Cryptology – Asiacrypt '94*, Proceedings (Lecture Notes in Computer Science 917), pp. 21–32.

14. Shannon, C.E.: Communication theory of secrecy systems. *Bell systems technical journal*, 28 (1949), 656–715

15. Vernam, G.S.: Secret signaling system. *U.S. Patent # 1,310,719, 22 Jul 1919*

16. *The New York Times*, April 14, 1998, pp.C1.

17. 3-D Adventure, *Starsis*, Berkeley, CA.

The Steganographic File System

Ross Anderson[1], Roger Needham[2], and Adi Shamir[3]

[1] Cambridge University; rja14@cl.cam.ac.uk
[2] Microsoft Research Ltd; needham@microsoft.com
[3] Weizmann Institute; shamir@wisdom.weizmann.ac.il

Abstract. Users of some systems are at risk of being compelled to disclose their keys or other private data, and this risk could be mitigated if access control mechanisms supported an element of plausible deniability. However, existing plausible deniability mechanisms, such as the one-time pad, are of rather limited scope.

In this paper, we present the steganographic file system. This is a storage mechanism designed to give the user a very high level of protection against being compelled to disclose its contents. It will deliver a file to any user who knows its name and password; but an attacker who does not possess this information and cannot guess it, can gain no information about whether the file is present, even given complete access to all the hardware and software. We provide two independent constructions, which make slightly different assumptions.

1 Introduction

Much work has been done on devising mechanisms, such as digital signatures, that can be used to provide non-repudiation; there has been much less work on the complementary property, namely plausible deniability. Yet there are many applications in which plausible deniability could be valuable:

- soldiers and intelligence agents may be captured and tortured into revealing cryptographic keys and other secret data;
- when conducting delicate negotiations, such as between a company and a trade union, informal offers may be made which will be denied in the event of later litigation. However, the other side might obtain court orders for access to documents;
- police power may be abused. An individual may be arrested on 'suspicion' of a crime, found with an encrypted hard disk partition, and told that if he does not supply the password, this will be taken as evidence of guilt. But the encrypted files might well contain confidential business information sought by people who have bribed the police;
- private individuals have been tortured by robbers into revealing information such as the secret codes for their bank cards and the location of safes [12].

David Aucsmith (Ed.): Information Hiding 1998, LNCS 1525, pp. 73–82, 1998.

There are few mechanisms available at present to provide protection against these threats. Crypto keys may be kept in tamper resistant devices, but tamper resistance is relative, especially against a capable motivated opponent [4]; incriminating documents can be shredded, but the word processor files used to create them may persist for months in backup tapes (as Oliver North found to his cost); and while the one-time pad may provide an element of plausible deniability in communications, it is difficult to use in data storage because the pad must also be stored somewhere (in the next section, we will discuss one way to overcome this difficulty). There are some deniable encryption schemes in the literature (e.g. [5,6,11]) but these protocols can still generally protect only short messages, and are not applicable to storage.

One possible defence against compulsion is dual control. Bank managers understand that the real purpose of having a dual combination lock on the vault is not to prevent them taking cash (they have many ways to do that!) but to stop their families being taken hostage. The manager's inability to open the lock on his own removes the temptation for criminals to try to force him.

Dual control may be inappropriate, such as for an attorney in single handed practice. It may also be inadequate, for example where crypto keys are shared between two soldiers in a signals unit who might be captured at the same time, or where someone has abused the legal process to obtain an injunction compelling an innocent party to disclose information against his interests. In all such cases, it may be sufficient if the victim can convincingly simulate an inability to perform the act required by the opponent.

These considerations motivate us to design a file system with the following property. A user may provide it with the name of an object, such as a file or directory, together with a password; and if these are correct for an object in the system, access to it will be provided. However, an attacker who does not have the matching object name and password, and lacks the computational power to guess it, can get no information about whether the named object even exists.

The concept of operations is that the user of such a file system could, if placed under compulsion, reveal (say) the three passwords used to protect the directories with his email archive, his tax records and his love letters, but keep quiet about the directory containing his trade secrets. The opponent would have no means of proving that such a directory exists.

We do not assume any properties of tamper resistance, whether of hardware or software. We assume that the opponents who may place the user under compulsion are competent; that they can examine the system at the level of bits and gates, and understand all its hardware and software completely. The only difference between them and the user is that the user knows one or more passwords (or more accurately, strong passphrases).

The first of our constructions assumes only that there are limits to the amount of knowledge of the plaintext that the opponent possesses, and to the number of computations that he can perform. In the second, we will assume the existence of a block cipher that the opponent cannot break.

2   A Simple Construction

Our first construction makes no assumptions about the existence of 'good' ciphers. Its protection goal is that if the opponent has no knowledge of the filename and password, then he can get no information about whether such a file is present in the system unless he already knows some of the file contents or tries all possible passwords. For the sake of simplicity in exposition, we will assume a password P of k bits. We might imagine that the filename plus a strong passphrase has somehow been compressed to a P of k bits in length; but we stipulate nothing about P other than that the opponent must not be able to guess it.

The idea is to have a number of cover files in the system, which start out as random, and then embed the user's files as the exclusive or of a subset of the cover files. This subset is chosen by the password.

To give a concrete example, suppose that all files are of the same length and that there are k cover files in the system to begin with, say $C_0, \ldots, C_{k-1}$. Let the first user file be F and its password be P. We then select those C_j for which the jth bit of P is one and combine them using bitwise exclusive or; the result is in turn XOR'ed with the user supplied file F and the result of this operation is finally exclusive or'ed with one of the C_j. The result is that the user's file F is now the exclusive or of the subset of the C_j selected by the nonzero bits of P. Symbolically,

$$F = \bigoplus_{P_j=1} C_j \tag{1}$$

A user can embed a number of files as combinations of the cover files. Adding subsequent files entails solving sets of linear equations to decide which combinations of the C_j to alter.

An important property of this system is that if we have a linear access hierarchy – that is, a user storing a file at a given security level knows the passwords of all the files stored at lower levels – then files can be added in a natural way without disturbing already hidden files. Assuming that the k cover files $C_0, \ldots, C_{k-1}$ are used to hide a smaller number m of user files $F_0, \ldots, F_{m-1}$, and that each file is n bits long, let $\mathbf{C}$ be the k x n matrix over GF(2) whose i-th row is the current contents of cover file C_i. Initially this matrix is filled with random bits. As we store or update an actual user file F_j, we modify the k cover files in a way which is guaranteed to change F_j without affecting any of the other user files; this can be done even by someone who has access only to files up to a certain security level, and has no information about the contents (or extraction method) of the "higher" files.

The basic idea is to use an orthonormal k x k binary matrix $\mathbf{K}$ as the extraction key. If K_j is the j-th row of $\mathbf{K}$, then F_j is defined as the vector-matrix product K_j x $\mathbf{C}$ (mod 2), which XORs the rows of $\mathbf{C}$ indicated by the 1's along the j-th row in $\mathbf{K}$. The orthonormality condition implies that K_j x K_i^t (row times column product, giving a scalar) is 1 if $i = j$, and 0 otherwise.

Suppose we want to modify only the i-th user file F_i by XORing it with the binary difference file D of length n. We change the cover file system represented by the matrix $\mathbf{C}$ by XORing to it the matrix $K_i^t \times D$ (t denotes transpose, so this is a column vector multiplied by a row vector, giving a $k \times n$ matrix). Consider now for any j the new value of the user file F_j, computed by $K_j \times (\mathbf{C} \text{ XOR } K_i^t \times D) = (K_j \times \mathbf{C}) \text{ XOR } (K_j \times K_i^t) \times D$. The second part is zero for all $i \neq j$, and D for $i = j$, which gives the desired effect on the secret files.

What is left is to show how a user can be given only his part of the key matrix $\mathbf{K}$, without revealing other parts or asking him to memorize lots of bits. We can use the standard trick of mapping a random initial password p_0 by iterating a one way function h (or even better, a one-way permutation) via $p_{i+1} = h(p_i)$. If we now give some user the value of p_i as his password, then he can compute all the later p's but not the earlier p's. We now map each p_i into a random binary vector with an odd number of 1's (so that its dot product with itself is 1). Finally, we use the Gram-Schmidt method to orthonormalise all the vectors from i onwards by subtracting from the candidate K_i all its components along later K_j which the user knows by the chaining property of the p_j's. In other words, a user who knows p_i can compute all the orthonormal key vectors K_j for $j \geq i$, but not any earlier ones.

This gives us a linear hierarchy of access rights, where each user has access to all the files from some index onwards. We cannot extend it all the way to k secret files, since when $K_2, K_3, \ldots, K_k$ are known binary vectors and K_1 is known to complement them to an orthonormal basis, it is uniquely defined. But if we ensure that the number m of secret files is a number randomly chosen in $1, \ldots, k/2$, the orthonormalization process is very likely to succeed, and it will be exponentially hard in k to find one more key vector given all the later key vectors.

To extend this 'multilevel secure' file system to provide the plausible deniability which we seek, the user must have a number of passwords p_i rather than just one (or two) of them. The p_i can therefore be generated at random rather than by repeated hashing, and users can manage them in any of the standard ways: a number of the p_i could be stored on disc, encrypted under user passphrases, together with a number of nulls (objects that look like encrypted passwords but are not), so that the opponent cannot tell how many genuine ones there are. Alternatively, mnemonics can be used to map the p_i to passphrases, in which case there would be no need to keep passwords encrypted on the disk. The rest of the linear algebra goes over as before.

Linear algebra also gives us a known-message attack: if the size of the password is k and the opponent knows more than k bits of plaintext, then after obtaining all the random files from the computer he can write k linear equations in the k unknown bits of the key. This is why we add the explicit assumption that the opponent knows nothing about the plaintext. If this assumption holds, then the scheme appears vulnerable only to an opponent who can guess the password.

Requiring that the opponent be totally ignorant of the file contents may be simple where these contents consist of random data such as crypto keys, but could often be onerous. For example, a tax inspector searching for early drafts of a set of accounts might know the location and value of the tax reference number in the files in question, and this could be enough to break the system for (say) $k = 100$. There is a simple practical solution: to disallow knowledge of the plaintext by preencrypting it with a key derived from the password. We will discuss below how an alternative construction is available, given the assumption that strong ciphers exist.

Meanwhile, we have shown how a simple steganographic file system can be constructed; it enables a user under compulsion to reveal (say) seventeen passwords that retrieve files on his tax affairs, love affairs, and so on, but hold back the eighteenth password which would have revealed the design for the new security system that the opponent was interested in. On the assumptions above, and absent implementation defects, there is no way that the opponent can tell that a valid eighteenth combination of filename and passphrase exists at all in the system.

In a practical system, we may wish to provide for files of different lengths, and we will also probably want the granularity of protection to correspond to directories rather than individual files. This can be accommodated in the above system by packing each directory into one of the files F_j whose length might be fixed at (say) 10MB; 100 such directories easily fit on a typical modern PC with 3.5 GB of hard disk, leaving plenty of room for the operating system and non-secret software and data. We could then end up with a hierarchy of several dozen directories for 'tax', 'love letters', 'company secrets' and so on, will only have to remember one passphrase for each level at which disclosure is to be made. Disc space is nowadays so cheap that having to allocate large fixed size directories is not a real problem for most applications; however there are two problems, one major and one minor.

The minor problem is that it might not always be convenient to have a strict linear access hierarchy, and the major problem is that there would be a significant performance penalty: reading or writing a file would involve reading or writing about 50 times and if this involved processing the entire directory contents it would entail about 500MB read or written on average. It need not however, since the modification or access can be done on arbitrarily narrow "slices" of the k x n matrix $\mathbf{C}$. For example, if the modification vector D is nonzero in a single bit (say, the q-th), then the product k_i^t x D is nonzero only in its q-th column, and thus both the computation and the data access are unnecessary except at these k bytes.

A further reduction in the overhead of reading and writing can be obtained by doing arithmetic over a field other than $\mathrm{GF}(2)$. This makes it possible to separate the security parameter from the number of levels in the access hierarchy. The reason we have 100 cover files is to have a complexity of 2^{100} in guessing the linear combination. This also gives us 100 levels in the hierarchy, which is likely to be too large. Instead, we can use 16 cover files which are added with coefficients from, say, $\mathrm{GF}(2^8)$ or $\mathrm{GF}(251)$ (the largest single byte prime). Guessing a vector of 16 such coefficients has probability about 2^{-128}, and we have about 8 levels in the access hierarchy. In terms of efficiency, to compute one byte of real file we need only 16 bytes (one from each cover file). This is probably a good choice of parameters. However, we still have a 16-fold penalty on reading and writing, and are constrained to a linear access hierarchy. This motivates us to ask if there is another way of implementing a steganographic file system.

3   An Alternative Construction

One might ask: why not just fill the whole hard disk with random bits, and then write each file block at an absolute disk address given by some pseudorandom process, such as by encrypting the block's location in the file using as a key a one-way hash of the filename and the directory password? The block could also be encrypted using a key derived using a similar process, and so – on the assumption that we have a block cipher which the opponent cannot distinguish from a random permutation – the presence or absence of a block at any location should not be distinguishable.

The problem with such a naïve approach is that, thanks to the birthday theorem in probability theory, we would start to get 'collisions' (where we overwrote already written data) once we had written a little more than $\sqrt{N}$ blocks, where there are N blocks in the disk. Given that a modern hard disk might have a million blocks, it would be 'full' after somewhat over a thousand of them had been written – a very wasteful use of resources.

However, there is a solution: write the block at more than one location. If, for example, we write each block in two pseudorandomly chosen locations, then both of these blocks will be overwritten by a third when the number of blocks is approximately that required to produce triples under resampling, namely $O(N^{2/3})$. It is straightforward to add redundancy to each block before encrypting it, so that the system can identify when a block has been overwritten and look for it in the other location instead.

Continuing in this way, we might hope that if we write to ten locations, then before all locations containing a block are accidentally overwritten, we could write $O(N^{9/10})$ blocks, and so on. However, the situation is somewhat more complicated.

Suppose that that K different blocks are written and that we write each block m times, giving a total of mK write operations (including overlaps). Consider the probability that an individual block will be overwritten by subsequent writes. If there are M of these, then the total number of distinct blocks that are written n_i times out of the total of N blocks is [1]:

$$\pi(n_1, n_2, \ldots, n_M) = 1/N^M \binom{N}{n_1, n_2, \ldots, n_M} \frac{M!}{\prod_{i=1}^{M} (i!)^{n_i}} \tag{2}$$

which can be approximated for computational purposes as:

$$\pi(n_1, n_2, \ldots, n_M) \simeq 1/(N^m e^{M^2/2N}) \frac{M^{M-n_1}}{\prod_{i=1}^{M} (i!)^{n_i} n_i!} \tag{3}$$

so the total number of distinct blocks that are overwritten is:

$$\Phi(M, N) = \sum_1^M \pi(n_1, n_2, \ldots, n_M) \tag{4}$$

where the sum is over all possible combinations of the n_j. The probability that one of the k versions of block number j survives this overwriting process is given by $1 - [\Phi((j-1)m, N)]^k$, and indeed the probability p that any one of the K files gets overwritten is:

$$p = \sum_{j=1}^K [\Phi((j-1)m, N)]^k \tag{5}$$

No analytic solutions are known for equations of type (2)–(5), and so we do not expect to find a closed form solution for the number m of replications that will maximise the 'load factor' of our system – this is K/N, the ratio of the total number of different blocks stored to the total disc space allocated to the system. However, a numerical model suggests the following results. If we consider the disk to be full the first time a block is corrupted (in that all copies of it are overwritten), then the load factor is rather low, with about 7% load achieved for $m = 4$ over a range of values for the number of blocks N from 20,000 to 1,000,000. This figure improves dramatically as soon as we allow even a small number of blocks to become corrupted; and if we allow 10% of blocks to be corrupted, we can obtain a raw load factor of 20% – giving an effective load factor of perhaps 15% once forward error correction is applied. These figures are somewhat tentative and we expect that they could be improved given an implementation. There are however some remarks that can be made in advance of that.

Firstly, this construction largely overcomes the performance problem of our previous construction. Files are still read and written multiple times, but the multiple is now about 5 rather than the 16–50 range of the first construction. Furthermore, we have a critical trick, in that when operating in a given directory (i.e., using a single user password, and operating at a single security level), we keep a Larson table which tells us which block to look at first [10].

Larson's system was designed to allow any record in a database to be retrieved with only one disk access. The basic idea is that a record is written at one of m locations on disc, which are specified pseudorandomly as in our construction, and a table is kept in memory telling the user at which location to look. In more detail, a record with key K is hashed to provide a 'probe sequence' of m values $h_1(K) \ldots h_m(K)$, plus a 'signature sequence' of m values $s_1(K) \ldots s_m(K)$; the latter are each of k bits in length. A table of 2^k values is kept in memory. A record with the key K is stored at the address $h_1(K)$, unless it is already full, in which case an attempt is made to store it at $h_2(K)$, and so on. The signature sequence is then used to encode the record's location in the table in memory. If all the addresses $h_1(K) \ldots h_m(K)$ are occupied, then the system declares 'disk full'. Experiments by Larson and Kajla showed that with values of m in the range 10–25, the disk would not be full until 80–90% of its blocks were occupied.

So a Larson table at a given security level (i.e., directory) can be built whenever the directory is opened and which points to locations which contain a true copy of each block; these can simply be the first uncorrupted copy of the block that can be found. This block can also be written first should the application write the block back. This table building can be carried out as a background process, so there need only be a performance penalty for those files which the user opens immediately on changing to a new directory. The table builder can also alarm when it first finds that a block has been completely corrupted (the disk is full) or that the limits of the error correction code are being reached (the disk is nearly full).

The performance of file systems based on Larson tables is relatively well understood. Reading a file that is stored at hashed absolute locations indexed by a Larson table is often faster than with a conventional file system, as the table can be held in memory and only one disk access is needed to read any block. On the other hand, writing is slightly slower. In the context of the steganographic file system, there is extra overhead when we close a file; blocks that have been written need to be replicated. We expect that the replication can largely be done in background, unless the user closes a file and changes immediately to a directory with a lower classification.

Secondly, as in our first construction, the assumption of a linear access hierarchy enables us to improve things substantially. In the present construction, the improvement is that we can greatly increase the load factor. Consider the lowest level in the hierarchy; the password for this directory will be known to all higher level processes, and so will always be available whenever a file is being written. Thus higher level processes can avoid the blocks of the lowest level files, and in consequence the lowest level directory can be implemented using Larson tables directly with no replication. A load factor at this level of 85% rather than 15% can therefore be expected. Similarly, high level processes can avoid overwriting existing copies of files at medium levels. Thus one might end up with the amount m of replication increasing with the security level; determining optimal values will probably require an implementation.

Of course the lowest level password would be divulged at once by a user under compulsion; but in the absence of compulsion, the present construction can ensure that the lowest level in the system is not only secure but highly efficient. Although writing a file would be slightly slower than in a standard non-secure operating system, reading might well be quicker. In a typical application where the bulk of the data on a system is stored at the lowest level and only a small amount at higher levels, the performance penalty (in terms of both time and space) could be very low.

Thirdly, even when the disk is full (in the sense that a block has been corrupted, or that the capacity of any error correction code used has been exceeded), most of the user file content will still be recoverable; in particular the most recently written files are very likely to be intact. So the availability of files degrades gracefully, unlike in the previous construction.

Many further optimisations are possible. Even without a linear access hierarchy, we might still benefit from having a high performance lowest level; and we might define directories at higher levels using orthogonal families of codes rather than purely pseudorandom replication in order to increase efficiency. No doubt implementation will uncover many more optimisations: we leave that for future papers.

4   Relevance to Classical Steganography

The classical way of hiding information in a deniable way would be to use a steganographic program to embed the information in large files such as audio or video [3]. This has a number of problems. Firstly, one can only hide so much information, or its presence becomes noticeable; and if the opponent is allowed to subject these objects to small distortions of his choice, then the usable bandwidth can be very low indeed [8]. Secondly, our aim here has been to design a practical system, and that means one that can be implemented so that normal Unix or Windows applications might run on top of it. Command-line file recovery using a steganographic tool is inconvenient in such an environment; transparent operation is greatly preferable. Thirdly, given the assumption that the opponent knows the system, one might as well dispense with the cover objects and write the secret information to disk directly.

However, there may well be an interesting interaction between our second construction and the world of copyright marking. It is often a requirement that many copyright marks be superimposed; for example, the International Federation of the Phonographic Industry stipulated this in a recent call for proposals for audio marking schemes [9]. There are marking schemes which are linear (in the sense of adding signals) and can accommodate this easily. However, this linearity brings problems with it [7] and many researchers are working on nonlinear schemes. The problem now is that multiple marks can interfere with each other; and we do not want a copyright pirate to be able to remove the rightful owner's mark by adding several marks of his own.

The insight behind our construction suggests that in such environments an efficient strategy may be to add a number of independent marks to each work (or to each segment of a work that has to be separately marked), with each mark replicated about six times and forward error correction used between them. (Of course, each mark may be separately encrypted in order to prevent correlation attacks.) In this way, we expect a good trade-off between on the one hand having the bandwidth to add a number of independent marks, and on the other hand forcing a pirate who wishes to obliterate the marks (but who does not know the key) to add so many marks at random places that the resulting distortion will degrade or destroy the resale value of the object. Such robust marking is the subject of separate work.

5   Conclusions

We have presented a new protection mechanism, the steganographic file system. It is designed to give users a high degree of protection against coercion, in that they can plausibly deny the existence of whole directories of files on their hard disk, even against an opponent with complete access to the system and the resources to reverse engineer every chip and understand every byte of software. We presented two possible mechanisms, one inspired by the one-time pad and providing security exponential in its system parameters, and another based on the computational security of block ciphers. These mechanisms tackle an important, practical problem that has hitherto been ignored in the security literature.

Acknowledgement: We are grateful to Charalampos Manifavas for writing the simulation that determined the available load factors for our second construction.

References

1. "Measuring the Diversity of Random Number Generators", R Anderson, R Gibbens, C Jagger, F Kelly, M Roe, *preprint*, 1992
2. "Stretching the Limits of Steganography", RJ Anderson, in [3] pp 39–48
3. *'Information Hiding'*, May 30 – June 1 1996; proceedings published by Springer as Lecture Notes in Computer Science vol 1174
4. "Tamper Resistance – a Cautionary Note", RJ Anderson, MG Kuhn, in *Proceedings of the Second Usenix Workshop on Electronic Commerce* (Nov 96) pp 1–11
5. 'Plausible Deniability', DR Beaver, *Pragocrypt 96* pp 272–288
6. "Plug and Play Encryption", DR Beaver, in *Advances in Cryptology – Crypto 97*, Springer LNCS v 1294 pp 75–89
7. "Can invisible watermark resolve rightful ownerships?", S Craver, N Memon, BL Yeo, MM Yeung, Fifth Conference on Storage and Retrieval for Image and Video Database, 13–14 February 1997, San Jose, CA; *SPIE* vol 3022 pp 310–321
8. "Attacks on Copyright Marking Systems", FAP Petitcolas, RJ Anderson, MG Kuhn, *in these proceedings*; this paper is also available online at `http://www.cl.cam.ac.uk/~fapp2/papers/ih98-attacks/`
9. *'Request for Proposals – Embedded Signalling Systems'*, June 97, International Federation of the Phonographic Industry, 54 Regent Street, London W1R 5PJ
10. "File Organisation: Implementation of a Method Guaranteeing Retrieval in One Access", PÅ Larson, A Kajla, in *Communications of the ACM* v 27 no 7 (July 1984) pp 670–677
11. *'Cryptography and Evidence'*, M Roe, Cambridge University (PhD Thesis, 1997)
12. "Developer tortured by raiders with crowbars", M Weaver, *Daily Telegraph*, 31 October 97

Stop-and-Go-MIXes Providing Probabilistic Anonymity in an Open System

Dogan Kesdogan*, Jan Egner, and Roland Büschkes

Aachen University of Technology – Department of Computer Science
Informatik 4 (Communication Systems)
D-52056 Aachen, Germany
kesdogan@informatik.rwth-aachen.de

Abstract. Currently known basic anonymity techniques depend on identity verification. If verification of user identities is not possible due to the related management overhead or a general lack of information (e.g. on the Internet), an adversary can participate several times in a communication relationship and observe the honest users. In this paper we focus on the problem of providing anonymity without identity verification. The notion of probabilistic anonymity is introduced. Probabilistic anonymity is based on a publicly known security parameter, which determines the security of the protocol. For probabilistic anonymity the insecurity, expressed as the probability of having only one honest participant, approaches 0 at an exponential rate as the security parameter is changed linearly. Based on our security model we propose a new MIX variant called "Stop-and-Go-MIX" (SG-MIX) which provides anonymity without identity verification, and prove that it is probabilistically secure.

1 Introduction

Recently much attention has been given to the application of anonymity techniques to various networks (Internet, ISDN, GSM etc.) and for various applications and purposes (email, WWW, location management, etc.). Basic well known techniques providing anonymity are:

1. Implicit Addresses and Broadcasting [5,16],
2. DC-Networks [2], and
3. MIXes [1].

A good overview about these techniques can be found in [18]. A short summary will also be given in the following section. Based on this introduction we show that these techniques are well applicable to closed environments[1], but have shortcomings in open environments[2]. The reason for this is that the techniques

---

* The work of D. Kesdogan was supported by the Gottlieb Daimler and Karl Benz Foundation.
[1] I.e. the number of users is some known and not too large number n (e.g. $n < 1000$).
[2] I.e. the number of potential users of a MIX is more than one million and usually not known exactly.

David Aucsmith (Ed.): Information Hiding 1998, LNCS 1525, pp. 83–98, 1998.

depend on identity verification in order to provide security (Sect. 2). Unfortunately, such information is not always available (e.g. on the Internet) and hence these basic methods are insecure against the usual attacker model. For that reason, most of the recent findings restrict the attacker to a weaker model in which he or she is not able to tap all used lines [6,7,10,11,21,22].

We therefore conclude that the basic techniques provide security only if either user specific information is available or the adversary is restricted to a weaker model. The resulting question is whether secure techniques for an open environment exist, which do not depend on identity verification and withstand the strong attacker model. Our answer to this question follows a probabilistic model. We define this model in section 3 analogous to the one used for public key cryptosystems. Following our new probabilistic model, we present in section 4 a technique called Stop-and-Go-MIX and prove its probabilistic security.

We finish our paper with a short conclusion and an outlook on potential applications and extensions of our model.

2 Basic Notions and Techniques

For the following discussion of anonymity techniques we make two general assumptions:

1. The underlying communication network is global and is not subject to any topology restrictions.
2. The attacker model[3] used throughout this paper assumes an omnipresent attacker E. E is able to tap all transmission lines of the communication network and to control all but one intermediary switching node. The attacker E is not able to break the used cryptographic techniques.

The question now is how to hide the existence of any communication relationship, i.e. that a message was sent (sender anonymity) or received (receiver anonymity) by a user. Although the content of a message can be well protected by cryptographic techniques, the use of cryptography solely can not guarantee anonymity. The omnipresent attacker E can observe the sender of a message and follow the message up to the receiver, thereby detecting the communication relation without a need to read the content of the packets.

Hence, the decisive point of anonymity techniques is to organize additional traffic in order to confuse the adversary and conceal the particular communication relationship. The sender and/or receiver of a message must be embedded in a so-called anonymity set.

The main questions related to an anonymity set are:

1. How is the anonymity set established?
2. What is the size of the anonymity set?

All of the following anonymity techniques differ in their approach towards establishing anonymity sets and therefore also differ in their possible field of application.

---

[3] The attacker model is based on the one given in [1].

2.1   Implicit Addresses and Broadcasting

One basic technique for anonymity is the combined use of *Implicit Addresses* and *Broadcasting*. If user A wants to keep the recipient B of a message secret, he chooses additional pseudo recipients (e.g. C and D). Together with the real recipient B, these additional recipients form the anonymity set. The message is broadcasted to all members of the anonymity set (Fig. 1). To identify the real recipient within the anonymity set A uses an implicit address "x". An implicit address is an attribute by which no one else than A and B can recognize the message as being addressed to B (for other types of implicit addresses see [18]).

The technique has a clear security limit. If the additional recipients (C and D) cooperate with attacker E, B can easily be identified as the recipient of the message.

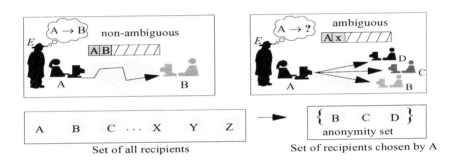

Fig. 1. Recipient anonymity by broadcast and addressing attributes

This attack scenario can be enhanced to the case that attacker E adopts different false identities (e.g. that of C and D) and therefore controls $(n - 1)$ members of the anonymity set by simply impersonating them. In order to defend against this kind of masquerading attack, identity verification through an adequately secure and flexible identification technique is required.

Drawbacks and Recent Directions What becomes clear from the simple example given above is that the broadcasting[4] overhead is prohibitive for a large scale network. Furthermore, the security attainable by this simple scheme is restricted to recipient anonymity. The sender of a message is observeable at least by the recipients.

A major drawback is that the technique depends on a closed anonymity set, which must be actively created by the sender of the message.

Implicit addresses and broadcasting as independent techniques are used in different anonymity techniques as basic building blocks [8]. These techniques are

---

[4] We assume here a switching network, not a broadcast network (e.g. satellite network).

also applied in real networks. GSM networks e.g. use implicit addresses on the air interface to hide the real identity of the users.

In research, different findings for anonymous mobility management are based on implicit addresses and broadcasting [12,13,14,21]. An extension to the basic scheme called *Variable Implicit Addresses* is presented in [8].

2.2 DC-Network

The DC-Network [2], a powerful technique for sender anonymity, uses superposed sending. To use a DC-network, users exchange secret keys along a given key graph, i.e. a graph with the users as nodes and the secret keys as edges. This initial phase of the protocol establishes the needed anonymity set. Obviously attacker E must again be prevented from controlling a majority of the exchanged items (keys or messages). Therefore, identity verification is necessary during this initial set-up phase.

To send a message (a sequence of bits), user A superposes (adds modulo 2) the message with the previously exchanged secret key. Other users superpose in the same manner (Fig. 2). If the superposed packets are transmitted via a network, an eavesdropper is not able to decide whether a packet really contains a message or not. All sums of all users are superposed globally and the result is distributed to all user stations. This distribution process guarantees the recipient anonymity. Because every secret key is added twice, the distributed message is the message of A. If more than one message was sent in the same period a collision occurs. This collision can be detected by the respective senders and collision avoidance protocols, known from multi access channels, can be applied.

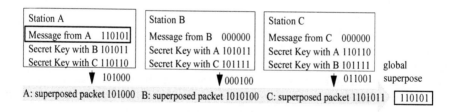

Fig. 2. DC-Network(taken from [17])

The anonymity set for the above example consists of A, B and C. Building secure groups beforehand by exchanging secret information enables the participiants to generate packets for which the adversary is unable to decide whether they contain a message or not. Therefore, DC-Networks provide an information-theoretic deterministic anonymity (see Def. 1) [2,17].

Drawbacks and Recent Directions The application of the basic method suffers from the related high overhead. For every real message n packets have to be transmitted. Therefore, [18] suggests to implement superposed sending on a physical ring network.

For special environments like e.g. broadcast networks superposed sending could be applied to reduce the cost (i.e. bandwidth). [3] proposes a superposing technique for reading anonymously from databases.

A major drawback is that DC-Networks require the installation of a closed anonymity set before the application of the superposing technique. Hence, this basic technique is not flexible. In order to include a new participant in the DC-network, a new key distribution graph has to be generated.

2.3   The MIX-Method

The two anonymity techniques presented so far both suffer from the same major drawback that they require the pre-installation of a closed anonymity set. The members of the anonymity set are then involved in every communication. This severely limits the flexibility of the involved users.

The MIX-Method [1] avoids this drawback by shifting the task of generating anonymity sets from the user to special intermediate network nodes called MIX nodes or MIXes. Centralized MIXes can serve a great amount of users without the constraint that each user has to participate in every communication. Hence, in designing a system that provides flexible access to an anonymity service the MIX approach is the most interesting and the only one suitable for open networks. MIXes collect a number of packets from distinct users (anonymity set) and process them in a way that no participant, except the MIX itself and the sender of the packet, can link an input message to an output message (Fig. 3). Therefore, the appearance (i.e. the bit pattern) and the order of the incoming packets have to be changed within the MIX. The change of appearance is a cryptographic operation, which is combined with a management procedure and a universal agreement to achieve anonymity:

1. User protocol: All generated data packets with address information are padded to equal length (agreement), combined with a secret random number (RN) and encrypted with the public key of the MIX node. A sequence of MIXes is used to increase the reliability of the system.

2. MIX protocol: A MIX collects n packets from distinct users (identity verification), decrypts the packets with its private key, strips off the RNs and outputs the packets in a different order (lexicographically sorted or randomly delayed). Furthermore, any incoming packet has to be compared with former received packets (management: store in a local database) in order to reject any duplicates. Every MIX (except the first) must include an anonymous

loop back[5], because only the first MIX can decide whether the packets are from distinct senders[6] or not.

E.g. assume that A wants to send a message M to Z (Fig. 3). A must encrypt the message two times with the public keys c_i of the respective MIXes and include the random numbers RN_i: $c_1(RN_1, c_2(RN_2, Z, M))$.

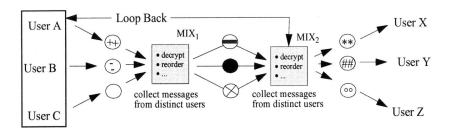

Fig. 3. Cascade of two mixes

Applying this protocol the MIX method provides full security. The relation between the sender and the recipient is hidden from an omnipresent attacker as long as he neither controls every MIX which the message passes nor cooperates with the other senders $(n - 1)$. [17] states that the MIX method provides information-theoretic deterministic anonymity based on complexity-theoretic secure cryptography.

Drawbacks and Recent Directions Before a MIX can forward a packet, it has to collect n messages from different users. This is a typical example for an asynchronous communication model (like e.g. email). The resulting end-to-end transmission delay can be minimized if every participant sends a packet at a given time. Of course, most of these messages would be dummy messages (see e.g. ISDN-MIXes [19]). In an open environment (global network) the sending of sender originated dummies should be avoided. Therefore [6,7,10] propose to hide the relation between sender and recipient by using a number of distinct MIXes without distributing the collecting property over the network. But these schemes are insecure against an omnipresent attacker E. It is hence still an

---

[5] Loop back: Every MIX knows the sender anonymity set. It signs the received packets and broadcasts them to the respective users. Each user inspects whether his own message is included or not and transmits a yes or no. The MIX goes on if it receives yes from all members of the anonymity set.

[6] Most of the suggestions for MIX realizations in the literature work without this property and are therefore not secure, because the former MIX(es) can conspire with the opponent and generate $(n - 1)$ dummy packets and observe the only remaining packet which is from the user of interest.

unsolved problem to provide security for synchronous communication in an open environment facing an omnipresent attacker.

All suggestions for the Internet scenario have to deal with the lack of identity verification information. If a MIX cannot decide whether the packets are from different senders or not[7], the attacker can intercept the incoming packets, isolate each packet, and forward it together with $(n-1)$ of his own packets[8]. This attack is well known as the $(n-1)$-attack, blocking or trickle attack [11].

Examining the $(n-1)$-attack we can identify two reasons for its success:

1. Time: The time until n messages are collected by a MIX and hence the end-to-end delay of a message is not known. Therefore it is possible to delay a single message without any risk of detection.
2. Deterministic output behavior: Sending messages with a high rate to the MIX results in a high output rate of the MIX.

The solution given in [11] is to delay every packet individually from one batch to the other and additionally choose detours for every packet from every MIX with a given probability. The detours are over several other MIXes. As stated by the authors, this scheme is insecure against the omnipresent attacker. In the literature known to us there is no existing solution for the Internet which is also secure against an omnipresent attacker.

3   Probabilistic Security

The techniques discussed in the previous section share the basic requirement of identity verification. While the protocols provide complete and even perfect security under the assumption that the knowledge necessary for identity verification is available, this requirement can severely handicap or even prevent their application.

What is needed is a technique that provides security for an open network without the need of identity verification. The question is what level of security can be guaranteed without the need of identity verification. Before answering this question, we now give a formal definition for the basic terms already used in the above description:

Definition 1. *Given an attacker model $\mathcal{E}$ and a finite set of all users Ψ. Let $\mathcal{R}$ be a role for the user (sender or recipient) in respect to a message $\mathcal{M}$. If, for an attacker according to model $\mathcal{E}$, the a-posteriori probability p that a user u has the role $\mathcal{R}$ in respect to $\mathcal{M}$ is non-zero $(p > 0)$, then u is an element of the anonymity set $\mathcal{U} \subseteq \ominus$.*

---

[7] Again this is the case if it is not possible to verify the identities of the senders of the mixed packets.
[8] If the anonymity set is built over an indeterministic procedure (e.g. every packet is delayed randomly) then the adversary fills up the MIX with his own packets and, after forwarding the one real message, keeps on sending his own packets until the MIX outputs the one real packet.

A technique (method) provides an $\mathcal{R}$ anonymity set of size n if the cardinality of $\mathcal{U}$ is n ($n \in \mathbb{N}$).
An algorithm provides deterministic anonymity if n is always greater than 1.

Obviously, the basic techniques presented so far provide deterministic and at their best information-theoretic anonymity, but have to verify the users identities to be secure at all. We relax the information-theoretic anonymity property of the above techniques to a notion of probabilistic anonymity in order to find a scheme which does not depend on identity verification and can be applied to open networks and groups:

Definition 2. *Given an attacker model $\mathcal{E}$, let AL be an algorithm providing anonymity with a complexity parameter μ. We say that AL is probabilistically secure against the attacker model $\mathcal{E}$ if AL, for a distinct message $\mathcal{M}$, can be broken with probability α and if*

1. *the a-posteriori probability of insecurity after any possible attack within the attacker model $\mathcal{E}$ is the same as the a-priori probability before an attack occurs, i.e. α remains constant for a given μ, and*
2. *the probability of insecurity approaches 0 at an exponential rate as μ is increased linearly.*

If AL is probabilistically secure it provides probabilistic anonymity.

Our aim is to define a protocol providing anonymity, where μ is given as a publicly known parameter. If the users use this parameter they can send a message spontaneously with the probability of insecurity α determined by μ, i.e. $\alpha = f(\mu)$.

Security Evaluation Model	Anonymity Evaluation Model
Information-theoretic security	Information-theoretic anonymity
Complexity-theoretic security	Probabilistic anonymity

Table 1. Anonymity Evaluation Models

Note that the above definition is analogous to the computational security of asymmetric cryptography [4,9,23]. To break the asymmetric protocols should be computationally as hard as solving a problem of the complexity class NP. Because the algorithms for encryption and decryption should be carried out in polynomial time P this would lead to the proof that $P \neq NP$. While this is a well known unproven hypothesis in complexity theory the security of the schemes depend on security parameters, which determine the length of the key etc. in accordance with the special considered problem (factoring assumption, discrete logarithm etc.) and the time complexity of the best known algorithm. The security here also depends exponentially on the parameter [20].

Table 1 compares the resulting models for security and anonymity evaluation.

4   The Stop-and-Go-MIX (SG-MIX)

Based on the definition of probabilistic anonymity we will now define the SG-MIX protocol and evaluate its security properties.

4.1   The SG-MIX Protocol

A SG-MIX (Fig. 4) operates in the same way as a classical MIX, but does not collect a fixed number of messages. Sender A selects the SG-MIXes to be used with equal probability. He calculates for every node i a time window $(TS^{min}, TS^{max})_i$ and draws a random delay time T_i from an exponential distribution with suitable parameter μ. This information is appended to the packet before encrypting it with the SG-MIX's public key. The SG-MIX i extracts $(TS^{min}, TS^{max})_i$ and T_i after decryption. If the arriving time of the packet is earlier or later than given by the time window the message will be discarded. After T_i units of time have elapsed, the SG-MIX i forwards the packet to the next hop or its final destination.

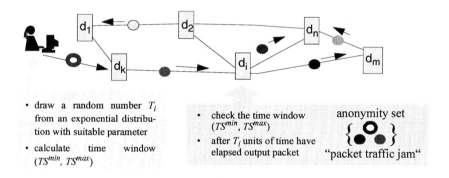

- draw a random number T_i from an exponential distribution with suitable parameter
- calculate time window (TS^{min}, TS^{max})

- check the time window (TS^{min}, TS^{max})
- after T_i units of time have elapsed output packet

anonymity set

"packet traffic jam"

Fig. 4. SG-MIX

Selecting the SG-MIX nodes with equal probability guarantees that an user does not prefer certain SG-MIXes over others, which would enable an attack via the analysis and comparison of the amount of traffic origin from the user and processed by his favorite SG-MIXes. Furthermore, the anonymity size (see Definition 1) will be always maximal with a high probability.

4.2   The Security of the SG-MIX

The security of a SG-MIX does not rely on shuffling a batch of messages, but on delaying each message individually and independently by a random amount of time. If the delay times are individually drawn from the same exponential distribution, the knowledge of the time a specific message has arrived at the SG-MIX node does not help the attacker in identifying the corresponding outgoing message as long as there is at least one other message in the queue at some time of the delay. Because of the memoryless property of the exponential distribution, if n messages are in the queue, it is equally probable for any one of them to depart next, regardless of their arrival times. Therefore, an attacker can correlate arrival and departure of a message only if during the whole delay time no other message is in the queue. This means that

1. A: the queue is empty at the arrival of the message (and the attacker knows this) and
2. B: no other message arrives during the delay time.

More formally speaking the probability of an successful attack is:

$$\mathcal{P}(\text{success}) = \mathcal{P}(\mathcal{A} \cap \mathcal{B}) = \mathcal{P}(\mathcal{A}) \cdot \mathcal{P}(\mathcal{B}) \quad .$$

Clearly, the arrivals are Poisson distributed due to the independent choice of the nodes and both events are independent from each other. Their probabilities will now be calculated.

The queue of a SG-MIX node can be modeled as an $M/M/\infty$ server, because the arrivals are Poisson distributed, the "service times" are exponentially distributed and the queue can "serve" any number of customers independently. We denote the rate of message arrivals by λ and the parameter of the exponential distribution from which the delay times are drawn by μ. Queuing theory then gives a (steady state) probability of $\mathcal{P}(A) = e^{-\lambda/\mu}$ that this server system is idle when a message arrives [15].

Because both interarrival times and delay times are exponentially distributed with respective parameters λ and μ, the probability that no message arrives during the delay time is equal to the probability that a sample drawn from $\text{Exp}(\lambda)$ is greater than a sample from $\text{Exp}(\mu)$. Hence we get

$$\mathcal{P}(\mathcal{B}) = \frac{\mu}{\lambda + \mu} = \frac{1}{1 + \lambda/\mu} \quad .$$

The probability that an arbitrary message can be tracked by an eavesdropper (an active attacker has no additional advantage) is therefore

$$\mathcal{P}(\text{success}) = \frac{e^{-\lambda/\mu}}{1 + \lambda/\mu} \quad . \tag{1}$$

Let us consider an example: Assume a SG-MIX node with a mean arrival rate $\lambda = 10\,\text{packets}/s$ and parameter $\mu = 0.2\,\text{packets}/s$, that is a mean delay of 5 seconds. Then the probability of an arriving packet finding the server empty is $e^{-50} \approx 1.9 \cdot 10^{-22}$.

(n-1)-Attack In order to provide probabilistic anonymity a SG-MIX must be able to fend off blocking attacks. When running such an attack the intruder must delay all incoming data packets for a certain amount of time in order to "flush" the SG-MIX. Therefore we introduce the time stamps (TS^{min}, TS^{max}) to detect the delay of an incoming data packet and discard this packet. This prevents blocking attacks. The SG-MIX technique allows the calculation of the time windows very accurately as the user knows the time a message will be delayed in advance.

We define for the pair of time stamps of node i $(TS^{min}, TS^{max})_i$ the time window Δt_i during which a packet must arrive at SG-MIX i. If a Δt value is given, we can calculate the success probability of a blocking attack:

A packet leaves a SG-MIX after at most Δt units of time with probability $\mathcal{P}(X \leq t) = 1 - e^{-\mu \Delta t}$. Assuming there are n packets in the SG-MIX the success probability of a blocking attack is $\mathcal{P}(\text{success} | X = n) = (1 - e^{-\mu \Delta t})^n$. The number of packets in the SG-MIX at an arbitrary point of time is Poisson distributed with parameter $\rho = \lambda/\mu$:

$$\mathcal{P}(X = i) = \frac{\rho^i}{i!} e^{-\rho} \quad .$$

Therefore the overall success probability of an $(n - 1)$-attack is

$$\mathcal{P}(\text{success}) = \sum_{i=0}^{\infty} \frac{(1 - e^{-\mu \Delta t})^i \cdot \rho^i \cdot e^{-\lambda/\mu}}{i!} = \exp\left(\frac{-\lambda e^{-\mu \Delta t}}{\mu}\right) \quad . \tag{2}$$

Obviously, when Δt is given, a linear decrease of μ leads to an exponentially decreasing success probability of a blocking attack. The only successful attack is if the adversary blocks the incoming messages of all SG-MIXes quite long before the attacked message arrives, due to the lack of knowledge which SG-MIX node would be selected from the user. This is usually impossible to do "on demand" and, in any case, would block the whole network, i.e. result in the loss of many messages due to time-outs, which would surely not go undetected.

Calculating Time Stamps When defining the time stamps one has to take into account that computer clocks are not perfectly synchronized. Many different clock synchronization mechanisms have been proposed, each of them providing a different quality of synchronization. For the following discussion we assume that the clocks of all involved hosts are synchronized with parameter syn. That is, the maximal clock offset between any pair of hosts is at most syn.

All together, the following parameters are relevant for time stamp calculation:

1. syn : maximum clock deviation of two clocks (max. offset)
2. t_S : local time of the sender
3. n : number of SG-MIXes
4. T_i : delay time of SG-MIX i
5. d_{ij} : unidirectional transmission delays

Define SG-MIX 0 as the sender. The time stamps are calculated as follows:

$$TS_i^{min} = t_S + \sum_{j=1}^{i-1} T_j + \sum_{j=1}^{i} d_{j-1,j}^{min} - \text{syn}$$

$$TS_i^{max} = t_S + \sum_{j=1}^{i-1} T_j + \sum_{j=1}^{i} d_{j-1,j}^{max} + \text{syn} \quad .$$

Therefore, the length of the time window is given by

$$\Delta t = TS_i^{max} - TS_i^{min} = 2\text{syn} + \sum_{j=1}^{i} \Delta d_{j-1,j}$$

with

$$\Delta d_{i,j} = d_{j-1,j}^{max} - d_{j-1,j}^{min} \quad .$$

The length of the time windows increases with the number of SG-MIXes used. Additionally it depends on the propagation delay jitter and the accuracy of synchronized clocks.

The crucial measure for the quality of the time stamps is the question whether an $(n-1)$-attack can be fended off. Let T_{empty} denote the time that is needed by an attacker to flush a SG-MIX if all incoming packets are blocked. Then the time windows should satisfy $\Delta t \leq T_{empty}$. The security parameter μ must be decreased until this requirement is fulfilled with a given probability. Of course, this results in longer security delays and the time an attacker needs to flush a SG-MIX increases.

Size of the Anonymity Set As the last subsection has shown how to calculate the timestamps, we will now prove our statement that the size of the anonymity set will always be maximal with a high propability.

The anonymity set $\mathcal{U}$ produced by a SG-MIX for a single message $\mathcal{M}$ is composed of the recipients of the messages already present at the SG-MIX at the arrival of $\mathcal{M}$ and the messages which are received by the SG-MIX during the same busy period. This property of the anonymity set is obvious. For no message which arrives after $\mathcal{M}$ and departs before the SG-MIX runs empty, the attacker can exclude that it is the one of interest.

To determine the mean size of the anonymity set we can follow the already used model of an $M/M/\infty$ server with arrival rate λ and service rate μ. The life cycle of such a system consists of alternating busy and idle periods. The process $\{N_t\}$, denoting the number of messages in the SG-MIX at time t, is regenerative due to the memoryless property of the exponential distribution. According to the fundamental theorem for regenerative processes the following relation between the probability π_0 that the system is empty, the expectation of the length of an idle period $E(t_i)$, and the mean length of a cycle $E(t_i + t_b)$ (t_b denotes the length of the busy period) holds:

$$\pi_0 = \frac{E(t_i)}{E(t_i + t_b)} \quad . \tag{3}$$

In addition the following properties hold:

1. $E(t_i + t_b) = E(t_i) + E(t_b)$, due to the linearity of the expectation
2. $\pi_0 = e^{-\lambda/\mu}$
3. $E(t_i) = \frac{1}{\lambda}$, because the t_i's are distributed equally according to the exponential distribution $\mathcal{E}(\lambda)$

This results in

$$e^{-\lambda/\mu} = \frac{1/\lambda}{1/\lambda + E(t_b)} \quad ,$$

and therefore

$$E(t_b) = \frac{e^{\lambda/\mu} - 1}{\lambda} \quad .$$

Hence the mean number Y of served packets during a busy period is:

$$E(Y) = \lambda \cdot E(t_b) + 1 = e^{\lambda/\mu} \quad . \tag{4}$$

Now we can examine a single message $\mathcal{M}$ arriving during a busy period in which n messages are processed.

X denotes the number of messages in the busy period arriving after $\mathcal{M}$ and Y denotes the total number of messages served during the busy period.

Because the message arrivals are Poisson distributed and therefore fulfill the memoryless property the following relation holds:

$$P(X = m | Y = n) = \begin{cases} \frac{1}{n} & : \quad m \le n \\ 0 & : \quad else \end{cases} \quad .$$

This leads to a conditional expectation of

$$E(X | Y = n) = \sum_{m=1}^{n} \frac{m}{n} = \frac{n+1}{2} \quad .$$

The summation over Y (theorem of total probability) results in:

$$E(X) = \sum_{n=1}^{\infty} \frac{n+1}{2} \cdot P(Y = n) = \frac{1}{2} E(Y) + \frac{1}{2} \quad . \tag{5}$$

Because the expectation of the number of message already in the SG-MIX at the arrival of $\mathcal{M}$ is λ/μ, the expectation of the size of the anonymity set is:

$$E(|\mathcal{U}|) = \frac{\lambda}{\mu} + E(X) = \frac{\lambda}{\mu} + \frac{e^{\lambda/\mu} + 1}{2} \quad . \tag{6}$$

Hence we can deduce that the size of the anonymity set will always be maximal with high propability.

The $M/M/\infty$ Model All security statements in this paper are based on the assumption of using an infinite server system ($M/M/\infty$ model). Obviously this assumption is not realistic for a concrete realization of a SG-MIX. A real-world SG-MIX can only approximate the ideal model depicted above, because it can only serve a finite number of packets. Therefore it must be analyzed according to the multiple server system model ($M/M/n$ model). Using the $M/M/n$ model it is possible that an arriving packet finds a situation in which all servers within a SG-MIX are busy. The probability that an arriving packet finds no idle server can be calculated by Erlang's C formula [15]. Taking this formula and the parameters μ and λ into account it is possible to design a concrete SG-MIX in a way that fulfills the demanded level of approximation to the ideal model.

Nonetheless the potential ranges of the arrival rate λ and the service rate μ must be taken carefully into account during the design of an SG-MIX to provide a reasonable servicing capacity.

And finally, as every real-world implementation can only provide a limited servicing capacity, the SG-MIX is like every other MIX vulnerable to denial of service attacks, in which an attacker floods the SG-MIX with packets. As a consequence, most of the other packets will time out during such an attack, but this will not go undetected.

5   Conclusions

The currently known basic anonymity techniques depend on identity verification, but provide perfect anonymity. Following the general idea of complexity-theoretic security we have introduced the notion of probabilistic anonymity in order to find a scheme which does not need these identity verification procedures.

Probabilistically secure algorithms provide untraceability with a probability which depends exponentially on a publicly known parameter. We have proposed the Stop-And-Go-MIX as a probabilistically secure protocol, where μ is given as a publicly known security parameter. This parameter can be chosen to fulfil the practical considerations and security demands. The users can predict the delays of their message very accurately and hence time stamp protocols can be applied to counter $(n-1)$-attacks. For the same reason the network delay can be calculated from packet turnaround times and congestion control algorithms can be employed, allowing the use of SG-MIX on ISO/OSI layer 3.

Untraceable Return Address can also be supported by the SG-MIX for an open system so fully anonymous communication is possible.

6   Acknowledgement

We would like to thank Andreas Pfitzmann for his support of this work and many fruitful discussions.

References

1. D.L. Chaum, "Untraceable Electronic Mail, Return Addresses, and Digital Pseudonyms", Comm. ACM, Feb. 1981, Vol. 24, No. 2, pp. 84–88.
2. D.L. Chaum, "The Dining Cryptographers Problem: Unconditional Sender and Recipient Untraceability", J. Cryptology, Vol. 1, No. 1, Springer-Verlag, 1988, pp. 65–75.
3. D.A. Cooper and K.P. Birman, "Preserving Privacy in a Network of Mobile Computers", 1995 Symposium on Research in Security and Privacy, IEEE Computer Society Press, Los Alamitos, 1995, pp. 26–38.
4. W. Diffie and M.E.Hellman, "New Directions in Cryptography", IEEE Transactions on Information Theory, 22 (1976), pp. 644–654.
5. D.J. Farber and K.C. Larson, "Network Security Via Dynamic Process Renaming", Fourth Data Communication Symp., Quebec City, Canada , Oct. 1975, pp. 8–18.
6. A. Fasbender, D. Kesdogan, and O. Kubitz, "Analysis of Security and Privacy in Mobile IP", 4th International Conference on Telecommunication Systems, Modelling and Analysis, Nashville, 1996.
7. A. Fasbender, D. Kesdogan, and O. Kubitz, "Variable and Scalable Security: Protection of Location Information in Mobile IP", VTC'96, Atlanta, 1996.
8. H. Federrath, A. Jerichow, D. Kesdogan, A. Pfitzmann, and D. Trossen, "Minimizing the Average Cost of Paging on the Air Interface – An Approach Considering Privacy", IEEE VTC' 97, May 1997, Phoenix, Arizona.
9. S. Goldwasser and S. Micali, "Probabilistic Encryption", Journal of Computer and System Science 28 (1984), pp. 270–299.
10. D.M. Goldschlag, M.G. Reed, and P.F. Syverson, "Hiding Routing Information", Information Hiding, Springer-Verlag LNCS 1174, 1996, pp. 137–150.
11. C. Gülcü and G. Tsudik, "Mixing Email with Babel", Proc. Symposium on Network and Distributed System Security, San Diego, IEEE Comput. Soc. Press, 1996, pp. 2–16.
12. S. Hoff, K. Jakobs, and D. Kesdogan, "Secure Location Management in UMTS", Communications and Multimedia Security, Proceedings of the IFIP TC6/TC11 International Conference on Communications and Multimedia Security at Essen, Germany, September 1996, Chapman & Hall, ISBN 0-412-79780-1.
13. D. Kesdogan, H. Federrath, A. Jerichow, and A. Pfitzmann, "Location Management Strategies increasing Privacy in Mobile Communication Systems", IFIP SEC 96, 12th International Information Security Conference, May 1996, pp. 39–48.
14. D. Kesdogan and X. Fouletier, "Secure Location Information Management in Cellular Radio Systems", IEEE Wireless Communication Systems Symposium WCSS 95, Wireless Trends in 21st Century", New York, 1995, pp. 35–40.
15. L. Kleinrock, "Queuing Systems, Vol. I: Theory", John Wiley & Sons, 1975.
16. P.A. Karger, "Non-Discretionary Access Control for decentralized Computing Systems", Master Thesis, MIT, Laboratory for Computer Science, Report MIT/LCS/TR-179, 1977.
17. A. Pfitzmann, "Dienstintegrierende Kommunikationsnetze mit teilnehmerüberprüfbarem Datenschutz", IFB 234, Springer-Verlag, Heidelberg, 1990.
18. A. Pfitzmann and M. Waidner, "Networks without User Observability", Computers & Security 6, 1987, pp. 158–166.

19. A. Pfitzmann, B. Pfitzmann, and M. Waidner, "ISDN-MIXes: Untraceable Communication wit Very Small Bandwidth Overhead", Information Security, Proc. IFIP/SEC 91, Brighton, UK, 15-17 May 1991, D,T. Lindsay, W.L. Price (eds.), North-Holland, Amsterdam 1991, pp. 245–258.

20. B. Pfitzmann, "Digital Signature Schemes. General Framework and Fail-Stop Signatures", Springer-Verlag LNCS 1100, Springer 1996.

21. M.G. Reed, P.F. Syverson, and D.M. Goldschlag, "Protocols using Anonymous Connections: Mobile Applications", 1997 Workshop on Security Protocols, Paris, France, April 1997.

22. M.K. Reiter and A.D. Rubin, "Crowds: Anonymity for Web Transactions", DIMACS Technical Report 97–15, http://www.research.att.com/projects/crowds/.

23. R.L. Rivest, A. Shamir, and L.M. Adleman, "A Method for Obtaining Digital Signatures and Public-Key Cryptosystems", Communications of the ACM, 21 (1978), pp. 96-99.

Biometric yet Privacy Protecting Person Authentication

Gerrit Bleumer *

AT&T Labs-Research Florham Park, NJ 07932, USA
bleumer@acm.org

Abstract. Many eligibility or entitlement certificates in every day life are non-transferable between persons. However, they are usually implemented by personal physical tokens that owners can easily pass around (e.g. credit card), driver's license). So there must either be negligible incentives to pass these certificates or the tokens around, or the tokens must allow to authenticate the persons who show certificates, e.g., by imprinted photographs. However, any kind of easily accessible personal identifying information threatens the owners' privacy. To solve these somehow paradoxical requirements, we assume for each owner a kind of pilot that is equipped with a tamper resistant biometric authentication facility. We draft cryptographic protocols for issuing and showing non-transferable yet privacy protecting certificates. Unforgeability of certificates relies on a well-established computational assumption, non-transferability relies upon a physical assumption and owners' privacy is protected unconditionally.

Keywords: Non-transferable certificates, Wallets-with-observer, Blind Signatures, Interactive proofs, Biometric person authentication.

1 Introduction

Many eligibilities or entitlements in every day life are bound to a person and are not intended to be transferred between persons, e.g., room/building/account access rights, driver's licenses, academic degrees, certain drug eligibilities, stock options. It is certainly desirable if not inevitable in an information society to implement such non-transferable certificates in an electronic way and many such solutions exist already, e.g. id badges, credit cards, insurance certificates, membership cards. These solutions work well if the incentives to give away, lend or sell certificates are sufficiently outweighed by the disadvantages for the respective owners. An instructive example where this is not the case are driver's licenses. Suppose electronic driver's licenses and (unmanned) electronic road checkpoints that can verify these driver's licenses. In such a scenario, lending one's driver's license to someone else would bear no disadvantage other than not being able to

---

* The research for this paper was supported by the German Research Foundation under grant DFG-Bi 311/9-1.

David Aucsmith (Ed.): Information Hiding 1998, LNCS 1525, pp. 99–110, 1998.

drive oneself at the same time. The problem is that personal information (passwords, PINs) and personal tokens (id badge, magnetic card) as such can easily be shared, lended or can even be traded. The only way to prevent this is *biometric person authentication*. In the road example, a straighforward solution is to equip the road checkpoints with video cameras peeking at the drivers. Not only would this solution render the electronic driver's licenses unnessasary, but it is almost certainly unacceptable from a privacy point of view. A smarter solution though is to equip drivers with personal devices into which biometric verification modules are implanted such that (i) drivers cannot deceive their biometric facility and (ii) road checkpoints cannot access the biometric modules (and their memory) directly, i.e., without the help of the respective owner's personal device.

In the following, we explore the latter solution. We assume each driver is equipped with a personal communication device (called *wallet* for historical reasons) that can run a trusted local process (called *observer*) [13]. For example, wallets and observers could be implemented by palmtops or pilots with a built-in tamper resistant chip [17]. Drivers need to trust their observers to support all legitimate operations, whereas road checkpoints need to trust observers to prevent any illegitimate operation. In order to achieve privacy, there must be no *outflow* of information from the observer to a road checkpoint. If loss or theft of observers is to be tolerated, there must also be no *inflow* of information from a driver's license issuing organization, typically the Motor Vehicle Services (MVS), to the observer. Preventing outflow and inflow requires that the observer has no communication link other than to its hosting wallet, and all communication protocols must prevent outflow from the observer (or inflow to the observer). This concept has been introduced by Chaum and Pedersen [13] as the *wallet with observer* architecture. Adding a biometric authentication facility to the observer has not been studied for this architecture before (Fig. 1).

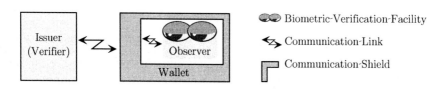

Fig. 1. Wallet with observer architecture

Each observer needs to be personalized to its respective owner in a way that is trusted by the MVS. Afterwards, they only need to verify their owner's biometric identity with sufficiently small false acceptance and false rejection rates. In principle, there are two kinds of biometric authentication. *Biometric verification* facilities need to distinguish only one particular identity from all others, whereas *biometric recognition* facilities need to distinguish a (large) number of biometric identities from each other. Recently, there is increasing scientific and commercial interest in biometric person authentication [3,15]. A growing number of easy-to-use computer peripherals is available in the consumer market [4]. Most of them are fingerprint recognizers with false acceptance and false rejection rates in the range of $10^{-4} \ldots 10^{-6}$ and $1 \times 10^{-2} \ldots 3 \times 10^{-2}$, respectively. The crossover error rate is typically 1–3%, but higher for elderly people and manual workers. Recognition time is typically $0.5 \ldots 1.0$ seconds. Since biometric verification is technically easier to achieve, it appears to become feasible even for small observers (and wallets) in the not too far future.

Electronic certificates can be built into wallets right at the end of the production line (*static issuing*). This is efficient for mono-purpose wallets e.g., id badges. Multi-purpose wallets, however, must allow to obtain new certificates during their entire lifetime and must also take care of dependencies among certificates (*dynamic issuing*). The concept of privacy oriented and dynamically issuable certificates is what Chaum has introduced as *credentials* [6,7,8,9,10]. In the following, we elaborate on the additional aspect of non-transferability. We propose a cryptographic implementation of driver's licenses based on the wallet with observer architecture, where the observer has implanted some tamper resistant biometric verification facility.

2   Cryptographic Primitives

We first introduce some notation. Then we present three cryptographic primitives, two kinds of blind signature and an interactive proof of knowledge.

2.1   Notation

Since the following protocols are based on the intractability of computing discrete representations, the following definitions are useful. Let p be a k-bit prime ($k \in \mathbb{N}$), q be a large prime divisor of $p - 1$, i.e., $q \log^2 q \geq p$, and G_q be the unique subgroup of order q in $\mathbb{Z}_p^*$. Furthermore, let $g_1, \ldots, g_l$ denote elements chosen uniformly at random from $G_q \setminus \{1\}$. (Each g_i generates G_q). It is generally assumed that a discrete representation $(\alpha_1, \ldots, \alpha_l)$ of a randomly chosen element $z \in G_q$ with respect to $(g_1, \ldots, g_l)$, i.e., $z = \prod_{i=1}^{l} g_i^{\alpha_i}$, is infeasible to compute in polynomial time (in the bitlength of p). We call this the *subgroup representation assumption* (SR). In the special case of $l = 1$, the discrete representation α_1 is called the *discrete logarithm* of z with respect to g_1, and the SR assumption in this case is called *subgroup discrete logarithm assumption* (SDL). We say that two representations $(\alpha_1, \ldots, \alpha_l)$ and $(\beta_1, \ldots, \beta_l)$ are *equivalent* iff there exists a factor $d \in \mathbb{Z}_q$ such that $\alpha_i = d\beta_i$ for all $1 \leq i \leq l$.

We denote protocols in the same way as algorithms are usually denoted: by a declaration and a definition. A *protocol declaration* consists of the (i) formal output parameters, followed by (ii) an assignment arrow, followed by (iii) the protocol name and the (iv) formal input parameters in parenthesis. To enhance readability, all input and output parameters of a participant are enclosed in square brackets labeled by the participant's initial. Values of formal input parameters are called *private input* or *common input* if these parameters are given to only one or to all participants of the protocol, respectively. A *protocol definition* is denoted in matrix form. Actions of each participant are aligned in columns, and each column is labeled by its participants name. Consecutive actions are displayed in consecutively numbered rows, which are called the *steps* of the protocol.

Protocol actions are denoted by usual mathematical notation and a few special symbols. Choosing an element uniformly at random from a set A and assigning it to a variable a is denoted $a \in_R A$. Evaluating an expression E and assigning the result to a is denoted by a left arrow $a \leftarrow E$. By h we denote a pseudo-random hash function [5] that, on input any binary string, returns a value in $\mathbb{Z}_q$. We relax the notation by allowing any number of arguments to h meaning that their binary representations are concatenated and then fed to h. Arithmetic operations are either in G_q, i.e., multiplication mod p or in $\mathbb{Z}_q$, i.e., addition and multiplication mod q. We omit the "(mod p)" and "(mod q)" whenever the modulus is clear from the context. Transmitting the value of a variable a from participant Alice to participant Bob is simply denoted by a labeled arrow $\xrightarrow{a}$ that stretches from Alice's to Bob's column[1] . A call of protocol *prot* is denoted by a similar but double headed arrow labeled by the declaration of *prot* instantiated with respective actual parameters. The phrase "proceed iff P" with P a Boolean predicate indicates that the protocol execution proceeds if and only if P holds. Otherwise, the protocol is aborted and the participants return a corresponding exception. *Polynomial composition* of protocols [14] means to execute a given set of protocols a polynomial number of times in arbitrarily interleaved fashion.

2.2   Restrictive Blind Signature Scheme

The signer Alice chooses her private key $x \in_R \mathbb{Z}_q$ uniformly at random and publishes the corresponding public key $y \leftarrow g^x \bmod p$. The message space is G_q. A signature σ is *valid* for message m with respect to public key y iff it satisfies the verification predicate

$$verify(y, m, \sigma) \ .$$

On common input a message m, Alice, on private input her signing key x, and Bob, on private input a *modifier* $\omega \in \mathbb{Z}_q$, produce a restrictive blind signature σ' for $m' = m^\omega$:[2]

$$([m', \sigma']^B) \leftarrow sign([x, m]^A, [y, m, \omega]^B) \ .$$

---

[1] We abstract here from essential fault-tolerant mechanisms like typing and (logically) time-stamping messages.

[2] We call parameter ω a modifier because it determines which output message Bob obtains relative to the common input message.

Prerequisite 1 *Protocol sign is (i) effective, (ii) unforgeable under the SDL assumption and (iii) restrictive in the sense of Brands [1,2], i.e., the only way for a cheating Bob to obtain a signature for a message m' is to choose $\alpha, \beta \in \mathbb{Z}_q$ "before" obtaining a signature for $m' = m^\alpha g^\beta$, where g is a global constant, chosen uniformly at random from $G_q \setminus \{1\}$.[3],[4] (iv) sign is unconditionally blind in the sense that Bob's results from executing protocol sign are unconditionally unlinkable to Alice's views of these executions even if Alice had unlimited computing resources.* ◇

2.3   Restrictive Cascade Signature Scheme

We consider the same setup as for the restrictive blind signature scheme. The common input is a message m, Alice's private input is her signing key $\bar{x}$ corresponding to her public key $\bar{y}$, and Bobs private input is a modifier ω. Now, we allow Bob an additional private input $\sigma \in \Sigma_q$, a valid signature for the common message m with respect to some verification key y, which is usually different from Alice's verification key $\bar{y}$. Bob seeks to obtain from Alice a signature σ' for $m' = m^\omega$ with respect to the product $y\bar{y}$. We call this signing operation *cascade* because it can be iterated so that Bob can use his output signatures as private inputs in any subsequent execution of *cascade*:

$$([m', \sigma']^B) \leftarrow cascade([x, m]^A, [y, m, \sigma, \omega]^B) \ .$$

Prerequisite 2 *Protocol cascade is (i) effective, (ii) unforgeable under the SDL assumption, (iii) restrictive (see Prerequisite 1) and (iv) unconditionally blind in the sense that Bob's results from executing protocol cascade are unconditionally unlinkable to Alice's views of these executions.* ◇

2.4   Diverted Proof of Knowledge

Brands [1] has proposed an interactive proof based on work of Chaum, Evertse and van de Graaf [12] where a prover P proves to a verifier V that she knows a witness, namely a representation $u = (u_1, \ldots, u_l) \in \mathbb{Z}q^l$, for a given candidate $\psi \in G_q$, i.e., $\psi = \prod_{i=1}^l g_i^{u_i}$ with all g_i chosen independently and uniformly at random in advance. For all $l > 1$, this interactive proof is witness indistinguishable over the predicate family W [14], where $W = \{W_q\}$ and $W_q = \{(\psi, w) | \psi = \prod_{i=1}^l g_i^{u_i}\}$. Brands has further shown in [1] how his proof protocol can be "diverted" such that

(i) P, during the interactive proof protocol with V, has online access to a third party, called the co-prover Q, and

---

[3] For simplicity, we assume only one such generator g. However, all following constructions work for any constant number of generators.

[4] The notion of "before" is left informal. We expect to formalize it in future work.

(ii) the witness u is shared between P and Q in a way that neither P nor Q knows u by herself.

In contrast to the well-defined notion of divertibility by Okamoto and Ohta [16], the "diverted" proof protocol by Brands takes private input not only from the co-prover, but also from the prover, and there is no input common to all three parties, but only a semi-common input to Q and P and one to P and V.[5] We need an interactive proof diverted in this way with the additional property that

(iii) if P (by help of Q) can prove knowledge of a representation of an element $\psi \in G_q$ and P chooses some $\omega \in \mathbb{Z}_q$, then P (with the same help of Q), can also prove knowledge of a representation of ψ^ω.

As our last prerequisite we assume an interactive proof protocol satisfying (i), (ii) and (iii) abovel. The candidate (semi-common input to P and V) is denoted ψ. The partial witnesses of P and Q are denoted as (ω, w) and v, respectively, where $\omega \in \mathbb{Z}_q$, $v, w \in \mathbb{Z}_q^2$. The witness of ψ is $u = v\omega + w$:

$$([acc]^V) \leftarrow prove([v]^Q, [\psi, \omega, w]^P, [\psi]^V) \ .$$

Prerequisite 3 *Protocol prove is a "diverted" and witness indistinguishable proof of knowledge over $W = \{W_q\}$.*   ◇

3   Driver's License Scheme

The following driver's license scheme basically consists of three protocols, namely to bind a pseudonym to a driver (Fig. 9), to issue a driver's license (or *license* for short) to a driver (Fig. 3.2) and to show licenses at a road checkpoint (V) (Fig. 3.3). For simplicity, we assume that the binding of new pseudonyms and the issuing of licenses is both done by the Motor Vehicle Services (MVS) I.[6] The basic idea for the following scheme is to enable an observer O to support its host wallet W in obtaining pseudonyms and licenses and in showing licenses, while not allowing O to issue new licenses. After explaining the setup of the scheme, we introduce the protocols in turn.

Observers shall authorize the pseudonym binding requests of their hosts, so there must be a *native key* (x_O, y_O) for each observer; the private part x_O is built into the observer to sign authorizations, and the public part y_O is broadcast to MVS, all road checkpoints and drivers, where wallets can look them up, too. We assume that each observer chooses its own native key.

---

[5] Other examples of this more general notion of divertibility of proofs of knowledge have been considered by Chen [11], but a formal definition is outstanding.

[6] In a more integrated system, the issuers of different kinds of certificates could rationalize this approach by establishing a pseudonym binding center and relying upon the same binding procedure.

The Motor Vehicle Services I chooses a *signing key* (x_I, y_I).[7] The public part y_I is broadcast to all drivers and road checkpoints. All observers share a co-signing key x_O, whose corresponding co-verification key y_O is also broadcast to all road checkpoints and is built into all wallets.

Since observers shall authorize the license showing requests of their hosts, each observer also needs to have a *co-signing key* (x^*, y^*). Again, the private part x^* is built into the observer, and the public part y^* is broadcast to all road checkpoints and wallets. The initialization of observers and their tamper-resistance must be trusted by the Motor Vehicle Services and road checkpoints.

Before observers can be used, each one must be personalized for the particular biometric identity of its owner. Once personalized, there is no way to re-personalize it, and from that on, we assume it verifies its owner with sufficiently small false acceptance and false rejection rates. Now, we let each driver personalize its observer, and insert the observer into his or her personal wallet. Once the wallet has mounted the observer, that driver is prepared to execute any of the following protocols.

In the following, the generators g_1, g_2 are chosen uniformly at random and independently of each other and of the generator g in the definition of restrictiveness of the blind and cascade signature primitives (Prerequisites 1 and 2).

3.1   Binding a Pseudonym to a Driver

The MVS I, a wallet W[8], and an observer O, on input its private native key and a biometric identity $\odot\odot$ (read "face"[9]) execute the binding protocol. If the observer verifies the biometric identity successfully, then I obtains the driver's new *source pseudonym* ψ; so does the driver's wallet and, in addition, the wallet and the observer each obtain their respective partial witnesses (ω, w) and v that are later needed to prove ψ.

3.2   Issuing a Driver's License

The MVS I inputs the private signing key x_I and both, I and the wallet W input W's source pseudonym ψ. In addition, W inputs the partial witness (ω, w) for ψ, and the observer O inputs its own partial witness v plus a biometric identity $\odot\odot$. If the observer verifies $\odot\odot$ successfully, then W obtains a license χ for the *interim pseudonym* ψ' and the corresponding partial witness (ω', w') for ψ'. O obtains the interim pseudonym too.

---

[7] This signing key serves to issue one kind of driver's license. For different kinds of licenses, e.g., basic, commercial, agricultural, boat, different signing keys must be used.

[8] Here and in the following, we do not mention the public keys being input

[9] the parameter $\odot\odot$ contains a binary string representation of the biometric identity of the driver performing this action. This string representation is only visible within the tamper resistant observer, so we may regard it as O's private input.

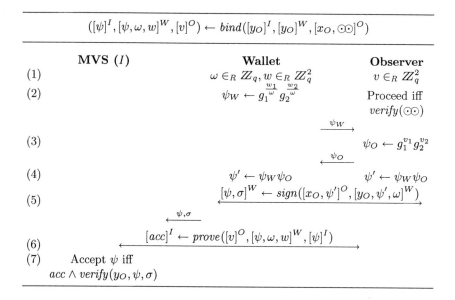

Fig. 2. Binding a pseudonym to a Driver

3.3   Showing a Driver's License

The wallet W inputs a license χ for interim pseudonym ψ' plus the corresponding partial witness (ω', w). The observer O inputs its partial witness v plus a biometric identity $\odot\odot$. If the observer verifies $\odot\odot$ successfully, then the road checkpoint obtains a valid license χ' for *target pseudonym* ϕ. The wallet also obtains its target pseudonym for further reference.

Proposition 1. *The proposed driver's license scheme is (i) effective, (ii) the licenses are unforgeable under the SDL assumption, (iii) the licenses are non-transferable between drivers unless observers are broken, and (iv) the views of Motor Vehicle Services, observers and road checkpoints after any polynomial composition of protocols bind, issue and show are mutually unconditionally unlinkable.*   ◇

Proof. (Proposition 1)

   EFFECTIVENESS: Let the observer's native key be (x_O and y_O), the MVS's signing key be (x_I, y_I) and the observers co-signing key be (x^*, y^*). Furthermore, let a driver D personalize its observer O with biometric identity $\odot\odot$ and mount it by wallet W. Then, if I binds the source pseudonym ψ to D,

$$([\psi]^I, [\psi, \omega, w]^W, [v]^O) \leftarrow bind([y_O]^I, [y_O]^W, [x_O, \odot\odot]^O) \ ,$$

and I issues a license χ for intermediate pseudonym ψ' to D,

$$([\psi', \chi, \omega', w']^W, [\psi']^O) \leftarrow issue([x_I, \psi]^I, [y_I, \psi, \omega, w]^W, [v, \odot\odot]^O) \ ,$$

$$([\psi', \chi, \omega', w']^W, [\psi']^O) \leftarrow issue([x_I, \psi]^I, [y_I, \psi, \omega, w]^W, [v, \odot\odot]^O)$$

	MVS (I)	Wallet	Observer
(1)		$\xleftarrow{\quad\psi\quad}$	Proceed iff $verify(\odot\odot)$
(2)	$\xleftarrow{\qquad [acc]^I \;\leftarrow\; prove([v]^O, [\psi, \omega, w]^W, [\psi]^I) \qquad}$		
(3)	Proceed iff acc	Choose $\omega' \in_R \mathbb{Z}_q$	
(4)	$\xleftarrow{\quad [\psi', \chi]^W \;\leftarrow\; sign([x_I, \psi]^I, [y_I, \psi, \omega']^W) \quad}$		
(5)		$w' \leftarrow \omega w; \; \omega' \leftarrow \omega'\omega$	
			$\xrightarrow{\quad\psi'\quad}$

Fig. 3. Issuing a driver's license

and D then shows its license χ for interim pseudonym ψ' to road checkpoint V,

$$([acc, \phi, \chi']^V, [\phi]^W) \leftarrow show([y_I, y^*]^V, [y_I, y^*, \psi', \chi, w', \omega']^W, [y_I, x^*, v, \odot\odot]^O) ,$$

then V sees a license χ' valid for target pseudonym ϕ. This holds for subsequent shows for further target pseudonyms $\phi', \phi'', \ldots$ to road checkpoints $V', V'', \ldots$. Before each show, the wallet prepares its observer by passing pseudonym ψ', so that O knows which partial knowledge v to input to protocol *show*.

UNFORGEABILITY of licenses under the SDL assumption follows from Prerequisite 2 because licenses are defined as cascade signatures.

NON-TRANSFERABILITY BETWEEN DRIVERS: Protocol *bind* ensures that the wallet does not have any Shannon information about any representation of its

$$([\phi, \chi']^V, [\phi]^W) \leftarrow show([y_I, y^*]^V, [y_I, y^*, \psi', \chi, \omega', w']^W, [y_I, x^*, v, \odot\odot]^O)$$

	Checkpoint (V)	Wallet	Observer
(1)		Choose $\omega'' \in_R \mathbb{Z}_q$	Proceed iff $verify(\odot\odot)$
		$\xrightarrow{\quad\psi', \chi\quad}$	
(2)		$\xleftarrow{\quad [\phi, \chi']^W \;\leftarrow\; cascade([x^*, \psi']^O, [y^*, \psi', \chi, \omega'']^W) \quad}$	
	$\xleftarrow{\quad\phi, \chi'\quad}$		
(3)		$\xleftarrow{\quad [acc]^I \;\leftarrow\; prove([v]^O, [\phi, \omega' \cdot \omega'', w']^W, [\phi]^I) \quad}$	
(4)	Proceed iff $acc \;\wedge$ $verify(y_I y^*, \phi, \chi')$		

Fig. 4. Showing a Driver's License

source pseudonym ψ. Note, that in step (4) of *bind*, the observer enforces ψ to contain a random factor ψ_O that is not chosen by the wallet. Moreover, the SR-assumption ensures that the wallet cannot compute any representation on its own. Therefore, different drivers will represent their pseudonyms inequivalently with overwhelming probability. Furthermore, the restrictiveness of *sign* (Prerequisite 1) and of *cascade* (Prerequisite 2) ensures that the intermediate pseudonym ψ' and all target pseudonyms $\phi, \phi', \ldots$ derived from ψ are equivalent to ψ. To see this, observe first that the generators g_1, g_2 in protocols *bind, issue* and *show* are chosen uniformly at random and independently of any pseudonyms and constants of the underlying blind signature and cascade signature schemes. (In particular, they are chosen independently of g.) From the restrictiveness of the blind and cascade signature schemes, we have that the wallet knows (i) a representation (α, β) of the intermediate pseudonym such that $\psi' = \psi^\alpha g^\beta$ and (ii) a representation (γ, δ) of the target pseudonym such that $\phi = \psi'^\gamma g^\delta$. Therefore, the wallet also knows a representation of the target pseudonym ϕ with respect to ψ and g, namely $(\alpha\gamma, \beta\gamma + \delta)$.

So we conclude, that a wallet has no Shannon information about the representations of any its intermediate and target pseudonyms. And therefore, the wallet has only but negligible chance to succeed in executing *issue* or *show* without the help of its observer. We assume now that the observer is neither broken (in which case its partial witness v might have been compromised) nor is its biometric verification facility bypassed or tampered with. Then we conclude that the three drivers (i) to whom the source pseudonym ψ is bound, (ii) who obtains a license for the intermediate pseudonym ψ', and (iii) who shows this license under a target pseudonym $\phi, \phi', \ldots$ are all the same (in terms of biometric identity).

UNCONDITIONAL UNLINKABILITY of the views of MVS, observers and road checkpoints holds for two reasons: Firstly, all pseudonyms related to the same license, i.e., $\psi, \psi', \phi, \phi', \ldots$ look statistically independent to anyone but the wallet W who chooses the modifiers $\omega, \omega', \omega'', \ldots$ to derive its pseudonyms. Secondly, the views of MVS, observers and road checkpoints on the wallet contain – except for those pseudonyms – only the subviews produced by the subprotocol *prove*, which the wallet uses to prove (its knowledge of representations of) its pseudonyms. From Prerequisite 3 we have that protocol *prove* is witness indistinguishable for predicate W_q, and according to Feige, Shamir [14] this also holds for any polynomial composition of protocol *prove*. Hence, follows the claim.

4 Conclusions and Open Questions

We have proposed an efficient implementation for electronic driver's licenses that drivers can freely carry around in small personal devices. Our proposal is based on the wallet with observer architecture proposed by Chaum and Pedersen [13]. Since transferability of driver's licenses can only be prevented by some kind of biometric driver authentication, we propose to implant some biometric verification facility into the observer. We have shown how the drivers' privacy can then still be protected even against coalitions of MVS, road checkpoints and observers, which have access to unlimited computing resources. The solution can easily be adapted to other kinds of electronic certificates that must not be tranferred between individuals. Our proposal is based upon restrictive blind signatures and a new primitive called restrictive cascade signatures. Implementations for these primitives will be published soon.

5 Acknowledgement

I thank Birgit Pfitzmann and Joachim Biskup for their continued encouragement of this work. Matthias Schunter contributed looks from several interesting angles, and Matt Franklin kindly but firmly urged me to write down this work.

References

1. Stefan Brands: An Efficient Off-line Electronic Cash System Based On The Representation Problem; Centrum voor Wiskunde en Informatica, Computer Science/Departement of Algorithmics and Architecture, *Technical Report CS-R9323*, March 1993.
2. Stefan Brands: Untraceable Off-line Cash in Wallet with Observers; *Crypto '93*, LNCS 773, Springer-Verlag, Berlin 1994, 302–318.
3. Josef Bigün, Gérard Chollet, Gunilla Borgefors (eds.): *Audio- and Video-based Biometric Person Authentication* (AVBPA) '97, LNCS 1206, Springer-Verlag, Berlin 1997
4. Biometric fingerprint readers:

> BioMouse http://www.abio.com
> PC-Lockdown http://users.ids.net
> SecureTouch http://www.biometricaccess.com
> TouchSafe http://www.identix.com
> U.are.U http://www.digitalpersona.com
> Veriprint http://www.biometricID.com

5. Mihir Bellare, Phillip Rogaway: Random Oracles are Practical: A Paradigm for Designing Efficient Protocols; *1st ACM Conference on Computer and Communications Security*, ACM Press, New York 1993, 62–73.
6. David Chaum: Blind Signature System; *Crypto '83*, Plenum Press, New York 1984, 153.
7. David Chaum: A New Paradigm for Individuals in the Information Age; *1984 IEEE Symposium on Security and Privacy*, IEEE Press, Washington 1984, 99–103.
8. David Chaum: Security without Identification: Transaction Systems to make Big Brother Obsolete; *Communications of the ACM* 28/10 (1985) 1030–1044.
9. David Chaum: Showing credentials without identification: Transferring signatures between unconditionally unlinkable pseudonyms; *Auscrypt '90*, LNCS 453, Springer-Verlag, Berlin 1990, 246–264.
10. David Chaum: Achieving Electronic Privacy; *Scientific American* (August 1992) 96–101.
11. Lidong Chen: Witness Hiding Proofs and Applications; *PhD Thesis DAIMI PB-477*, Computer Science Department Aarhus University, August 1994.

12. David Chaum, Jan.-Hendrik Evertse, Jeroen van de Graaf: An improved protocol for demonstrating possession of discrete logarithms and some generalizations; *Eurocrypt '87*, LNCS 304, Springer-Verlag, Berlin 1988, 127–141.
13. David Chaum, Torben Pryds Pedersen: Wallet Databases with Observers. *Crypto '92*, LNCS 740, Springer Verlag, Berlin 1993, 89–105.
14. Uriel Feige, Adi Shamir: Witness Indistinguishable and Witness Hiding Protocols; *22nd Symposium on Theory of Computing (STOC) 1990*, ACM Press, New York 1990, 416–426.
15. Benjamin Miller: Vital signs of identity; *IEEE spectrum* 31/2 (1994) 22–30.
16. Tatsuaki Okamoto, Kazuo Ohta: Divertible zero-knowledge interactive proofs and commutative random self-reducibility; *Eurocrypt '89*, LNCS 434, Springer-Verlag, Berlin 1990, 134–149.
17. Andreas Pfitzmann, Birgit Pfitzmann, Matthias Schunter, Michael Waidner: Trusting Mobile User Devices and Security Modules; *Computer* 30/2 (1997) 61–68.

On Software Protection via Function Hiding

Tomas Sander and Christian F. Tschudin[*]

International Computer Science Institute
1947 Center Street, Berkeley, CA 94704, USA
{sander, tschudin}@icsi.berkeley.edu

Abstract. Software piracy is a major economic problem: it leads to revenue losses, it favors big software houses that are less hurt by these losses and it prevents new software economy models where small enterprises can sell software on a per-usage basis. Proprietary algorithms are currently hard to protect, both at the technical as well as the legal level. In this paper we show how encrypted programs can be used to achieve protection of algorithms against disclosure. Moreover, using this approach we describe a protocol that ensures – under reasonable conditions – that only licensed users are able to obtain the cleartext output of the program. This protocol also allows to charge clients on a per-usage basis.

These results are applied to a special class of functions for which we obtain a secure and computationally feasible solution: the key point is to encrypt functions such that they remain executable. We further show how to robustly fingerprint the resulting programs. Our approach is fully software based and does not rely on tamper resistant hardware.

1 Introduction

Assume that Alice, an ingenious and smart professor of mathematics, finds an algorithm that solves an important mathematical problem (e.g., the discrete log problem for finite fields) much faster than any other previously known algorithm. How can she turn this finding into a profitable business without revealing the algorithm? As the program generates a considerable workload she does not want everybody to send their problem instances to her. Instead, Alice would like to sell the software that her clients would run in the most autonomous way possible. However, this should not jeopardize her trade secret and should still let her control who licensed (and thus is allowed to run) the program. We draw some consequences from these requirements:

(i) Alice needs to hide the algorithm in a program such that it is not disclosed even by extensive and competent code analysis (e.g., by government agencies). This makes it necessary to cryptographically protect the algorithm.

---

[*] New address: Uppsala University, Dept of Computer Systems, Box 325, S - 75105 Uppsala, Sweden

David Aucsmith (Ed.): Information Hiding 1998, LNCS 1525, pp. 111–123, 1998.

(ii) Furthermore, Alice wants to avoid that her program is simply duplicated and used by unlicensed parties who don't pay some license fee. Thus, she wants to prevent that unauthorized users run her program.

(iii) Alice may also want to fingerprint the program and the results in order to identify the source of unauthorized copies.

Our goal is to find a fully software based solution for these problems that runs on any suitable general purpose computer. This excludes special configurations where the computation is delegated to tamper-resistant hardware e.g., a smart card with its own processor. Without such a hardware "save haven" there is no way to prevent that a program is copied – it is just a series of bits. The other major problem is that it seems impossible to protect the software from being spied out because the program is executed "in the public" and is at the full mercy of the executing host.

Surprising new solutions for the protection of software can be envisaged when one relies on encrypted programs that can be executed without preceding decryption. This means that an unsecure host never has to decrypt parts or the whole program but can just go on and execute the instructions found. A method to encrypt functions and to execute them without decryption is the first point we make in this paper. Our second point is that such a "hardened" program moreover has to produce encrypted results. Otherwise little can be done to prevent software pirates from copying and using the program without paying anything for it. The third point is that our method leads to an elegant way of fingerprinting these encrypted functions as well as their results.

Section 2 discusses in more detail the implications of executable encrypted programs. In section 3 we show how to cryptographically hide functions in a program. In fact, *several* functions must be hidden and packaged into a program for security reasons although only one function contributes to the desired result. Section 4 discusses the limitations and the generalization of our results and references related work before we summarize this paper in section 5.

2   The Usefulness of Function Hiding

2.1   Evaluating Encrypted Functions

Code privacy i.e., the ability to hide functions inside a program, enables new solutions for software protection because it eliminates the danger of reverse engineering or program analysis. Important applications for code privacy can be found in the software industry and with service providers that look for ways to make it technically impossible to copy or learn proprietary algorithms. In the introduction we already mentioned software houses that would prefer technical solutions over having to impose their trade secrets via courts. As another example we mention banks which are reluctant to put their proprietary economic models and computations for customer advice services into Java applets because competing institutes could reconstruct them. Finally, consider mobile software

agents that represent human users in E-commerce applications: with
tive software protection their bargaining logic is fully visible to the po
malicious executing hosts. In all cases we have to face arbitrary and u
hosts and therefore would like to conceal a function inside a program i.
code privacy, such that the code can still be executed.

2.2 Computing Encrypted Results

Code privacy alone can not prevent that unauthorized copies of a program
made for which the software's author is not renumerated: Although a func
may be fully protected by the encryption scheme, it could still be copied a
used as a blackbox in order to compute the desired results. From this we co
clude that every usage of the program has to depend on an interaction wi
some authorizing entity. We propose in this paper to study function encryptio
schemes that lead to programs that produce encrypted output. If we let agai
Alice be the software producer and Bob the software user, this means that Bob
is bound to ask Alice for decryption. This leads to the following basic protocol
(see Fig. 1):

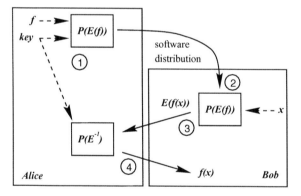

Fig. 1. A basic protocol for executing encrypted functions and keeping control
over who may obtain cleartext outputs.

Let E be a mechanism to encrypt a function f:

1) Alice encrypts f and creates a program $P(E(f))$.
2) Alice sends her software $P(E(f))$ to interested parties e.g., Bob.
3) Bob executes $P(E(f))$ at his input x and send the result y to Alice,
4) Alice decrypts y, obtains $f(x)$ and sends this result back to Bob.

Based on such a protocol Alice can charge the users on a per-usage basis. This
is an important aspect of a software economy: instead of having to fix the price
tag for the software package itself, we rather charge for its usage. Together with a

... amounts this would foster the way towards highly
...tures where the required subroutines are selected
...e decryption requests provide the natural hook for
...charges and could be handled by worldwide replicated
payment centers.

...g Encrypted Functions and Their Results

...del Alice would distribute a single version of her encrypted
...putting it on her WEB page. Because a customer pays for
...e module via the necessary decryption step she gladly grants
...ight to copy the encrypted program and is not interested in the
...customers sending her requests. There may be cases, however,
...ousiness models are required. For example, the United Nations could
...tions against a country because of its continuous violations of human
...e would then be forced to stop business with this country. In this case
...st keep track about who requests the decryption of an output of her
...

...rst approach is to avoid that copies of Alice's program reach the convicted
...ry. Alice would fingerprint each program she hands out and would not sell
...to clients from the incriminated country. Unauthorized copies, if they can
...seized, could then be linked to the client who copied his program in a first
...ace and who would consequently face severe fines. A more powerful control
...an be exerted by exploiting the necessary interaction between Bob and Alice.
A modified protocol could force Bob to digitally sign each decryption request
and thereby lead to an authentication of the requestor. To obtain additional
security a very elegant solution consists in fingerprinting the (encrypted) results
that Bob generates so that each decryption request automatically identifies the
program by which the result was obtained.

All the requirements described in this section (encrypted functions that can
be directly evaluated and which return fingerprintable encrypted results) can be
fulfilled by the encryption scheme we introduce below.

3 How to Hide Polynomials

In this section we sketch how additive homomorphic encryption schemes enable
to hide polynomial functions in programs. We furthermore show how such a
mechanism can be used in our basic software protection protocol and how it
enables the fingerprinting of the program's results.

3.1 Homomorphic Encryption Schemes

Definition 1. *Let R and S be rings. We call an (encryption) function $E : R \to$
S additively homomorphic if there is an efficient algorithm* PLUS *to compute*
$E(x + y)$ *from $E(x)$ and $E(y)$ that does not reveal x and y.*

Using an additive and mixed multiplicative encryption function one
polynomials over rings $\mathbb{Z}/M\mathbb{Z}$ in a program as was pointed out by the
in [10]. We review this technique here briefly.

Proposition 1. *Let $E : \mathbb{Z}/N\mathbb{Z} \to R$ be an additively homomorphic enci
scheme. Then we can hide polynomials $p \in \mathbb{Z}/N\mathbb{Z}[X_1, \ldots, X_s]$ with the k
E in a program* Prog. *The program outputs $E(p(x))$ for an input x.*

Proof. It is easy to see that one can construct an algorithm MIXED-MULT
computes $E(xy)$ from $E(x)$ and y without revealing x just by appropriate c
to PLUS .

Let now f be the polynomial $\sum a_{i_1 \ldots i_s} X_1^{i_1} \ldots X_s^{i_s}$. Alice creates a progi.
Prog(X) that implements f in the following way:

- each coefficient $a_{i_1 \ldots i_s}$ of f is replaced by $E(a_{i_1 \ldots i_s})$,
- the monomials of f are evaluated on the input $x_1, \ldots, x_s$ and stored in a list
  $L := [\ldots, (x_1^{i_1} \ldots x_s^{i_s}), \ldots]$,
- the list $M := [\ldots, E(a_{i_1 \ldots i_s} x_1^{i_1} \ldots x_s^{i_s}), \ldots]$ is produced by calling MIXED-
  MULT for the elements of L and the coefficients $E(a_{i_1 \ldots i_s})$
- the elements of M are added up by calling PLUS.

The claim on the output of the program is now proved by an easy induction.
∎

3.2 Hiding a Polynomial in a Program

Using the homomorphic encryption scheme we just described one can encrypt a
polynomial such that the resulting program effectively hides the function. For
this we rely on the Goldwasser–Micali scheme [6] that, when applied to a one
bit message, is an additive homomorphic encryption scheme E on $\mathbb{Z}/2\mathbb{Z}$. In the
Goldwasser–Micali public key crypto system, Alice's secret key are two large
primes P and Q. Her public key is the modulus $N = PQ$ and a quadratic
nonresidue t modulo N with Jacobi symbol 1. The plaintext 0 is encrypted
by a random quadratic residue modulo N, 1 is represented by non-residues.
Such non-residue values can be computed by multiplying t with an arbitrary
quadratic residue. The scheme is additive because the encrypted sum of two
values x and y is obtained by multiplying their encrypted values modulo N i.e.,
$E(x+y) = E(x)E(y)$.

Lipton and Sander described in [7] a more general additive homomorphic encryption scheme on rings $\mathbb{Z}/M\mathbb{Z}$ for smooth integers M. For ease of presentation
we work in the following only with the Goldwasser–Micali scheme but want to
note that the subsequent constructions generalize to the scheme described in [7].
For previous work see [3].

Using the Goldwasser-Micali scheme (or its generalization), Alice can encrypt
a polynomial f inside a program Prog such that Bob can execute the program
on his input x and obtains the encrypted value of $f(x)$.

Prog **Leak About** f? We call a set $\mathcal{U}$ which con-
fore encryption the *skeleton* of f. (We do not require
m the skeleton occur in f with non–zero coefficients.)
be easily reconstructed from the program **Prog**. Thus
leaks the skeleton of f. By identifying the polynomial
cients m one sees that the information leaked about the
ls the information leaked from the ciphertext of m under
that an encryption scheme that does not leak any informa-
ssages is called polynomial time indistinguishable (see [8] for

*et E be an additively homomorphic encryption scheme. Then the
ructed in proposition 1 hides polynomials $f \in \mathbb{Z}/N\mathbb{Z}[X_1, \ldots, X_s]$.
er that the used encryption scheme E is polynomial time indistin-
hen no information is leaked about f except its skeleton.*

e [10,7] for a more detailed proof.

Goldwasser–Micali scheme is polynomial time indistinguishable under
sumed hardness of the Quadratic Residue Hypothesis [6]. Thus the above
cructed program **Prog** hides everything about the polynomial $f \in \mathbb{Z}/2\mathbb{Z}[X_1,$
$, X_s]$ except it's skeleton (the skeleton may even be increased before encryp-
n for additional security). We note here that there are cases where the leakage
f the skeleton is not tolerable (see [10]).

3.3 A Naïve Protocol for Protecting Polynomials

Hiding a polynomial f in a program **Prog** according to the method described
above enables Alice to realize the basic protocol of section 2:

Bob runs Alice's program **Prog** on his private input $x_1, \ldots, x_s$ and obtains $\mathsf{Prog}(x_1, \ldots, x_s) = E(f(x))$. He sends the result back to Alice for
decryption. Alice decrypts the result by applying E^{-1}, obtains $f(x)$ and
sends the cleartext result to Bob.

Although the construction of the program **Prog** guarantees that no information is
leaked about the coefficients of the polynomial f, there is a *coefficient attack* on
this "naïve" protocol: An attack allows Bob to recover the cleartext coefficients
of f. Instead of sending outputs of **Prog** to Alice, he sends her the encrypted
coefficients that he finds in the program **Prog**. Bob may even scramble them
by multiplication with some random quadratic residue such that Alice can not
recognize these values as her coefficients. According to the protocol, Alice has
to decrypt them and thus would hand him out the main information she wants
to keep secret. This is a general problem that function hiding schemes have to
face if the encryption of some "data" about the function and the output of the
encrypted function are encrypted by the same encryption scheme.

A Remedy We show now how Alice can defeat this coefficient attack in the case of polynomials. We do this by making sure that Alice is able to detect if an element send to her was in fact produced as an output of her encrypted program. The key idea is that Alice hides additional polynomials besides the function f that get simultaneously executed when Prog is run and that serve as checksums for her. By careful construction we make sure that it is unfeasible for a software pirate to construct numbers that pass Alice's checksum test for elements that are not outputs of her encrypted program. This holds in particular for the coefficients of the encrypted program Prog and thus defeats the coefficient attack.

We first describe a modification of the Goldwasser–Micali scheme that allows to hide additional polynomials.

3.4   Hidden Checksums

To the end of piggybacking hidden (checksum) functions to an encrypted program Prog, we first describe how to make an additive homomorphic encryption scheme on $(\mathbb{Z}/2\mathbb{Z})^k$. For describing this public key crypto system we use the names A for the entity that generates a public/private key pair and B for the entity that wants to send a message to A.

Public/Private Key Generation:
> A constructs her public/private key pair as follows:
> (i) A picks k pairs of large primes $(P_1, Q_1), \ldots, (P_k, Q_k)$ such that all the chosen primes are distinct. She set's $N_i := P_i Q_i$ and $N := N_1 \ldots N_k$.
> (ii) She generates for each i a quadratic residue q_i modulo N_i and quadratic non-residue r_i modulo N_i with Jacobi symbol 1.
> (iii) A lifts for each i the tuples $(q_1, \ldots, q_{i-1}, r_i, q_{i+1}, \ldots q_k)$ via Chinese remaindering to an element $T_i \in \mathbb{Z}/N\mathbb{Z}$.
> (iv) A's private key is the list $(P_1, Q_1), \ldots, (P_k, Q_k)$.
> (v) A's public key is the list $(N, T_1, \ldots, T_k)$.

Encryption:
> B encrypts a message $m = (m_1, \ldots, m_k) \in (\mathbb{Z}/2\mathbb{Z})^k$ as follows:
> (i) B computes the product $y := \prod_{\{i \mid m_i = 1\}} T_i \in \mathbb{Z}/N\mathbb{Z}$.
> (ii) B picks at random an element $l \in (\mathbb{Z}/N\mathbb{Z})^{\times}$, and computes $z := yl^2$.
> (iii) z is the encryption of m.

Decryption:
> A computes the Legendre symbol of z in $\mathbb{Z}/P_i\mathbb{Z}$ and in $\mathbb{Z}/Q_i\mathbb{Z}$ and obtains so m_i. By doing this for each i, $1 \leq i \leq k$, A recovers the plaintext m.

Proposition 2. *The described scheme is an additive homomorphic encryption scheme on $(\mathbb{Z}/2\mathbb{Z})^k$. For this encryption function E we have $E(a+b) = E(a)E(b)$.*

Proof. We have the canonical isomorphism $\varphi : \mathbb{Z}/N\mathbb{Z} \to \bigoplus_{i=1}^{k} \mathbb{Z}/N_i\mathbb{Z}$, $x \mapsto (x \bmod N_1, \ldots, x \bmod N_k)$. So an element $x \bmod N$ is a square in $\mathbb{Z}/N\mathbb{Z}$ if and only if $x \bmod N_i$ is a square in $\mathbb{Z}/N_i\mathbb{Z}$ for all i.

By $E_i : \mathbb{Z}/2\mathbb{Z} \to \mathbb{Z}/N_i\mathbb{Z}$ we denote the classical Goldwasser–Micali encryption of one bit. Abstractly one may identify the new encryption process of an element $a = (a_1, \ldots, a_k)$ under E with the process of first encrypting a_i via E_i by the value $E_i(a_i)$ in $\mathbb{Z}/N_i\mathbb{Z}$ and then combining these values together via Chinese remaindering. So we can write:

$$
\begin{aligned}
E(a)E(b) &= \varphi^{-1}(\varphi(E(a)E(b))) \\
&= \varphi^{-1}\big((E_1(a_1), \ldots, E_k(a_k))(E_1(b_1), \ldots, E_k(b_k))\big) \\
&= \varphi^{-1}\big((E_1(a_1)E_1(b_1), \ldots, E_k(a_k)E_k(b_k))\big) \\
&= \varphi^{-1}\big((E_1(a_1 + b_1), \ldots, E_k(a_k + b_k))\big) \\
&= E(a + b)
\end{aligned}
$$

∎

Piggybacking the Evaluation of Checksums In the above naïve protocol we have seen how Alice may hide her polynomial f via $E(f)$ but that this protocol is subject to the coefficient attack. The modified Goldwasser–Micali scheme introduced above allows Alice to hide additional polynomials that serve as checksums. As a first step we show how additional polynomials $g_2, \ldots, g_k$ may be hidden.

Let $\mathcal{U}$ be the skeleton of $f \in \mathbb{Z}/2\mathbb{Z}[X_1, \ldots, X_n]$. Let $g_2, \ldots, g_k$ be polynomials in $\mathbb{Z}/2\mathbb{Z}[X_1, \ldots, X_n]$ with the same skeleton $\mathcal{U}$. Then Alice can build the system of polynomial maps $H : (\mathbb{Z}/2\mathbb{Z})^n \to (\mathbb{Z}/2\mathbb{Z})^k, x \mapsto (f(x), g_2(x), \ldots, g_k(x))$. The system H can be written in a canonical way as *one* polynomial with coefficients in $(\mathbb{Z}/2\mathbb{Z})^k$. We denote this representation by $\tilde{H}$. The following example explains this:

Assume f is the polynomial $f = X^2 + 0X + 1$ and g_2 is the polynomial $g_2 = 0X^2 + 1X + 1$. Thus $k = 2$. The system of the maps $H = (f, g_2) :$ $\mathbb{Z}/2\mathbb{Z} \to (\mathbb{Z}/2\mathbb{Z})^2$, $x \mapsto (f(x), g_2(x))$ may now also be written as the polynomial $\tilde{H} : \mathbb{Z}/2\mathbb{Z} \to (\mathbb{Z}/2\mathbb{Z})^2$, $x \mapsto (1, 0)X^2 + (0, 1)X + (1, 1)1$ whose coefficients are elements from $(\mathbb{Z}/2\mathbb{Z})^2$.

In general the coefficients of $\tilde{H}$ are found as follows. The polynomial $\tilde{H}$ has the skeleton $\mathcal{U}$. For a monomial T from $\mathcal{U}$ the corresponding coefficient in $\tilde{H}$ c_T is the tuple $(a_T, b_{2,T}, \ldots, b_{k,T})$, where a_T is the coefficient belonging to the monomial T in f and $b_{i,T}$ is the coefficient of T in g_i. The coefficients of $\tilde{H}$ are elements in $(\mathbb{Z}/2\mathbb{Z})^k$ and can be encoded via the modified Goldwasser–Micali scheme E. We denote the obtained encrypted polynomial by $E(\tilde{H})$. As the modified Goldwasser–Micali scheme is additive homomorphic, Alice can produce a program Prog for the evaluation of $E(\tilde{H})$ in exactly the same way as described in proposition 1. Thus, we obtain with the same proof:

Lemma 1. *The so constructed program* Prog *evaluated at an input* $x = (x_1, \ldots, x_n)$ *yields the output* $E(\tilde{H}(x))$. *By decrypting* $E(\tilde{H}(x))$ *Alice obtains* $H(x) = (f(x), g_2(x), \ldots, g_k(x))$.

The construction of Prog uses only the homomorphic property of the modified Goldwasser–Micali scheme. Bob does not automatically gain knowledge about the non–residue elements $T_1, \ldots, T_k$.

As a first intermediate result we have thus succeeded in hiding additional polynomials in the program Prog. In the following paragraphs we demonstrate how this technique can be used to defeat the coefficient attack on the "naïve protocol".

A Modified Protocol for Protecting Polynomials We fix the protocol flaw as follows. Alice demands that Bob sends besides the program output Z (which might be a priori any ciphervalue, e.g., a coefficient) also his input x. After decoding Z she obtains the tuple $E^{-1}(Z) = (y, y_2, \ldots, y_k)$. She now evaluates her checksum polynomials g_i at Bob's input x. The value Z passes the checksum test if and only $y_i = g_i(x)$ for all $2 \leq i \leq k$. If Z passes the checksum test Alice sends y back to Bob. If Z does not pass the checksum test she knows that Z has not been obtained as an output of her program Prog at the input x. Thus she refuses to send y back to Bob, or returns an arbitrary value.

Why does this fix the flaw? A software pirate Eve who wants to have a special value Z (which might be a coefficient) to be decrypted by Alice has to produce an input x such that $E^{-1}(Z) = (y, y_2, \ldots, y_k)$ passes the checksum test i.e., $y_i = g_i(x)$ for all i. For several reasons it is very hard for Eve to come up with such a value x:

(i) Note first that such an x might not exist i.e., $(y_2, \ldots, y_k)$ lies not in the range of the map $(g_2, \ldots, g_k)$. The range of the map $(g_2, \ldots, g_k) : (\mathbb{Z}/2\mathbb{Z})^l \rightarrow (\mathbb{Z}/2\mathbb{Z})^{k-1}$ has cardinality at most 2^l. However, the decoding of Z might be any element in $(\mathbb{Z}/2\mathbb{Z})^{k-1}$ and thus from a space of cardinality 2^{k-1}. By increasing k Alice might thus increase the probability that a random element does not lie in the range.

(ii) Even if $(y_2, \ldots, y_k)$ lies in the range of $(g_2, \ldots, g_k)$ Eve has no better choice then sending pairs (Z, x) where x is randomly picked from the input space $(\mathbb{Z}/2\mathbb{Z})^n$. Because of the probabilistic nature of the modified Goldwasser–Micali scheme, Eve is not able to test whether the j'th component of the decryption of Z and Prog(x) coincide $(2 \leq j \leq k)$. So she can not test herself if she has found an input value x that will be accepted by Alice. This requires $\mathcal{O}(2^n)$ queries for decryption and is thus also infeasible.

Efficiency Considerations and the Choice of the $g_i's$ The checksums g_i should be easy to evaluate for Alice. In particular they should be much faster to evaluate then the original polynomial f itself. Else Alice might just evaluate f on x that is send to her by Bob right away. On the other hand the decodings of the coefficients of $\tilde{H}$ (let us call them traces) should be sufficiently random to ensure that Bob can not guess an acceptable x. The traces of the coefficients of $\tilde{H}$ emerge directly from the coefficients of the g_i. To obtain that these traces are sufficiently random thus the $g_i's$ should have many non–zero coefficients and not be too sparse. Both requirements can be met with the following trick, which we explain with an example:

The polynomial $g = (x + 1)^d \in \mathbb{Q}[X]$ can be easily evaluated with $\mathcal{O}(\log(d))$ multiplications. However, the dense representation of $g = \sum_{i=0}^{d} \binom{d}{k} x^i$ has $d + 1$ non–zero coefficients. Mathematically speaking Alice works with the "easy to evaluate" representation of g as a so called "Straight Line Program" but she encodes via $\tilde{H}$ the dense representation of g. More about the theory of straight line programs can be found in [4]. So, a good choice for Alice is to pick the $g_i's$ as sufficiently random straight line programs whose skeletons do not extend the size of $\mathcal{U}$ too much.

3.5   Fingerprinting Encrypted Functions

Encrypted functions offer an elegant new way to fingerprint a program: versions for different users of the program can be encrypted with different encryption functions.

In the treated case of polynomial functions, f can be encrypted with a different modulus for each user e.g., with N for Bob and $\tilde{N}$ for Carol. Denote the encrypted programs by Prog resp. $\tilde{\text{Prog}}$. This has the interesting side effect that the encrypted outputs are fingerprinted too. Bob sends $(\text{Prog}(x), N)$ to Alice and Carol sends $(\tilde{\text{Prog}}(x), \tilde{N})$ (the modulus is required for correct decryption). Thus Alice has complete knowledge about by which program copy the request for decryption has been produced.

Certainly one has to make sure that the encryption of the same function with different moduli does not introduce weaknesses for the encryption scheme. For the basic Goldwasser–Micali scheme on which our construction relies we do not see how the knowledge that elements $a \bmod N$ and $b \bmod \tilde{N}$ are both simultaneously either quadratic residues or quadratic non–residues (of Jacobi–symbol 1) should facilitate cryptanalysis (except in some trivially avoidable cases like $\gcd(N, \tilde{N}) \neq 1$).

4   Discussion

4.1   Learning Attack

A user can build a table of Input/Output values of the algorithm, no matter how well and by which means the algorithm is hidden.

Thus an algorithm which can be easily learned from this table, i.e. reconstructed, is hard to protect. Then the size of this table necessary for reconstruction becomes an important parameter of how well an algorithm may be protected by any means.

In the case of polynomials studied in this paper, the hidden polynomial f may be reconstructed from $\mathcal{O}(\sharp\mathcal{U})$ input/output pairs by obvious interpolation techniques. Moreover, more sophisticated sparse interpolation techniques apply in cases where the degree of the polynomial f is low [12]. However, we view this attack as much less serious than the "coefficient attack" that – if successful – would immediately render explicit information about interesting coefficients of f whereas for interpolation attacks a huge number of input/output pairs must be gained before substantial statements can be made about the underlying polynomial f.

Positively speaking, an estimation of the necessary size of such a table for reconstruction gives Alice an absolute upper bound how well her algorithm can be protected at all. She might use this estimate as an additional parameter to fix her pricing policy for the decryption service she provides. If the polynomial f she hides has, e.g., 10^8 non–zero coefficients and if she charges 10 Cents for each decryption Alice would still be a multi–millionaire before the coefficients of f could be completely recovered.

4.2   Hiding General Programs

We have presented a protocol that allows to hide polynomials over rings $\mathbb{Z}/2\mathbb{Z}$. Using the additive homomorphic encryption scheme described in [7] this ideas generalize to hide polynomials over rings $\mathbb{Z}/M\mathbb{Z}$ for smooth integers M. However, considering only polynomial functions may be a restriction. This restriction is motivated by our requirement for rigorous security proofs. It will be interesting to extend these results to algebraic circuits and finally to Boolean circuits. We regard our results as a first important step in this direction. If one succeeds to hide Boolean circuits, major problems of software protection would – at least theoretically – be solved for general programs because every Turing machine program can (for a fixed input size) be efficiently simulated by Boolean circuits [11].

The first major obstacle for such a general solution is that we do not know of an encryption function E on $\mathbb{Z}/2\mathbb{Z}$ such that both $E(x+y)$ and $E(xy)$ can be easily computed from $E(x)$ and $E(y)$. Such an encryption function seems to be necessary to hide Boolean circuits in a program. However, we believe that such an encryption function will be found in the near future as this an area of ongoing research. Even if such an encryption function is finally found one has to deal with the "coefficient attack" in the context of Boolean circuits. We hope that similar ideas to those we described for polynomials will help to defeat the coefficient attack also in the Boolean context.

4.3   Some Related Work

Previous work dealt mainly with the (related) problem of processing encrypted data. The general importance of homomorphic encryption functions for these type of problems was pointed out by Rivest, Adleman and Dertouzos (cf. [9]). An important step was done by Abadi and Feigenbaum [1] who described a protocol how to securely evaluate a Boolean circuit in encrypted data. Their protocol however requires a high amount of communication rounds between Alice and Bob. Adaptions of this techniques to evaluate encrypted circuits would intrinsically put a high communication burden on Alice and can thus not be considered to be satisfactory for our purposes.

Provable software protection via special software-hardware packaging was proposed by Goldreich and Ostrovsky [5]. The authors of this paper studied in [10] the problem how to cryptographically make mobile code tamper–resistant without recurring to hardware. This is achieved by the same hiding techniques we use in this paper. However, in the mobile code context the additionally difficulty of the "coefficient attack" does not occur. Aucsmith [2] describes a different software–only approach based on code analysis frustration techniques like obfuscation, code rearrangement and gradual code decryption.

5   Summary

Encrypted functions that can be executed without prior decryption give way to surprising solutions for seemingly unsolvable problems of software protection. Alice can safely give the program that implements her encrypted function to Bob without fearing that the function is divulged. In this paper we have shown how this scheme works for polynomials over $\mathbb{Z}/2\mathbb{Z}$.

Our approach for computing with encrypted functions has the desirable property that Bob can produce encrypted results only. He needs Alice's cooperation for recovering the computed value. This enables a cryptographically secured scheme where clients can be charged on a per-usage basis. Requiring Alice to decrypt arbitrary values means that the function hiding protocol has to be secured against adaptive chosen ciphertext attacks. To defeat this protocol attack we construct a suitable public key encryption scheme based on the Goldwasser-Micali scheme. This scheme allows us to merge additional checksum polynomials into the program that implements the encrypted function. The checksums are hidden functions that are executed at the same time as the encrypted function is evaluated. Using these checksums, Alice can decide whether it is permissible to decrypt the presented ciphertext.

A given polynomial can be encrypted in different ways, leading to an elegant way of unremovably fingerprinting the resulting programs. Our scheme has the additional property that also the program outputs are fingerprinted.

References

1. M. Abadi and J. Feigenbaum. Secure circuit evaluation. *Journal of Cryptology*, 2(1):1–12, 1990.
2. David Aucsmith. Tamper resistant software: An implementation. In Ross Anderson, editor, *Information Hiding – Proceedings of the First International Workshop, May/June 1996*, number 1174 in LNCS, pages 317–333, 1996.
3. J. Benaloh. Dense probabilistic encryption. In *Proceedings of the Workshop on Selected Areas of Cryptography*, pages 120–128, 1994.
4. P. Bürgisser, M. Clausen, and M. A. Shokrollahi. *Algebraic Complexity Theory*. Number 315 in Grundlehren der mathematischen Wissenschaften. Springer, 1997.

5. O. Goldreich and R. Ostrovsky. Software protection and simulation on oblivious RAMs. revised October 1995, ftp://theory.lcs.mit.edu/pub/people/oded/soft.ps.
6. S. Goldwasser and S. Micali. Probabilistic encryption. *Journal of Computer and System Sciences*, 28(2):270–299, April 1984.
7. Richard Lipton and Tomas Sander. An additively homomorphic encryption scheme or how to introduce a partial trapdoor in the discrete log. In preparation.
8. S. Micali, C. Rackoff, and B. Sloan. The notion of security for probabilistic cryptosystems. *SIAM Journal on Computing*, 17(2):412–426, 1988.
9. Ronald L. Rivest, Len Adleman, and Michael L. Dertouzos. On data banks and privacy homomorphisms. In R. A. DeMillo, D. P. Dobkin, A. K. Jones, and R. J. Lipton, editors, *Foundations of Secure Computation*, pages 169–179. Academic Press, 1978.
10. T. Sander and Chr. Tschudin. Towards mobile cryptography. In *IEEE Symposium on Security & Privacy'98, Oakland, California*, May 1998.
11. Ingo Wegener. *The Complexity of Boolean Functions*. Eiley-Teubner, 1987.
12. R. E. Zippel. Interpolating polynomials from their values. *Journal of Symbolic Computation*, 9:375–403, March 1990.

Soft Tempest: Hidden Data Transmission Using Electromagnetic Emanations

Markus G. Kuhn* and Ross J. Anderson

University of Cambridge, Computer Laboratory, New Museums Site,
Pembroke Street, Cambridge CB2 3QG, United Kingdom
{mgk25,rja14}@cl.cam.ac.uk

Abstract. It is well known that eavesdroppers can reconstruct video screen content from radio frequency emanations. We discuss techniques that enable the software on a computer to control the electromagnetic radiation it transmits. This can be used for both attack and defence. To attack a system, malicious code can encode stolen information in the machine's RF emissions and optimise them for some combination of reception range, receiver cost and covertness. To defend a system, a trusted screen driver can display sensitive information using fonts which minimise the energy of these emissions. There is also an interesting potential application to software copyright protection.

1 Introduction

It has been known to military organizations since at least the early 1960s that computers generate electromagnetic radiation which not only interferes with radio reception, but also leaks information about the data being processed. Known as *compromising emanations* or *Tempest* radiation, a code word for a U.S. government programme aimed at attacking the problem, the electromagnetic broadcast of data has been a significant concern in sensitive computer applications.

In his book 'Spycatcher' [1], former MI5 scientist Peter Wright recounts the origin of Tempest attacks on cipher machines. In 1960, Britain was negotiating to join the European Economic Community, and the Prime Minister was worried that French president De Gaulle would block Britain's entry. He therefore asked the intelligence community to determine the French negotiating position. They tried to break the French diplomatic cipher and failed. However, Wright and his assistant Tony Sale noticed that the enciphered traffic carried a faint secondary signal, and constructed equipment to recover it. It turned out to be the plaintext, which somehow leaked through the cipher machine.

Sensitive government systems today employ expensive metallic shielding of individual devices, rooms and sometimes entire buildings [2]. Even inside shielded environments, the 'red/black' separation principle has to be followed: 'Red' equipment carrying confidential data (such as computer terminals) has to be isolated by filters and shields from 'black' equipment (such as radio modems) that

---

* Supported by a European Commission Marie Curie training grant

David Aucsmith (Ed.): Information Hiding 1998, LNCS 1525, pp. 124–142, 1998.

handles or transmits unclassified data. Equipment with both 'red' and 'black' connections, such as cipher machines and multilevel secure workstations, requires particularly thorough testing. The U.S. standard NACSIM 5100A that specifies the test requirements for Tempest protected equipment, and its NATO equivalent AMSG 720B, are classified documents [3,4,5]. In Germany, even the names of the government standards on compromising radiation are kept secret.

So we lack full information about the measurement technology required for Tempest tests, but descriptions in published patents [6,7] suggest that the tools employed are orders of magnitude more sensitive than the spectrum analysers used in standard electromagnetic compatibility (EMC) and radio frequency interference (RFI) testing. Some tests involve long-term cross-correlation measurements between signals measured directly inside the target system and the noisy and distorted signals received from external sources including not just antennas but also power and ground lines, peripherals and network cables. Even microphones can be suitable sensors, especially to test noisy equipment like line printers. By averaging correlation values over millions of samples, even very weak traces of the processed information can be identified in electric, electromagnetic and acoustic emanations.

When conducting attacks, similar periodic averaging and cross-correlation techniques can be used if the signal is periodic or if its structure is understood. Video display units output their frame buffer content periodically to a monitor and are therefore a target, especially where the video signal is amplified to several hundred volts. Knowledge of the fonts used with video displays and printers allows maximum likelihood character recognition techniques to give a better signal/noise ratio for whole characters than is possible for individual pixels. Malicious software implanted by an attacker can also generate periodic or pseudorandom signals that are easy to detect.

Similar techniques can be applied when snooping on CPUs that execute known algorithms. Even if signals caused by single instructions are lost in the noise, correlation techniques can be used to spot the execution of a known pattern of instructions. Bovenlander reports identifying when a smartcard performs a DES encryption by monitoring its power consumption for a pattern repeated sixteen times [8]. Several attacks become possible if one can detect in the power consumption that the smartcard processor is about to write into EEPROM. For example, one can try a PIN, deduce that it was incorrect from the power consumption, and issue a reset before the non-volatile PIN retry counter is updated. In this way, the PIN retry limit may be defeated.

Electromagnetic radiation as a computer security risk was mentioned in the open literature as early as 1967 [9]. One of the first more detailed public descriptions of the Tempest threat appears to have been a 1983 report in Swedish [10], but the problem was brought to general attention by a 1985 paper [11] in which van Eck demonstrated that the screen content of a video display unit could be reconstructed at a distance using low-cost home built equipment—a TV set whose sync pulse generators were replaced by manually controlled oscillators. His results were later confirmed by Möller, Bernstein and Kolberg, who also discuss various shielding techniques [12].

Smulders later showed that even shielded RS-232 cables can often be eavesdropped at a distance [13]. Connection cables form resonant circuits consisting of the induction of the cable and the capacitance between the device and ground; these are excited by the high-frequency components in the edges of the data signal, and the resulting short HF oscillations emit electromagnetic waves.

It has also been suggested that an eavesdropper standing near an automatic teller machine equipped with fairly simple radio equipment could pick up both magnetic stripe and PIN data, because card readers and keypads are typically connected to the CPU using serial links. A related risk is cross-talk between cables that run in parallel. For instance, the reconstruction of network data from telephone lines has been demonstrated where the phone cable ran parallel to the network cable for only two metres [14]. Amateur radio operators in the neighbourhood of a 10BASE-T network are well aware of the radio interference that twisted-pair Ethernet traffic causes in the short-wave bands. Laptop owners frequently hear radio interference on nearby FM radio receivers, especially during operations such as window scrolling that cause bursts of system bus activity. A virus could use this effect to broadcast data.

Compromising emanations are not only caused directly by signal lines acting as parasitic antennas. Power and ground connections can also leak high-frequency information. Data line drivers can cause low-frequency variations in the power supply voltage, which in turn cause frequency shifts in the clock; the data signal is thus frequency modulated in the emitted RFI. Yet another risk comes from 'active' attacks [15], in which parasitic modulators and data-dependent resonators affect externally applied electromagnetic radiation: an attacker who knows the resonant frequency of (say) a PC's keyboard cable can irradiate it with this frequency and then detect keypress codes in the retransmitted signal thanks to the impedance changes they cause. In general, transistors are non-linear and may modulate any signals that are picked up and retransmitted by a line to which they are connected. This effect is well known in the counterintelligence community, where 'nonlinear junction detectors' are used to locate radio microphones and other unauthorised equipment.

Yet some protection standards apparently do not specify resistance against active attacks, but only specify testing for signals that originate inside a device, and within a predefined frequency band (typically up to the low gigahertz). A reader of an early version of this paper reported that he was able to get data signals out of U.S. Tempest certified equipment by directing a 10 GHz microwave beam at it. Such vulnerabilities may explain the old Soviet practice of flooding U.S. and allied diplomatic premises in the USSR with microwave radiation.

Considering the excitement that van Eck's findings created [9,16,17,18], and the enormous investment in shielding by the diplomatic and defence community, it is surprising that practically no further research on Tempest attack and defence has appeared in the open literature. However, an RF lab is expensive, while purely theoretical contributions are difficult due to the lack of published data about the information-carrying emanations of modern hardware.

Commercial use of Tempest technology is also marginal. Attempts have been made by the UK and German governments to interest commercial firms in Tempest, in order to help maintain capabilities developed during the Cold War. This has been without success: Tempest shielded PCs and peripherals are many times more expensive than standard models, and sales are typically export controlled. So it is no surprise that shielded facilities and equipment are practically never used outside the diplomatic and defence communities.

In this paper, we describe a number of simple experiments that we have performed with a Tempest receiver and a cheap AM radio. This project started out of the curiosity of the authors and was not funded. We had no access to the expensive equipment that one would expect to find in a signals intelligence agency; even our elderly Tempest receiver is not much more sophisticated than a modified TV set. Our experiments thus show what kinds of attacks are practical in 1998 for a creative amateur eavesdropper. We have also developed some extremely low-cost protective measures.

2   Shortwave Audio Transmissions

If we want to write a computer virus to infiltrate a bank or certification authority, obtain key material and broadcast it to us over an improvised radio channel, then an important design criterion is the cost of the receiver. While intelligence services may already possess phased array antennas and software radios [19], such equipment is not yet generally available. The graduate student's Tempest spying kit is more likely to be just a radio receiver connected to an audio cassette recorder, costing in total about US$100.

In order to get a computer VDU to produce audible tones on our radio, we designed a screen image that causes the VDU beam current to approximate a broadcast AM radio signal. If this latter has a carrier frequency f_c and an audio tone with a frequency f_t, then it can be represented as

$$s(t) = A \cdot \cos(2\pi f_c t) \cdot [1 + m \cdot \cos(2\pi f_t t)]$$
$$= A \cdot \left\{ \cos(2\pi f_c t) + \frac{m}{2} \cdot \cos[2\pi(f_c - f_t)t] + \frac{m}{2} \cdot \cos[2\pi(f_c + f_t)t] \right\}.$$

The timing of a digital video display system is first of all characterised by the pixel clock frequency f_p, which is the reciprocal of the time in which the electron beam in the CRT travels from the centre of one pixel to the centre of its right neighbour. The pixel clock is an integer multiple of both the horizontal and vertical deflection frequencies, that is the rate $f_h = f_p/x_t$ with which lines are drawn and the rate $f_v = f_h/y_t$ with which complete frames are built on the screen. Here, x_t and y_t are the total width and height of the pixel field that we would get if the electron beam needed no time to jump back to the start of the line or frame. However the displayed image on the screen is only x_d pixels wide and y_d pixels high as the time allocated to the remaining $x_t y_t - x_d y_d$ virtual pixels is used to bring the electron beam back to the other side of the screen.

Attack software can read these parameters directly from the video controller chip, or find them in configuration files. For instance, on the authors' Linux workstation, a line of the form

```
ModeLine "1152x900"  95  1152 1152 1192 1472  900 900 931 939
```

in the X Window System server configuration file /usr/lib/X11/XF86Config indicates that the parameters $f_p = 95$ MHz, $x_d = 1152$, $y_d = 900$, $x_t = 1472$ and $y_t = 939$ are used on this system, which leads to deflection frequencies of $f_h = 64.5$ kHz and $f_v = 68.7$ Hz.

If we define $t = 0$ to be the time when the beam is in the centre of the upper left corner pixel ($x = 0$, $y = 0$), then the electron beam will be in the centre of the pixel (x,y) at time

$$t = \frac{x}{f_p} + \frac{y}{f_h} + \frac{n}{f_v},$$

for all $0 \leq x < x_d$, $0 \leq y < y_d$ and $n \in \mathbb{N}$. Using the above formula with the frame counter $n = 0$, we can now calculate a time t for every pixel (x,y) and set this pixel to an 8-bit greyscale value of $\lfloor \frac{255}{2} + s(t) + R \rfloor$ with amplitudes $A = \frac{255}{4}$ and $m = 1$, where $0 \leq R < 1$ is a uniformly distributed random number that spreads the quantization noise (dithering). See Fig. 1 for screen contents generated this way to broadcast an AM tone.

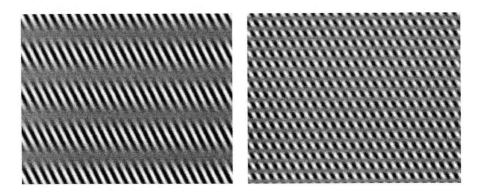

Fig. 1. Example screen contents that cause the authors' computer monitor to broadcast an $f_t = 300$ Hz (left) and 1200 Hz tone (right) on an $f_c = 2.0$ MHz carrier in amplitude modulation.

It is not necessary to fill the entire screen with the pattern, but the energy of the transmitted signal is proportional to the number of pixels that display it. Ideally, both f_c and f_t should be integer multiples of f_v to avoid phase discontinuities from one line or frame to the next.

We had no problems hearing a test melody broadcast by our PC, using a cheap handheld radio. This worked everywhere in our lab and in nearby rooms, while reception over longer distances was good so long as the receiver antenna was held close to power supply lines. As one might expect from the wavelengths involved, the power lines appear to propagate more RF energy than the parasitic antennas in the PC do. In addition, our handheld radio had only a simple untuned dipole antenna, so with a better antenna we would expect to get reasonable reception at several hundred metres.

The shortwave (HF) radio bands in the 3–30 MHz range seem to be the best for this attack. They are the highest bands that normal radios can pick up and that are well below the pixel frequency f_p. Although computer monitors and video cables are too small to be efficient antennas for these frequencies, the lower frequency bands would be even worse, while the VHF frequencies at which electronic components radiate well are too close to current pixel frequencies for software to modulate efficiently, especially using FM. (Of course, as time passes, rising pixel frequencies might bring VHF FM radio within reach.)

The reception range depends largely on how noisy the radio spectrum is near the selected carrier frequency f_c, so this frequency should be selected to avoid nearby broadcast stations. Reception thus depends on the time of day, as the shortwave bands are crowded at night.

In a typical low-cost attack, the eavesdropper would place a radio and cassette recorder near the target and implant the attack software using standard virus or Trojan techniques. Since the broadcast patterns will be visible, the attack should take place after business hours while avoiding times when the chosen frequency is swamped by ionospheric propagation of interfering stations. Many PCs are not turned off at night, a habit encouraged by the power management features of modern systems. If monitors are also left powered up, then the attack software might monitor network traffic to detect the presence of people in the department. Where monitors are turned off but PCs are not, a serviceable signal can usually be picked up: as well as the power line, the VDU cable can be a quite adequate antenna. In these cases, the attack software can broadcast unobtrusively in the evening and early morning hours.

The attack software can use frequency shift keying, with 0 and 1 represented by tone patterns like those shown in Fig. 1. These would be loaded into two video buffers which would be switched at the frame rate f_v. Fast switches between screen patterns and real-time amplitude modulation can also be accomplished using the colour lookup table. The bit pattern would be encoded first to provide forward error correction before its bits are used to select the sequence of tones transmitted.

Our eavesdropper can then take the cassette with the recorded broadcast to her PC and digitise the signal with her sound card. The remaining steps involve symbol detection, synchronization and decoding as they are described in any digital communications textbook [20]. Typical bit rates that can be obtained are of the order of 50 bit/s, so our attack software has to choose the data it transmits. Obvious targets include password files, key material and documents selected by text searching of the hard disk.

A side note for designers of unusual radio transmitters: a PC graphics adapter can be transformed into a digital short-wave transmitter by connecting a suitable antenna to the video output. With no monitor connected, we can set $x_d = x_t$ and $y_d = y_t$ to suppress the sync pulses and blanking intervals and get a clean spectral shape. With carefully optimized software, modern processors can fill video memory faster than the graphics hardware reads it out, opening the possibility of real-time voice and data transmission either using a standard laptop or with at most a very simple RF output stage.

3   The Video Display Eavesdropping Receiver

We performed further experiments using an ESL model 400 Tempest monitoring receiver (Fig. 2) from DataSafe Ltd. of Cheltenham, UK. This device is not intended for signals intelligence missions; it was designed in the late 1980's as a test and demonstration tool to work with the video display technology of that period [21]. It is basically a small black-and-white TV set with some modifications, of which the most important is that the sync signal recovery circuits have been replaced by two manually adjustable oscillators. The horizontal deflection frequency or line rate can be selected in the range 10–20 kHz with almost millihertz resolution, while the vertical deflection frequency or frame rate can be chosen in the range 40.0–99.9 Hz with 0.1 Hz resolution.

Like a normal TV set, this receiver performs an upper sideband linear demodulation with 8 MHz bandwidth and displays inverted video (a higher baseband voltage is shown darker on the 13 cm screen). Unlike a normal TV set, it can be freely tuned in four bands in the range 20–860 MHz and has a sensitivity ranging from 60 μV at 20 MHz to 5 μV at 860 MHz. A more expensive version of this receiver featured a larger screen, line frequencies up to 35 kHz, a demodulator that could be switched between linear AM, logarithmic AM and FM, a receiver bandwidth adjustable from 1.5–8 MHz, a notch filter and a manual override of the automatic gain control.

With a folded 4 m dipole antenna, we got the best image quality in the 100–200 MHz range. This antenna is by no means optimal; experiments with a borrowed spiral log conical antenna with a nominal 200–2000 MHz range gave much better reception results even at frequencies of 140–200 MHz. This more expensive antenna appears better suited to the elliptically polarised emanations from a typical video monitor.

The monitor used in our experiments is a common 43 cm Super-VGA PC monitor (model MT-9017E produced by *iiyama*, 160 MHz video bandwidth) that fulfills the MPR II low-radiation requirements. The video mode is the same as that used in the audio broadcast experiment described in section 2.

The MPR and TCO low-radiation requirements specify only measurements in the bands up to 400 kHz. The fields emitted in these bands are mostly created by the deflection coils and do not carry much information about the screen content.

Fig. 2. DataSafe/ESL Model 400 Tempest Emission Monitor used in our experiments.

The emissions related to the screen content are mostly found far above 30 MHz in the VHF and UHF band (unless we use pathological screen contents as in the audio broadcasting experiment described above). These standards, which were introduced because of health concerns, do not require shielding in the VHF and UHF bands and are thus largely irrelevant from a Tempest point of view. Monitor buyers should not assume that so-called low-radiation monitors, or even LCD screens, provide any Tempest protection; we found that some modern TFT-LCD laptop displays give clearer reception than many cathode ray tubes.

With a 64 kHz line frequency and 95 MHz pixel clock, our PC video mode was well outside the range of displays for which the ESL 400 had been designed. We had to set the horizontal synch generator to around 16.1 kHz, a quarter of the PC's actual frequency. This causes the screen content to be displayed in four columns on the receiver monitor; as successive pixel lines are now split up modulo four, normal text characters although visible are unreadable.

A Tempest monitor sufficient to repeat the following experiments can be built by interconnecting common household components: a PC multi-sync monitor provides the display, a PC graphics adapter card provides the sync pulses, and a VCR tuner connected to a VHF TV antenna and amplifier performs the demodulation.

4   Hiding Information in Dither Patterns

We observed that our Tempest receiver mostly displays the high-frequency part of the video signal. The strongest useful spectral components are at frequencies close to the pixel frequency and its harmonics. However, monitor technology has changed critically over the past decade. The early 1980's terminals studied by van Eck in [11] switched the electron beam on and off for every single pixel. This improved image quality on the low video bandwidth CRTs of the time, as it made all the pixels in a line appear identical. Without this pixel pulsing, pixels in the middle of a horizontal line would appear brighter than those at the edge because of the slow voltage rise and fall times supported by early electronics. Thus short horizontal lines would have appeared as ovals.

Modern video display units have a much higher video bandwidth and so do not need pixel pulsing. As a result, all the eavesdropper can receive of a horizontal line on a modern monitor screen are two short impulses, emitted when the beam is switched on at the left end and switched off again at the right end. Indeed, the Tempest signal is roughly the derivative of the video signal. This is not usually a problem with text, because characters (in most languages) are identifiable from their vertical components; but it hinders eavesdropping of screen contents such as photographic images that cannot be reconstructed easily from their sharp vertical edges.

The human eye is less sensitive to high than to low spatial frequencies. Dithering or halftoning is a technique that uses this to increase the number of colour shades available on displays with a small colour lookup table [22]. On modern high-resolution monitors, users cannot easily distinguish between a medium grey and a chequered halftoning pattern of black and white pixels, especially as the distance between pixels is often smaller than the diameter of the electron beam focus. For the eavesdropper, on the other hand, the high-frequency black/white dither pattern creates the strongest possible signal while a constant colour results in the weakest.

We can use this difference in the spectral sensitivity of the user and the eavesdropper to present different information to them. Figure 3 shows on the left a test signal on the authors' workstation monitor, and on the right the image seen on our Tempest receiver.

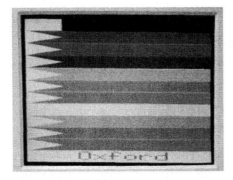 

Fig. 3. Test image as displayed on computer monitor (left) and the captured signal shown on the eavesdropping receiver. Our receiver supports only vertical deflection frequencies of 10–20 kHz, so we had to set it to 16.1 kHz, a quarter of the actual line frequency, and three copies of the image appear next to each other. (The fourth is lost during beam flyback.)

This test image contains on the left side one square and several triangular markers drawn with a dither pattern of vertical black and white lines. These markers help to locate other image features and even with our simple dipole antenna are very clearly visible on the receiver monitor, even in other rooms over 20 metres away. On the right side of every marker is a colour bar that looks uniform on the computer monitor but fades out on the left side of the Tempest image. The bars next to the seven triangles below the square were drawn in uniform colours (dark red, green, blue, yellow, magenta, cyan and grey) on the left end, fading smoothly to dither patterns (red/black, green/black, blue/black, yellow/black, magenta/black, cyan/black, white/black) at the right. The next three bars below are again yellow, magenta, cyan on the left side, but this time the dither pattern shows a phase shift between the primary colours so that the dither pattern on the right end is red/green, red/blue and blue/green. Between the left and right end of the bars, the amplitude of the dither pattern increases linearly. This test image enables us to see at a glance which of the three electron guns produces a usable Tempest signal and at which edge height.

One observation is that the signals generated with identical video input voltages for the three primary colours red, green and blue show different Tempest amplitudes. One reason is that the white calibration of the monitor transfers equal input voltages into different control voltages and beam currents. Another seems to be that the emissions for the three primary colours create different polarisations of the emitted waves; varying the antenna position changes the relative luminosity of the received test bars. Even the phase shift of one primary colour in the dither patterns of the second set of yellow, magenta and cyan can be distinguished in some antenna positions. By evaluating polarisation modes with several antennas, it might even be possible for an eavesdropper to reconstruct some colours.

A fascinating application of the eavesdropper's sensitivity to dither amplitudes is given in the colour bar right of the eleventh triangle marker below the square. While the computer monitor clearly displays "Oxford" here in large letters, the eavesdropper sees instead the message "Cambridge". Figure 4 shows the magnified pixel field around the letters "Ox" that radiate as "Ca". While "Oxford" is drawn in magenta instead of grey by deactivating only the green component, "Cambridge" is embedded in the image by increasing the amplitude of the dithering.

As Fig. 5 shows, this can be generalized. We can embed not only text but arbitrary greyscale images inside other cover images. Embedded images give an impression of the large bandwidth that is available to the attacker by dither modulation. Let $C_{x,y,c}$ be the value of a cover image at pixel coordinates (x,y) for primary colour $c \in \{\text{red}, \text{green}, \text{blue}\}$ and let $E_{x,y}$ be the pixel value of the image that shall be embedded covertly for reception by the eavesdropper. Then the colour component values that we have to display on the screen are

$$S_{x,y,c} = \left(C_{x,y,c}^{\tilde{\gamma}} + \min\{\alpha(1 - E_{x,y}), C_{x,y,c}^{\tilde{\gamma}}, 1 - C_{x,y,c}^{\tilde{\gamma}}\} \cdot d_{x,y} \right)^{1/\tilde{\gamma}}$$

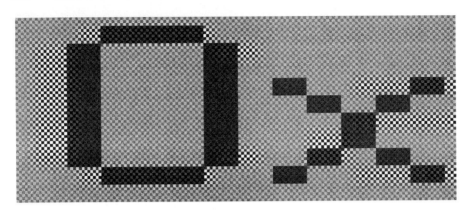

Fig. 4. A magnification of the section that reads "Ox" on the computer monitor but "Ca" on the eavesdroppers screen (see Fig. 3) shows how the broadcast message was hidden. The text made visible to the eavesdropper is present as gamma-corrected amplitude modulation in the background pattern, while the foreground message is just a low-frequency signal.

where $d_{x,y} = 2[(x + y) \bmod 2] - 1 \in \{-1, 1\}$ is the dither function, $0 < \alpha \leq 0.5$ is a parameter that determines the maximum amplitude of the added dithering and $\tilde{\gamma}$ is as described below. Here, all pixel values are normalised values in the range 0 (black) to 1 (maximum luminosity), so with 8-bit displays the value written into the frame buffer is $\lfloor 255 \cdot S_{x,y,c} + R \rfloor$.

The colour component value chosen by the display software is usually mapped linearly to the video voltage supplied to the monitor. But the relation between the video voltage V and the luminosity L of the screen is non-linear and can be approximated as $L = \mathrm{const} \cdot V^{\gamma}$ for CRTs, where γ is usually in the range 1.5–3.0 and depends on the hardware design of the monitor. Software that compensates this non-linearity performs what is known as *gamma correction* [22,23]. The overall luminosity of a two-colour dither pattern depends on the arithmetic mean of the luminosities L rather than the voltages V. To remain inconspicuous for the viewer, amplitude variations in the dither pattern must be performed such that the average luminosity is preserved.

We observed that the arithmetic average of the gamma-corrected luminosities only predicts the luminosity accurately for a dither pattern consisting of horizontal lines. For dither patterns with vertical lines or chequered patterns, the restricted bandwidth of the beam current introduces many intermediate values. An accurate luminosity estimation for such dither patterns with high horizontal frequency components—the ones of interest for hiding information in emissions—would involve integration of the distorted gamma-corrected video signal [24]. We performed tests in which we determined the video voltage $\bar{V}$ that gives rise to a colour of the same brightness as a dither mix of the voltages V_1 and V_2. For a dither pattern of horizontal lines, the formula $\bar{V} = (\frac{1}{2}V_1^{\gamma} + \frac{1}{2}V_2^{\gamma})^{1/\gamma}$ produced excellent predictions with $\gamma = 2.0$, the exponent for our CRT. For a

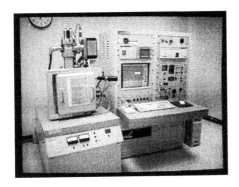 

Fig. 5. The left photo shows what the user sees on her computer monitor. At the same time, the eavesdropping receiver shows in the right photo two greyscale images that we embedded. Bright and dark parts of the cover image reduce the amplitude that the embedding can utilize inconspicuously, so these areas become visible as bright shadows on the eavesdropping receiver ($\alpha = 0.4$).

chequered dither pattern, which looks much smoother, the same formula still worked, but the exponent changed to $\tilde{\gamma} = 1.28$. This is the value that we have to use to determine $S_{x,y,c}$. The gamma-correction parameters that computers can download from modern monitors are thus not sufficient to gamma-correct a high-amplitude chequered dither pattern.

The embedded image should be smoothed in order not to arouse the very sensitive edge detectors implemented in the human retina. Where the transmitted image must be very difficult to see, the correction parameter $\tilde{\gamma}$ should be manually calibrated for a specific monitor. The calibration depends not only on the type of monitor, but also on its brightness, contrast and colour temperature settings, which the user might modify. So a careful attacker will not attempt to hide readable text or barcodes in uniformly coloured areas, but in structurally rich content like photos or the animations shown by screen savers.

The implication for systems with mandatory access control is that any software with pixel-level access to an unshielded display must either be part of the trusted computing base or be prevented from accessing protected data.

5   Broadband Transmissions

Our dither amplitude modulation of large readable letters was designed to allow easy low-cost reception of hidden broadcast information with a modified TV set. A professional eavesdropper is more likely to select a method that affects only a small part of the screen layout and that is optimized for maximum range and robust reception with sophisticated equipment. In this section, we outline what such a system might look like.

Reception of monitor emanations with modified TV sets requires either exact knowledge of the horizontal and vertical deflection frequencies or a strong enough signal to adjust the sync pulse generators manually. With larger distances and low signal levels, the emitted information can only be separated from the noise by averaging the periodic signal over a period of time, and manual adjustment of the synch is difficult.

In a professional attack, one might use spread-spectrum techniques to increase the jamming margin and thus the available range. The attack software would dither one or more colours in several lines of the screen layout using a pseudorandom bit sequence. A cross-correlator in the receiver gets one input from an antenna and sees at its other input the same pseudorandom bit sequence presented with the guessed pixel clock rate of the monitor. It will generate an output peak that provides the phase difference between the receiver and the target. A phase-locked loop can then control the oscillator in the receiver such that stable long-term averaging of the screen content is possible. Information can be transmitted by inverting the sequence depending on whether a 0 or 1 bit is to be broadcast. Readers familiar with direct sequence spread-spectrum modulation [20] will find the idea familiar, and many spread-spectrum engineering techniques are applicable.

The advantages of using spread-spectrum techniques are that higher data rates and reception ranges can be achieved, and that only the pixel clock frequency and (perhaps) the carrier frequency have to be selected. This enables fast lock-on and fully automatic operation.

A practical benefit is that it may only be necessary to use a small number of lines—perhaps in the toolbar, or even off the visible edge of the screen. If a spreading sequence coded as a series of black and white pixels is too different from the normal grey toolbar expected by the user, then phase modulation can be used instead. The amplitude of the dither pattern can be reduced smoothly for a few pixels at phase jumps to avoid visible bright or dark spots.

An interesting commercial application of this could be in software license enforcement. Most software licenses allow the use of a product on only one computer at a time, but this condition is frequently violated. Commercial software vendors tackle piracy by forming trade associations which prosecute offenders, but the main enforcement problem is not so much identifying offending companies as getting the initial search warrant. This motivates the design of a system that will detect piracy from outside an offender's premises.

Our suggestion is that software packages include in their screen layout a few lines with a signal that encodes the license serial number plus a random value [27]. Just as "TV detector vans" circulate in countries with mandatory television license fees to discover unlicensed TV sets from their stray RF emissions, a "software detector van" can be used to patrol business districts and other areas where software piracy is suspected. If the van receives twenty signals from the same copy of a software from a company that has only licensed five copies, then probable cause for a search warrant has been established.

The random value encoded in the signal helps distinguish echoes from messages received from different computers. Finally, if the signal were displayed by the operating system, it could contain the identities and license numbers of all currently active programs.

6 A New Protective Measure: Tempest Fonts

As we noted above, only the high-frequency components of the video signal can be picked up by the eavesdropper. Figure 6 shows on the left a test image that helps us to determine which part of the image spectrum actually produces a Tempest signal. This "zoneplate" signal is used by TV technicians, and is generated from the function $\cos(x^2 + y^2)$ where the coordinate system origin is in the centre. At every point of this test signal, the local spectrum has a single peak at a horizontal and vertical frequency that is proportional to the horizontal and vertical coordinates of this point. This frequency peak reaches the Nyquist frequency $f_p/2$ for the points at the border of the zoneplate image.

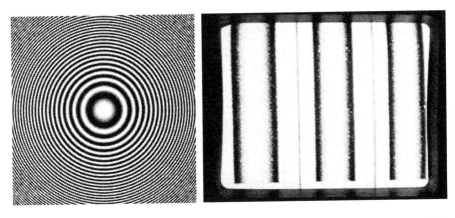

Fig. 6. In the zoneplate test signal (left), every point has a local spectrum with a horizontal and a vertical frequency proportional to its coordinates (origin in the centre). The received image (right) shows that only those parts of the zoneplate signal where the horizontal frequency is in the upper 30% of the spectrum (i.e., $> 0.7 \cdot f_p/2$) cause a significant signal to be received from our monitor.

In the right part of Fig. 6, we can see the Tempest signal received from a monitor showing the zoneplate image (for this and the other experiments described in this section, we brought our antenna as close as possible to the monitor to give best reception). As one might expect, only the horizontal frequency of the signal determines what is received. Note that only the outer 30% of the zoneplate image area appears dark on the receiver. This means that if we look at the Fourier transform of a horizontal sequence of pixels, only information present as frequencies f in the range $0.7 \cdot f_p/2 < f \leq f_p/2$ in the spectrum can be received in our setup. This value 0.7 clearly depends on the equipment used, but seems to be not untypical.

We wondered whether this leads us to a potentially very cheap software-based eavesdropping protection technique. Figure 7 shows in the upper left side a magnified pixel field that displays some text. On the upper right, the same pixel field is shown after we removed the top 30% of the Fourier transform of the signal by convolving it with a suitable $\sin(x)/x$ low pass filter.

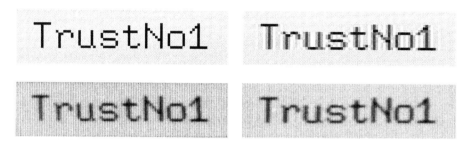

Fig. 7. The text on the left is displayed with a conventional font, while the text on the right has been filtered to remove the top 30% of the horizontal frequency spectrum. The graphics in the upper row show the pixel luminosities, while below there are magnified screen photographs of a 21×5 mm text area. While the user can see practically no difference between the fonts, the filtered text disappears from our eavesdropping monitor while the normal text can be received clearly.

The filtered text looks rather blurred and unpleasant in this magnified representation, but surprisingly, the loss in text quality is almost unnoticeable for the user at the computer screen, as the magnified photos in the lower half of Fig. 7 show. The limited focus of the electron beam, the limited resolution of the eye, as well as effects created by the mask and the monitor electronics filter the signal anyway.

While there is little visible change for the user, such filtering causes a text which could previously be received easily to vanish completely from the Tempest monitor, even when the antenna is right next to the VDU (Fig. 8). Filtered text display requires greyscale representation of glyphs, but this technology is already available in many display drivers in order to support anti-aliasing fonts. We are optimistic that if the low pass filtering is combined carefully with anti-aliasing techniques, readability can be better than with simple bi-level fonts. Simple low pass filtering could also be performed without software modifications by programming the filter available in the next generation of graphic adapters. Good anti-Tempest display routines will also apply the opposite of the techniques used in OCR fonts: there could be small random variations to the glyphs to make automatic character recognition by the eavesdropper more challenging.

Eavesdropping text from a monitor is only one of the Tempest risks associated with personal computers. Nevertheless, we still consider it the most significant one. The video display unit is usually the strongest source of radiation and due

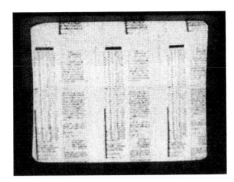

Fig. 8. On the left we see what the eavesdropping monitor shows when text is displayed with normal fonts. The small screen size and the modulo four separation of image lines renders the text unreadable on our simple monitor, but the presence of the signal is clear. On the right, the screen content was low pass filtered as in Fig. 7 and the received Tempest signal has vanished except for the horizontal sync pulses.

to its periodic nature, a video signal can easily be separated from other signals and from noise by periodic averaging.

We have identified two more potential sources of periodic signals in every PC, both of which can be fixed at low cost by software or at worst firmware changes [28]. Keyboard controllers execute an endless key-matrix scan loop, with the sequence of instructions executed depending on the currently pressed key. A short random wait routine inside this loop and a random scan order can prevent an eavesdropper doing periodic averaging. Secondly, many disk drives read the last accessed track continuously until another access is made. As an attacker might try to reconstruct this track by periodic averaging, we suggest that after accessing sensitive data, the disk head should be moved to a track with unclassified data unless further read requests are in the queue.

DRAM refresh is another periodic process in every computer that deserves consideration. The emanations from most other sources, such as the CPU and peripherals, are usually transient. To use them effectively, the eavesdropper would have to install software that drives them periodically, or at least have detailed knowledge of the system configuration and the executed software.

We are convinced that our Soft Tempest techniques, and in particular Tempest fonts, can provide a significant increase in emanation security at a very low cost. There are many applications where they may be enough; in medium sensitivity applications, many governments use a zone model in which computers with confidential data are not shielded but located in rooms far away from accessible areas. Here, the 10–20 dB of protection that a Tempest font affords is of major significance. There are also applications where Tempest fonts are the only option, such as when a nation suddenly has to buy large quantities of commercial off-the-shelf computers and field them in a sudden deployment such as Desert Storm.

Finally, in applications such as diplomacy that require the highest levels of protection, users should install soft as well as hard Tempest protection; hardware shielding often fails due to dirty gaskets or to procedural problems such as ambassadors refusing to keep doors closed on a hot day.

7 Conclusions

Compromising emanations continue to be a fascinating field of research, although they are mostly unexplored in the research literature. The high cost of physical shielding and the continuously increasing clock frequencies of modern computers ensure that the problem will not go away quickly. Things will be made worse by the arrival of cheap software radios—universal receivers in which all demodulation of the signal after the intermediate frequency conversion is done completely in software on high-speed DSPs [19]. This technology will allow low-budget attackers to implement sophisticated Tempest attacks which were previously only possible with very expensive dedicated equipment.

However, we have shown that Tempest is not just about RF engineering. Software techniques can make a huge difference: they can be used to mount new attacks, construct new defences and implement some quite novel applications.

The attack consists of implanting malicious software in a target computer to steal secret data and transmit it in a manner optimised for some combination of reception range, receiver cost and observability. This 'Tempest virus' can attack computers not connected to any communication lines and situated in rooms from which the removal of storage media is prohibited. It can also be used in commercial applications such as software copy protection.

On the defensive side, we have shown how fonts can be designed with spectral characteristics that significantly reduce the effective range of eavesdropping at a negligible cost in image quality.

References

1. Peter Wright: Spycatcher – The Candid Autobiography of a Senior Intelligence Officer. William Heinemann Australia, 1987, ISBN 0-85561-098-0
2. Electromagnetic Pulse (EMP) and Tempest Protection for Facilities. Engineer Pamphlet EP 1110-3-2, 469 pages, U.S. Army Corps of Engineers, Publications Depot, Hyattsville, December 31, 1990
3. Deborah Russell, G. T. Gangemi Sr.: Computer Security Basics. Chapter 10: TEMPEST, O'Reilly & Associates, 1991, ISBN 0-937175-71-4
4. A. J. Mauriello: Join a government program to unveil Tempest-spec mysteries. EDN vol 28 no 13, pp 191–195, June 23, 1983
5. Anton Kohling: TEMPEST – eine Einführung und Übersicht zu kompromittieren-den Aussendungen, einem Teilaspekt der Informationssicherheit. In H.R. Schmeer (ed.): Elektromagnetische Verträglichkeit/EMV'92, Stuttgart, February 1992, pp 97–104, VDE-Verlag, Berlin, ISBN 3-8007-1808-1.

6. Joachim Opfer, Reinhart Engelbart: Verfahren zum Nachweis von verzerrten und stark gestörten Digitalsignalen und Schaltungsanordnung zur Durchführung des Verfahrens [Method for the detection of distorted and strongly interfered digital signals and circuit arrangement for implementing this method]. German Patent DE 4301701 C1, Deutsches Patentamt, May 5, 1994

7. Wolfgang Bitzer, Joachim Opfer: Schaltungsanordnung zum Messen der Korrelationsfunktion zwischen zwei vorgegebenen Signalen [Circuit arrangement for measuring the correlation function between two provided signals]. German Patent DE 3911155 C2, Deutsches Patentamt, November 11, 1993

8. Ernst Bovenlander, invited talk on smartcard security, Eurocrypt '97, May 11–15, 1997, Konstanz, Germany

9. Harold Joseph Highland: Electromagnetic Radiation Revisited. Computers & Security vol 5, pp 85–93 and 181–184, 1986

10. Kristian Beckman: Läckande Datorer [Leaking Computers]. Cited in [9,18]

11. Wim van Eck: Electromagnetic Radiation from Video Display Units: An Eavesdropping Risk? Computers & Security vol 4, pp 269–286, 1985

12. Erhard Möller, Lutz Bernstein, Ferdinand Kolberg: Schutzmaßnahmen gegen kompromittierende elektromagnetische Emissionen von Bildschirmsichtgeräten [Protective Measures Against Compromising Electro Magnetic Radiation Emitted by Video Display Terminals]. Labor für Nachrichtentechnik, Fachhochschule Aachen, Aachen, Germany

13. Peter Smulders: The Threat of Information Theft by Reception of Electromagnetic Radiation from RS-232 Cables. Computers & Security vol 9, pp 53–58, 1990

14. Überkoppeln auf Leitungen [Cross-talk on cables], Faltblätter des BSI 4, German Information Security Agency, Bonn, 1997.

15. Schutzmaßnahmen gegen Lauschangriffe [Protection against eavesdropping attacks], Faltblätter des BSI 5, German Information Security Agency, Bonn, 1997.

16. Bloßstellende Abstrahlung [Compromising Emanation], Faltblätter des BSI 12, German Information Security Agency, Bonn, 1996.

17. Joel McNamara: The Complete, Unofficial TEMPEST Information Page. Internet Web page, URL <http://www.eskimo.com/~joelm/tempest.html>.

18. Harold Joseph Highland: The Tempest over Leaking Computers. Abacus vol 5 no 2, pp 10–18 and 53, 1998

19. Raymod J. Lackey, Donald W. Upmal: Speakeasy: The Military Software Radio. IEEE Communications Magazine vol 33 no 5, pp 56–61, May 1995

20. John G. Proakis: Digital Communications. 3rd ed., McGraw-Hill, New York, 1995, ISBN 0-07-051726-6

21. Operating Manual for DataSafe/ESL Model 400B/400B1 Emission Monitors. DataSafe Limited, 33 King Street, Cheltenham, Goucestershire GL50 4AU, United Kingdom, June 1991

22. James D. Foley, Andries van Dam: Fundamentals of Interactive Computer Graphics, Addison-Wesley, 1982

23. Michael Bach, Thomas Meigen, Hans Strasburger: Raster-scan cathode-ray tubes for vision research—limits of resolution in space, time and intensity and some solutions. Spatial Vision vol 10 no 4, pp 403–414, 1997

24. Stanley A. Klein, Q. James Hu, Thom Carney: The Adjacent Pixel Nonlinearity: Problems and Solutions. Vision Research vol 36 no 19, pp 3167–3181, 1996

25. Lars Høivik: System for Protecting Digital Equipment Against Remote Access. United States Patent 5165098, November 17, 1992

26. John H. Dunlavy: System for Preventing Remote Detection of Computer Data from TEMPEST Signal Emissions. United States Patent 5297201, March 22, 1994

27. Markus G. Kuhn, Ross J. Anderson: Software Piracy Detector Sensing Electromagnetic Computer Emanations. UK patent application no 9722799.5, October 29, 1997

28. Markus G. Kuhn, Ross J. Anderson: Low Cost Countermeasures Against Compromising Electromagnetic Computer Emanations. UK patent application no 9801745.2, January 28, 1998

Robust Digital Watermarking Based on Key-Dependent Basis Functions

Jiri Fridrich[1]

Center for Intelligent Systems
SUNY Binghamton
Binghamton, NY 13902-6000
fridrich@binghamton.edu

2 Lt Arnold C. Baldoza and Richard J. Simard

Air Force Research Laboratory/IFEC
32 Hangar Road
Rome, NY 13441-4114
{baldozaa, simardr}@rl.af.mil

Abstract. In this paper, we introduce the concept of key-dependent basis functions and discuss its applications to secure robust watermarking for copyright protection and to designing secure public black-box watermark detectors. The new schemes overcome a possible security weakness of global, non-adaptive schemes that apply watermark patterns spanned by a small number of publicly known basis functions. The watermark is embedded into the projections of an image onto the secret set of key-dependent functions (patterns). The robustness of the watermarking scheme with respect to filtering, lossy compression, and combinations of many other attacks is studied. Finally, we propose a candidate for a watermarking scheme that enables the construction of a secure public watermark detector.

Keywords. Robust image watermarking, attacks, orthogonal patterns, secure public watermark detector

1 Introduction

Digital images and digital video-streams can be easily copied. Even though such copying may violate copyright laws, it is widespread. The ease with which electronic images may be copied without loss of content significantly contributes to illegal copying. One of the goals of digital watermarks is authentication for copyright protection. To prove the ownership of an image, a perceptually invisible pattern (a watermark) is embedded into the image and ideally stays in the image as long as the image is recognizable. This means that the watermark must be embedded in a robust way and

---

[1] The author has been supported by an SBIR research grant "Intelligent C4I Technologies".
David Aucsmith (Ed.): Information Hiding 1998, LNCS 1525, pp. 143-157, 1998.

withstand any attempts to remove it using image processing tools as well as a targeted intentional removal based on the full knowledge of the watermarking scheme.

As pointed out by Cox *et al.* [1] and Miller [2] the watermark should be embedded in the most perceptually important features in the image, otherwise it would be too sensitive to compression schemes capable of removing *redundant* information. While schemes that adapt the watermark strength according to local image properties provide higher robustness [3–5], it is not entirely clear whether or not they provide higher degree of security because the watermarked image provides a clue about the strength and location of the watermark. This may be a handicap if such schemes were to be combined with public watermark detectors [11, 12]. In addition to that, future compression schemes capable of removing *irrelevant* information may disrupt such watermarks [6–8].

Schemes that embed watermarks into the projections onto smooth orthogonal basis functions such as, discrete cosines, are typically very robust and less sensitive to synchronization errors due to skipping of rows of pixels, and/or permuting of nearby pixels than techniques that embed watermarks using pseudo-noise patterns [9, 10]. However, if the watermark pattern is spanned by a relatively small number of publicly known functions, it may be possible to remove the watermark or disrupt it beyond reliable detection if a portion of the watermark pattern can be guessed or is known[2], or when the embedding key becomes partially available. The plausibility of such an attack is demonstrated in section 2, where a simplified NEC scheme is analyzed.

This observation lead us towards investigating general, key-dependent orthogonal basis functions as a replacement for publicly known bases, such as discrete cosines. We believe that such techniques may significantly increase the security of watermarking schemes. A technique that utilizes key-dependent orthogonal functions (patterns) is described and analyzed in section 3. Another important motivation for this paper was the problem of designing a secure black-box public watermark detector. In section 4, we describe a candidate for such a secure detector based on key-dependent bases. Secure public detectors find important applications in copy-control of Digital Video Disks [11–15]. In section 5, we summarize the paper and outline future research directions.

2   An Attack on Global Watermarking Schemes

It is important that a partial knowledge of the watermark should not enable a pirate to remove the entire watermark or disturb it beyond reliable detection. Below, we show that it is indeed possible in certain cases to reconstruct the watermark pattern based on the assumption that the watermark becomes known in some small area. This assumption is not that unreasonable as it may seem at first. For example, one can make a guess that certain portion of the original image had pixels of uniform brightness or of a uniform gradient, or an attacker may be able to foist a piece of his image into a collage created by somebody else. If this is the case, then the knowledge of a portion of the watermark pattern may give us additional constraints to disturb or eliminate the

---

[2] This can happen in a collage consisting of several images.

whole watermark. This is especially relevant for watermark patterns spanned by publicly known functions. Below, we describe an attack that can be applied to any non-adaptive robust watermarking technique, invertible or not, if some portion of the original unwatermarked image is known or can be guessed, and if the watermark is mostly spanned by some small number of Fourier modes. The attack attempts to find the coefficients of the lowest frequency DCT coefficients based on the "known" pixel values. A set of linear equations completed with a stabilizing functional makes the inversion possible.

In the watermarking technique proposed by Cox *et al.* [1], the watermark is embedded into a selected set of discrete cosine coefficients (the highest energy 1000 frequency coefficients). The logic behind this technique is to hide the watermark into the most perceptive modes of the image to achieve a high degree of robustness with respect to lossy compression and most common image processing techniques. The watermark is spanned by 1000 highest frequency discrete cosines. The non-locality of the watermark pattern could be potentially dangerous if an attacker is able to guess the original, unwatermarked values of some pixels. What makes the attack hard to mount, however, is the fact that discrete cosines are not linearly independent on proper subsets of the image, and, depending on the number of discrete cosines spanning the watermark, we may not have enough constraints to exactly recover the whole watermark.

In order to demonstrate the plausibility of the proposed attack, we performed the following experiment with a weakened version of the scheme proposed in [1]. The watermark is embedded into the lowest 50 coefficients v_k of the DCT according to the formula

$$v_k' = v_k (1 + \alpha \, \eta_k), \tag{1}$$

where v_k' are the modified DCT coefficients, η_k is a Gaussian sequence with zero mean and unit variance, and α is the watermark strength (also related to watermark's visibility). The watermarked image is obtained by applying the inverse DCT to the coefficients v_k'. In our experiments, we took $\alpha = 0.1$.

Let us assume that there is a region containing P pixels (i, j) in the image for which the original pixel values are known. Using the inverse DCT transformation, we can express the difference, $Iw-I$, between the watermarked and the original image as

$$(Iw - I)(i,j) = \tag{2}$$

$$\frac{2}{\sqrt{M \times N}} \sum_{k=1}^{J} c_1(r_k) c_2(s_k) \cdot \alpha \cdot \eta(k) \cdot V(r_k, s_k) \cos \frac{\pi}{2M} r_k (2i+1) \cos \frac{\pi}{2N} s_k (2j+1)$$

where

$$c_1(r) = 1/\sqrt{2} \text{ when } r = 0 \text{ and } c_1(r) = 1 \text{ otherwise}$$

$$c_2(s) = 1/\sqrt{2} \text{ when } s = 0 \text{ and } c_2(s) = 1 \text{ otherwise}$$

and $V(r, s)$ denotes the coefficient matrix of DCT. The indices (r_k, s_k), $k = 1, ..., J$ correspond to the 50 lowest frequency discrete cosines that have been modified. The above equation describes a linear system of P equations for J unknowns $\eta_k \cdot V(r_k, s_k)$. Since our goal is to obtain the sequence η_k, we need to use the DCT of the watermarked image to calculate η_k. This can be done easily because the DCT of Iw gives us

$V(r_k, s_k)$ $(1 + \alpha\eta_k)$. The number of equations is determined by the number, P, of pixels (i, j) for which the original gray levels can be estimated or are known. Even though the number of pixels, P, may exceed J, the rank of the matrix may be smaller than J because discrete cosines do not generally form a set of linearly independent functions on proper subsets of the image.

In our experiment, we used a test image containing 128×128 pixels with 256 gray levels. The image has a small area of pixels in the upper right corner that has a constant luminance of 192 (see Fig. 1). We took $P = 862$ pixels that had constant brightness in the original unwatermarked image. Then, a watermark was inserted into the lowest $J = 50$ coefficients of the DCT using the algorithm above. The resulting overdetermined system of equations was solved for η_k. The original and recovered watermark sequences are shown in Fig. 2. The watermark has been recovered almost exactly. It was not recovered completely accurately because the matrix of the system of equations was ill conditioned.

Fig. 1. A test image with a small area of pixels of constant brightness (the upper right corner)

By increasing the number of modified coefficients in watermark embedding, this attack becomes harder to perform because the rank of the matrix is basically determined by the number of pixels, P, their spatial arrangement, and the image size. By increasing the number of modified coefficients, J, to 100, the MATLAB linear solver could not recover the watermark sequence due to an ill-conditioned matrix. It is not surprising that a general linear system solver breaks down in such cases. More sophisticated techniques that were not investigated so far could be put to work. For example, one could add constraints that will make the problem of finding the watermark sequence better conditioned. One obvious possibility is to use stabilizing functionals that would give penalty to sequences that do not satisfy Gaussian statistics. Even though such methods are usually computationally expensive, speed is obviously not a critical issue in watermark breaking.

The above attack can be mounted against any non-adaptive watermarking technique that inserts watermarks by modifying a relatively small set of selected coefficients in the DCT or other publicly known image transformation. The attack can be thwarted by using a larger number of coefficients in those transforms, or by adapting the watermark to the image content. As argued in the introduction and in [2], global schemes that embed watermarks into projections on orthogonal basis functions may have certain advantages over adaptive techniques. In the next section, we investigate water-marking techniques in which the orthogonal basis of discrete cosines is replaced by a set of general, random, smooth, orthogonal patterns that sensitively depend on a secret key.

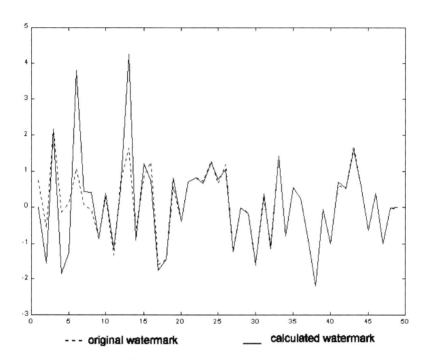

--- original watermark   ___ calculated watermark

Fig. 2. Comparison of the original and the recovered watermark of length 50.

3   Orthogonal Patterns and Their Use in Digital Watermarking

The high robustness of the method of Cox *et al.* [1] is due to the fact that the water-mark is placed into the most perceptive Fourier modes of the image. As argued above, the fact that a publicly known transformation is used can potentially become danger-ous if portions of the original unwatermarked image can be guessed. The security of the scheme and its versatility could be increased if a different set of orthogonal basis functions would be used depending on a secret key. Since the basis functions or, equivalently, the key for their generation, will be kept secret, the watermark pattern could be spanned by a smaller number of functions thus enabling us to embed more bits in a robust and secure manner. To achieve this goal, we need a method for gener-ating a set of orthogonal random functions (patterns) that sensitively depend on each bit of a secret key and possibly on an image hash. To guarantee good robustness properties, the generated patterns should have their energy concentrated mainly in low frequencies.

It is not necessary to generate a *complete* set of orthogonal basis functions since only a relatively small number of them is needed to span a watermark pattern. One can calculate projections[3] of the original image onto a set of J orthogonal functions, and modify the projections so that some secret information is encoded. Let us denote such functions f_i, $i = 1, \ldots, J$. Assuming that the functions are orthogonal to each other, the system of J functions can be completed by $MN-J$ functions g_i to a complete orthogonal system. The original image I can then be written as

$$I = \sum_{i=1}^{J} c_i f_i + g, \qquad c_i = <f_i, I>, \tag{3}$$

where g is a linear combination of functions g_i that are orthogonal to f_i. The watermarking process is realized by modifying the coefficients c_i. Furthermore, the watermarked image Iw can be expressed as

$$Iw = \sum_{i=1}^{J} c'_i f_i + g, \qquad c_i' = <f_i, Iw> = (1 + \alpha w_i)c_i, \tag{4}$$

where c_i' are the modified coefficients, α determines watermark's strength and visibility, and w_i is a watermark sequence. Given a modified watermarked image Im,

$$Im = \sum_{i=1}^{J} c_i'' f_i + g', \qquad c_i'' = <f_i, Im>, \tag{5}$$

we can calculate the modified coefficients by evaluating the projections of Im onto the functions f_i. A cross-correlation *corr* of the differences $c''-c$ with $c'-c$,

$$corr = \frac{(c''-c)(c'-c)}{\|c''-c\|\|c'-c\|}, \tag{6}$$

is compared to a threshold to decide about the presence of a watermark.

If the watermarking method is used for copyright protection, the sequence w_i should depend on the image hash in order to prevent a forgery of the original image [16]. The orthogonal patterns do not have to be image dependent because they depend on some initial secret key and it would be clearly computationally infeasible to forge them given a certain watermark sequence w_i. In section 4, we describe a modification of this scheme in which the original image is not needed for watermark extraction. In this case, the watermark sequence does not have to be a part of the secret key and can carry several bits of useful information.

For practical implementation, we need a method for generating a set of random, smooth, orthogonal patterns whose power is concentrated in low frequencies. The patterns should sensitively depend on each bit of the secret key. There is obviously

---

[3] The dot product of two images A_{ij} and B_{ij} is defined as $<A,B> = \sum_{i=1}^{M} \sum_{j=1}^{N} A_{ij} B_{ij}$

more than one way to achieve this task. One possibility would be to use some known orthogonal basis, such as the discrete cosines, and build a new basis from them. For example, one could choose M lowest frequency discrete cosines, randomly divide them into M/G groups of G cosines, and linearly combine the functions in each group to get M/G random, smooth, orthogonal patterns. This method is equivalent to embedding watermark patterns into linear combinations of selected G-tuples of DCT coefficients. Although this approach does not produce patterns that are "truly random", it has low computational complexity and can be easily implemented. Detailed investigation of this approach will a part of future research.

In this paper, we opted for a general approach that does not use any orthogonal basis as the building blocks. We generate a set of J pseudo-random black and white patterns using a cryptographically strong pseudo-random number generator seeded with the secret key. The patterns are further smoothened by applying a low-pass filter to them. To make the patterns orthogonal, the Gram-Schmidt orthogonalization procedure is applied. Finally, the functions are normalized to obtain an orthonormal system. This way, we obtain a set of J orthonormal functions that have their power concentrated in low frequencies. Moreover, the patterns sensitively depend on each bit of the secret bit-string. Although this approach is rather computationally expensive, we feel that it is important to investigate the properties of this most general scheme in order to prove the viability of the concept as a whole.

The scheme for embedding watermarks can be described as follows: Secret key → (pseudo-random number generator + smoothing) → a set of J random, smooth patterns → (Gram-Schmidt orthogonalization process) → a set of J orthonormal, random, smooth patterns → (modifying projections according to some key {and image hash}) → watermarked image. In our scheme, the first coefficient plays the role similar to the DC term in a DCT. To preserve the energy of the watermarked image, the first coefficient c_1 is left unmodified.

To retrieve the watermark, we calculate the projections c_i'' onto the J secret functions f_i. The projections c_i'' are then compared with those of the watermarked image and the original unwatermarked image by calculating the correlation (6). Based on the value of this correlation, we decide whether or not a watermark is present. To avoid large memory requirements to store all orthogonal patterns, only the image hash and the secret key need to be stored. The orthogonal patterns can be generated for each detection attempt.

3.1   A Pseudo-Code for the Watermarking Algorithm (Gray Scale $N \times N$ Images)

begin_algorithm
    read image I;   // I is a matrix of integers $0, \ldots, 255$
    convert I to an intensity matrix $\mathbf{X}$;   // $x_{ij} \in [0, 1]$
    seed = secret_bitstring;   // Initialize a PRNG with a secret bit string

Step 1 (Generate J pseudo-random binary patterns and smooth them)
> for k = 1 to J
>> using a PRNG, generate an N×N binary pattern $Z^k = Z^k_{ij}$, $1 \leq i, j \leq N$;
>> $Z^k = \text{smooth}(Z^k)$;
>
> end_for

Step 2 (Orthogonalize the smoothened patterns using Gram-Schmidt orthogonalization procedure)
> for k = 1 to J

$$Z^k = Z^k - \sum_{s=1}^{k-1} < Z^s, Z^k > Z^s$$

$$Z^k = \frac{Z^k}{\left\| Z^k \right\|}$$

> end_for

Step 3 (Calculate the projections and modify them to embed a watermark)
> for k = 1 to J

$$c_k = < Z^k, X >$$
$$c_k' = c_k (1 + \alpha w_k)$$

> end_for

Step 4 (Calculate the watermarked image Xw)

$$Xw = X + \alpha \sum_{j=2}^{J} w_k c_k f_k$$

> Convert Xw to a gray-scale image $\boldsymbol{Iw}$;
> *end_algorithm*

The coefficient α determines the visibility of the watermark and its robustness. The watermarking scheme could be applied either globally to the whole image, or locally. In the global scheme, the support of the functions f_i is the whole image. This makes the scheme computationally very expensive with large memory requirements. For an $N \times N$ grayscale image, one needs JN^2 bytes to store all J orthogonal patterns. This number could become prohibitively large with even for moderate values of N (such as $N = 256$). The most time consuming part of the algorithm is the Gram-Schmidt orthogonalization procedure. Its computational complexity is $O(J^2 N^2)$. Thus, the choice of the number of orthogonal patterns, J, turns out to be critical. If J is chosen too small, the correlation used for detection of watermarks can have occasionally large values due to random correlations. If J is chosen too large (of the order of 1000 or larger), the computational complexity of the scheme becomes unreasonably large. A good compromise is to break the image into smaller subregions that are watermarked separately using different sets of orthogonal patterns and average the correlations from multiple subregions. The averaging will decrease the values of random correlations, while keeping the robustness sufficiently high and at reasonable computational requirements.

The combination of the following parameters is crucial to obtaining a computationally effective and robust watermarking scheme: (*i*) size of the subregions, (*ii*) watermark length *J*, (*iii*) watermark strength α.. A detailed study of how the performance of the new scheme is influenced by different combinations of these parameters is necessary and will be a part of the future research. The tests that were performed so far indicate that the new scheme is very robust with respect to blind attempts to remove the watermark. It also provides higher degree of security when compared to global schemes that form the watermark from publicly known basis functions, due to the fact that the orthogonal patterns are kept secret and are generated from a secret key. Both the global and local versions of the new watermarking scheme were implemented as m-functions in Matlab and tested for robustness. Some preliminary results are included below.

3.2   Test 1: Global Scheme

Even though the global scheme is not suitable for practical use due to the immense computational and memory requirements, we nevertheless performed tests on a 64×64 image (see Fig. 3).

Fig. 3. Original image.   **Fig. 4.** Watermarked image.

Table 1 Robustness with respect to image modifications.

Image operation	Correlation
Blurring (in PaintShop Pro 4.12)	0.75
16% uniform noise (as in PSP 4.12)	0.95
Downsampling by a factor of 2	0.92
Stirmark applied once	0.80
Unzign12 applied once	0.82

Table 2 Robustness after an adjustment for StirMark geometrical deformation.

Distortion	Correlation without adjustment	Correlation with adjustment
StirMark 2×	0.21	0.81
StirMark 3×	0.10	0.78
StirMark 3× + 20% uniform noise (as in PSP 4.12)	< 0.1	0.53
StirMark 3× + blurring 1× (as in PSP 4.12)	< 0.1	0.69
StirMark 3× + JPEG 25% quality compression	< 0.1	0.79
StirMark 3× + JPEG 15% quality compression	< 0.1	0.78

The image was watermarked using $J = 100$ orthogonal patterns, and tested for presence of 100 randomly generated watermarks. The watermark strength α was set to 0.15, and the watermark sequence was chosen for simplicity as $w_k = (-1)^k$. The correlation for 100 random watermarks is shown in Fig. 5. The robustness with respect to JPEG compression was tested for quality factors from 5% to 85% and is shown in Fig. 6. The robustness with respect to other image processing operations is summarized in Table 1. Both StirMark and Unzign were used with their default settings. Since Unzign12 cut the horizontal dimension of the image by 3 pixel values, the corresponding portion of the original image was used to bring the dimensions back to those of the watermarked image. Repetitive applications of StirMark did remove the watermark beyond detection. However, if the original image is available, the watermark can be easily detected even after multiple applications of StirMark. We used a simple motion vector estimator and resampled the image to correct for the geometrical deformation introduced by StirMark. The results are reported in Table 2.

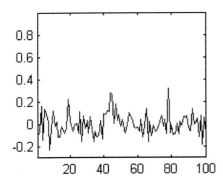

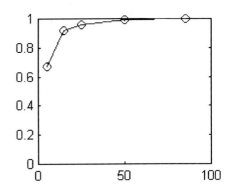

Fig. 5. Correlation for 100 random watermarks.

Fig. 6. Robustness to JPEG compression.

To test the robustness with respect to the collusion attack, total of six images watermarked by different marks were averaged. The correlation coefficients were in the range from 0.51 to 0.71. The robustness experiments together with the test for correlations (Fig. 5) between random watermarks suggest that a threshold of 0.4 should be used with this scheme. On the assumption that the projections are Gaussian distributed, this threshold gives the probability of false detection of the order of 10^{-4}.

Fig. 7. Original image.   **Fig. 8.** Watermarked image.

3.3   Test 2: Local Scheme

In the local scheme, the image is divided into square subregions and each subregion is watermarked with a different set of orthogonal patterns. In our simulations, we used a 256×256 image of Lenna divided into 16 subregions of 64×64 pixels. The watermark strength was set to $\alpha = 0.05$, and the watermark sequence was again $w_k = (-1)^k$. The watermark length was fixed at $J = 30$ to cut down on computing time. First, the original image was watermarked and then tested for presence of 100 randomly generated watermarks (Fig. 9).

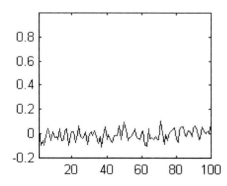

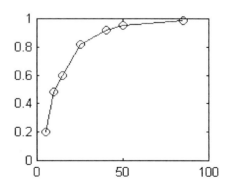

Fig. 9. Correlation for 100 random watermarks.

Fig. 10. Robustness to JPEG compression.

Table 3 Robustness with respect to image processing operations.

Image operation	Correlation
Blurring (in PaintShop Pro 4.12)	0.68
16% uniform noise (as in PSP 4.12)	0.76
Downsampling by a factor of 2	0.53
2× downsampling, 16% uniform noise, 25% quality JPEG	0.47

The robustness with respect to JPEG compression is shown in Fig. 10. By comparing the correlation values to random correlations in Fig. 9, it appears that the threshold of 0.25 is appropriate in this case. Using this threshold, no false detections are produced for 100 random watermarks. The threshold enables a reliable detection of 10% quality (0.38bbp) compressed JPEGs. Other image processing operations, such as blurring, noise adding, and downsampling, and their combinations have been studied. A sample of the results is shown in Table 3. Further tests of robustness with respect to consecutive printing, copying, and scanning are currently undergoing.

4   Secure Public Black-Box Watermark Detector

One of the most important arguments for using key-dependent basis functions is the fact that this concept may enable us to construct a secure public detector of watermarks that is implemented as a black-box in a tamper-proof hardware. Such watermark detectors will find important applications in copy control of DVD [11–15]. The box accepts integer matrices on its input and outputs one bit of information. It is assumed that the complete design of the detector and the corresponding watermarking scheme are known except a secret key, and that an attacker has one watermarked image at his disposal. The latest attacks on public watermark detectors [11–15] indicate that it is not clear if a secure public watermark detector can be built at all. It has been proven that all watermark detectors that are thresholded linear correlators can be attacked using a variety of techniques [11–14]. Kalker [13, 14] describes a simple statistical technique using which the secret key can be recovered in $O(N)$ operations, where N is the number of pixels in the image. The main culprit seems to be the fact that the quantities c_i that are correlated with the watermark sequence w_i can be directly modified through the pixel values, and the fact that the correlation function is linear. Linnartz and Cox [11,12] attack public detectors by investigating the sensitivity of the watermark detector to individual pixels for a critical image – the image at the detection threshold. Once the most influential set of pixels is found, its gray levels are scaled and subtracted from the watermarked image. They repeat the process in a hope to converge to an image that does not have the watermark. The assumption here is that we can actually learn the sensitivity of the detection function *at the watermarked image* from its sensitivity *at the critical image* that will generally be far from the watermarked image.

In order to design a watermarking method with a detector that would not be vulnerable to those attacks, we need to mask the quantities that are being correlated so that we cannot purposely change them through pixel values and we must introduce nonlinearity into the scheme to prevent the attack by Linnartz and Cox [11, 12]. Towards this purpose, we propose to use key-dependent basis functions and a special nonlinear index function. This technique will be described in more detail in a forthcoming paper. The watermarking technique will work on the same principle as before: the watermark sequence $w_i \in \{-1, 1\}$ is embedded into an image by adjusting the projections c_i, $i = 1, \ldots, J$ of the image onto the orthogonal patterns so that $ind(c_i) = w_i$ for a carefully chosen index function $ind(x)$. The index function is a continuous function similar to $sin(x)$ with an increasing wavelength. It plays the role of a quantization-like function. We propose the following function

$$ind(x) = \sin\left(\frac{\pi}{\ln(q)}\ln\left(\frac{x}{x_0}\right)\right), \tag{7}$$

where $q = (1+\alpha)/(1-\alpha)$, $x_0 = 1$. This function has the following properties: (i) any $x \geq 1$ can be modified by at most $2\alpha\%$ in order to change its index $ind(x)$ from any value to either 1 or -1. By embedding a watermark into the projections, most of them will be modified by a small value, but some can be modified by almost $2\alpha\%$.

To detect the watermark sequence w_i in image I, the watermark detector first projects the image I onto the secret patterns f^i, calculates the values of the correlation, applies the index function and correlates the result with the watermark sequence w_i:

$$D(I) = H\left(\sum_{i=1}^{J} w_i\, ind(c_i) - Th\right), \tag{8}$$

where Th is the detection threshold, $H(x)$ is the step Heaviside function, and $D(I)$ is the detection function applied to I.

Now we need to argue why this scheme may not be vulnerable to previously described attacks. First of all, since c_i are projections on unknown patterns, one cannot purposely change the pixels values – the input of the detector. The relationship between the projections and pixel values is unknown. If we were able to calculate c_i from the pixel values, we could learn the watermark values w_i from cleverly chosen perturbations. Second, the sensitivity of the detector function at a critical image C (or, equivalently, the values of partial derivatives with respect to pixel values) cannot be directly related to sensitivity values at the watermarked image. By changing the pixel g_{rs} by Δ, we can express the corresponding change in the detector function as

$$\Delta D(C) = \Delta \sum_{i=1}^{J} w_i\, f^i_{rs}\, ind'(c_i), \tag{9}$$

where f^i_{rs} is the gray level of the (r, s)-th element of the i-th pattern. What we can learn from sensitivity analysis at the critical image is the value of the summation. However, this value depends on the unknown parameters f^i_{rs} and on the values of the derivative of the index function at the projections c_i corresponding to the critical image. However, the projections of the critical image and the original watermarked image will generally be very different. This indicates that it may be rather difficult to utilize the leakage of information gained by perturbing the critical image.

Preliminary tests of the robustness of this scheme suggest that it has extremely good robustness with respect to filtering, JPEG compression, and resampling. More detailed theoretical investigation and experiments are needed, however, before this scheme can be termed as a successful solution to the public watermark detector. Detailed analysis of the proposed scheme and a watermark detector will the subject of further research.

5   Conclusions and Future Directions

In this paper, we introduced the concept of key-dependent basis functions and described how it can be used for designing secure robust watermarking schemes and secure public black-box watermark detectors. The new schemes overcome a possible security weakness of global, non-adaptive schemes that apply watermark patterns spanned by a small number of publicly known basis functions. The watermark is embedded into the projections of an image onto the secret set of key-dependent patterns. The robustness of the watermarking scheme with respect to filtering, lossy compression, and combinations of other attacks was studied. Finally, we proposed a candidate for a watermarking scheme that has a secure public watermark detector.

Future research will include further study of the robustness of the new scheme with respect to image distortions. One important future research direction is the development of secure public black-box watermark detectors using key-dependent basis functions. It appears that the concept of key-dependent basis functions together with special quantization index functions leads to very robust watermarking schemes for which the construction of a secure public black-box watermark detector is possible. Most importantly, we plan to rigorously estimate the complexity of possible attacks on the public detector.

Acknowledgments

The work on this paper was supported by Air Force Research Laboratory, Air Force Material Command, USAF, under a Phase I SBIR grant number F30602-97-C-0209. The U.S. Government is authorized to reproduce and distribute reprints for Governmental purposes notwithstanding any copyright notation there on. The views and conclusions contained herein are those of the authors and should not be interpreted as necessarily representing the official policies, either expressed or implied, of Air Force Research Laboratory, or the U. S. Government.

References

1.   I.J. Cox, J. Kilian, T. Leighton, and T. Shamoon, Secure Spread Spectrum Watermarking for Multimedia," NEC Research Institute, *Technical Report* 95–10.
2.   I.J. Cox and M.L. Miller, "A review of watermarking and the importance of perceptual modeling", *Proceedings of Electronic Imaging'97*, February 1997.
3.   M.D. Swanson, M. Kobayashi, and A. H. Tewfik, "Multimedia Data Embedding and Watermarking Technologies", *Invited Paper, to appear in the Proceedings of the IEEE*, 1998.

4. A.H. Tewfik, M.D. Swanson, B. Zhu, K. Hamdy, and L. Boney, "Transparent Robust Watermarking for Images and Audio." *IEEE Trans. on Signal Proc.*, 1996.
5. J.-F. Delaigle, C. De Vleeschouwer, B. Macq, "Digital watermarking of images," *Proceedings of the IS&T/SPIE Symposium on Electronic Imaging Science and Technology*, 1996.
6. N. Jayant, J. Johnston, and R. Safranek, "Signal Compression Based on Models of Human Perception", *Proceedings of the IEEE*, Vol. 81, No. 10, Oct 1993.
7. N. Jayant, J. Johnston, and R. Safranek, "Perceptual Coding of Images", *SPIE Vol. 1913*, 1993.
8. B. Zhu and A.H. Tewfik, "Low Bit Rate Near-Transparent Image Coding", *SPIE Vol. 2491*, 1995.
9. B.O. Comiskey and J.R. Smith, "Modulation and Information Hiding in Images," in: *Information Hiding, First International Workshop*, edited by Ross J. Anderson. Cambridge, U.K., May 30–June 1, 1996, Proceedings. Lecture Notes in Computer Science, Vol. 1174, Springer-Verlag, 1996.
10. Hartung and B. Girod, "Digital Watermarking of Raw and Compressed Video", *Proc. European EOS/SPIE Symposium on Advanced Imaging and Network Technologies*, Berlin, Germany, Oct. 1996.
11. I.J. Cox and Jean-Paul M.G. Linnartz, "Public watermarks and resistance to tampering", in *Proceedings of the ICIP*, October 1997, CD version of Proceedings.
12. I.J. Cox and Jean-Paul M.G. Linnartz, "Some general methods for tampering with watermarks", *preprint*, 1998.
13. T. Kalker, "Watermark Estimation Through Detector Observation", Philips Research Eindhoven, Netherland, *preprint* 1998.
14. T. Kalker, J.P. Linnartz and M. van Dijk, "Watermark Estimation Through Detector Analysis", preprint submitted to *ICIP-98*.
15. J.P. Linnartz and M. van Dijk, "Analysis of the sensitivity attack against electronic watermarks in images", in *Proceedings of the Workshop on Information Hiding*, Portland, April 1998, submitted.
16. S. Craver, N. Memon, B.-L. Yeo, and M. Yeung. "Can invisible watermarks resolve rightful ownerships?" *Proceedings of the IS&T/SPIE Conference on Storage and Retrieval for Image and Video Databases V*, San Jose, CA, USA, Feb. 13–14, 1997, vol. 3022, pp. 310–321.
17. M.G. Kuhn and F.A.P. Petitcolas, *StirMark*. Available at *http://www.cl.cam.ac.uk/~fapp2/watermarking/stirmark/*, Security Group, Computer Laboratory, University of Cambridge, UK (E-mail: {mgk25, fapp2}@cl.cam.ac.uk), 1997.
18. *Unzign*. Available at *http://altern.org/watermark/* (E-mail: unzign@hotmail.com), 1997.

Intellectual Property Protection Systems and Digital Watermarking

Jack Lacy, Schuyler R. Quackenbush, Amy Reibman, James H. Snyder

AT&T Labs – Research
Florham Park, NJ; Red Bank, NJ
{lacy, srq, amy, jhs}@research.att.com

Abstract. Adequate protection of digital copies of multimedia content – both audio and video – is a prerequisite to the distribution of this content over networks. Until recently digital audio and video content has been protected by its size: it is difficult to distribute and store without compression. Modern compression algorithms allow substantial bitrate reduction while maintaining high-fidelity reproduction. If distribution of these algorithms is controlled, cleartext uncompressed content is still protected by its size. However, once the compression algorithms are generally available cleartext content becomes extremely vulnerable to piracy. In this paper we explore the implications of this vulnerability and discuss the use of compression and watermarking in the control of piracy.

1   Introduction

Protection of digital copies of multimedia content – both audio and video – is a prerequisite to the distribution of this content over networks. Until recently digital audio and video content has been protected by its size. For example, audio on compact discs is encoded using PCM at 1.4 megabits per second – about half a gigabyte for a 45 minute CD. Such large quantities of data are difficult to distribute and store. Modern compression algorithms provide high-fidelity reconstruction while allowing substantial size reductions. If distribution of these algorithms is controlled, cleartext, uncompressed content is still protected by its size. However, once the compression algorithms are generally available cleartext content becomes extremely vulnerable, as is evidenced by the proliferation of illegally distributed MP3 compressed music. In this paper we explore the implications of this vulnerability and how watermarking techniques can contribute to a system strategy that protects intellectual property.

2   A Systemic View of IP Protection

The design of secure systems should be based upon an analysis of the application risks and threats. As Fig. 1 illustrates, such analysis will identify some of the risks of a particular domain. The technological net should handle many identified risks. The legal net will handle others. No matter how thorough the analysis, not all risks will be

David Aucsmith (Ed.): Information Hiding 1998, LNCS 1525, pp. 158-168, 1998.

identified, and not all identified risks will be caught by the technological and legal nets. Ideally the system design includes the possibility of renewable security so that these residual risks do not undermine the foundations of the business.

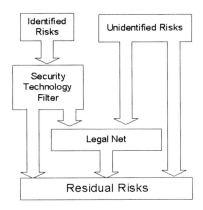

Fig. 1.

The business model for the application is one of the strongest security mechanisms. If the system is easy to use, rich in features, support and information, and reasonably priced, why should consumers go to the black market? Designing the system with this in mind will minimize the attacks from legitimate users, most of whom are willing to play by the rules. System security should not interfere with legitimate use. We also want to design the system so that even if an attacker does break the system he cannot then use the same system to distribute that IP for his gain. Such a system should consist of:

1. a compression engine for managing music or video. This mechanism should discourage multiple compression/decompression cycles;
2. a mechanism for protecting the integrity of the content and for enforcing rights-to-use rules;
3. a flexible mechanism for licensing content and for granting various rights to consumers with appropriate credentials;
4. a secure client for accessing, rendering, playing or viewing content in a manner consistent with system policy and with the credentials or licenses associated with that content;
5. a mechanism for labeling the content to be distributed in a persistent manner. For example, the label might indicate ownership, name the distributor, identify the property or contain information about transactions involving the content.

Component 2 involves the use of cryptographic containers as in [8], [12] and [16]. The content is encrypted and perhaps digitally signed. The encryption keys are distributed via other channels using cryptographic protocols. A flexible licensing mechanism (Component 3), based for example upon PolicyMaker [3], manages these keys and governs their use [12]. Client security (Component 4) is what distinguishes the IP protection problem from the protected communications channel problem. That is, content must be protected in the client, not just in the channel. Protection mechanisms include tamper resistant software and hardware. These techniques are discussed in [2] and [12].

2.1   Compression

As discussed earlier, compression enables the distribution of music or video over networks. For audio, the MPEG-2 Advanced Audio Coder [1] provides CD quality reproduction for most music and most listeners at a compression ratio of 11 to 1 (128 kilobits per second). Compression may also be relevant as a protection mechanism for the following two reasons.

Attackers will always have access to decompressed output. If recompression of the decompressed content results in noticeable degradation of quality, then the 2nd generation output will be of sufficiently low quality that it is not a threat to the IP owner. Of equal importance, when cleartext content is available, nothing we do to protect compressed content matters. Should controlled degradation via compression prove possible, then a solution to this cleartext audio problem would be to compress and then decompress the music as part of the mastering process. Controlled degradation via compression is an area of current research.

Because it can easily be distributed, the compressed file is the valuable commodity. It therefore makes sense to associate labels with the compressed file in a way that is persistent in the compressed domain.

3   Digital Watermarking

3.1   Overview

As stated earlier, a mechanism is needed for binding content identification to content in a persistent manner. Digital watermarking is such a mechanism. (See for example [11].) Watermarking has also been proposed as a mechanism for gating the use of content. In this case, when decisions regarding access to or use of the content are made, the mark must be retrieved in real-time and used as input in the decision-making process. No one marking algorithm is best suited for these two functions, both because of complexity issues and because different functions and different marking algorithms are resistant to different attacks. Indeed, we expect that any single album or film will be marked by a variety of different algorithms, to improve the overall resistance to attack.

3.2   System Attacks

We list several general classes of attacks against information embedded in multimedia content. The use of a watermarking algorithm for a particular application needs to be 'sanity-checked' against this list to determine whether or not the watermark serves any useful purpose.

If cleartext content is available and the compression algorithm is readily available to a pirate, then the pirate can generate an equivalent, unprotected, and untraceable copy of the compressed content, and bypass every protection/tracing mechanism the copyright owner might employ. Watermarking is irrelevant in this case.

One attack is forgery of identity. Whether the watermark is a point-of-sale watermark (a "fingerprint") or pressing-plant watermark, if the input to the marking process is fraudulent, then the watermark doesn't protect the IP.

Works distributed in versions distinguished only by different watermarks are susceptible to collusion attacks. The existence of multiple copies of a work, especially if the bitstreams differ *only* in the markings, provides a probe of the sites of the watermarks and indirectly of the marking algorithm itself. The existence of differently marked copies of a work may reduce the effectiveness of the security of the system.

The simplest collusion attack is the *bitwise XOR attack*. The attacker compares the differences between two representations of the same work, and jams differing bits to 0s or 1s. The jam pattern can be either random or – if the attacker has knowledge of the marking algorithm – one that creates a counterfeit of a legitimate mark. When a work is to be marked in multiple versions each with its own markings, the marking algorithm must be designed so that in the presence of tampering one of three conditions holds. The work should be impossible to decompress, the quality of the decompressed output should be significantly degraded, or the mark should nonetheless be recoverd from the bits which were not changed by the attacker. Generally this means either that very few bits should differ from one mark to the next, or else that all of the bits in the bitstream should change when the mark changes.

Another collusion attack specific to frame-based compression algorithms can be effective against marks that extend in time through the work. In these algorithms, a bitstream is composed of frames, each representing a segment of the original signal. For a given algorithm all segments have the same duration. Given multiple versions of the signal, each marked differently, take the first frame from the first copy, the second frame from the second copy, and so on. More sophisticated versions of this attack are possible. It is difficult to see how any mark that is extended in time across several frames can survive this attack, be it a cleartext PCM watermark or a bitstream watermark. Extended watermarks should not be used for differentially marking multiple copies of a work. If an extended marking algorithm must be used for this purpose, then it should be complemented by watermarks which have a reasonable probability of recovery from bitstreams composed of fragments of watermarked streams.

System designers should think carefully before using watermarks to gate usage, since by feeding different bitstreams into the gating mechanism the attacker may be able to probe the watermark algorithm, discover mark sites and possibly generate fraudulent marks [5]. If a marking algorithm is to be used to gate usage, the algorithm should be designed in such a way that tampering with the mark should degrade the quality of the decompressed content. This suggests that the marking algorithm could beneficially be associated with the compression algorithm. We describe one such marking algorithm in section 3.5.

3.3   Desirable Characteristics of Watermark Algorithms

The following requirements are typically expected of watermarks (see also [10]):
1. *Imperceptibility.* A watermarked signal should (usually) not be distinguishable from the original signal.
2. *Information capacity.* The mark bitrate must be compatible with the rate limits imposed by the system.
3. *Robustness.* The mark must be recoverable, not only in the complete work, but also in truncated, filtered, dilated, and otherwise processed clips, in a concatenation of unrelated content, and in the presence of noise.
4. *Low complexity.* Marking schemes intended for use with real-time applications should be low complexity.
5. *Survive multiple encode-decode generations.* A watermark should survive tandem encoding-decoding.
6. *Tamper resistant or tamper evident.* It should be possible to recognize that a mark has been modified. It should not be possible to modify a mark in such a way as to create a different valid mark.
7. *Difficult to create or extract legitimate watermark without proper credentials.* In the context of the watermarking engine alone, a proper credential is knowledge of the algorithm used to insert the mark. An ideal would be a public key analogue to watermarking: hard to insert mark, easy to retrieve, hard to counterfeit.

For copyright identification every copy of the content can be marked identically, so the watermark can be inserted once prior to distribution. Ideally, detection should not require a reference because the search engine has no *a priori* way to associate the reference material with the work from which the mark is to be recovered. Not only must the watermark be short enough to be recovered in a truncated version, some means must be provided to synchronize the detection process so that the watermark can be located in the processed bitstream. Finally, any attempt to obscure the mark, including re-encoding the content, should lead to perceptible distortion.

Transaction identification requires a distinct mark for each transaction. The primary challenge of point-of-sale marking ("fingerprinting") is to move the content through the marking engine quickly. That is, the algorithm must be low complexity. One strategy is to insert the watermark in the compressed domain, in which case mark insertion should increase the data rate very little. Watermarking algorithms designed for fingerprinting must be robust to collusion attacks.

3.4   General Mechanisms

Watermarks for compressed content fall into three categories: cleartext or original (PCM in the case of audio or video) marking, compressed bitstream marking which does not alter the bitstream semantics, and marking integrated with the compression algorithm in which the semantics of the bitstream are altered. We describe these below and discuss their advantages and limitations. We anticipate that in a well-designed system, each of these marking techniques will be used.

Cleartext PCM: We define cleartext watermarks as marks inserted in the original or during decompression into output (e.g. while writing a decompressed song to CD).

Cleartext marking embeds a data stream imperceptibly in a signal. The model for many cleartext-marking algorithms is one in which a signal is injected into a noisy communication channel, where the audio/video signal is the interfering noise [17]. Because the channel is so noisy, and the mark signal must be imperceptible, the maximum bit rates that are achieved for audio are generally less than 100bps.

Cleartext marks are intended to survive in all processed generations of the work. They are therefore well suited to identification of the work. There are two major concerns with cleartext marking. Because such algorithms (usually) compute a perceptual model, they tend to be too complex for point-of-sale applications. Second, these algorithms are susceptible to advances in the perceptual compression algorithms.

Retrieval mechanisms for cleartext watermarks fall into two classes: reference necessary and reference unnecessary. In either case the mechanism for mark recovery is generally of high complexity and is often proprietary. Further, if means for detecting these watermarks are embedded in a player, an attacker, by reverse engineering the player, may be able to identify and remove the marks. We believe that cleartext watermarks should *not* be used to gate access to content.

Bitstream Watermarking (semantic-non-altering): Bitstream marking algorithms manipulate the compressed digital bitstream without changing the semantics of the audio or video stream. Bitstream marking, being low-complexity, can be used to carry transaction information. Because the mark signal is unrelated to the media signal, the bit rate these techniques can support can be as high as the channel rate. However these marks cannot survive D/A conversion and are generally not very robust against attack; e.g. they are susceptible to collusion attacks (we describe techniques for increasing robustness to collusion in section 4.7). This type of mark can easily be extracted by clients and is thus appropriate for gating access to content; it is an example of a security measure intended primarily to "keep honest users honest".

Bitstream Marking Integrated with Compression Algorithm (semantic altering): Integrating the marking algorithm with the compression algorithm avoids an 'arms race' between marking and compression algorithms, in which improvements in hiding data imperceptibly in content are undercut by and even motivate further improvements in perceptual compression algorithms. Since the perceptual model is available from the workings of the compression algorithm, the complexity associated with marking can be minimized. Integrated marking algorithms alter the semantics of the audio or video bitstream, thereby increasing resistance to collusion attacks. An example of this approach is [7], which however does not use perceptual techniques. We now present another example.

3.5   Integrating the Watermarking Algorithm with Compression

We have developed a first generation system that combines bitstream and integrated watermarking. It can be configured to support the three marking functions mentioned above. It does not include but is compatible with use of a front-end cleartext-marking algorithm as well. We assume that the cleartext original is not available except possibly to auditors seeking to recover the watermark. In particular, the cleartext original is not available to attackers. The decompressed and marked content will generally be available to everyone.

Our method relies on the fact that quantization, which takes place in the encoder, is a lossy process. By combining mark insertion with quantization we ensure that the attacker cannot modify the mark without introducing perceptible artifacts. The fact that marking data is present is indicated by characteristics of the bitstream data. Our marking technique involves the perceptual modeling, rate control, quantization, and noiseless coding blocks of a generic perceptual coder. In MPEG AAC spectral lines are grouped into 49 "scale factor" bands (SFB), each band containing between 4 and 32 lines. Associated with each band is a single scale factor, which sets the quantizer step-size, and a single Huffman table (AAC employs 11 non-trivial Huffman tables). The coefficient for each spectral line is represented by an integer (i.e. quantized) value. In MPEG video, a block consists of 64 coefficients, and each set (termed a macroblock) of 6 blocks has an associated quantization step-size Q_p. The same Huffman table is used for the coefficients for all Q_p values. As with audio, each coefficient is represented by an integer after quantization. Because the watermarking algorithms for audio and video are similar, for consistency we use the audio terminology (scale factor) throughout when we are discussing techniques. When we discuss the results for video, we will use terminology specific to video.

Let $A = \{f_i, H_i, \{q_{ij}\}\}$ be the set of triples of scale factors f_i, Huffman tables H_i, and quantized coefficients $\{q_{ij}\}$. (Only one Huffman table is used in video.) We assume that we have selected some set of scale factor bands into which mark data will be inserted. The marking set will generally be dynamic. Let M be the set of indices associated with the set of SFB chosen for marking.

Choose a set of multipliers $\{x_i: i \in M\}$, with all x_i close to unity. Modify the triple $\{f_i, H_i, \{q_{ij}\}: i \in M\}$ as follows. Let $\{v_{ij}\}$ be the set of spectral coefficients prior to quantization, and Q_i be the quantizer for SFB i, i.e. $\forall i \{q_{ij}\} = Q_i[\{v_{ij}\}]$. Then

$$\{f_i, H_i, \{q_{ij}\}\} \rightarrow \{f_i', H_i', \{q_{ij}'\}\}, \text{ where}$$
$$f_i' = f_i/x_i$$
$$q_{ij}' = Q_i'[x_i \times v_{ij}]$$
$$H_i' = H_i \text{ or the next larger codebook}$$
$$x_i \cong 1$$

(See [13] for changes for the slight modifications necessary for video.) Because the modification to the spectral coefficients occurs before quantization, the changes to the reconstructed coefficients will be below perceptual threshold. If this change were introduced after quantization, the change in some quantized values would be greater than the perceptual noise floor. Equivalently, an attacker who modifies the quantized values to eradicate or modify the mark will be introducing energy changes that exceed the noise floor. Because the changes in step-sizes will be small, because not all coefficients will change, and because the attacker will not have access to the uncompressed cleartext source material, the attacker will generally not be able to identify those SFB which are used for marking. Further, the increase in bit rate associated with marking should be small, and so must be monitored. A feedback mechanism similar to the one in [7] can be used to prevent modification of scale factors that would increase the bit rate significantly.

Watermark bits can be inserted in a variety of ways. Generally watermark sequences are inserted a few bits per frame. The data to be carried by the stream is typically mapped into a marking sequence prior to embedding, where the characteristics of the mapping function depend on the type of attack expected. Indeed, since there may be a wide range of attacks, the data may be redundantly mapped in different ways in the hope that at least one mapping will survive all attacks. We describe one such mapping in section 3.8.

In our system we insert the marking sequence by modifying the scale factors included at the beginning of the frame by modifying the LSBs so that they represent a sequence which contains one or more synchronization codes. Specifically, when we select a frame for watermark insertion, and a scale factor LSB does not match (0 where a 1 is indicated, or a 1 instead of a 0), we decrement that scale factor and adjust all the coefficients in the SFB accordingly. Although the watermark data can be damaged, random flipping of scale factor LSB by an attacker will introduce perceptible artifacts.

The marking sequence can be recovered by comparison to a reference or through the use of synchronization codes. Note that if synchronization codes are used, *the watermark can be recovered in the compressed domain through a lightweight recovery process*. It can therefore be used for gating access to content. Although the attacker can use the gating mechanism to probe for the watermark sites [5] and perhaps damage the synchronization codes, damage to the codes will generally produce perceptible artifacts.

3.6   Audio Results

To evaluate our audio watermarking algorithm we used AT&T's implementation of AAC. Watermark synchronization is indicated by the sequence comprising the LSB of the first 44 decoded scale factors in a long block. When the value of the LSB of a scale factor does not match the corresponding bit in the synchronization code then the scale factor is decremented and the spectral coefficients adjusted accordingly, resulting in perceptually irrelevant overcoding of the associated spectral data.

The following table shows the cost of carrying watermark data inserted into *every frame* of an AAC bitstream for a stereo signal sampled at 44.1 kHz and coded at 96 kbps. Cost is expressed as increase in bits per frame (21.3 ms of audio) and increase in rate.

An important issue for any watermarking algorithm is the quality of the reconstructed signal following an attack that obscures the watermark. We have simulated a naïve attack on this marking algorithm by zeroing all scale factor LSB, and find that this attack results in unacceptable distortion in the reconstructed audio signal.

Table 1. Increase in audio bit-rate.

	increase in bits (per marked frame)	increase in rate
Synchronization	5.2	0.25%
sync + 32 bits	9.0	0.44%

3.7   Video Results

Our baseline system for video compression uses a rudimentary perceptual model. A variance-based activity measure is used to select the quantization step-size for each macroblock as in step 3 of the MPEG-2 TM5 rate control [14]. We generate I frames every half second; all other frames are P frames. We inserted watermark data into both I and P frames, and present results taken from an average over two different 10 second sequences.

The first 44 macroblocks of a frame are used for synchronization as described in section 3.5. The next several macroblocks (100 or 600 in the Table, of 1320) of a frame carry mark bits. For each macroblock, when the LSB of the step-size Q_p does not match, Q_p is decremented. However, a dead-zone is applied to the original Q_p to ensure that zero coefficients remain zero.

We have simulated a naïve attack on this algorithm by zeroing all scale factor LSB, and find that this attack results in a perceptible 1.6dB degradation in PSNR of the reconstructed video signal.

Table 2. Increase in video bit-rate.

	increase in bits (per marked frame)	increase in rate
Synchronization	124	0.005%
sync + 100 bits	138	0.006%
sync + 600 bits	557	0.024%

3.8   Formatting Watermark Data

We said in section 3.4 that for transaction watermarking, the bits representing differently marked versions of the same content should have bitstreams which are either nearly the same or as different as possible. We have developed a simple method for formatting watermark data that is relatively resistant to XOR collusion attacks. ([4] describes an algorithm with similar intent.) Although we are using this technique for formatting watermark data for a semantic non-altering scheme, it is more generally applicable.

We assume that the set identifying data (e.g. transaction identities), one datum of which is to be formatted, can be put into a linear sequence. For example, we might uniquely mark each transaction that occurs on 31 April 1998, so we wish to identify Transaction 1, Transaction 2, and so on. Instead of representing the Nth transaction by the ordinal N, we represent it by 2^{N-1}. Assume that no further formatting of the mark data has been performed. When an attacker bitwise XORs two copies of the same content, the resulting sequence will indicate both the first transaction and the second. If the attacker sets or clears the bits identified by the XOR operation, then the resulting mark is identical to one of the original marks. If the projected bits are randomized, then the mark is invalid.

This exponential sequence is inadequate by itself as a hiding mechanism. What needs to be protected from the attacker is the location of the transitions. This can be accomplished by permuting the bits of the sequence, possibly after XORing them with a mask. The bits of the watermark sequence can also be interleaved with other data. Finally, the watermark sequence can be redundantly inserted. These manipulations hide the transition in the watermark sequence, so that the result of an XOR of two bitstreams (which differ only in the sequences with which they are marked) appears as a random jumble of 1s and 0s.

4   Conclusion

We have discussed threat models against IPP systems, including threats posed by the existence of high-quality compression, and attacks against watermarking algorithms in particular. We have identified three classes of watermark algorithms, distinguished by the domains in which the watermark is inserted and the extent of integration with the compression algorithm. We have reviewed suggested uses for watermarking and find that a particular algorithm can be effective in some instances, ineffective in others, and compromising in yet others. There is no panacea.

We describe what we believe is the first published example of a watermarking algorithm that has been integrated with a perceptually based compression algorithm. It has the desirable property that it can be recovered in the compressed domain with a lightweight process. Although the watermark can be damaged, early work suggests that such damage will introduce perceptible artifacts.

We have also described a method for mapping watermark data into a mark sequence that is relatively robust to XOR collusion attacks.

References

1. M. Bosi, K. Brandenburg, S. Quackenbush, L. Fielder, K. Akagiri, H. Fuchs, M. Dietz, J. Herre, G. Davidson, Y. Oikawa, "ISO/IEC MPEG-2 Advanced Audio Coding", presented at the 101st Convention of the Audio Engineering Society, Nov. 1996, preprint 4382.
2. D. Aucsmith, "Tamper Resistant Software", in *Proceedings of the First International Information Hiding Workshop*, LNCS 1174, Springer-Verlag, Cambridge, U.K., May/June, 1996, pp. 317-334.
3. M. Blaze, J. Feigenbaum, J. Lacy, "Decentralized Trust Management", in *Proceedings of the 1996 IEEE Symposium on Security and Privacy*, pp. 164-173.
4. D. Boneh, J. Shaw, "Collusion-secure Fingerprinting for Digital Data", Crypto '95, LNCS 963, Springer-Verlag, Berlin 1995, pp. 452-465
5. I. J. Cox and J.M.G. Linnartz, "Public Watermarks and Resistance to Tampering", Proceedings of the Fourth International Conference on Image Processing, Santa Barbara CA, October 1997.
6. U.S. National Bureau of Standards, "Data Encryption Standard," Federal Information Processing Standards Publication, FIPS PUB 46-1, Jan. 1988.
7. F. Hartung and B. Girod, "Digital Watermarking of MPEG-2 Coded Video in the Bitstream Domain", *Proc. IEEE ICASSP*, pp. 2621-4, April 1997.
8. "Cryptolope Container Technology", an IBM White Paper, http://www.cryptolope.ibm. com/white.htm.
9. Proceedings of the Fourth International Conference on Image Processing, Santa Barbara CA, October 1997.

10. International Federation of the Phonograph Industry, Request for Proposals – Embedded signaling systems issue 1.0. 54 Regent Street, London W1R 5PJ, June 1997.
11. *Proc. First International Information Hiding Workshop*, LNCS 1174, Springer-Verlag, Cambridge, U.K., May/June, 1996, pp. 207-226.
12. J. Lacy, D. P. Maher, and J. H. Snyder, "Music on the Internet and the Intellectual Property Protection Problem", *Proc. International Symposium on Industrial Electronics*, Guimaraes, Portugal, July 1997.
13. J. Lacy, S.R. Quackenbush, A.R. Reibman, D. Shur, J.H. Snyder, "On Combining Watermarking with Perceptual Coding", submitted to *Proc. IEEE ICASSP*, 1998.
14. MPEG video committee, "Test Model 5", ISO-IEC/JTC1/SC29/WG11 N0400, April 1993.
15 F. Petitcolas, R. Anderson, M. Kuhn, "Attacks on Copyright Marking Systems", Second Information Hiding Workshop, 1998.
16. O. Sibert, D. Bernstein, D. Van Wie, "Securing the Content, Not the Wire, for Information Commerce",
17 J. Smith, B. Comisky, "Modulation and Information Hiding in Images", *Proc. First International Information Hiding Workshop*, LNCS 1174, Springer-Verlag, Cambridge, U.K., May/June, 1996, pp. 207-226.

Secure Copyright Protection Techniques for Digital Images

Alexander Herrigel[1], Joseph Ó Ruanaidh[2], Holger Petersen[1], Shelby Pereira[2], and Thierry Pun[2]

[1] security engineering ag
{herrigel,petersen}@r3.ch
P.O. Box
CH-8301 Glattzentrum
[2] University of Geneva
CUI – Vision Group
24, rue du Général-Dufour
CH-1211 Geneva

Abstract. This paper[2] presents a new approach for the secure and robust copyright protection of digital images. A system for generating digital watermarks and for trading watermarked images is described. The system is based on a new watermarking technique, which is *robust* against image transformation techniques such as *compression, rotation, translation, scaling* and *cropping*. It uses modulation of the magnitude components in Fourier space to embed a watermark and an accompanying template and, during watermark extraction, reads a template in the log polar transform of the frequency domain. The template is used for analyzing scaling and rotation suffered by the watermarked stego-image. The detection of the watermarks is also possible without any need for the original cover-image. In addition, the system applies asymmetric cryptographic protocols for different purposes, namely embedding/detecting the watermark and transferring watermarked data. The public key technique is applied for the construction of a one-way watermark embedding and the verification function to identify and prove the uniqueness of the watermark. Legal dispute resolution is supported for the multiple watermarking of a digital image without revealing the confidential keying information.

1 Introduction

The current rapid development and deployment of new IT technologies for the fast provision of commercial multimedia services has resulted in a strong demand for reliable and secure *copyright protection* techniques for multimedia data.

---

[1] All methods, procedures and schemes presented in this paper are based on the European patent application No. 97 810 708.4

[2] This work has been founded by the Swiss National Science Foundation under the SPP program (Grant. 5003-45334)

David Aucsmith (Ed.): Information Hiding 1998, LNCS 1525, pp. 169–190, 1998.
© Springer-Verlag Berlin Heidelberg 1998

Copyright protection of digital images is defined as the process of proving the intellectual property rights to a court of law against the unauthorized reproduction, processing, transformation or broadcasting of a digital image. Depending on the law in various countries, this process may be based on a prior registration of the copyright with a trusted third party. After successful registration, the copyright ownership is legally bound by a copyright notice, which is required to notify and prove copyright ownership.

Digital watermarking is a method for marking data sets, such as images, sound or video. A stego data set consists of the original data, the cover data set and a digital watermark that does not affect the data set's usability but that can be detected using dedicated analysis software or systems. Watermarking can, for example, be used for marking authorship or ownership of a data set.

Quite a number of different approaches [1,2,4,5,6,11,14,15,18,19,20,21,23,24] to digital watermarking have been proposed but only some of them implemented in commercial products. Due to the very short time and minimal effort needed for copying and distributing digital multimedia data, protection against copyright infringements is an important issue for the copyright owner and should form an integral part of the exploitation process for Internet based trading services. Today, the Internet community has not identified or accepted adequate copyright protection techniques. This is in direct contrast to the provision of secure transaction protocols, such as SSL [7].

2   State-of-the-Art

Digital watermarking can be seen as being fundamentally a problem in digital communications [1]. Early methods of encoding watermarks consisted of no more than incrementing an image component to encode a binary '1' and decrementing to encode a '0' [2]. Tirkel et al. [20] and van Schyndel *et al.* [21] have applied the properties of $m-$sequences to produce oblivious watermarks resistant to filtering, cropping and reasonably robust to cryptographic attack. Matsui and Tanaka [11] have applied linear predictive coding for watermarking. Their approach to hide a watermark is to make the watermark resemble quantization noise. Tirkel and Osborne [20] were the first to note the applicability of spread spectrum techniques to digital image watermarking. Spread spectrum has several advantageous features. It offers cryptographic security (see [20]) and is capable of achieving error free transmission of the watermark at the limits given by the maximum channel capacity [18]. Fundamental information theoretic limits to reliable communication have been discussed by some authors (see [18]). The shorter is the payload of a watermark, the better are the chances of it being communicated reliably.

Spread spectrum is an example of a symmetric key cryptosystem [19]. System security is based on proprietary knowledge of the keys (or pseudo random seeds) which are required to embed, extract or remove an image watermark. One provision in the use of a spread spectrum system is that it is important that the watermarking be non-invertible because only in this way can true ownership of the copyright material be resolved [4]. Ó Ruanaidh *et al.* [14] and Cox *et al.* [1] have developed perceptually adaptive transform domain methods for watermarking. In contrast to previous approaches the emphasis was on embedding the watermark in the most significant components of an image. The general approach used in these papers is to divide the image into blocks. Each block is mapped into the transform domain using either the Discrete Cosine Transform (DCT) [16], the Hadamard Transform [3] or the Daubechies Wavelet Transform [17]. Information has been embedded using the DCT [15] or FFT magnitude and phase, wavelets (see refs. of [15]), Linear Predictive Coding [11] and fractals [5]. J.-F. Delaigle *et al.* [6] have applied signature labelling techniques for the copyright protection of digital images.

The industrial importance of digital copyright protection has resulted in a number of products, either based on specific watermark techniques or additional registration services. They include the PictureMarc system by Digimarc, SureSign (former FBI's Fingerprint) by HighWater Signum, IP2 system by Intellectual Protocols, the Argent system by Digital Information Commodities Exchange and the Tigermark system from NEC. Further some prototypes have been developed among which are the PixelTag system by the MIT Media Lab and the SysCop system from Zhao and Koch of the Frauenhofer-Institut für Graphische Datenverarbeitung [23,24]

3   Overview

We envision the watermark system operating an open environment like the Internet with different interconnected computers. Users can be located anywhere and can sell or buy images. If legal dispute resolution for multiple watermarks is needed the Copyright Holder (H) sends copyright information and authentic image information to the Copyright Certificate Center (C). After having received a copyright certificate from C, the copyright holder can sell his digital images, for example, via an image shopping mall, to an image buyer (B). The Public Key Infrastructure (PKI) supports the distribution of authentic public keys between all parties which are needed for mutual authentication, non-repudiation and confidentiality. The communication channels between the parties are shown in Fig. 1.

Our approach enables the secure generation and transmission of watermarked data using an asymmetric key pair like applied in public-key cryptography. The cover data set is watermarked, while the watermark is encoded using one or both of these keys. The resulting stego data set is then transmitted to a second party, while the same keys are used for establishing a secure transmission between the parties.

During the trading process, the involved parties use asymmetric key pairs and a key agreement protocol for establishing a symmetric key between them. The party creating the watermark can embed a *private*, a *detection* and a *public watermark* in the data set. The public watermark can be detected by third parties while the private and detection watermark can only be detected by the copyright holder.

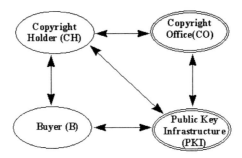

Fig. 1. Communication channels between identified parties

After embedding the digital watermark into the image, the information describing it, such as the image identifier, a textual description and related information is transmitted authentically to a registration party that permanently stores a record relating to this stego data set and issues a copyright certificate which it stores and transmits to the copyright holder.

A template pattern is added to the Fourier transform of an image to be watermarked. For checking the watermark, the Fourier transform of the stego-image is calculated. From this Fourier transform, the log polar mapping transform is generated, which is then searched for the modulation pattern. Using the log polar transform of the Fourier transform has the advantage that scaling and rotation of the stego-image are expressed as translations. This allows an easy search for rotation and scaling using cross-correlation techniques. The magnitude components of the Fourier transform of each image block is modulated using the same pattern in each block. This method provides robustness against cropping of the stego-image because the magnitude spectrum is invariant to circular translations (cyclic shifts) and cropping leads to a circular translation of the watermark in each block.

4   Copyright Protection and Image Owner Authentication

Depending on the proof-level to be provided for copyright protection, our approach provides three increasing levels of reliability, namely: individual copyright protection, copyright protection with registered cryptographic keys and copyright protection with C on the basis of registered cryptographic keys. The present method is based on an image owner authentication technique, described below, which embeds and detects the Image Authentication Data (IAD) as the payload of a watermark. The applied image owner authentication technique is based on a perceptually adaptive spread spectrum technique. This technique provides a reliable means of embedding robust watermarks. Such a technique will be discussed in section 5. In addition, spread spectrum is a form of symmetric cryptosystem. In order to embed or extract a watermark, it is necessary to know the exact values of the seed used to produce pseudo random sequences used to encode a watermark. The seeds are considered to be cryptographic keys for watermark generation and verification. System security is therefore based on proprietary knowledge of private keys, which provide in addition the necessary security parameters needed for a secure communication (mutual authentication, integrity, confidentiality, non-repudiation) in the trading process of digital images. Because spread spectrum signals are statistically independent (and therefore virtually orthogonal), the present method and apparatus encodes more than one watermark in an image at the same time, namely a private, a detection and a public watermark.

The *detection watermark* is embedded under a fixed random seed which allows H to efficiently search for his images on the Internet. The *public watermark* indicates that the image is copyright material and provide information on true ownership. At the same time there is a secure *private watermark* whose secrecy depends on the private key of H. Since the public key of H is registered, H can prove that he is the only person in the possession of the adequate private key and therefore the generator of the private watermark. The system also provides the secure registration (mutual authentication, integrity, non-repudiation) of watermark encoded images (data sets) at C. Derived data of the stego-image is registered at C. A signed digital copyright certificate is generated by C and transmitted to H. If an unauthorized third party has also encoded watermarks in the same image, conflicting claims in copyright disputes can be resolved, as only one of the two parties has a copyright certificate for the image containing only its watermark. The other party, who redistributed the original watermarked image, has only a certificate on the image where both watermarks are embedded and thus can be identified as the cheating party.

Watermark protection with registered cryptographic keys and C based copyright protection are based on a PKI. The PKI issues on request public key certificates such as X.509 certificates, containing the public key of the party, its distinguished name and a time stamp. Every certificate is signed with the PKI's private key and trust is built on the validity of the authentic copy of the PKI's public key (we assume that the public key of the PKI is accessible, authentically distributed and verifiable by every party).

4.1 Cryptographic Mechanisms

The following cryptographic mechanisms are used in the description [12]:

- A probabilistic digital signature scheme $(\mathcal{G}, \mathcal{S}, \mathcal{V})$, with key generation algorithm $\mathcal{G}$, signature algorithm $\mathcal{S}$ and verification algorithm $\mathcal{V}$. The key generation algorithms $\mathcal{G}$ returns a key pair $(x_{\mathcal{Z}}, y_{\mathcal{Z}})$ for entity $\mathcal{Z}$. Signature generation for a message m is described as $\sigma := \mathcal{S}(x_{\mathcal{Z}}, m)$ and the verification of this signature by $\mathcal{V}(y_{\mathcal{Z}}, m, \sigma) \in \{true, false\}$.
- $AKAP(A, B, K_{AB}, x_A, y_A, x_B, y_B)$: Asymmetric key agreement protocol (e.g. [9]) with entity A's keypair (x_A, y_A), entity B's keypair (x_B, y_B), between the entities A and B. After the protocol, the two entities have agreed on a symmetric key K_{AB}.

- *OIAE(X, Y, CI, SI)*: Oblivious image owner authentication embedding algorithm with seed X, payload Y, cover-image CI and resulting stego-image SI.
- *OIAV(X, SI, Y)*: Oblivious image owner authentication detection algorithm with seed X, stego-image SI and the resulting payload Y.
- h_1, h_2: collision resistant hash functions with a hash value of appropriate length.

4.2   Individual Copyright Protection

During individual copyright protection only the copyright holder H with distinguished $name_H$ and asymmetric key pair (x_H, y_H) is involved. The following steps are applied:

1. H retrieves the cover-image CI, generates a unique image identifier $ID_I :=$ $h_1(name_H) \parallel SN_I$, where SN_I is an image serial number and stores ID_I.
2. *Embedding of private watermark:*
   (a) H generates the stego-image SI_0 applying the transformation $OIAE(h_2(\sigma), ID_I, CI, SI_0)$, where CI denotes the cover-image, SI_0 denotes the resulting stego-image and $\sigma := \mathcal{S}(x_H, ID_I)$.
   (b) H stores σ together with CI in a protected database.
3. *Embedding of detection watermark:*
   H generates $OIAE(h_2(x_H), SN_I \parallel SN_I, SI_0, SI^*)$. The key x_H could also be replaced by a random secret key k_H, which is used for every embedding and securely stored in a database.
4. *Embedding of public watermark:*
   (a) *H* generates a public $IAD_I :=$ "Copyright by" $\parallel CDSig \parallel$ "All Rights Reserved" applying $CDSig := \mathcal{S}^3(x_H, Initials \parallel year)$.
   (b) H partitions IAD_I into blocks $BL_i, 1 \le i \le P$ of length 128 bits[4].
   (c) H generates the stego-image SI applying for every $i, 1 \le i \le P$, the transformation $OIAE(h_2(y_H \parallel i \parallel y_H), BL_i, CI_i, SI_i)$, where $CI_i := SI_{i-1}$ is the cover-image (stego-image from the previous iteration), $CI_1 = SI^*$ and SI_i is resulting stego-image after iteration i.
   The resulting stego-image is $SI := SI_P$.
5. H stores SI and might generate a signed copyright certificate $SigSI :=$ $\mathcal{S}(x_H, SI \parallel TS)$ where TS is a time stamp.

Cryptographic Properties Besides the robustness of the watermarks against various image transformations, which is discussed in section 5.4, the embedding of the private watermark offers useful cryptographic properties:

---

[3] A signature scheme with message recovery is used here.
[4] This is the maximum length of a payload that can be robustly embedded by the spread spectrum technique.

- The seed for embedding the private watermark is *probabilistic*, as it depends on the output of a probabilistic signature scheme. Thus even if the private watermark in one image is detected this doesn't allow an attacker to find the private watermarks in other protected images.
- The seed for embedding is *image-dependent*. Thus an attacker who knows a valid image ID can't embed this using a different seed, as this wouldn't fit with the recovered ID from the signature with message used to generate the seed. The same is true for an attacker who knows a valid signed seed and wants to use this to embed his own image ID.
- The private watermark offers *non-repudiation*, as it can only be generated by the copyright holder, who knows the corresponding private key. This allows the proof of ownership to a judge.
- The signature σ remains *secret* until H has to prove his ownership to a court. Even in this case, he doesn't have to reveal a secret to the court, which would enable it to generate valid private watermarks instead of H afterwards.
- The payload is *very short*. One could think of embedding the signed image ID using a random seed instead of the described method. This leads to a longer message, which is not as robust as the chosen one, if we assume that the image ID consists of, for example, 12 bytes. The shortest known signature schemes with message recovery already produce a signature 20 bytes long [13,8], i.e. their output is 80% longer than our payload.

4.3 Trading of Digital Images

The copyright holder H and the image buyer B with distinguished $name_B$ are involved in the trading of digital images. Suppose (x_H, y_H) is the asymmetric key pair of H and (x_B, y_B) is the asymmetric key pair of B. Suppose H has an authentic copy of y_B and B has an authentic copy of y_H before they start any communication. The following steps are applied during the trading of digital images:

1. H and B execute $AKAP(H, B, K_{HB}, x_H, y_H, x_B, y_B)$ for the generation of a shared symmetric session key K_{HB}.
2. B generates the Trading Request Envelope $TRE := < TD \parallel SigTD >$, with transmission data $TD := \{ID_I \parallel ExpTime \parallel name_B \parallel name_H\}$ and $SigTD := \mathcal{S}(x_B, h_2(TD))$. $ExpTime$ is the expiry time of the TRE, which avoids later replay of the same envelope. B transmits TRE to H.
3. H receives TRE and verifies TD, applying $\mathcal{V}(y_B, h_2(TD), SigTD) \overset{?}{=} true$ where $TD := ID_I \parallel ExpTime \parallel name_B \parallel name_H$. If TD has been successfully verified the next step is executed. In any other case, the processing and communication between H and B is stopped.
4. If the verification was successful, H retrieves with ID_I the corresponding stego-image SI and generates the Trading reSponse Envelope $TSE := < TD \parallel SigTD >$, with $TD := K_{HB}[SI] \parallel ExpTime \parallel name_H \parallel name_B$ and $SigTD := \mathcal{S}(x_H, h_2(TD))$. H transmits TSE to B.

5. B receives TSE and verifies TD by applying $\mathcal{V}(y_H, h_2(TD), SigTD) \stackrel{?}{=} true$, where $TD := K_{HB}[SI] \parallel ExpTime \parallel name_H \parallel name_B$. If the verification is true, then TD has been successfully verified.

B then deciphers $K_{HB}[SI]$ and checks IAD applying for every $i, 1 \leq i \leq P$, the following transformation: $OIAV(h_2(y_H \parallel h_2(i) \parallel y_H), SI, PL_i)$, where SI_i denotes the stego-image and PL_i the detected payload of the i-th public watermark. (If P is not known, the procedure is iterated until no more public watermarks can be detected).

IAD_I is then generated by concatenating PL_i, i.e. $IAD_I := PL_1 \parallel \ldots \parallel PL_N$, $1 \leq i \leq P$. IAD_I should be of the format "Copyright by" $\parallel CDSig \parallel$ "All Rights Reserved". The message $Initials \parallel year$ is recovered from $CDSig$ and the signature is verified applying $\mathcal{V}(y_H, Initials \parallel year, CDSig) \stackrel{?}{=} true$. If the verification is correct, B has verified H as the copyright holder.

Remark

In the case of a legal copyright dispute, H can retrieve IAD_I and construct the corresponding unique image ID_I. Since the generation of the same asymmetric key pair by two distinguished entities is very unlikely, the construction of the unique image ID_I provides a high level of proof against copyright infringement. In the case of watermark protection with registered keys, the generation of the same asymmetric key pair by two distinguished entities can be prevented.

4.4 Copyright Protection with Registered Keys

Copyright protection with registered cryptographic keys needs three parties, namely H with $name_H$, B with $name_B$ and the PKI with $name_I$. Suppose (x_H, y_H), (x_B, y_B), (x_I, y_I) are the unique key pairs of H, B and I respectively. Suppose, H has an authentic and actual copy of $Cert_B$ which signature was verified with the authentic copy of y_I and B has an authentic and actual copy of $Cert_H$ which signature was verified with the authentic copy of y_I. Then the same steps as for the individual watermark protection are applied.

Remark:

Since the generated asymmetric key pairs are unique, H can be uniquely identified if no additional watermarks by unauthorized persons have been encoded into a given SI. The C based watermark protection described below provides the necessary countermeasures to prevent this threat.

4.5 Copyright Protection with a Copyright Center

The system for copyright protection with Copyright Center has four participants, namely H with $name_H$, B with $name_B$, the PKI with $name_I$ and C with $name_C$. Suppose (x_H, y_H), (x_B, y_B), (x_I, y_I) and (x_C, y_C) are the unique key pairs of H, B, I and C, respectively. H has an authentic copy of $Cert_B$ and $Cert_C$ whose signatures were verified with the authentic copy of y_I, B has an authentic copy of $Cert_H$ and $Cert_C$ whose signatures were verified with the authentic copy of

y_I and C has an authentic copy of $Cert_H$ and $Cert_B$ whose signatures were verified with the authentic copy of y_I. The following steps are applied:

1. Steps 1-4 of the individual watermark protection protocol are applied, where the unique image ID_I is computed as $ID_I := h_1(name_H \ || \ name_C) \ || \ SN_I$.

2. H generates a thumbnail $Thumb$ from SI and stores it together with the stego-image SI.

3. H and C execute the following steps for the secure registration and the generation of copyright certificates:

   (a) H generates the Copyright Request Data $CRD := \{h_2(SI) \ || \ h_2(Thumb) \ || \ ID_I\}$ and the Copyright Request Envelope $CRE :=< TD \ || \ SigTD >$, with $TD := \{CRD \ || \ ExpTime \ || \ name_H \ || \ name_C\}$ and $SigTD := \mathcal{S}(x_H, h_2(TD))$. H transmits CRE to C.

   (b) C receives CRE and verifies it. For this, C requests the certificate $Cert_H$ that belongs to $name_H$ in CRE and obtains the authentic public key y_H. C checks the signature on TD by applying $\mathcal{V}(y_H, h_2(TD), SigTD) \stackrel{?}{=} true$, where $TD = \{CRD \ || \ ExpTime \ || \ name_H \ || \ name_C\}$. Then C checks the semantical correctness of TD. If all verifications are passed, then CRE has been successfully verified and the next step is executed.

   (c) C generates the digital *Copyright Certificate* by executing $SigCCD := \mathcal{S}(x_C, CCD)$, with $CCD := \{name_C \ || \ name_H \ || \ SN \ || \ ID_I \ || \ h_2(SI) \ || \ h_2(Thumb) \ || \ UCCN\}$ and $UCCN :=$ "Copyright" $|| \ year \ || \ name_H \ ||$ "All rights reserved". C stores the copyright certificate $CC := CCD \ || \ SigCCD$ together with $h_2(Thumb)$ in its database, generates the Copyright Certificate Envelope $CCE :=< TD \ || \ SigTD >$, with $TD := \{CC \ || \ ExpTime \ || \ name_C \ || \ name_H\}$ and $SigTD := \mathcal{S}(x_C, TD)$ and transmits it to H.

   (d) H receives CCE and verifies it by requesting the certificate $Cert_C$ that belongs to $name_C$ in CCE. H obtains the authentic public key y_C which he uses to check $SigTD$ on TD by applying $\mathcal{V}(y_C, h_2(TD), SigTD) \stackrel{?}{=} true$, where $TD := \{CC \ || \ ExpTime \ || \ name_C \ ||name_H\}$. H checks the semantic correctness of TD and if all verifications are correct then H stores CC in its database.

4. H and B might execute the image trading protocol described in section 4.3

Remark

B may check the copyright certificate requesting C to transfer an authentic copy of the copyright certificate for a given image identifier ID_I. Except the data transfer, the applied protocol is similar to the one described above. If B would like to transfer a specific copyright of a CI to another legal party, he may initiate a copyright revocation request with C. The different phases of this request are analogous to the copyright request.

5   Oblivious Image Owner Authentication

The watermarking technique comprises the following components:

1. An error-control coding technique for the payload to be transmitted in the watermark.
2. An encoding technique to encode the resulting message.
3. A reliable method for embedding the encoded message in the image without introducing visible artefacts.

Components 1 and 2 apply to embed watermarks in any type of data while component 3 is specific to the embedding of watermarks in images.

5.1   Error Control Coding

Error control coding is applied to the message prior to encoding. Symbol based Reed Solomon (RS) codes are applied for this purpose. The advantages are the following:

- RS codes correct symbol errors rather than bit errors and
- RS codes can correct erasures as well as errors.

Erasures can be factored out of the key equation, which means that "erased" symbols can be ignored. They do not play any role in the error control mechanism. In a sense, an erasure is useless redundancy. Being able to discard erased symbols has two advantages:

- If the posterior probability of a received symbol is low, it may be ignored.
- RS codes only come in standard sizes. For example a 255 x 8 bit code is common. Most commonly used RS error control codes appear to be too large to be used in watermarking. However, it is possible to make almost any RS code fit a watermarking application by judiciously selecting symbols as being erased (because they were never embedded in the image in the first place).

5.2   Encoding the Message

During encoding, the message to be transmitted in the watermark is transformed into a form suitable for use in the modulation of image components. At the same time, it is encrypted using a suitable key.

One can easily combine spread spectrum based watermarking with the cryptographic key distribution techniques described earlier. The encoding procedure has access to the cryptographic keys x_H and y_H (or their hash values), which are used to generate the seeds for the pseudo-random sequences as described below. Knowledge of the corresponding key is required for recovering the message from the watermark.

A watermark can be embedded or extracted by the key owner using the same key. From the point of view of embedding watermarks in images given the cryptographic keys the sequences themselves can be generated. A good spread spectrum sequence is one which combines desirable statistical properties such as uniformly low cross correlation with cryptographic security.

Suppose we are given a message M (for example, that was provided with error coding). The message has the binary form $b_1 b_2 \ldots b_L$, where b_i are its bits. This can be written in the form of a set of symbols $s_1 s_2 \ldots s_M$ – most generally by a change in a number base from 2 to B. The next stage is to encode each symbol s_i in the form of a pseudo random vector of length N, wherein each element of this vector either takes the value 0 or 1. N is, for example, in the order of 1000 to 10000 (typically in the order of 10% of the total number of image coefficients (Fourier components) that can, theoretically, be modulated).

To encode the first symbol a pseudo random sequence v of length $N + B - 1$ is generated. To encode a symbol of values where $0 < s < B$ the elements $v_s, v_{s+1} \ldots v_{s+N-1}$ are extracted as a vector r_1 of length N. For the next symbol another independent pseudo random sequence is generated and the symbol encoded as a random vector r_2. Each successive symbol is encoded in the same way. Alternatively, one can use any the N cyclic shifts of the pseudo random sequence v. Note that even if the same symbol occurs in different positions in the sequence, no collision is possible because the random sequences used to encode them are different — in fact they are statistically independent. Finally the entire sequence of symbols is encoded as the summation: $m = \sum_{i=1..M} r_i$

The pseudo-random vector m has N elements, each varying between 0 and M. In a next step, the elements of m are offset to make their mean zero. When decoding the watermark, a vector m' (read-out message) is derived from the stego-image. In oblivious watermarking, m' corresponds to the modulated Fourier coefficients. Due to distortions suffered by the stego-image due to image processing, in general m' will not be equal to but will be "statistically similar" to m. To decode s from m', the elements of m' are first offset to make their mean zero. Then, starting from the (known) seed, the first random sequence v of length $N + B - 1$ is generated and the correlation of v with m' is calculated. The peak of the correlation indicates the offset s_1 in the random sequence that was used for generating r_1. Then, the next random sequence v is generated and cross-correlated with m' to retrieve s_2, etc. Reliable communications of the system are best accommodated by using $m-$sequences that possess minimum cross correlation with each other. This is the same as maximizing the Euclidean distance between vectors $v_1, v_2, v_3 \ldots$. If M is sufficiently large, the statistical distribution of the message m should approach a Gaussian distribution (according to the Central Limit Theorem). A Gaussian distributed watermark has the advantage that it is somewhat more difficult to detect. The variance increases with order $M^{1/2}$; in other words, the expected peak excursion of the sequence is only order $M^{1/2}$.

5.3   Oblivious Image Authentication Algorithm

In this section, we describe how to embed the encoded message m in the image in the form of a watermark. The method is designed for robustness to operations generally applied to images such as translation, cropping, rotating and scaling. (The method is not designed for other types of data such as sound or text.) In order to achieve robustness against circular translation, each image block is first subjected to a Fourier transform and the same watermark is embedded in each block so the watermark tiles the entire image. Then, message m modulates the Fourier components. In addition to this, a template is embedded in the image, which can be used for detecting a rotation and scaling of the image when reading the watermark. Given a cover image the steps for embedding a watermark in the image are as follows:

1. If the image is a colour image, then compute the luminance component (for example, by simply replacing each pixel by $g/2 + r/3 + b/6$, where g, r and b are its green, red and blue components) and use these values for the following calculations.
2. Divide the image into adjacent blocks of size 128×128 pixels.
3. Map the image luminance levels (or grey levels for a black and white image) to a perceptually "flat" domain by replacing them with their logarithm. The logarithm is a good choice because it corresponds to the Weber-Fechner law which describes the response of the human visual system to changes of luminance. This step ensures that the intensity of the watermark is diminished in the darker regions of the image where it would otherwise be visible.
4. Compute the FFT (Fast Fourier Transform) of each block. From the real and imaginary components obtained in this way, calculate the corresponding magnitude and phase components. The magnitude components are translation invariant and will therefore be used in the following modulation steps. (However, it is possible to derive translation invariants from the phase spectrum as well, which could also be modulated).
5. Select the magnitude components to be modulated. To encode a message m of length N, a total number of N components are modulated. In non-oblivious watermarking, any components can be modulated. For oblivious watermarking, because of the interference of the cover-image with the watermark, the largest magnitude components are avoided and only a band of frequencies are used. These mid band frequencies are chosen because they generally give a good compromise between robustness and visibility of the watermark. There are two methods for selecting the components to be modulated:
   - The selection of the components to be modulated does not depend on the given image. Rather, the same components are selected for every image. The author as well as the reader of the watermark know the positions of the components to be selected in advance.
   - The largest components (inside the allowable frequency range) are used for modulation using a perceptually adaptive approach.
6. Add a template by a second modulation of the magnitude components. This is described in more detail below.
7. Compute the inverse FFT using the phase components and the modulated magnitude components.

8. Compute the inverse of the perceptual mapping function of step 3. For Weber-Fechner law mapping, the inverse function is an exponential.
9. Replace each watermarked block in the image to obtain the stego-image.
10. If the image is a colour image, then re-scale the red, green and blue components by the relative change in luminance introduced by embedding a watermark. Typically, the red, green and blue pixels occupy a byte each in program memory. If overflow or underflow occurs then the pixel is set to the upper bound 255 or lower bound 0 respectively.

When selecting the components to be modulated, care must be taken to preserve the symmetry imposed on the Fourier components $F(k_1, k_2)$ by the fact that the image block is real valued: $F(k_1, k_2) = F^*(N_1 - k_1, N_2 - k_2)$, where N_1, N_2 designate the size of the image block. Once the magnitude components $(M_1, ... M_N)$ to be modulated are chosen, the corresponding value m_i of message m is added to or subtracted from the corresponding selected magnitude component M_i. Addition is applied, if the difference between the corresponding phase component P_i and a "reference phase" is between 0 and π. Subtraction is applied if the difference is between π and 2π. Note that the reference phase for each watermark component should be the same for each block. This provides robustness against translation and cropping (see below). Before adding/subtracting the values m_i to/from M_i, the vector m can be scaled to adjust the magnitude of its elements to those of the components M_i. Generally, the elements m_i should be in the same order of magnitude as the components M_i. The depth of modulation or amplitude of the embedded signal should depend on the objective measure of the perceptual significance. The lower the perceptual significance, the higher should be the amplitude of the watermark. However, for simplicity, the amplitude for all components is usually kept constant.

Template As mentioned above, a template is added to the image in step 6. The following steps have to be executed:

1. Apply a log-polar map to the magnitude components, i.e. transform them into a polar coordinate system $(\Theta, log - r)$ with an angular and a logarithmic radius axis respectively. In this representation, a scaling of the image leads to an offset of the components along the $log - r$ axis. A rotation of the image leads to an offset along the Θ axis. Preferably, low pass filtering is used for interpolating the frequency space components during this mapping. The magnitude components belonging to very low or high frequencies are not mapped. The following modulation is only applied to components in midband frequency range.
2. Select the magnitude components in the log-polar coordinate system to be modulated. Typically, as few as 10 components can be modulated. The pattern T formed by the selected components in log polar space should be such that its auto-correlation under translation is weak. There should be as little ambiguity as possible in matching the shifted stego-image with the template. For this purpose, the indices of the selected components should be co-prime or at least be derived from a two-dimensional random sequence.

3. Map the modulated points by a change of coordinates back into frequency space. The pattern T formed by the selected components in log polar space is predefined and known to the reader of the watermark. It must be noted that the calculation of the log-polar transform is not required for embedding the template. The pattern T of the components to be modulated in log-polar space can be mapped back to the corresponding components in frequency space.

As will be explained below, the template is not required for non-oblivious watermarking (since the original image can be used as the "template, in other words, the stego-image can be registered with the original image). Also if the image is a colour image then the luminance image is used during the following operations:

1. Divide the image into adjacent blocks of size 128×128.
2. Map the image luminance levels (or gray levels) to the perceptually "flat" domain by replacing them with their logarithm.
3. For each block compute the FFT.
4. Determine the rotation and scaling that the image suffered by finding the template in log-polar space and compensate for the rotation and scale.
5. Read the modulated components to generate message m'.
6. Once that the message m' is recovered, it is demodulated and error corrected using the methods described earlier.

Finding the template
The steps for finding the template are as follows:

1. Apply a log-polar mapping to the magnitude components of the Fourier transform. The magnitude components in the very low or high frequency range are not mapped. The log-polar mapping is only applied to components in midband frequency range.
2. For oblivious watermarking, calculate the normalized cross correlation of the components in log-polar space with the template pattern T that was used for generating the template in step 6 and find the point of best correlation. If the image has neither been rotated or scaled, this point is at origin. Scaling leads to a corresponding offset along the $log - r$ axis, rotation to a corresponding offset along the Θ axis.
3. For non-oblivious watermarking, the log polar transform of the Fourier components of the cover-image can be used instead of template pattern T for retrieving scaling and rotation. The cross correlation can be calculated efficiently using conventional Fourier techniques.

5.4   Properties of the Watermark

In the following, some of the properties of the watermark generated using the steps described above are discussed.

Robustness to Cropping One feature of translation invariants developed using the Fourier transform is that they are invariant to circular translations (or cyclic shifts). This is used to construct watermarks that are invariant to cropping. As mentioned above, the image is split into blocks and the watermark is applied to each block. In other words, the same modulation pattern is applied to the Fourier components of each block, wherein the modulation pattern is given by the corresponding encoded messages m. Suppose that the watermark in a standard size block will be of the form: $T = [AB; CD]$ where the submatrices A, B, C and D are of arbitrary size. A circular translation of such a watermark is of the form: $S = [DC; BA]$. The original stego-image is tiled with watermarks in the pattern $[TTTT; TTTT; TTTT]$. A little thought demonstrates that a cropped section of the matrix will carry a watermark in the form $[SSSS; SSSS; SSSS]$. When reading the watermark of the cropped image, each block carries the watermark S. Since S is a circular transform of T, it can be read directly in the Fourier domain using the steps outlined above. Note, however, that the cover-image is not tiled, only the watermark is. Therefore, while cropping merely induces a circular translation of the watermark in each block, the change of image in each block is not a circular translation.

The optimum size of block depends on a number of different factors. A size that is a power of two is useful because the FFT can be used. The block size also must be small enough to withstand cropping but large enough to comfortably contain a watermark. Heuristically, the best compromise for block size is 128.

Robustness to Scaling and Rotation As mentioned earlier, reading the template in log-polar space allows to detect and measure any scaling and/or rotation that was applied to the image. This information can then be used for reading the watermark. Since the reader knows the pattern that was used for modulating the magnitude components, he can identify the modulated components in the scaled and rotated image and extract the message m'. Note that the apparatus does not explicitly use a rotation and scale invariant watermark but instead searches the parameter space of rotations and scales. Since searching the space of rotation and scales in the frequency or space domain is quite complicated, the log-polar map is used to map these parameters to Cartesian coordinates where searching can be carried out using efficient correlation techniques.

Robustness to Translations: By translation, we mean zero padding of the image such as would occur if an image were placed on a scanner and scanned. In this case the effect on the watermark blocks may be understood in terms of simple signal and image processing theory. Effectively, zero padding is a multiplication by a rectangular window function in the spatial domain. In the frequency domain this approximates to a convolution with a cardinal sine function. Generally, this blurring of frequency space is not severe. If more than about one third of an watermark block is present the watermark can still be decoded.

Robustness to Compression The watermark is also resistant to compression. It is well known that transform based image compression techniques favour low frequencies in the sense that low frequency content in the original image is better preserved in the compressed image. For this reason, it would seem that a low frequency watermark would be better. However, as mentioned earlier in oblivious watermarking it is necessary to avoid low frequencies for embedding information because the image interferes with the watermark at those frequencies. Fortunately, a compromise is possible: judicious selection of a band of frequencies leads to a watermark that is both oblivious and is sufficiently resistant to lossy image compression. One helpful factor is that there are relatively few low frequency components in which to embed a spread spectrum signal. Using midband frequencies actually improves the robustness of the mark because of the increased redundancy of the encoding of the payload.

Fig. 2 shows an image that was quite strongly watermarked using the techniques described in this paper. Fig. 3 shows this image after JPEG compression was applied at 15% quality factor where it is found that that the storage required is less than 1% of that needed for the original image. Not surprisingly, the quality is very low and the image is of little commercial use. A 104 bit watermark "The watermark" (in ASCII code) can be recovered from the JPEG compressed image.

Fig. 2. A watermarked image of Lena

Fig. 3. A watermarked image of Lena compressed at 15% quality factor. The compression ratio is 100:1

Robustness to Other Attacks Specialised watermark removal algorithms have been proposed in the literature. StirMark [10] uses both contrast based attacks and geometric attacks. The geometric attacks are not directly addressed using the method proposed in this paper. However, we can give one good example of the robustness of the spread spectrum watermark described in this paper to a contrast based attack. The results are as follows:

- Operation: stirmark -i0 -o0 -d128 :
  - decoded watermark: "The watermark",
  - agreement with original = 100.00 percent.
  Operation: stirmark -i0 -o0 -d256 :
  - decoded watermark: "The wAtereak",
  - agreement with original = 96.15 percent.

The stirmark distorted image is shown in Fig. 4. It has obviously been very severely distorted. It was even surprising to the authors that this distortion only destroyed 4% of the bits of the watermark. Other attacks such as UnZign [22] have no effect on the mark.

Robustness of the Template Pattern The template pattern is essential to determine the rotation and scaling of the image. Thus its robustness is highly

Fig. 4. The watermarked image of Lena after being attacked using "StirMark"

important. There is a good case for arguing that the template is somewhat more robust than the watermark. The reason for this is, that the template actually has to carry less information than the watermark. For example, suppose it is only possible to recover the watermark if the rotation angle and scaling factor recovered using the template are both 99.9% accurate. To give 99.9% accuracy one needs $\log_2(1000) \approx 9$ bit. Specifying both the angle and the scaling factor therefore needs around 18 bit which is considerably less than the amount of information contained in a typical watermark (about 128 bit).

Redundancy The watermark is embedded in blocks of a fixed size with exactly the same watermark embedded in each block. This means that the watermark can be recovered from a single block only. However the chance of extracting the watermark correctly increases if one has more than one block. Therefore, the reliability of watermark extraction increases with the size of image, as one might expect.

6   Conclusions and Future Work

We have presented a new approach for the copyright protection of digital images. This approach is based on asymmetric cryptographic protocols and techniques. In contrast to any other scheme, the combination of a spread spectrum based technique in conjunction with an asymmetric cryptographic technique allows the construction of a one-way function, since only H is able to verify the private watermark. In addition, he may prove that he has the adequate key by verifying the signature of the seed for the payload data. Even if the different phases of the approach are known in the public, the security of our approach is not compromised. Compared to other approaches, the following new properties have been identified:

1. Different security services for the communication, such as *mutual authentication, integrity, confidentiality* and *non-repudiation* are supported along with the protection against copyright infringement by the system with one asymmetric cryptographic key pair.
2. The present technique enables a strong binding relation between the image ID, the image and H if H registers his copyright at C. If an image is watermarked later by an unauthorized person, the time stamp in the copyright certificates resolves the copyright ownership.
3. H does not have to reveal his private cryptographic key if ownership verification has to be applied by a different legal party.
4. The present technique supports the *transferral of copyrights.* If a copyright is transferred to another legal party, corresponding copyright revocation certificates may be generated.
5. Digital signatures are used for the security of the communication between different parties and for the authenticity of the data embedded in a public watermark of an image. No signature labelling techniques of the complete image are applied by the system.
6. Circular translation invariants are used as a means of constructing digital watermarks that are invariant to cropping.
7. In contrast to some known techniques, the system does not require a database of watermarks since only the keys are required to embed or extract a watermark.
8. Information is retrieved from the log polar domain of the Fourier transform. Frequency components are modulated which are oblivious to the cover-image but which also have the property that they form an unambiguous non-repeated pattern in log-polar space. They are used for determining the degree of rotation and scaling suffered by a stego-image in the absence of the cover-image. Co-prime frequencies are useful for generating such a pattern or template. Uniform random sampling of log polar space is another method that can be applied.

To demonstrate the feasibility of the approach, a Java/C++ based copyright protection and authentication environment for digital images has been implemented. An example of this copyright protection environment in action is shown in Fig. 5. The PKI, H, C and B application processes all implement a Graphical User Interface and a server, supporting both console users and other requests through a socket interface.

The approach presented for the copyright protection of digital images can also be extended to other data such as video, audio and binary data. We are

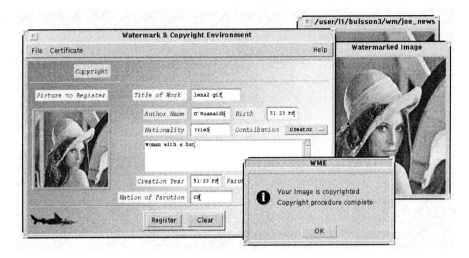

Fig. 5. The watermarked image of Lena being registered for copyright protection using a Java console

actually investigating new spread spectrum techniques for the watermarking of audio and binary data.

References

1. C. Cox, J. Killian, T. Leighton and T. Shamoon, "Secure spread spectrum communication for multimedia", Technical report, N.E.C. Research Institute, 1995.
2. G. Caronni "Assuring Ownership Rights for Digital Images" in H. H. Brueggemann and W. Gerhardt-Haeckl, editors, Reliable IT Systems VIS '95, Vieweg, Germany, 1995, pp. 251-264.
3. W. G. Chambers, "Basics of Communications and Coding", Oxford Science Publications. Clarendon Press Oxford, 1985.
4. S. Craver, N. Memon, B. Yeo and M. Yeung, "Can invisible marks resolve rightful ownerships ?", IS&T/SPIE Electronic Imaging '97 : "Storage and Retrieval of Image and Video Databases", 1997.
5. P. Davern and M. Scott, "Fractal based image steganography", Proc. International Workshop in Information Hiding, LNCS, Springer, 1996, pp. 279–294.
6. J.-F. Delaigle, J.-M. Boucqueau, J.-J. Quisquater and B. Macq, "Digital Images protection techniques in a broadcast framework: An overview", Laboratoire de Télécommunications et de Télédéction, Université Catholique de Louvain, 1996.
7. A. Freier, P. Karlton and P. Kocher, "SSL Version 3.0", Netscape Communications, Version 3.0, November 1996.
8. P. Horster, M. Michels, H. Petersen, "'Meta signature schemes giving message recovery based on the discrete logarithm problem'", Proc. 2nd Int. Workshop on IT-Security, September, 1994, pp. 82–92.
9. ISO/ IEC 11770-3, "Information technology-Security techniques-Key management, Part 3: Mechanisms using asymmetric techniques", 1995.

10. M.G. Kuhn, "StirMark",
    http://www.cl.cam.ac.uk/~fapp2/watermarking/stirmark/ November 1997.
11. K. Matsui and K. Tanaka, "Video-Steganography : How to secretly embed a signature in a picture", IMA Intellectual Property Project Proceedings, January 1994, pp. 187–206.
12. A.J. Menezes, P.C. Van Oorschot and S.A. Vanstone, "Handbook of Applied Cryptography", CRC Press, 1996.
13. K.Nyberg, R.Rueppel, "Message recovery for signature schemes based on the discrete logarithm problem", LNCS 950, Advances in Cryptology: Proc. Eurocrypt '94, Springer, (1994), pp. 182–193.
14. J. K. Ó Ruanaidh, W. J. Dowling and F. M. Boland, "Phase watermarking of images", IEEE International Conference on Image Processing, September 1996.
15. J. J. K. Ó Ruanaidh, W. J. Dowling and F. M. Boland, "Watermarking digital images for copyright protection", IEEE Proceedings on Vision, Image and Signal Processing, Vol. 143, No. 4, August 1996, pp. 250–256.
16. W. B. Pennebaker and J. L. Mitchell, "JPEG Still Image Compression Standard", Van Nostrand Reinhold, New York, 1993.
17. W.H. Press, S.A. Teukolsky, W.T. Vetterling and B.P. Flannery, "Numerical Recipes in C", Cambridge University Press, second edition, 1992.
18. J. Smith and B. Comiskey, "Modulation and information hiding in images", Proc. Workshop in Information Hiding, LNCS 1173, Springer, 1996, pp. 207–226.
19. B. Schneier, "Applied Cryptography", Wiley, 2nd edition, 1995.
20. A. Z. Tirkel, G. A. Rankin, R. G. van Schyndel, W. J. Ho, N. R. A. Mee and C. F. Osborne, "Electronic watermark", Dicta-93, December 1993, pp. 666–672.
21. A. Z. Tirkel, R. G. van Schyndel and C. F. Osborne, "a two-dimensional digital watermark", Proc. ACCV'95, December 1995, pp. 378–383.
22. "UnZign", http://www.altern.org/watermark/, 1997.
23. J. Zhao and E. Koch, "Embedding robust labels into images for copyright protection", Technical report, Fraunhofer Institute for Computer Graphics, Darmstadt, Germany, 1994.
24. J. Zhao, "A WWW Service To Embed And Prove Digital Copyright Watermarks", Proc. Of the European Conference on Multimedia Application, Services and Techniques, May 1996.

A   Glossary

Some key terms used in the description of the digital copyright protection scheme are explained here.

Image An image in either digital or physical form. It may constitute a still image or a video frame. It can also refer to other types of data, such as video and audio data.

Signal A signal in either digital or physical form. It may refer to one dimensional or multidimensional signals such as image and video signals.

Image Copyright Holder (H) A party (or a process acting on behalf of it) "owning" a digital image. This is the party that generates the watermarks.

Image Buyer (B) A party (or a process acting on behalf it) which obtains (e.g. by purchase) via electronic means a specific image from H.

Image Authentication Data (IAD) The authentication data used in the image authentication process.

Stego-image Implies that an image or data is marked (i.e. it has an IAD embedded in it). The stego-image is also referred to as the stego data set.

Cover-image Implies that an image or data is unmarked (i.e. it has no IAD embedded in it). The cover-image is also referred to as the cover data set.

Watermark The form the IAD takes when it is suitable for embedding in a signal.

Image Copyright Certificate Center (C) An organization (or a process which acts on behalf it) which registers ownership for a specific image. Successful registration is based on a verification procedure such as checking the name and postal address of H, information how ownership was acquired, the title of the image, a description of the type of image (artistic, literary, musical, dramatic) and date and place of first publication. After registration a digital copyright certificate is generated.

Digital copyright certificate Digital copyright data which comprise the copyright certificate data and a digital signature.

Public watermark A watermark that can be detected using a publicly available key.

Detection watermark An image independent watermark that can be detected using a secret key.

Private watermark An image dependent watermark that can only be detected using a private key. It is not possible for an unauthorized third party to overwrite or delete the private watermark without the cryptographic secret keying information.

Payload The core of the hidden Image Authentication Data in bit form without error control coding applied.

Image ID The unique image ID is represented by an 8 byte hash determining H and C, followed by 4 bytes assigned by H for unique identification of each of his images.

Oblivious A watermarking technique which does not require the cover-image for extracting the mark. In other words, only the stego image is required to extract the mark when using an oblivious marking scheme.

Template A hidden message encoded in the image. By detecting the template, the scaling (zooming) and rotation suffered by a stego-image can be determined.

Shedding More Light on Image Watermarks

Juan Ramón Hernández and Fernando Pérez-González

Departamento de Tecnoloxías das Comunicacións
E.T.S.I. Telecomunicación
Universidad de Vigo
Vigo 36200, Pontevedra (SPAIN)
{jhernan, fperez}@tsc.uvigo.es

Abstract. In this paper a general model of a watermarking system for copyright protection of outputs from an arbitrary source is presented. This model is proposed as a framework for an information-theoretical analysis of watermarking schemes. The main elements which comprise such schemes are described, performance measures are defined and important issues such as imperceptibility, robustness and cryptographic security are discussed. The application of concepts such as channel capacity, authentication and secrecy in the context of watermarking is also discussed. As a particular case, a spatial-domain image watermarking system based on direct sequence spread spectrum modulation techniques is described. Special enphasis is placed in discussing the analogies and differences between spread spectrum communication systems and watermarking applications.

1 Introduction

One of the main impediments to a widespread use of digital communication networks such as Internet for commercial distribution of information in digital format is the ease of replication, manipulation and misuse of digital data that current technologies offer at fairly low cost. Digital watermarking techniques are promising schemes that can be applied to enforce ownership rights.

Previous research on copyright protection of still images has resulted in the appearance of several methods based on watermarking. Some of these methods perform the watermarking process in the spatial domain using spread spectrum techniques [1,2] and others operate ont he DCT domain of the whole image [3] or in a block basis [1,2,4,5]. The spread spectrum techniques have been applied without considering important differences between communication systems and watermarking schemes. One of the main goals of this paper is to discuss these differences.

This paper is organized in two parts. In the first part (Sect. 2), we propose a general model of a watermarking system, analyze its main components, define performance measures and discuss issues and limits in performance from an information-theoretical point of view. Some of the proposed performance measures have not been considered in the existing literature. In the second part

David Aucsmith (Ed.): Information Hiding 1998, LNCS 1525, pp. 191–207, 1998.

(Sects. 3 and 4) we describe a spatial domain watermarking system based on spread spectrum techniques. The main goal of this part is to compare the watermarking system with the framework defined in section 2 and to describe each element establishing analogies and differences with respect to a classical spread spectrum communication system.

2   A General Watermarking System

In this section we present a general model of a watermarking system applied to copyright protection of outputs from an arbitrary information source. The purpose of a watermarking system is to provide a means to enforce authorship of multimedia information by introducing imperceptible alterations into a source output in a secret fashion in such a way that those alterations encode copyright information and using a properly designed verification test the authorship can be verified. Secrecy is provided by a key only known to the copyright owner. In this paper we will assume that a symmetric key scheme is used, i.e. the secret key is necessary in the copyright verification test. We will also assume that the original source output is not available in the verification test. A watermarking system contemplating this possibility is more flexible since the verification can be performed without exposing the original work.

2.1   Definitions

Let X be the output of a source with alphabet $\mathcal{X}$ (see Fig. 1) and W be a message in a discrete alphabet $\mathcal{W} = \{1, \ldots, M\}$. For simplicity, we will assume in the sequel that $\mathcal{X}$ is a discrete alphabet, and the source output follows a discrete distribution p_X. Let $S \in \{0, 1\}$ be a random variable which indicates whether X will be watermarked. This variable is introduced in the model only to provide the possibility of expressing mathematically the existence or non-exsistence of a watermark in a simple way. Let K be a secret key defined on a discrete alphabet $\mathcal{K}$.

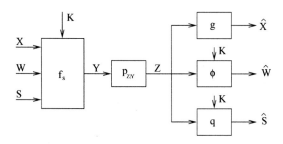

Fig. 1.   *General model of a watermarking system.*

When $S = 1$, the source output X is transformed into a watermarked version Y using a watermarking function $f_1 : \mathcal{X} \times \mathcal{W} \times \mathcal{K} \to \mathcal{Y}$, where $\mathcal{Y}$ is the output alphabet of the watermarking function. When $S = 0$, the source output X is transformed using a function $f_0 : \mathcal{X} \to \mathcal{Y}$. The output of the watermarking function f_1 depends on the value of K, a secret key which uniquely identifies the copyright owner.

The watermarked version Y then passes through a noisy channel and is transformed into $Z \in \mathcal{Y}$. This channel models both unintentional distortions suffered by Y and attacks aimed at deleting or corrupting the watermark information. In both cases we assume that the secret key is not known, so the noisy channel can be defined by the distribution $p_{Z|Y}(z \mid y)$ which is independent of K.

Finally, Z is processed to obtain a point $\hat{X} \in \mathcal{X}$ which will be used by the recipient instead of X. There are two tests that can serve to verify the ownership of Z: the watermark detection test and the watermark decoding test. We assume that the original source output X is not available in any of the verification tests. The watermark detection test is modeled by a function $q : \mathcal{Y} \times \mathcal{K} \to \{0, 1\}$ used to obtain an estimate $\hat{S}$ of S, in other words, to decide whether Z has been watermarked using K. The watermark decoding test consists in obtaining an estimate $\hat{W}$ of the hidden information W using a function $\phi : \mathcal{Y} \times \mathcal{K} \to \mathcal{W}$.

2.2   Imperceptibility

The first requirement for a watermark is imperceptibility. Let $d : \mathcal{X} \times \mathcal{X} \to \mathbb{R}^+$ be a perceptually significant distortion function. A watermarking system must guarantee that the functions f_0, f_1 and g introduce imperceptible alterations with respect to X. This requirement can be expressed mathematically as the mean distortion constraints

$$E[d(X, g(f_0(X)))] \leq D_0 \tag{1}$$
$$E[d(X, g(f_1(X, W, K)))] \leq D_1 \tag{2}$$

with expectations taken with respect to X, W, K, or maximum constraints

$$d(X, g(f_0(X))) \leq D_0 \quad \forall X \in \mathcal{X} \tag{3}$$
$$d(X, g(f_1(X, W, K))) \leq D_1 \quad \forall X \in \mathcal{X}, W \in \mathcal{W}, K \in \mathcal{K}. \tag{4}$$

2.3   Hiding Information

The performance of the watermark decoding process is measured by the probability of error, defined as

$$P_e \triangleq Pr\{\hat{W} \neq W\} = \sum_K p_K(K) Pr\{\phi(Z, K) \neq W \mid K\}. \tag{5}$$

For each value of K, the space $\mathcal{Y}$ is partitioned into decision regions $\mathcal{D}_1, \ldots, \mathcal{D}_M$, where $M = |\mathcal{W}|$ is the number of possible hidden messages. Decoding errors are due to the uncertainty about the source output X from which the watermarked version was obtained.

2.4   Detecting the Watermark

For each value of K, the watermark detection test can be mathematically defined as a binary hypothesis test in which we have to decide if Z was generated by the distribution of $f_0(X)$ or the distribution of $f_1(X, W, K)$, where $X \sim p_X(X)$ and W is modeled as a random variable. Let $\mathcal{E}_K \triangleq \{Z \in \mathcal{Y} \mid q(Z, K) = 1\}$ be the critical region for the watermark detection test performed with K, i.e. the set of points in $\mathcal{Y}$ where $\hat{S} = 1$ is decided for that key. The watermark detection test is completely defined by the sets $\{\mathcal{E}_K, K \in \mathcal{K}\}$. The performance of the watermark detection test is measured by the probabilities of false alarm (P_F) and detection (P_D), defined as

$$P_F \triangleq Pr\{\hat{S} = 1 \mid S = 0\} = \sum_K p_K(K) Pr\{Z \in \mathcal{E}_K \mid S = 0\} \tag{6}$$

$$P_D \triangleq Pr\{\hat{S} = 1 \mid S = 1\} = \sum_K p_K(K) Pr\{Z \in \mathcal{E}_K \mid S = 1, K\}. \tag{7}$$

Suppose there is no distortion during distribution, so $Z = Y$. Intuitively, optimizing the performance of the watermark detection test in terms of P_F and P_D is in a way equivalent to maximizing the Kullback-Leibler distance between distributions $p(Y \mid S = 1, K)$ and $p(Y \mid S = 0)$. The maximum achievable distance is limited by the perceptual distortion constraint and by the entropy of the source.

Another important performance measure is the probability of deciding $\hat{S} = 1$ in the watermark detection test for certain key K_1 when Z has been watermarked using a different key K_2. In the sequel we will call this performance measure the probability of collision between keys K_1 and K_2. In the context of copyright protection, this probability should be constrained below a maximum allowed value for all the pairs (K_1, K_2) since otherwise the author in possession of K_1 could claim authorship of information watermarked by the author who owns K_2. This constraint imposes a limit to the cardinality of the key space since the minimum achievable maximum probability of collision between keys increases with the number of keys for fixed P_F and P_D.

2.5   Attacks

A watermarking system may suffer several kinds of attacks. In this section we will give a classification of the main attacks and will relate them to the model defined in section 2.1. In the following discussion we will assume that the attacker has unlimited computational power and that the algorithms for watermarking, detection and decoding are public, so the security of the watermarking system relies exclusively on the secret key K of the copyright owner.

An attacker could try to impersonate an author by generating the point Z in $\mathcal{Y}$ which maximizes his chances of deciding $\hat{S} = 1$ for the secret key of the victim. The robustness of the watermarking system against this attack relies on the uncertainty about the secret key owned by the legitimate author. This kind of attack appears in authentication systems and was analyzed by Simmons [6,7] using a game-theoretic model. The probability of success in the impersonation attack is [6]

$$P_I \overset{\triangle}{=} \max_Z \sum_K p(K)q(Z,K). \tag{8}$$

An important kind of attack in watermarking systems is the elimination attack, aimed at deleting the watermark information. In other words, an elimination attack consists in altering a watermarked source output Y to obtain a negative result $(\hat{S} = 0)$ in the watermark detection test for the secret key used by the legitimate owner. The alteration made by the attacker should not be perceptible, since the resulting output Z will be used as a substitute for the watermarked source output Y. This constraint can be expressed in mathematical form as an average distortion constraint $E[d(Z,Y)] \leq D_E$ or as a maximum distortion constraint $d(Z,Y) \leq D_E$, $\forall Z, Y$, where $d(\cdot,\cdot)$ is the distortion function defined in section 2.2 and D_E is the maximum distortion allowed by the attacker. Authentication systems are not designed to resist this kind of attack since the goal in those systems is to detect any alteration suffered by a signed message. The elimination attack can be represented by a game-theoretic model. Given a certain watermarked source output Y, the attacker will choose the point $Z \in \mathcal{Y}$, subject to the distortion constraint, which maximizes his probability of success. Under a maximum distortion constraint, this maximum probability of success for a given Y can be expressed as

$$P_E(Y) \overset{\triangle}{=} \max_{Z:d(Z,Y) \leq D_E} \sum_K p(K \mid Y)(1 - q(Z,K)). \tag{9}$$

After averaging out over $\mathcal{Y}$, the average probability of success in the elimination attack is

$$P_E = \sum_Y p(Y) \max_{Z:d(Z,Y) \leq D_E} \sum_K p(K \mid Y)(1 - q(Z,K)). \tag{10}$$

We can also model the transformation made by the attacker as a channel with conditioned pmf $p_{Z|Y}$. Then, the optimum elimination estrategy can be seen as a worst-case channel $p_{Z|Y}$ in the sense that it minimizes the P_D for given critical regions $\{\mathcal{E}_K\}$ and watermarking function f_1. It is important to note that the attacker is limited to those channels which satisfy the average distortion constraint. In fact, the minimum achievable P_D is a non-increasing function of D_E. The optimum watermarking strategy consists in choosing the watermarking function f_1 and the critical regions $\{\mathcal{E}_K\}$ maximizing the minimum P_D achievable by the attacker through the choice of a channel $p_{Z|Y}$. Hence, the design of the watermarking system is a robust hypothesis testing problem.

Another possible attack consists in the corruption of the hidden information introduced by the watermarking function. In this case the attacker is not interested in eliminating the watermark, but in increasing the probability of error in the watermark decoding process.

2.6   Cryptographic Security

The security of the watermarking system relies on the use of a secret key known exclusively by the copyright owner. Therefore, the security level of the system can be measured by the uncertainty about the key given a watermarked source output Y. Using an information-theoretical terminology, this uncertainty is the conditioned entropy $H(K \mid Y)$, also called equivocation in the theory of secrecy systems [8].

A large equivocation helps in increasing the minimum P_D achievable by the opponent in an elimination attack since the attacker will have more uncertainty about the key used to watermark the source output and if the watermarking function and detection test are properly designed, this uncertainty can be used to reduce the probability of success in an elimination attack.

2.7   Size of Key Space

A minimum cardinality of the key space $\mathcal{K}$ is a necessary condition for increasing the equivocation $H(K \mid Y)$. We have seen in section 2.6, that increasing the equivocation helps in increasing the robustness against elimination attacks. However, increasing the number of available keys also increases the probability of collision among keys (Sect. 2.4). Therefore, if we specify a maximum allowable probability of collision, this constraint will impose a limit on the maximum number of keys.

2.8   Discussion

We can see that watermarking is a challenging problem in which many concepts from information theory appear. For instance, decoding of hidden information (Sect. 2.3) is affected by uncertainty due to the source output (not available at the receiver), distortions and attacks. Hence, we can think that there is a channel between W and Z which can be characterized by a certain capacity. Watermarking and watermark detection under a constrained maximum probability of collision between keys (Sect. 2.4) can be seen as an application of identification via channels [9], with additional constraints derived from the limited admissible perceptual distorion in the watermarking process. In fact, the combination of watermark detection and data hiding can be related to the theory of identification plus transmission codes [10]. At the same time, cryptographic security must be considered since one of the goals is to make it difficult for an opponent to find the secret key used in the watermarking process. We saw in Sect. 2.5 that concepts from authentication theory [6] also appear due to the possibility of an impersonation attack. The most challenging topic in the analysis of a watermarking system is the robustness against attacks. All the information-theoretical concepts enumerated above should be restated in the context of watermarking if the design of robust watermark decoders and detectors is considered.

3   Image Watermarking and Spread Spectrum Modulation

Spread spectrum systems were initially used in secure military communications because of their robustness against jamming, interference, and multipath distortion in fading channels. In these systems the binary information sequence is transformed into a noise-like signal by means of a pseudorandom sequence generator operating at a rate much larger than the symbol rate. Because of their applicability in secure communications, spread spectrum schemes are good candidates for hiding information into images. In a spread spectrum system a binary message is transformed into a sequence in a space of much higher dimensionality. This transformation depends on the value of a secret key, and the resulting sequence looks like white noise. Key-dependence and whiteness provide cryptographic security and robustness against jamming and interference, and these are desirable features of a watermarking system. In fact, the addition of a spread spectrum signal to an image can be seen as a particular case of the general watermarking system depicted in Fig. 1. The function f_0 is in this case the identity, and f_1 is a transformation consisting in the addition of a key-dependent pseudorandom sequence to the original image X.

Although spread spectrum systems possess desirable properties in terms of security and robustness, we must keep in mind that in classical spread spectrum applications not all channel distortions are possible and jamming is limited to additive attacks. The situation is completely different in image watermarking applications. Once the opponent has intercepted a watermarked image, he can employ all the computational power at his disposal to eliminate or corrupt the watermark employing any kind of transformation. The only limit in the choice of transformation is the perceptual distortion constraint.

In the following section we study the general structure of a spatial-domain image watermarking system and we compare each component with its counterpart in a spread spectrum communication system, commenting the main analogies and differences.

4   Spatial-Domain Image Watermarking

4.1   Modulation

In the sequel we will use vector notation for the indices in two-dimensional signals, i.e. $x[n_1, n_2] = x[\boldsymbol{n}]$, where $\boldsymbol{n} = [n_1 n_2]^T$. Let $x[\boldsymbol{n}]$ be a $N_1 \times N_2$ discrete-space image. The watermark is added to $x[\boldsymbol{n}]$, which is unknown to the receiver, so the image plays the same role as additive noise in a communication system. However, in a communication link the addtive noise is usually Gaussian and stationary, whereas images $x[\boldsymbol{n}]$ are usually non-stationary and cannot be satisfactorily modeled by means of a general statistical model.

Let $s[\boldsymbol{n}]$ be the output of a two-dimensional pseudorandom sequence generator initialized to a state determined by the secret key (Fig. 2). Treating the key as a random variable, the output of the pseudorandom sequence generator can be modeled as a stochastic process. We will assume that this stochastic process may have arbitrary marginal distributions and autocorrelation function. An open field of study is the extension of algorithms for generation of pseudorandom sequences to the two-dimensional case. Let $W = [b_1 \cdots b_N] \in \{1, -1\}^N$ be a N-bit binary antipodal word encoding the hidden information. Let $\mathcal{S}_i, i = 1, \ldots, M$ be sets of pixel indices $\boldsymbol{n}$ defining a tiling on the $N_1 \times N_2$ image. The counterpart of this tiling in a classical spread spectrum modulation scheme is the grouping of several consecutive chips in each symbol period. Each message bit is now replicated in all the pixels of the corresponding tile, obtaining the binary antipodal two-dimensional sequence $b[\boldsymbol{n}] = b_i, \boldsymbol{n} \in \mathcal{S}_i$. This replication introduces the necessary redundancy to compensate for the low energy that the watermark will have, compared to the energy of the image in which it is immersed. This is in fact a means of providing spatial diversity to increase the robustness of the watermark. The addition of the spread spectrum signal should not perceptually distort

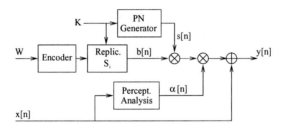

Fig. 2. *Modulator for a spatial-domain image watermarking system.*

the image. Properties of the human visual system such as spatial masking can be exploited to introduce imperceptible alterations in the luminance components. The original image is processed to obtain a perceptual mask $\alpha^2[\boldsymbol{n}]$ indicating the maximum allowable variance of the addtitive distortion at pixel $\boldsymbol{n}$. After modulation, the spread spectrum signal is shaped by $\alpha[\boldsymbol{n}]$ to guarantee that the perceptual constrains are fulfilled. As a consequence, the second order statistics of the watermark are space-variant. In communication systems, if interference produced by the transmitted signal in other receivers is not considered, additive noise and interferent signals do not impose a maximum power constraint since we are not considering noise and interference as useful information. However, in a watermarking scheme, noise (i.e. the original image) carries information that should not be noticeably distorted. This is another important difference with respect to classical spread spectrum schemes.

Summarizing, the discrete watermarked two-dimensional sequence can be expressed as

$$y[\boldsymbol{n}] = x[\boldsymbol{n}] + w[\boldsymbol{n}] \tag{11}$$

where $w[\boldsymbol{n}] = b[\boldsymbol{n}]\alpha[\boldsymbol{n}]s[\boldsymbol{n}]$ is the watermark.

4.2 Preprocessing

In a spread spectrum communication system the receiver demodulates the received signal and the resulting signal is passed through a matched filter and a sampler. The matched filter maximizes the output signal-to-noise ratio when noise and interference are assumed to be white and Gaussian. In a watermarking system we can also employ as a preprocessing step the linear filter which maximizes the SNR (Fig. 3). This filter corresponds to the linear MSE estimator of $w[\boldsymbol{n}]$ given $y[\boldsymbol{n}]$, also called Wiener filter.

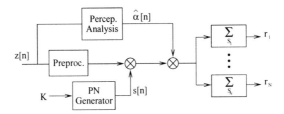

Fig. 3. *Demodulator for a spatial-domain image watermarking system.*

4.3 Demodulation

The output of the preprocessing filter is multiplied by a locally generated pseudorandom sequence $s[\boldsymbol{n}]$ and an estimate $\hat{\alpha}[\boldsymbol{n}]$ of the perceptual mask originally used by the modulator (Fig. 3). To generate the pseudorandom sequence, the secret key under test must be provided. For this reason the watermarking system we are studying is based on a symmetric key scheme. Furthermore, the locally generated pseudorandom sequence should be kept secret, since otherwise an attacker could use it to eliminate the watermark from the image under test or even from other images watermarked with the same key. This requirement is specially important if we want that any person can perform the watermark verification process. Therefore, the demodulator must be embedded in a secure unit. The perceptual mask $\hat{\alpha}[\boldsymbol{n}]$ must be computed from the watermarked image, since the original image is not available in the demodulator. Hence, there will be differences between $\hat{\alpha}[\boldsymbol{n}]$ and $\alpha[\boldsymbol{n}]$ that will result in a slight performance degradation. Fortunately, the estimate $\hat{\alpha}[\boldsymbol{n}]$ is fairly good since the watermarked image is perceptually indistinguishable from the original, so the performance degradation is negligible.

Then, the samples in each tile $\{\mathcal{S}_i\}, i = 1, \ldots, N$ are grouped together and summed up. This operation is commonly called despreading in spread spectrum communication systems and is equivalent to obtaining the inner product between the received sequence $z[\boldsymbol{n}]$ and each of the pseudorandom pulses $p_i[\boldsymbol{n}] \stackrel{\triangle}{=} \alpha[\boldsymbol{n}]s[\boldsymbol{n}], \boldsymbol{n} \in \mathcal{S}_i, i = 1, \ldots, N$. The inner products $r_i = \langle z[\boldsymbol{n}], p_i[\boldsymbol{n}] \rangle$ are sufficient statistics for detection when the additive noise is Gaussian. For this reason, this is the optimum demodulator structure in spread spectrum communication systems. In a watermarking system, however, the noise (the estimation error in the preprocessing step) is not Gaussian in general, so the inner products are not sufficient statistics. Nevertheless, the sufficient statistic assumption is a practical approximation since there is no simple statistical model for output noise in the preprocessing step.

The output of the demodulator can be analyzed statistically to obtain an equivalent channel model comprised of all the elements from the modulator to the demodulator. Under certain conditions the central limit theorem can be applied to approximate the equivalent channel by an additive Gaussian channel [11].

4.4 Interleaving

Interleaving is used in spread spectrum communication systems to get independent chip contributions separated in time. These contributions provide time diversity that can help to improve the resilience against channel variability. A similar approach can be followed in a watermarking system. In this case channel variability is related to the non-stationarity of common images, which results in the variability of the admissible watermark variance and the preprocessing output noise at each pixel. If pixels in the tiling are reordered in such a way that pixels modulated by each information bit are scattered over the whole image, then the resulting spatial diversity can be used to improve the performance of the watermark detector and decoder.

Interleaving drastically improves the resilience against cropping. The cropping attack can actually be seen as an extreme case of variable channel which completely destroys certain pixels and keeps unchanged the rest. For this reason the spatial diversity provided by the interleaving process helps to recover all information bits from the unaltered portion of the image. All the information bits will loose on average the same number of pixels if the watermarked image is cropped whereas without interleaving the effect of a cropping attack is greater for those bits located at the removed area of the image. As a consequence, the SNR at the output of the demodulator is more homogeneous with interleaving if the image is cropped, and this is beneficial for the design of channel codes for information hiding and tests for detection and decoding.

Furthermore, if the reordering performed by the interleaver is different for each key, an additional level of security is provided since the uncertainty about the spatial location of pixels modulated by each information bit avoids attacks concentrated on specific bits of the hidden message.

4.5 Watermark Detection

In the watermark detection test we decide whether a given image $z[n]$ has been watermarked with certain key. As we stated in section 4.3, even though some information is lost since the pdf of the noise at the demodulator output is not

Gaussian in general, we will consider for simplicity that the inner products $r_1, \ldots, r_N$ as sufficient statistics for this test. In terms of the equivalent vector channel also defined in section 4.3, the watermark detection test can be seen as a binary hypothesis test in which we have to decide whether any codeword in the code corresponding to the given secret key is "present" in the vector $r = [r_1, \ldots, r_N]$ (Fig. 4). The equivalent of the watermark detection test in a DS

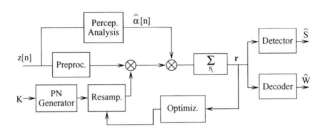

Fig. 4. *Demodulator with synchronization algorithm, watermark detector and watermark decoder.*

spread spectrum communication system is a test in which we decide whether a signal modulated using certain spreading code is present in the received signal. In practical systems such a test is usually not considered.

In the context of DS spread spectrum watermarking of images, the probability of false alarm P_F is defined as the probability of an arbitrary image yielding a decision $\hat{S} = 1$ in the watermark detection test. In other words, it can be defined as the probability of getting a decision $\hat{S} = 1$ when the output of the demodulator is noise. The probability of detection P_D is defined as the probability of deciding $\hat{S} = 1$ when the image has been watermarked with the key under test. In other words, P_D is the probability of deciding $\hat{S} = 1$ when the output of the demodulator contains one of the codewords for the secret key under test plus noise.

Due to the lack of good statistical models for common images, it is interesting to consider the probabilities P_F and P_D conditioned to a given original image. Given a fixed image $x[n]$ and assuming that all the keys are equiprobable, these probilities are the percentages of keys for which $\hat{S} = 1$ is decided when $x[n]$ is not watermarked (P_F) and when $x[n]$ is watermarked using the same key (P_D). Note that the probabilities P_F and P_D defined in section 2.4 can be obtained by averaging out the conditioned probabilities over the set of possible original images.

The performance in terms of the conditioned P_F and P_D is determined by several factors. First, the original image appears as noise at the demodulator output since we assumed that the original image is not available in the verification process. In addition, The perceptual analysis of the original image determines the maximum allowable watermark energy for a certain visibility level. Therefore, the original image itself imposes a limit to the maximum SNR that can be achieved at the output of the demodulator and that determines the performance of the watermark detector. Accidental distortions and intentional attacks (Sect. 4.8) degrade the performance of the detector. However, the distortion introduced by these alterations is limited since otherwise the resulting image would be useless. Therefore, we can define for a given detector structure and a given original image $x[n]$ the worst case probabilities P_F and P_D which correspond to the worst-case admissible alteration.

In practice, the threshold should be adjusted to guarantee certain fixed probability of false alarm P_F. Then, the decision about S should be accompanied by an estimate of the worst-case P_D that can be expected for that threshold. This estimated P_D can be considered as a confidence level for the decision taken in the watermark detection test.

4.6   Watermark Decoding

If the watermark detection test yields a positive result, then we can proceed to decode the hidden information carried by the watermark (Fig. 4). If the Gaussian approximation for the pdf of the demodulator output is assumed (Sect. 4.3), the optimum ML decoder takes the vector formed by the inner products $r = [r_1, \ldots, r_N]$ (Sect. 4.3) and chooses the closest codeword in the Euclidean distance sense. The optimum structure requires soft decoding, which in some coding schemes can be difficult to implement (e.g. block codes). In these situations a detector structure based on a hard decisor followed by a minimum Hamming distance decoder is a good alternative.

It is useful to analyze the performance of the watermark decoder in terms of the probability of error conditioned to a given original image [11]. If all the keys are assumed to be equiprobable, then this performance measure indicates the percentage of keys for which a decoding error occurs when they are applied to watermark certain fixed original image. Note that the probability of error as defined in section 2.3 can be obtained by averaging out the conditioned probability of error over the set of possible original images, though in practice it is extremely difficult due to the lack of good statistical models for common images.

As we discussed in section 2.8, we can apply the concept of channel capacity to the context of information hiding. If we fix a given original image and a detector structure and measure the performance in terms of the probability of decoding error conditioned to that image, then we can define a capacity function $C(x[n], P_e)$ indicating the maximum number of information bits that can be hidden in a given image $x[n]$ with conditioned probability of error at most P_e. Note that $C(x[n], P_e)$ is a non-decreasing function of P_e. The capacity function actually depends on several factors. First, the greater the admissible watermark variance obtained in the perceptual analysis of $x[n]$, the better the capacity function. The energy of the original image itself also determines the variance of the preprocessing output noise and, therefore, the probability of error (recall that the original image is not available in the receiver). Finally, accidental distortions and intentioned attacks degrade the performance of the hidden information decoder, resulting in a degradation of the capacity function. Since alterations are limited to those producing perceptually acceptable distortion, it is possible to define a worst-case capacity function corresponding to a the worst-case attack designed for a given detector structure. Therefore, the optimum robust detector structure is that achieving the best possible worst-case capacity function.

4.7   Synchronization

In the description of the decoding process we have assumed that the the locally generated pseudorandom sequence was perfectly synchronized to that used to watermark the image. However, there are both accidental and intentioned alterations which can alter the spatial geometry of the watermark. For instance, printing and subsequent scanning may accidentally scale, rotate or crop the watermarked image. As an example of deliberate manipulations, an opponent may resample the watermarked image with a geometrically transformed sampling grid to induce errors in the watermark detection test (Sect. 4.8). As a consequence of these alterations, there is uncertainty in the demodulator about the exact configuration of the sampling grid originally used to generate the watermark. A similar situation appears in DS spread spectrum systems since the receiver has no information about the instant at which the pseudorandom sequence begins.

Synchronization of the pseudorandom sequence is usually performed in two phases in spread spectrum communication systems. First, in the acquisition phase, a rough estimate of the sampling instant corresponding to the first chip of the pseudo random sequence is obtained. Then, in the tracking phase, a closed-loop tracking technique is employed to refine the accuracy of the sampling phase estimate. Similarly, in a watermarking system the synchronization can be implemented as a two-step process. In the first step, the space in which the sampling grid parameters are defined can be discretized and a brute force search algorithm can be employed to decide one of the points in the resulting discrete set. The decision taken can be considered a coarse estimate of the sampling grid parameters. In the second step, called fine acquisition phase, an iterative algorithm can be used to refine the estimate. Both steps can be based on the optimization of a function such as the maximum likelihood function for the binary hypothesis test [11] conditioned to each set of sample grid parameters. This function is intimately related to the autocorrelation function of the pseudorandom sequence. Therefore, the different pseudorandom sequence generation schemes have a different impact on the synchronization algorithm. In Fig. 4 we can see the structure of a watermark verification unit including a synchronization algorithm. The coarse acquisition is performed to guarantee the convergence of the iterative algorithm employed in the fine acquisition phase since this kind of algorithms usually require a search starting point sufficiently close to the solution. If the pseudorandom sequence is white, the peak in the autocorrelation function is very narrow and as consequence the coarse acquisition phase will be computationally expensive since a huge amount of points in the search space must be examined.

However, if some redundancy is introduced in the generation of the pseudorandom sequence so that the autocorrelation function is smoother, then the number of points tested during the coarse acquisition phase can be considerably reduced, and furthermore, the efficiency of the iterative algorithm in the fine acquisition phase can be improved. However, adding redundancy to the pseudorandom sequence reduces the uncertainty when the secret key is not known and, hence, the cryptographic security (Sect. 2.6) decreases. Therefore, there is a tradeoff between efficiency of the synchronization algorithm and cryptographic security.

Spatial synchronization and watermark detection can be combined in the same algorithm. For instance, it is possible to first estimate the possibly used sampling grid and then decide whether the image has been watermarked with it. An example of this combined approach is the maximization of the maximum likelihood function corresponding to the binary hypothesis test over the space of sampling grid parameters [11].

4.8   Attacks

Additive Noise An obvious attack the opponent may try is adding imperceptible noise to degrade the performance of the watermark detection and decoding tests. For this purpose, the attacker can perform a perceptual analysis of the watermarked image, determine the maximum allowable noise variance at each pixel to guarantee invisibility and add a two-dimensional white Gaussian noise sequence shaped to meet this maximum variance requirement. The choice of a white Gaussian process is justified since it achieves maximum entropy under a maximum variance constraint and, therefore, it introduces the maximum possible uncertainty in the decoder. Therefore, additive Gaussian noise corresponds to the worst case channel $p_{Z|Y}$ within the family of additive noise channels.

Linear Filtering If the objective of the attacker is to eliminate the copyright information to destroy any evidence regarding the true authorship of the image, a more intelligent attack consists in substracting from the watermarked image an estimate of the watermark, or equivalently, in obtaining an estimate of the original image. He could, for instance, low-pass filter the watermarked image to eliminate the high-frequency components of the watermark. However, a low pass filter smooths out the image and can introduce severe distortion in areas with complex textures.

A more effective technique consists in substracting a MSE linear estimate of the watermark from the watermarked image, or equivalently, obtaining a minimum MSE linear estimate of the original image [11]. This linear estimate can be implemented as an adaptive Wiener filter, commonly used for image restoration [12].

Resampling The opponent can also resample the watermarked image applying a geometrical transformation to the sampling grid. Let $h[n]$ be the combination of the reconstruction and antialiasing filters employed for interpolation and alias-free resampling. Then, we can define the continuous-space two-dimensional signal

$$y(t) = \sum_n y[n]h(t - Tn) \tag{12}$$

where $T \triangleq \begin{bmatrix} T_1 & 0 \\ 0 & T_2 \end{bmatrix}$ defines the original sampling grid in terms of the sampling period for each dimension. The attacker can change the sampling grid by multiplying T by an invertible matrix A and introducing an offset vector θ. If we denote $T' \triangleq AT$, then the resampled signal can be expressed as

$$z[n] = y(T'n + \theta) = \sum_m y[m]h(T'n + \theta - Tm). \tag{13}$$

This attack is equivalent to changing the chip rate and the chip timing phase in a spread spectrum system, with additional complexity due to the two-dimensional nature of the sampling process in images. If the pseudorandom sequence is white the resampling attack is very effective since a small mismatch in the sampling grid will produce a drastical reduction in the mean values of the inner products defined in section 4.3. In other words, resampling can easily degrade the SNR at the output of the demodulator. The structure of the receiver can be modified to include a synchronization algorithm for the estimation of the sampling grid parameters (Sect. 4.7).

Cropping We have already commented in section 4.4 that the watermarked image may be cropped by an attacker to eliminate part of the energy of the watermark. This attack can be seen as a variable communication channel in which certain chips (most of them consecutive) are completely lost (e.g. received as zero-amplitude) while the rest remain unaltered (Sect. 4.8). Spatial diversity improves the performance of a communication system in which information is passed through a space-variant channel. Therefore, spatial diversity provided by interleaving helps to improve the resilience against cropping attacks (Sect. 4.4). The cropping attack can also be compared to an impulsive jamming attack similar to the one discussed in [13] since the pixels destroyed by cropping are contiguous and have in a way a rather periodic structure.

Fortunately, there exists a limit to the amount of watermark energy that in practice can be lost since the attacker will never be interested in destroying visual information relevant for a potential user of the manipulated image. This fact is related to the discussion in section 2.5 about the perceptual distortion constraint on possible manipulations by opponents. For instance, if the perceptual analysis is based on the spatial masking properties of the human visual system, the watermark will have more energy in places where the original image presents luminance edges. These edges usually belong to relevant portions of the image, and they will be preserved in cropping attacks.

A cropping attack also introduces uncertainty about the spatial location of the modulation pulses, so it can also be seen as an attack directed against the synchronization algorithm and, as a consequence, to the watermark detection test. The effect of a cropping attack can be modeled mathematically, besides the loss of data, as an integer offset $\boldsymbol{\theta} = \boldsymbol{Tk}$ in equation (13), where $\boldsymbol{k}$ is a vector with integer elements.

5   Conclusions and Further Work

In this paper we have proposed a general model of a watermarking system suitable for an information-theoretical analysis of the main issues appearing in watermarking of arbitrary source outputs. The main elements have been described and different performance measures have been defined and discussed. Then, a spatial-domain image watermarking system has been presented as a particular case of the general model. The main components of this system have been described and issues related to practical implementations have been discussed.

In future work we will apply the concepts defined in this paper to other watermarking schemes for images, such as DCT-based watermarking, or other sources, such as audio and video. It is also left as a future research line the design of authentication schemes admitting a certain level of distortion.

References

1. M. D. Swanson, B. Zhu, and A. H. Tewfik, "Robust data hiding for images," in *Proc. IEEE Digital Signal Processing Workshop*, (Loen, Norway), pp. 37–40, September 1996.
2. F. Hartung and B. Girod, "Digital watermarking of raw and compressed video," in *Digital Compression Technologies and Systems for Video Communications* (N. Ohta, ed.), vol. 2952, pp. 205–213, SPIE Proceedings Series, October 1996.
3. I. J. Cox, J. Kilian, T. Leighton, and T. Shamoon, "Secure spread spectrum watermarking for multimedia," Tech. Rep. 95-10, NEC Research Institute, Princeton, NJ, USA, 1995.
4. M. D. Swanson, B. Zhu, and A. H. Tewfik, "Transparent robust image watermarking," in *Proc. IEEE Int. Conf. on Image Processing*, vol. III, (Lausanne, Switzerland), pp. 211–214, September 1996.
5. F. M. Boland, J. J. K. O. Ruanaidh, and C. Dautzenberg, "Watermarking digital images for copyright protection," in *IEE International Conference on Image Processing and its Applications*, (Edinburgh), pp. 326–330, 1995.
6. G. J. Simmons, "Authentication theory / coding theory," in *Advances in Cryptology: Proceedings of CRYPTO84* (G. R. Blakley and D. Chaum, eds.), pp. 411–431, Springer Verlag, 1985.
7. G. J. Simmons, "A survey of information authentication," *Proc. IEEE*, vol. 76, pp. 603–620, May 1988.
8. C. E. Shannon, "Communication theory of secrecy systems," *Bell Syst. Tech J.*, vol. 28, pp. 565–715, October 1949.
9. R. Ahlswede and G. Dueck, "Identification via channels," *IEEE Trans. Inform. Theory*, vol. 35, pp. 15–29, January 1989.
10. T. S. Han and S. Verdú, "New results in the theory of identification via channels," *IEEE Trans. Inform. Theory*, vol. 38, pp. 14–25, January 1992.

11. J. R. Hernández, F. Pérez-González, J. M. Rodríguez, and G. Nieto, "Performance analysis of a 2d-multipulse amplitude modulation scheme for data hiding and watermarking of still images." to be published in IEEE J. Select. Areas Commun., April 1998.
12. J. S. Lim, *Two-Dimensional Signal and Image Processing.* Prentice-Hall, 1990.
13. D. R. Martin and P. L. McAdam, "Convolutional code performance with optimal jamming," in *Conf. Rec. Int. Conf. Commun.*, pp. 4.3.1–4.3.7, May 1980.

Continuous Steganographic Data Transmission Using Uncompressed Audio

Chr. Neubauer, J. Herre, and K. Brandenburg

Fraunhofer Institut für Integrierte Schaltungen,
91058 Erlangen, Germany

Abstract. Today watermarking of still and moving images is a well-known technology enabling proof of authorship for the watermarked data. Similarly, there is a large interest in watermarking of audio data. Since the human auditory system is very sensitive to signal modifications, fairly elaborated schemes are required in order to perfectly/imperceptibly hide embedded data.

This paper describes how to transmit continuous data using uncompressed audio as cover data. Rather than just embedding a signature into the audio data with a watermark, a generally usable channel is provided in which any data – cryptographic or not – can be transmitted.

The paper includes a description of the transmission system, quantitative evaluations of achieved bit error rates and perceptibility tests using well-known audio quality measurements such as PAQM (Perceptual Audio Quality Measurement), NMR (Noise-to-Mask Ratio) and the ITU TG 10/4 perceptual measurement system.

1   Introduction

Today, large amounts of multimedia data are available to everyone and can easily be accessed e.g. via the Internet, digital broadcasting of radio and TV programs or – soon to come – satellite communication channels for the home user. Since all these channels provide content in a digital format, everyone is able to duplicate received data without loss of quality and without asking for permission to do so. This is often referred to as the *digital world's copying problem*.

A well-known concept for dealing with this problem is the so-called digital watermarking approach. A watermark is added to a multimedia content by embedding an imperceptible signature into the multimedia data (cover data). While this approach cannot prevent persons from copying the multimedia data itself, it offers a means to prove ownership of intellectual property rights for a piece of digital data (content). Furthermore, illegal copies can be traced back to the licensed user (traitor tracing) [1].

Currently, watermarking techniques are already employed extensively in the domain of still and moving images [2]. For audio signals, there is a large interest in watermarking techniques which is further stimulated by the rapid progress in audio compression technology over the recent years. Today, powerful compression algorithms, such as ISO/MPEG Audio *Layer-3* [3,4] or ISO/MPEG-2

David Aucsmith (Ed.): Information Hiding 1998, LNCS 1525, pp. 208–217, 1998.

Advanced Audio Coding (AAC) [5,6], allow the distribution (and duplication) of high-quality audio data at very low data rates like 48 kbit/s/channel. However, since the human auditory system is very sensitive to signal modifications, fairly elaborated schemes are required in order to perfectly/imperceptibly hide embedded data. This might be the reason why watermarking of audio signal is still an emerging technology compared to watermarking of images.

In this paper we present a watermarking scheme for digital uncompressed audio data with continuous data transmission. Our approach is an extension of a concept proposed in [7]. In particular, not only watermarking of the cover data is performed, but a stream of additional information can be carried within the cover data.

Furthermore, a quantitative evaluation of the performance of the proposed scheme is presented which is characterized by the trade-off between the three fundamental parameters, namely steganographic data transmission rate, bit error rate and subjective audio quality. Since the latter aspect plays an important role for the acceptance and usability of such a technique, objective perceptual measurement results will be given to show that imperceptible steganographic data transmission is possible at the given data rates and bit error rates.

2   Encoder

The encoder is shown in Fig. 1. It consists of the three main components *Modulation*, *Signal Conditioning* and *I/O* which will be described subsequently.

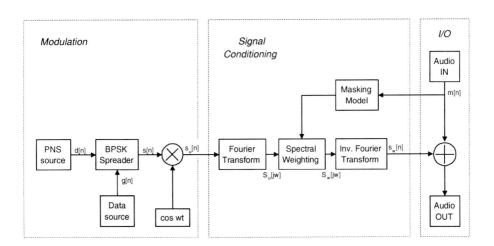

Fig. 1. Block diagram of the encoder.

2.1   Modulation

The modulation block consists of of five parts

- Pseudo Noise Sequence (PNS) source
- Data source
- BPSK Spreader
- Multiplier
- Local oscillator.

Together they form a Direct Sequence Spread-Spectrum (DS-SS) Binary Phase Shift Keying (BPSK) modulator [8,9,10].

From a user's view, the most important component is the data source. It produces a bit stream, $g[n]$, that is to be transmitted by the system. At this point any kind of information can be fed into the encoder. Thus it is possible to transmit various kinds of data such as copyright information, serial number, context related information and, of course, watermarking information. The symbol duration is denoted by T_{symb}.

Direct sequence spread-spectrum systems spread the bandwidth of the information signal, $g[n]$, by a large factor called processing gain G_p. The processing gain is determined by

$$G_p = \frac{W_{ss}}{R} \tag{1}$$

where W_{ss} is the spread-spectrum bandwidth and $R = 1/T_{symb}$ is the rate of the data signal. W_{ss} is determined by the rate of the so-called spreading sequence, $d[n]$. The transmission duration of one bit of $d[n]$ is $T_c \approx 1/W_{ss}$.

If $d[n]$ and $g[n]$ are antipodal, the spreading process inside the *BPSK Spreader* can easily be implemented by a simple multiplication of both signals. Thus the transmitted signal, $s[n]$, is described by

$$s[n] = g[n]d[n] \ . \tag{2}$$

The purpose of this spreading operation is to become resistant against interferers which could corrupt the transmitted data. In our case, the interferer is the audio signal which commonly exceeds the transmitted data signal, $s[n]$, by 10-20 dB in terms of energy. In order to obtain a satisfactory reconstruction of $g[n]$ in the decoder the spread-spectrum system has to provide sufficient processing gain. The proposed system currently works with a processing gain of

$$10\log(127) = 21.03 \ \text{dB} \tag{3}$$

Thus the rate of the $g[n]$ is 127 times smaller than the rate of $d[n]$. Using $T_c = 1/6000$ s this results in a data bit rate of 47.2 bit/s.

For the generation of the pseudo noise sequence, $d[n]$, the reader is referred to [7,8,11]. As is known from literature, a bipolar length-N maximum length sequence (m-sequence) has the special periodic autocorrelation function

$$\Phi(j) = \begin{cases} N & : \ (j = 0) \\ -1 & : \ (1 < j \le N - 1) \end{cases} \tag{4}$$

This property is used to reconstruct $g[n]$ at the receiver end.

Finally $s[n]$ is up-converted by multiplying it with a cosine wave of $\omega = 2\pi6$kHz. This yields a spectral shift of $s[n]$ such that its maximum spectral contribution is located at 6 kHz.

2.2 Signal Conditioning

The main purpose of the encoders signal conditioning section is to shape the modulated data signal, $d[n]$, in a way that it is imperceptible to the human auditory system. Therefore the signal $s_u[n]$ is windowed with a Hann window and transformed by a 256 point discrete Fourier transform with an overlap of 50%. In the next step, the spectrum of the signal $s_u[n]$ is weighted spectrally in order to ensure proper masking of the watermarking signal to be embedded, $s_u[n]$. This weighting process is controlled by the masking model which is described next.

Masking Model The masking model used in our system has originally been developed for the AAC codec. It calculates the maximum permissible distortion energy which is still masked by the audio signal. This energy is called the (masking) threshold. A more detailed description of the threshold computation can be found in [5,6]. It includes the following basic steps:

1. shift next 128 input samples into FIFO buffer
2. window with Hann window, compute 256 point FFT
3. calculate energy and unpredictability measure for each threshold calculation partition
4. convolve partitioned energy and unpredictability weighted energy with spreading function
5. calculate tonality for each partition
6. calculate required Signal-to-Noise Ratio (SNR) for each partition
7. calculate energy threshold for each partition
8. calculate pre-echo control for each partition
9. calculate Signal-to-Mask Ratio (SMR) for each partition

At its output the masking model provides an estimate of the threshold energy for every threshold calculation partition. This energy is used by the weighting process.

Weighting Process At this stage, the masking threshold for the processed block is available from the masking model and a spectral representation, $S_u[j\omega]$, of $s_u[n]$ is available from the Fourier transform. Inside the weighting block the energy of $S_u[j\omega]$ is computed for every critical band. The weighting process itself is carried out by reducing the energy of $S_u[j\omega]$ for each critical band by the amount computed by the masking model. The spectrum of the weighted signal is denoted by $S_w[j\omega]$. This operation guarantees that no spectral part of $S_u[j\omega]$ will become perceptible when adding $s_w[n]$ to $m[n]$. Since the weighting is carried out in the frequency domain, an inverse Fourier transform is used to calculate the weighted time domain signal, $s_w[n]$.

Fig. 2 shows a sample of an original audio signal, $m[n]$, and the weighted data signal, $s_w[n]$, for a 1 second excerpt from a castanets recording. A comparison of both curves illustrates how closely the temporal structure of the weighted data signal is adapted to the structure of the original signal by the perceptual weighting process in order to ensure proper masking.

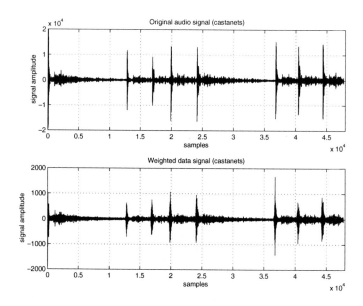

Fig. 2. Original audio and weighted data signal.

2.3   Audio Signal I/O

The audio input/output section reads the audio input data, $m[n]$, which is used as an input for the masking model. Furthermore, the input signal, $m[n]$, and the weighted signal $s_w[n]$ are added to form the encoded signal containing the embedded watermarking information.

3   Decoder

The decoder is shown in Fig. 3. It consists of a matched filter, a synchronizer, a sampling device, a threshold decision unit and, for the purpose of testing, a bit error measurement device. Its purpose is to recover $g[n]$ from the input signal of the decoder, $m[n] + s_w[n]$.

The matched filter is designed to match the m-sequence, $d[n]$, that was used for encoding. This is achieved by choosing the time reversed sequence, $d[N - n]$,

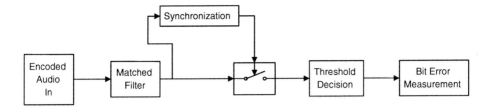

Fig. 3. Block diagram of the decoder.

as the coefficients of the filter. Due to the correlation property (4) of the m-sequence the filter shows one peak at its output during each time interval of T_{symb}. The decision unit will check the sign of the correlation peak and output 1 if positive and 0 otherwise. Fig. 4 shows an example for the output of the matched filter which clearly exhibits a positive peak around sample offset 105.

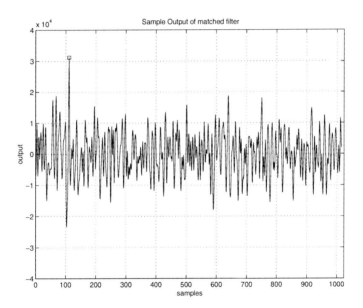

Fig. 4. Output of matched filter.

Special attention has to be paid to ensure a correct synchronization of the decoder which is particularly challenging in view of the low SNR provided by the masking model. In order to determine the sampling time instant at which the output of the matched filter should be tested, a histogram evaluation of the output magnitude of the matched filter is performed for successive time intervals of length T_{symb}. Thus, a clear peak will develop after a certain starting time indicating the correct sampling time instant within the data block.

4   Results

For the method to work as intended, the hidden data transmission must not have any influence on the quality of the audio signal. Ideally, no audible change of the audio signal is allowed for any test material. This condition is similar to the requirements for low bit rate audio coding schemes. As in the case of audio compression, large scale listening tests are necessary to verify the absence of audible artifacts. Since there was no possibility to conduct such tests, we used objective perceptual measurement methods to evaluate an estimate of the signal degradation. We selected four test items which are well-known critical items for the testing of perceptual coders and another, longer item to establish the stability of the system. The test items are

- Harpsichord (single instrument, EBU SQAM)
- Castanets (single instrument, EBU SQAM)
- German Speech (EBU SQAM)
- Bagpipes (BBC recording)
- Gershwin (longer item)

We present results for both the fidelity of the signal reproduction (absence of artifacts) and the quality of the communications channel. Both should be looked at in conjunction.

Another required property of hidden data transmission systems is the robustness under heavy processing of the signal including low bit rate coding or destructive attack (trying to get rid of the hidden data). While work on these issues is progressing, there are no results available at the moment.

4.1   Perceptual Distortion

To specify the perceptual distortion introduced by the steganographic message we employed three perceptual measurement methods. We selected Perceptual Audio Quality Measurement (PAQM), Noise-to-Mask Ratio (NMR) and the current version of the EQ (Evaluation of Quality) system under development for standardization in the ITU-R TG 10/4 [12]. Detailed descriptions of PAQM and NMR can be found in the references [13,14]. The following comments describe the output scales of the different measurement methods.

- PAQM derives an estimate of the signals on the cochlea and compares the representation of the reference signal with that of the signal under test. The weighted difference of these representations is mapped to the five-grade impairment scale as used in the testing of speech and audio coders. Table 1 shows this Subjective Grades (SG) scale.

Table 1. Five-grade impairment scales used in listening tests.

SG	Description	SDG	Description
5.0	imperceptible	0.0	imperceptible
4.0	perceptible, but not annoying	-1.0	perceptible, but not annoying
3.0	slightly annoying	-2.0	slightly annoying
2.0	annoying	-3.0	annoying
1.0	very annoying	-4.0	very annoying

In listening tests for very high quality signals, the test subjects sometimes confuse coded and original signal and grade the original signal below a SG of 5.0. Therefore the difference between the grades for the original signal and the signal under test is used as a normalized output value for the result of the listening test. Table 1 also lists the corresponding Subjective Diff-Grades (SDG).

- In the development of a standardized perceptual measurement scheme in ITU TG10/4, the task is to faithfully estimate the SDGs of real world listening tests. Correspondingly, the output value of the EQ measurement scheme is called ODG for Objective Diff-Grades.
- The third system used in the evaluations is the NMR. We used the overall NMR_{total} value expressed in dB to indicate the averaged energy ratio of the difference signal with respect to a just masked signal (masking threshold). Usually, at NMR_{total} values below -10 dB there is no audible difference between the processed and the original signal.

Table 2 lists the results of all three perceptual measurement techniques for the five test items. While there are some differences, the basic tendencies of all three measurements coincide. According to the table, there might be small audible artifacts only for two of the test signals, Harpsichord and Bagpipes.

These perceptual measurement results need some calibration with known artifacts. For this purpose, the four short test items have been subjected to coding/decoding with MPEG-2 AAC at a bit rate of 64 kbit/s for a mono signal. Table 3 lists the results for the three perceptual measurement methods. From earlier listening tests it is known that with AAC at 64 kbit/s mono all four items exhibit some small audible degradation of the signal. In the listening tests, only Castanets and German Speech were graded in the "perceptible, but not annoying" to "slightly annoying" range whereas the other items were graded between "imperceptible" and "perceptible, but not annoying"

The conclusion of these results is that, while exhibiting already a very good quality, more work is necessary to accomplish a truly inaudible transmission of the hidden data. More evaluations, including listening tests, are necessary to verify the results.

Table 2. Results of perceptual measurements.

Track	Duration [s]	PAQM/MOS	EQ/ODG	NMR_{total} [dB]
Harpsichord	13.21	4.36	-1.43	-13.33
Castanets	14.81	4.59	-0.85	-15.69
German Speech	16.62	4.72	-0.33	-16.35
Bagpipes	23.89	3.27	-1.87	-12.95
Gershwin	187.05	4.62	-0.84	-13.20

Table 3. Results of coding with the AAC codec at 64kbit/s.

Track	Duration [s]	PAQM/MOS	EQ/ODG	NMR_{total} [dB]
Harpsichord	13.21	4.68	-1.24	-13.98
Castanets	14.81	3.09	-2.12	-12.72
German Speech	16.62	2.95	-2.34	-10.48
Bagpipes	23.89	4.68	-0.75	-13.64

4.2 Bit Error Rates

In Table 4 the achieved bit error rates are listed. From a digital communications point of view the results do not look too impressive. However, it should be kept in mind that the table below just lists the raw channel bit error rate of the steganographic data transmission which can be improved significantly by applying standard channel coding techniques, like e.g. convolutional coding.

Table 4. Results of raw channel bit error rate measurements.

Track	tot. bits	err. bits	bit error rate
Harpsichord	778	1	0.00128
Castanets	670	20	0.02985
German Speech	757	45	0.05944
Bagpipes	1102	21	0.01906
Gershwin	8808	642	0.07289

5   Conclusions

In this paper a system for continuous steganographic data transmission using audio signals as cover data has been described. The encoder uses a direct sequence spread-spectrum modulation. The digitally modulated signal is then weighted with energy levels provided by a masking model. The sum of weighted signal and original signal is the encoded signal. Using a correlation decoder the steganographic data can be recovered. The basic function of the system was demonstrated by measuring bit error rates and the degradation of the audio quality via perceptual measurement schemes. Future work will include investigations about the robustness of the transmission and the application of error correction coding to improve the bit error rates.

References

1. B. Pfitzmann: *Trials of Traced Traitors*, Information Hiding, Ed. R. Anderson, Springer LLNCS 1174, 1996
2. I. Cox, J. Kilian: *A Secure Robust Watermark for Multimedia*, Information Hiding, Ed. R. Anderson, Springer LLNCS 1174, 1996
3. ISO/IEC JTC1/SC29/WG11 MPEG, International Standard IS 11172-3 *Coding of moving pictures and associated audio for digital storage media at up to about 1.5 Mb/s, Part 3: Audio*
4. K. Brandenburg, G. Stoll, G. Dehery, Y.-F. Johnston, J.D. v.d. Kerkhof, L. Schroeder, E.F., 1994, *The ISO/MPEG-1 Audio Codec: A Generic Standard for Coding High Quality Digital Audio*, JAES, Vol. 42, pp. 780–792
5. M. Bosi, K. Brandenburg, S. Quackenbush, K. Akagiri, H. Fuchs, J. Herre, L. Fielder, M. Dietz, Y. Oikawa, G. Davidson: *ISO/IEC MPEG-2 Advanced Audio Coding*, JAES, Vol. 45, No. 8
6. ISO/IEC JTC1/SC29/WG11 N1650, April 1997, *IS 13818-7 (MPEG-2 Advanced Audio Coding, AAC)*
7. L. Boney, A. Tewfik, K. Hamdy: *Digital Watermarks for Audio Signals*, IEEE Int. Conf. Multimedia, June 17-23, pp. 473–480, 1996
8. B. Sklar: *Digital Communications*, Prentice Hall, 1988
9. J.G. Proakis: *Digital Communications*, 3. Aufl., MacGraw-Hill, New York, 1995
10. K.D. Kammeyer: *Nachrichtenübertragung* , 2. Aufl., Teubner, Stuttgart, 1996
11. R. Dixon: *Spread Spectrum Systems*, 3rd. Ed., Wiley & Sons Inc., 1994
12. T. Sporer: *Evaluating Small Impairments with mean Opinion Scale–Reliable or just a guess*, AES 101st Convention, Los Angeles, 1996
13. J. Beerends, J. Stemerdink: *A Perceptual Audio Quality Measurement Based on a Psychoacoustic Sound Representation*, J. Audio Eng. Society, Vol. 40, No. 12, 1992 December, pp. 963–972
14. K. Brandenburg, T. Sporer: *NMR and Masking Flag: Evaluation of Quality using Perceptual Criteria*, Proc. of the 11th International AES Conference on Audio Test and Measurement, Portland 1992, pp. 169–179

Attacks on Copyright Marking Systems

Fabien A.P. Petitcolas *, Ross J. Anderson, and Markus G. Kuhn**

University of Cambridge, Computer Laboratory
Pembroke Street, Cambridge CB2 3QG, UK
{fapp2, rja14, mgk25}@cl.cam.ac.uk
http://www.cl.cam.ac.uk/Research/Security/

Abstract. In the last few years, a large number of schemes have been proposed for hiding copyright marks and other information in digital pictures, video, audio and other multimedia objects. We describe some contenders that have appeared in the research literature and in the field; we then present a number of attacks that enable the information hidden by them to be removed or otherwise rendered unusable.

1 Information Hiding Applications

The last few years have seen rapidly growing interest in ways to hide information in other information. A number of factors contributed to this. Fears that copyright would be eroded by the ease with which digital media could be copied led people to study ways of embedding hidden copyright marks and serial numbers in audio and video; concern that privacy would be eroded led to work on electronic cash, anonymous remailers, digital elections and techniques for making mobile computer users harder for third parties to trace; and there remain the traditional 'military' concerns about hiding one's own traffic while making it hard for the opponent to do likewise.

The first international workshop on information hiding [2] brought these communities together and a number of hiding schemes were presented there; more have been presented elsewhere. We formed the view that useful progress in steganography and copyright marking might come from trying to attack all these first generation schemes. In the related field of cryptology, progress was iterative: cryptographic algorithms were proposed, attacks on them were found, more algorithms were proposed, and so on. Eventually, theory emerged: fast correlation attacks on stream ciphers and differential and linear attacks on block ciphers, now help us understand the strength of cryptographic algorithms in much more detail than before. Similarly, many cryptographic protocols were proposed and almost all the early candidates were broken, leading to concepts of protocol robustness and techniques for formal verification [6].

So in this paper, we first describe the copyright protection context in which most recent schemes have been developed; we then describe a selection of these

---

* The first author is grateful to Intel Corporation for financial support under the grant 'Robustness of Information Hiding Systems'
** The third author is supported by a European Commission Marie-Curie grant

David Aucsmith (Ed.): Information Hiding 1998, LNCS 1525, pp. 218–238, 1998.

schemes and present a number of attacks, which break most of them. We finally make some remarks on the meaning of robustness in the context of steganography in general and copyright marking in particular.

1.1   Copyright Protection Issues

Digital recording media offer many new possibilities but their uptake has been hindered by widespread fears among intellectual property owners such as Hollywood and the rock music industry that their livelihoods would be threatened if users could make unlimited perfect copies of videos, music and multimedia works.

One of the first copy protection mechanisms for digital media was the serial copy management system (SCMS) introduced by Sony and Phillips for digital audio tapes in the eighties [31]. The idea was to allow consumers to make a digital audio tape of a CD they owned in order to use it (say) in their car, but not to make a tape of somebody else's tape; thus copies would be limited to first generation only. The implementation was to include a Boolean marker in the header of each audio object. Unfortunately this failed because the hardware produced by some manufacturers did not enforce it.

More recently the Digital Video Disk, also known as Digital Versatile Disk (DVD) consortium called for proposals for a copyright marking scheme to enforce serial copy management. The idea is that the DVD players sold to consumers will allow unlimited copying of home videos and time-shifted viewing of TV programmes, but cannot easily be abused for commercial piracy [19, 44]. The proposed implementation is that videos will be unmarked, or marked 'never copy', or 'copy once only'; compliant players would not record a video marked 'never copy' and when recording one marked 'copy once only' would change its mark to 'never copy'. Commercially sold videos would be marked 'never copy', while TV broadcasts and similar material would be marked 'copy once only' and home videos would be unmarked.

Electronic copyright management schemes have also been proposed by European projects such as Imprimatur and CITED [45, 66, 67], and American projects such as the proposed by the Working Group on Intellectual Property Rights [69].

1.2   Problems

Although these schemes might become predominant in areas where they can be imposed from the beginning (such as DVD and video-on-demand), they suffer from a number of drawbacks. Firstly, they rely on the tamper-resistance of consumer electronics – a notoriously unsolved problem [4]. The tamper-resistance mechanisms being built into DVD players are fairly rudimentary and the history of satellite TV piracy leads us to expect the appearance of 'rogue' players which will copy everything. Electronic copyright management schemes also conflict with applications such as digital libraries, where 'fair use' provisions are strongly entrenched. According to Samuelson, '*Tolerating some leakage may be in the long run of interest to publishers [...] For educational and research works, pay-per-use schemes may deter learning and deep scholarship'* [56]. A European legal expert put it even more strongly: that copyright laws are only tolerated because they are not enforced against the large numbers of petty offenders [32].

Similar issues are debated within the software industry; some people argue, for example, that a modest level of amateur software piracy actually enhances revenue because people may 'try out' software they have 'borrowed' from a friend and then go on to buy it (or the next update).

For all these reasons, we may expect leaks in the primary copyright protection mechanisms and wish to provide independent secondary mechanisms that can be used to trace and prove ownership of digital objects. It is here that marking techniques are expected to be most important.

2   Copyright Marks

There are two basic kinds of mark: fingerprints and watermarks. One may think of a fingerprint as an embedded serial number while a watermark is an embedded copyright message. The first enables us to trace offenders, while the second can provide some of the evidence needed to prosecute them. It may also, as in the DVD proposal, form part of the primary copy management system; but it will more often provide an independent back-up to a copy management system that uses overt mechanisms such as digital signatures.

In [7], we discussed the various applications of fingerprinting and watermarking, their interaction, and some related technologies. Here, we are concerned with the robustness of the underlying mechanisms. What sort of attacks are possible on marking schemes? What sort of resources are required to remove marks completely, or to alter them so that they are read incorrectly? What sort of effect do various possible removal techniques have on the perceptual quality of the resulting audio or video?

We will use the terminology agreed at the first international workshop on Information Hiding [52]. The information to be hidden (watermark, fingerprint, or in the general case of steganography, a secret message) is *embedded* in a *cover* object (a cover CD, a cover video, a cover text, etc.) giving a *stego* object, which in the context of copyright marking we may also call a *marked* object (CD, video, etc). The embedding is performed with the help of a *key*, a secret variable that is in general known to the object's owner. Recovery of the embedded mark may or may not require a key; if it does the key may be equal to, or derived from, the key used in the embedding process.

In the rest of this section, we will first discuss simple hiding methods and the obvious attacks on them. We will then present, as an example of the 'state of the art', robustness requirements that appeared in a recent music industry request for proposals [48]. We will then present the main contending techniques used in currently published and fielded systems. Attacks on these systems will then be presented.

2.1 Simple Hiding Methods

The simplest schemes replace all the bits in one or more of the less significant bit planes of an image or audio sample with the 'hidden' information [11, 23, 36, 65]. This is particularly easy with pictures: even when the four least significant bits of the cover image are replaced with the four most significant bits of the embedded image, the eye cannot usually tell the difference [36]. Audio is slightly harder, as the randomisation of even the least significant bit of 8-bit audio adds noise that is audible during quiet passages of music or pauses in speech. Nonetheless, several systems have been proposed: they include embedding, in the regular channels of an audio CD, another sound channel [24, 68] and a steganographic system in which secret messages are hidden in the digitised speech of an ISDN telephone conversation [23].

However, bit-plane replacement signals are not only easy to detect. They violate http://www.cl.cam.ac.uk/users/fapp2/kerckhoffs/ that the security of a protection system should not rely on its method of operation being unknown to the opponent, but rather on the choice of a secret key [33]. Better approaches use a key to select some subset of pixels or sound samples which then carry the mark.

An example of this approach is Chameleon [5], a system which enables a broadcaster to send a single ciphertext to a large population of users, each of which is supplied with a slightly different decryption key; the effect of this is to introduce a controlled number of least-significant-bit errors into the plaintext that each user decrypts. With uncompressed digital audio, the resulting noise is at an acceptably low level and then Chameleon has the advantage that the decrypted audio is fingerprinted automatically during decryption without any requirement that the consumer electronic device be tamper-resistant.

In general, schemes which use a key to choose some subset of least significant bits to tweak may provide acceptable levels of security in applications where the decrypted objects are unlikely to be tampered with. However, in many applications, a copyright pirate may be able and willing to perform significant filtering operations and these will destroy any watermark, fingerprint or other message hidden by simple bit tweaking. So we shall now consider what it means for a marking scheme to be robust.

2.2 Robustness Requirements

The basic problem is to embed a mark in the digital representation of an analogue object (such as a film or sound recording) in such a way that it will not reduce the perceived value of the object while being difficult for an unauthorised person to remove. A first pass at defining robustness in this context may be found in a recent request for proposals for audio marking technology from the International Federation for the Phonographic Industry, IFPI [48]. The goal of this exercise was to find a marking scheme that would generate evidence for anti-piracy operations, track the use of recordings by broadcasters and others and control copying. The IFPI robustness requirements are as follows:

- the marking mechanism should not affect the sonic quality of the sound recording;
- the marking information should be recoverable after a wide range of filtering and processing operations, including two successive D/A and A/D conversions, steady-state compression or expansion of 10%, compression techniques such as MPEG and multi-band nonlinear amplitude compression, adding additive or multiplicative noise, adding a second embedded signal using the same system, frequency response distortion of up to 15 dB as applied by bass, mid and treble controls, group delay distortions and notch filters;
- there should be no other way to remove or alter the embedded information without sufficient degradation of the sound quality as to render it unusable;
- given a signal-to-noise level of 20 dB or more, the embedded data channel should have a bandwidth of 20 bits per second, independent of the signal level and type (classical, pop, speech).

Similar requirements could be drawn up for marking still pictures, videos and multimedia objects in general. However, before rushing to do this, we will consider some systems recently proposed and show attacks on them that will significantly extend the range of distortions against which designers will have to provide defences, or greatly reduce the available bandwidth, or both.

2.3   General Techniques

We mentioned schemes that modify the least significant bits of digital media; by repeating such marks, or employing more robust encoding methods, we can counter some filtering attacks. We can also combine coding with various transform techniques (DCT, wavelet and so on).

The *Patchwork* algorithm [10], for instance, successively selects random pairs of pixels; it makes the brighter pixel brighter and the duller pixel duller and the contrast change in this pixel subset encodes one bit. To maintain reasonable robustness against filtering attacks, the bandwidth of such systems has to be limited to at most a few hundred bits per image [37, 38]. In a similar way, marks can be embedded in audio by increasing the amplitude contrast of many pairs of randomly chosen sound samples and using a suitable filter to minimise the introduction of high-frequency noise.

More sophisticated variants on this theme involve spread-spectrum techniques. Although these have been used since the mid-fifties in the military domain because of their anti-jamming and low-probability-of-intercept properties [59], their applicability to image watermarking has only been noticed recently by Tirkel *et al.* [64]. Since then a number of systems based on this technique have been proposed [65, 70, 71]: typically a maximal length sequence is added to the signal in the spatial domain and the watermark is detected by using the spatial cross-correlation of the sequence and the watermarked image.

Another kind of marking technique embeds the mark in a transform domain, typically one that is widely used by compression algorithms. Thus when marking sound one could add a pseudorandom sequence to the excitation signal in an LPC or CELP coded audio signal [43] and when marking an image one could use the DCT domain. Langelaar *et al.* remove certain high frequency DCT coefficients [38]; Cox *et al.* modulate the 1000 largest DCT coefficients of an image with a random vector [17]; Koch *et al.* change the quantisation of the DCT coefficients and modify some of them in such a way that a certain property (order in size) is verified [34]; while Ó Ruanaidh *et al.* modulate the DCT coefficient with a bi-directional coding [47].

Techniques of this kind are fairly robust against various kinds of signal processing and may be combined with exploitation of the perceptual masking properties of the human auditory system in [14, 15] and of the human vision system in [25, 62, 63]. The basic idea here is to amplify the mark wherever the changes will be less noticeable and also to embed it in the *perceptually significant* components of the signal [18]. Masking may also be used to avoid placing marks in places such as the large expanses of pure colour found in cartoons; the colour histogram of such images has sharp peaks, which are split into twin peaks by some naïve marking methods as the colour value c is replaced by $c - \delta$ and $c + \delta$, thus allowing the mark to be identified and removed [42].

3   Attacks

This leads us to the topic of attacks and here we present some quite general kinds of attack that destroy, or at least reveal significant limitations of, several marking schemes: PictureMarc 1.51 [22, 54], SysCoP [34, 72, 73], JK_PGS (EPFL algorithm, part of the European TALISMAN project), SureSign [61], EIKONA-mark [41, 53], Echo Hiding, and the NEC method [17]. We suspect that systems that use similar techniques are also vulnerable to our attacks.

3.1   The Jitter Attack

Our starting point in developing a systematic attack on marking technology was to consider audio marking schemes that tweak low order bits whose location is specified by a key. A simple and devastating attack on these schemes is to add jitter to the signal. In our first implementation, we split the signal into chunks of 500 samples, either duplicated or deleted a sample at random in each chunk (resulting in chunks of 499 or 501 samples long) and stuck the chunks back together. This turned out to be almost imperceptible after filtering, even in classical music; but the jitter prevents the marked bits from being located.

In a more sophisticated implementation, we resample these chunks at a lower or higher frequency. This relies on the properties of the ear's pitch resolution:

> In pitch perception experiments in the mid-audio frequency range, subjects are able to perceive changes in frequency of pure tones of approximately 0.1%. [...] At frequencies above 4 kHz pitch discrimination reduces substantially. [...] In the case of complex signals, such as speech, it is very much less clear what the capabilities and processes of the auditory system are. [...] There is evidence that peaks in the spectrum of

the audio signal are detected more easily than features between spectral peaks. *J.N. Holmes* [30]

If n_i is the number of samples in the ith chunk, n_i' the number of samples after resampling and α the maximum relative change of frequency allowed then, in the mid-audio range, we are roughly limited, for pure tones, by $|\Delta n_i| \leq \alpha n_i$ (because α is small), where $\Delta n_i := n_{i+1}' - n_i'$. This can be simplified as $0 < k \leq \frac{\alpha n}{2}$ when the n_i are equal and when the number k of removed or added samples is constant for each chunk. This is the approach we chose; it allowed us to introduce a long jitter. Then the strategy for choosing k and n depends on the input signal. With this technique we were able to tweak up to one sample in 50 of a 44 kHz sampled voice recording without any perceptible effect.

We also applied a similar attack to SysCoP Demo 1.0. In that case we simply deleted columns of pixels and duplicated others in order to preserve the image size. Fig. 1 gives an example of this attack.

Of course, there are much more subtle distortions that can be applied. For instance, in [27], Hamdy *et al.* present a way to increase or decrease the length of a music performance without changing the pitch; this was developed to enable radio broadcasters to slightly increase or decrease the playing time of a musical track. As such tools become widely available, attacks involving sound manipulation will become easy. Most simple spread-spectrum based techniques are subject to this kind of attacks. Indeed, although spread-spectrum signal are very robust to distortion of their amplitude and to noise addition, they do not survive timing errors: synchronisation of the chip signal is very important and simple systems fail to recover this synchronisation properly.

3.2   StirMark

Following this attack and after evaluating some watermarking software, it became clear that although many of the seriously proposed schemes could survive basic manipulations – that is, manipulations that can be done easily with standard tools, such as rotation, shearing, resampling, resizing and lossy compression – they would not cope with combinations of them. This motivated us to implement StirMark.

StirMark is a generic tool developed for simple robustness testing of image marking algorithms and other steganographic techniques. In its simplest version, StirMark simulates a resampling process, i.e. it introduces the same kind of errors into an image as printing it on a high quality printer and then scanning it again with a high quality scanner. It applies a minor geometric distortion: the image is slightly stretched, sheared, shifted and/or rotated by an unnoticeable random amount[1] (Fig. 2 – middle drawing) and then resampled using either bi-linear or

---

[1] If A, B, C and D are the corners of the image, a point M of the said image can be expressed as $M = \alpha[\beta A + (1 - \beta)D] + (1 - \alpha)[\beta B + (1 - \beta)C]$ where $0 \leq \alpha, \beta \leq 1$ are the coordinates of M relatively to the corners. The distortion is done by moving the corners by a small random amount in both directions. The new coordinates of M are given by the previous formula, keeping (α, β) constant.

(a)
bash$ imageread_demo watermarked.ppm

Key:

No certificate file.

────────────────────────────

A valid watermark found - estimated correction
percentage is : 100

Retrieved Secret Label (string) : SysCoP(TM)

(b)
bash$ imageread_demo jitter.ppm

Key:

No certificate file.

────────────────────────────

Cannon find valid watermark - failed.

Image jitter.ppm has been tampered or has not
been watermarked.

(c)

(d)

(e)

(f)

Fig. 1. A successful jitter attack on SysCoP. We used the demo software release 1.0 available on SysCoP's Web site [74]. (a) shows an image watermarked
with SysCoP and (b) the same image but after the attack. In the first case the
software detects the watermark correctly (c) but the check fails on the modified image (d). Here, the attack simply consists in deleting and duplicating some
columns of pixels such that the original size of the picture is conserved. (e) shows
the columns which have been deleted (-) and duplicated (+). Finally, (f) is a
magnified view of the white rectangle in (e); the bottom part corresponds to the
original image.

Nyquist interpolation. In addition, a transfer function that introduces a small and smoothly distributed error into all sample values is applied. This emulates the small non-linear analog/digital converter imperfection typically found in scanners and display devices. StirMark introduces a practically unnoticeable quality loss in the image if it is applied only once. However after a few iterated applications, the image degradation becomes noticeable.

With those simple geometrical distortions we could confuse most marking systems available on the market. More distortions – still unnoticeable – can be applied to a picture. We applied a global 'bending' to the image: in addition to the general bi-linear property explained previously a slight deviation is applied to each pixel, which is greatest at the center of the picture and almost null at the borders. On top of this a higher frequency displacement of the form $\lambda \sin(\omega_x x) \sin(\omega_y y) + n(x, y)$ – where n is a random number – is added. In order for these distortions to be most effective, a medium JPEG compression is applied at the end.

Fig. 2. We exaggerate here the distortion applied by StirMark to still pictures. The first drawing corresponds to the original picture; the others show the picture after StirMark has been applied – without and with bending and randomisation.

For those unfamiliar with digital image signal processing we shall now summarise briefly the main computation steps. Apart from a few simple operations such as rotations by 90 or 180 degrees, reflection and mirroring, image manipulation usually requires resampling when destination pixels do not line up with source pixels. In theory, one first generates a continuous image from the digital one, then modifies the continuous image, finally samples this to create a new digital image. In practice, however, we compute the inverse transform of a new pixel and evaluate the reconstruction function at that point.

There are numerous reconstruction filters. In a first version of the software we simply used a linear interpolation but, as foreseen, this tended to blur the image too much, making the validity of the watermark removal arguable. Then we implemented the sinc function as a reconstruction filter, which gives theoretically perfect reconstruction for photo images and can be described as follows. If (x, y) are the coordinates of the inverse transform – which, in our case is a distortion of the picture – of a point in the new image and f the function to be reconstructed, then, an estimate of f at (x, y) is given by $\hat{f}(x, y) = \sum_{i=-n}^{n} \sum_{j=-n}^{n} \text{sinc}(x - i)\text{sinc}(y - j)f_{i,j}$. This gives very much better results than the simple filter; an example of the removal of an NEC watermark is given in Fig. 3.

We suggest that image watermarking tools which do not survive StirMark – with default parameters – should be considered unacceptably easy to break. This immediately rules out the majority of commercial marking schemes.

(a)   (b)

Fig. 3. Kings' College Chapel, courtesy of John Thompson, JetPhotographic, Cambridge. For this example we watermarked a picture with NEC's algorithm [17]. We used the default parameters suggested by their paper ($N = 1000$ and $\alpha = 0.1$). (a) is the watermarked image. We then applied StirMark (b) and tested the presence of the watermark. The similarity between the original watermark and the extracted watermark was 3.74 instead of 21.08. This is well below the decision threshold.

One might try to increase the robustness of a watermarking system by trying to foresee the possible transforms used by pirates; one might then use techniques such as embedding multiple versions of the mark under suitable inverse transforms; for instance Ó Ruanaidh and Pereira suggest to use the Fourier-Mellin transform[2] to cope with rotation and scaling [55]. However, the general theme of the attacks we have developed and described above is that given a target marking scheme, we invent a distortion (or a combination of distortions) that will remove it or at least make it unreadable, while leaving the perceptual value of the previously marked object undiminished. We are not limited in this process to the distortions produced by common analogue equipment, or considered in the IFPI request for proposals cited above.

---

[2] The Fourier-Mellin transform is equivalent to the Fourier transform on a log-polar map: $(x, y) \rightarrow (\mu, \theta)$ with $x = e^{\mu} \cos \theta$ and $y = e^{\mu} \sin \theta$.

As an analogy, one might consider the 'chosen protocol attack' on authentication schemes [58]. It is an open question whether there is any marking scheme for which a chosen distortion attack cannot be found.

3.3   The Mosaic Attack

This point is emphasised by a 'presentation' attack, which is of quite general applicability and which possesses the initially remarkable property that a marked image can be unmarked and yet still rendered pixel for pixel in exactly the same way as the marked image by a standard browser.

The attack was motivated by a fielded automatic system for copyright piracy detection, consisting of a watermarking scheme plus a web crawler that downloads pictures from the net and checks whether they contain a watermark.

It consists of chopping an image up into a number of smaller subimages, which are embedded in a suitable sequence in a web page. Common web browsers render juxtaposed subimages stuck together, so they appear identical to the original image (Fig. 4). This attack appears to be quite general; all marking

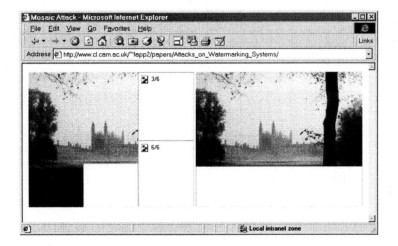

Fig. 4. Screen-shot of a web browser while downloading an image after the *mosaic attack*. This attack chops a watermarked image into smaller images which are stuck back together when the browser renders the page. We implemented software (2Mosaic) that reads a JPEG picture and produces a corresponding mosaic of small JPEG images as well as the necessary HTML code automatically [51]. In some cases downloading the mosaic is even faster than downloading the full image! In this example we used a 350×280-pixel image watermarked using PictureMarc 1.51.

schemes require the marked image to have some minimal size (one cannot hide a meaningful mark in just one pixel). Thus by splitting an image into sufficiently small pieces, the mark detector will be confused [51]. The best that one can hope for is that the minimal size could be quite small and the method might therefore not be very practical.

There are other problems with such 'crawlers'. Java applets, ActiveX controls, etc. can be embedded to display a picture inside the browser; the applet could even de-scramble the picture in real time. Defeating such techniques would entail rendering the web page, detecting pictures and checking whether they contain a mark. An even more serious problem is that much current piracy is of pictures sold via many small services, from which the crawler would have to purchase them using a credit card before it could examine them. A crawler that provided such 'guaranteed sales' would obviously become a target.

3.4   Attack on *Echo Hiding*

One of the few marking schemes to be robust against the jitter attack is echo hiding, which hides information in sound by introducing echoes with very short delays. *Echo hiding* [26] relies on the fact that we cannot perceive short echoes (say 1 ms) and embeds data into a cover audio signal by introducing an echo characterised by its delay τ and its relative amplitude α. By using two types of echo it is possible to encode ones and zeros. For this purpose the original signal is divided into chunks separated by spaces of pseudo-random length; each of these chunks will contain one bit of information.

The echo delays are chosen between 0.5 and 2 milliseconds and the best relative amplitude of the echo is around 0.8. According to its creators, decoding involves detecting the initial delay and the auto-correlation of the cepstrum of the encoded signal is used for this purpose.

The 'obvious' attack on this scheme is to detect the echo and then remove it by simply inverting the convolution formula; the problem is to detect the echo without knowledge of either the original object or the echo parameters. This is known as 'blind echo cancellation' in the signal processing literature and is known to be a hard problem in general.

We tried several methods to remove the echo. Frequency invariant filtering [49, 57] was not very successful. Instead we used a combination of cepstrum analysis and 'brute force' search.

The underlying idea of cepstrum analysis is presented in [13]. Suppose that we are given a signal $y(t)$ which contains a simple single echo, i.e. $y(t) = x(t) + \alpha x(t - \tau)$. If we note Φ_{xx} the power spectrum of x then $\Phi_{yy}(f) = \Phi_{xx}(f)[1 + 2\alpha \cos(2\pi f \tau) + \alpha^2]$ whose logarithm is approximately $\log \Phi_{yy}(f) \approx \log \Phi_{xx}(f) + 2\alpha \cos(2\pi f \tau)$. This is a function of the frequency f and taking its power spectrum raises its 'quefrency' τ, that is the frequency of $\cos(2\pi \tau f)$. The auto-covariance of this later function emphasises the peak that appears at 'quefrency' τ (Fig. 5).

To remove the echos, we need a method to detect the echo delay τ. For this, we used a slightly modified version of the cepstrum: $C \circ \Phi \circ \ln \circ \Phi$ where C is the auto-covariance function[3], Φ the power spectrum density function and $\circ$ the

---

[3] $C(x) = E[(x - \overline{x})(x - \overline{x})^*]$.

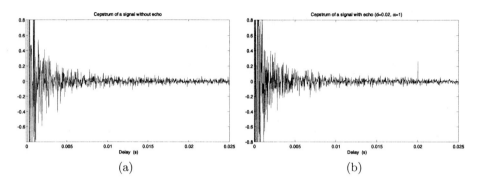

Fig. 5. Graph (a) represents the cepstrum of a signal without echo. Graph (b) is the cepstrum of the same signal with a 20 ms echo which is emphasised by the very clear peak at 0.02 s.

composition operator. Experiments on random signals as well as on music show that this method returns quite accurate estimators of the delay (Fig. 6) when an artificial echo has been added to the signal. In the detection function we only consider echo delays between 0.5 and 3 milliseconds. Below 0.5 ms the function does not work properly and above 3 ms the echo becomes too audible.

Our first attack was to remove an echo with random relative amplitude, expecting that this would introduce enough modification in the signal to prevent watermark recovery. Since echo hiding gives best results for α greater than 0.7 we could use $\tilde{\alpha}$ – an estimation of α – drawn from, say a normal distribution centred on 0.8. It was not really successful so our next attack was to iterate: we re-apply the detection function and vary $\tilde{\alpha}$ to minimise the residual echo. We could obtain successively better estimators of the echo parameters and then remove this echo. When the detection function cannot detect any more echo, we have got the correct value of $\tilde{\alpha}$ (as this gives the lowest output value of the detection function). Results obtained using this algorithm are presented in Fig. 6.

3.5　Protocol Considerations

The main threat addressed in the literature is an attack by a pirate who tries to remove the watermark directly. As a consequence, the definition commonly used for robustness includes only resistance to signal manipulation (cropping, scaling, resampling, etc.). Craver *et al.* show that this is not enough by exhibiting a 'protocol' level attack [20].

The basic idea is that many schemes provide no intrinsic way of detecting which of two watermarks was added first: the process of marking is often additive, or at least commutative. So if the owner of the document d encodes a watermark w and publishes the marked version $d + w$ and has no other proof of ownership, a pirate who has registered his watermark as w' can claim that the document is his and that the original unmarked version of it was $d + w - w'$.

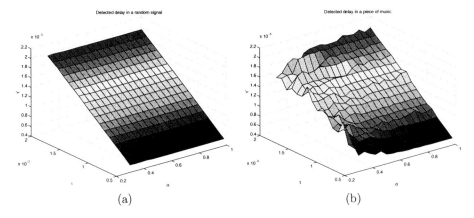

Fig. 6. Performances of the echo detector. We added different echoes characterised by their relative amplitude α and their delay τ to a signal and each time we used our echo detector to find an estimation $\hat{\tau}$ of τ. These graphs show the detected echo delay as a function of α and τ for random signals (a) and for a piece of music (b).

Their paper ([21]) extends this idea to defeat a scheme which is non-invertible (an inverse needs only be approximated).

Craver *et al.* argue for the use of information-losing marking schemes whose inverses cannot be approximated closely enough. However, our alternative interpretation of their attack is that watermarking and fingerprinting methods must be used in the context of a larger system that may use mechanisms such as timestamping and notarisation to prevent attacks of this kind.

Registration mechanisms have not received very much attention in the copyright marking literature to date. The existing references such as [16, 28, 29, 50] mainly focus on protecting the copyright holder and do not fully address the rights of the consumers who might be fooled by a crooked reseller.

3.6   Implementation Considerations

The robustness of embedding and retrieving techniques is not the only issue. Most attacks on fielded cryptographic systems have come from the opportunistic exploitation of loopholes that were found by accident; cryptanalysis was rarely used, even against systems that were vulnerable to it [1].

We cannot expect copyright marking systems to be any different and the pattern was followed in the first attack to be made available on the Internet against the most widely used picture marking scheme, PictureMarc, which is bundled with Adobe Photoshop and Corel Draw. This attack [12] exploited weaknesses in the implementation rather than the underlying marking algorithms, even although these are weak (the marks can be removed using StirMark).

Each user has an ID and a two-digit password, which are issued when she registers with Digimarc and pays for a subscription. The correspondence between

IDs and passwords is checked using obscure software in the implementation and although the passwords are short enough to be found by trial and error, the attack first uses a debugger to break into the software and disable the password checking mechanism.

We note in passing that IDs are public, so either password search or disassembly can enable any user to be impersonated.

A deeper examination of the program also allows a villain to change the ID, thus the copyright, of an already marked image as well as the type of use (such as adult versus general public content). Before embedding a mark, the program checks whether there is already a mark in the picture, but this check can be bypassed fairly easily using the debugger with the result that it is possible to overwrite any existing mark and replace it with another one.

Exhaustive search for the personal code can be prevented by making it longer, but there is no obvious solution to the disassembly attack. If tamper resistant software [8] cannot give enough protection, then one can always have an online system in which each user shares a secret embedding key with a trusted party and uses this key to embed some kind of digital signature. Observe that there are two separate keyed operations here; the authentication (which can be done with a signature) and the embedding or hiding operation.

Although we can do public-key steganography – hiding information so that only someone with a certain private key can detect its existence [3] – we still do not know how to do the hiding equivalent of a digital signature; that is, to enable someone with a private key to embed marks in such a way that anyone with the corresponding public key can read them but not remove them. One problem is that a public decoder can be used by the attacker; he can remove a mark by applying small changes to the image until the decoder cannot find it anymore. This was first suggested by Perrig in [50]. In [39] a more theoretical analysis of this attack is presented as well as a possible countermeasure: randomisating the detection process. One could also make the decoding process computationally expensive. However neither approach is really satisfactory in the absence of tamper-resistant hardware.

Unless a breakthrough is made, applications that require the public verifiability of a mark (such as DVD) appear doomed to operate within the constraints of the available tamper resistance technology, or to use a central 'mark reading' service. This is evocative of cryptographic key management prior to the invention of public key techniques.

4   Conclusion

We have demonstrated that the majority of copyright marking schemes in the literature are vulnerable to attacks involving the introduction of sub-perceptual levels of distortion. In particular, many of the marking schemes in the marketplace provide only a limited measure of protection against attacks. Most of them are defeated by StirMark, a simple piece of software that we have placed in the public domain [35]. We have also shown a specific attack on the one serious exception to this rule (echo hiding).

This experience confirms our hypothesis that steganography would go through the same process of evolutionary development as cryptography, with an iterative process in which attacks lead to more robust systems.

Our experience in attacking the existing marking schemes has convinced us that any system which attempted to meet all the accepted requirements for marking (such as those set out by IFPI) would fail: if it met the robustness requirements then its bandwidth would be quite insufficient. This is hardly surprising when one considers that the information content of many music recording is only a few bits per second, so to expect to embed 20 bits per second against an opponent who can introduce arbitrary distortions is very ambitious.

Our more general conclusion from this work is that the 'marking problem' has been over-abstracted; there is not one 'marking problem' but a whole constellation of them. We do not believe that any general solution will be found. The trade-offs and in particular the critical one between bandwidth and robustness, will be critical to designing a specific system.

We already remarked in [7] on the importance of whether the warden was active or passive – that is, whether the mark needed to be robust against distortion. In general, we observe that most real applications do not require all of the properties in the IFPI list. For example, when auditing radio transmissions, we only require enough resistance to distortion to deal with naturally occurring effects such as multipath. Many applications will also require supporting protocol features, such as the timestamping service that we mentioned in the context of reversible marks.

So we do not believe that the intractability of the 'marking problem' is a reason to abandon this field of research. On the contrary; practical schemes for most realistic application requirements are probably feasible and the continuing process of inventing schemes and breaking them will enable us to advance the state of the art rapidly.

Finally, we suggest that the real problem is not so much inserting the marks as recognising them afterwards. Thus progress may come not just from devising new marking schemes, but in developing ways to recognise marks that have been embedded using the obvious combinations of statistical and transform techniques and thereafter subjected to distortion. The considerable literature on signal recognition may provide useful starting points.

Acknowledgements

Some of the ideas presented here were clarified by discussion with Roger Needham, David Wheeler, John Daugman, Peter Rayner, David Aucsmith, Stewart Lee, Scott Craver, Brian Moore, Mike Roe, Peter Wayner, Jon Honeyball, Scott Moskowitz and Matt Blaze.

References

[1] Ross J. Anderson. Why cryptosystems fail. *Communications of the ACM*, 37(11):32–40, November 1994.

[2] Ross J. Anderson, editor. *Information hiding: first international workshop*, volume 1174 of *Lecture Notes in Computer Science*, Isaac Newton Institute, Cambridge, UK, May 1996. Springer-Verlag, Berlin, Germany. ISBN 3-540-61996-8.

[3] Ross J. Anderson. Stretching the limits of steganography. In IH96 [2], pages 39–48. ISBN 3-540-61996-8.

[4] Ross J. Anderson and Markus G. Kuhn. Tamper resistance – A cautionary note. In *Second USENIX Workshop on Electronic Commerce*, pages 1–11, Oakland, CA, USA, November 1996. ISBN 1-880446-83-9.

[5] Ross J. Anderson and Charalampos Manifavas. Chameleon – a new kind of stream cipher. *Fourth Workshop on Fast Software Encryption*, 1267:107–113, 1997.

[6] Ross J. Anderson and Roger M. Needham. Programming satan's computer. In J.van Leeuwen, editor, *Computer Science Today – Commemorative Issue*, volume 1000 of *Lecture Notes in Computer Science*, pages 426–441. Springer-Verlag, Berlin, Germany, 1995. ISBN 3-540-60105-8.

[7] Ross J. Anderson and Fabien A.P. Petitcolas. On The Limits of Steganography. *IEEE Journal of Selected Areas in Communications*, 16(4):474–481, May 1998. Special Issue on Copyright & Privacy Protection. ISSN 0733-8716.

[8] David Aucsmith. Tamper resistant software: An implementation. In Anderson [2], pages 317–333. ISBN 3-540-61996-8.

[9] David Aucsmith, editor. *Information Hiding: Second International Workshop*, volume 1525 of *Lecture Notes in Computer Science*, Portland, Oregon, USA, 1998. Springer-Verlag, Berlin, Germany. This volume.

[10] Walter Bender, Daniel Gruhl, and Norishige Morimoto. Techniques for data hiding. In Niblack and Jain [46], pages 164–173.

[11] Walter Bender, Daniel Gruhl, Norishige Morimoto, and Anthony Lu. Techniques for data hiding. *IBM Systems Journal*, 35(3&4):313–336, 1996.

[12] Anonymous (zguan.bbs@bbs.ntu.edu.tw). Learn cracking IV – another weakness of PictureMarc. news:tw.bbs.comp.hacker mirrored on http://www.cl.cam.ac.uk/~fapp2/watermarking/image_watermarking/digimarc_crack.html, August 1997. Includes instructions to override any Digimarc watermark using PictureMarc.

[13] Bruce P. Bogert, M.J.R. Healy, and John W. Tukey. The quefrency alanysis of time series for echoes: Cepstrum, pseudo-autocovariance, cross-ceptstrum and saphe cracking. In M. Rosenblatt, editor, *Symposium on Time Series Analysis*, pages 209–243, New York, USA, 1963. John Wiley & Sons, Inc.

[14] Laurence Boney, Ahmed H. Tewfik, and Khaled N. Hamdy. Digital watermarks for audio signals. In *European Signal Processing Conference, EUSIPCO '96*, Trieste, Italy, September 1996.

[15] Laurence Boney, Ahmed H. Tewfik, and Khaled N. Hamdy. Digital watermarks for audio signals. In *International Conference on Multimedia Computing and Systems*, pages 473–480, Hiroshima, Japan, June 1996. IEEE.

[16] Marc Cooperman and Scott A. Moskowitz. Steganographic method and device. US Patent 5,613,004, March 1995.

[17] Ingemar J. Cox, Joe Kilian, Tom Leighton, and Talal Shamoon. A secure, robust watermark for multimedia. In Anderson [2], pages 183–206. ISBN 3-540-61996-8.

[18] Ingemar J. Cox and Matt L. Miller. A review of watermarking and the importance of perceptual modeling. In Bernice E. Rogowitz and Thrasyvoulos N. Pappas, editors, *Human Vision and Electrtonic Imaging II*, volume 3016, San Jose, CA, USA, February 1997. IS&T, The Society for Imaging Science and Technology and SPIE, The International Society for Optical Engineering, SPIE.

[19] Ingemar J. Cox and Kazuyoshi Tanaka. NEC data hiding proposal. Technical report, NEC Copy Protection Technical Working Group, July 1997. Response to call for proposal issued by the Data Hiding SubGroup.

[20] Scott Craver, Nasir Memon, Boon-Lock Yeo, and Minerva M. Yeung. Can invisible watermark resolve rightful ownerships? In Sethin and Jain [60], pages 310–321.

[21] Scott Craver, Nasir Memon, Boon-Lock Yeo, and Minerva M. Yeung. Resolving rightful ownerships with invisible watermarking techniques: Limitations, attacks, and implications. *IEEE Journal of Selected Areas in Communications*, 16(4):573–586, May 1998. Special Issue on Copyright & Privacy Protection. ISSN 0733-8716.

[22] Digimarc home page. http://www.digimarc.com/, April 1997.

[23] Elke Franz, Anja Jerichow, Steffen Möller, Andreas Pfitzmann, and Ingo Stierand. Computer based steganography: how it works and why therefore any restriction on cryptography are nonsense, at best. In Anderson [2], pages 7–21. ISBN 3-540-61996-8.

[24] Michael A. Gerzon and Peter G. Graven. A high-rate buried-data channel for audio CD. *Journal of the Audio Engineering Society*, 43(1/2):3–22, January/February 1995.

[25] François Goffin, Jean-François Delaigle, Christophe De Vleeschouwer, Benoît Macq, and Jean-Jacques Quisquater. A low cost perceptive digital picture watermarking method. In Sethin and Jain [60], pages 264–277.

[26] Daniel Gruhl, Walter Bender, and Anthony Lu. Echo hiding. In Anderson [2], pages 295–315. ISBN 3-540-61996-8.

[27] Khaled N. Hamdy, Ahmed H. Tewfik, Ting Chen, and Satoshi Takagi. Time-scale modification of audio signals with combined harmonic and wavelet representations. In *International Conference on Acoustics, Speech and Signal Processing – ICASSP '97*, volume 1, pages 439–442, Munich, Germany, April 1997. IEEE, IEEE Press. Session on Hearing Aids and Computer Music.

[28] Alexander Herrigel, Adrian Perrig, and Joseph J.K. Ó Ruanaidh. A copyright protection environment for digital images. In *Verläßliche IT-Systeme '97*, Albert-Ludwigs Universität, Freiburg, Germany, October 1997.

[29] Alexander Herrigel, Joseph J.K. Ó Ruanaidh, Holger Petersen, Shelby Pereira, and Thierry Pun. Secure copyright protection techniques for digital images. In Aucsmith [9], pages 170–191. This volume.

[30] J.N. Holmes. *Speech Synthesis and Recognition*, chapter 3.6 Analysis of simple and complex signals, pages 47–48. Aspects of Information Technology. Chapman & Hall, London, UK, 1988.

[31] International Electrotechnical Commission, Geneva, Switzerland. *Digital audio interface, IEC 60958*, February 1989.

[32] Alastair Kelman. Electronic copyright management – the way ahead. Security Seminars, University of Cambridge, February 1997.

[33] A. Kerckhoffs. La Cryptographie Militaire. *Journal des Sciences Militaires*, 9:5–38, January 1883.

[34] E. Koch and J. Zhao. Towards robust and hidden image copyright labeling. In *Workshop on Nonlinear Signal and Image Processing*, pages 452–455, Neos Marmaras, Greece, June 1995. IEEE.

[35] Markus G. Kuhn and Fabien A.P. Petitcolas. StirMark. http://www.cl.cam.ac.uk/~fapp2/watermarking/stirmark/, November 1997.

[36] Charles Kurak and John McHugh. A cautionary note on image downgrading. In *Computer Security Applications Conference*, pages 153–159, San Antonio, TX, USA, December 1992.

[37] Gerrit C. Langelaar, Jan C.A van der Lubbe, and J. Biemond. Copy protection for multimedia data based on labeling techniques. In *17th Symposium on Information Theory in the Benelux*, Enschede, The Netherlands, May 1996.

[38] Gerrit C. Langelaar, Jan C.A. van der Lubbe, and Reginald L. Lagendijk. Robust labeling methods for copy protection of images. In Sethin and Jain [60], pages 298–309.

[39] Jean-Paul M.G. Linnartz and Marten van Dijk. Analysis of the sensitivity attack against electronic watermarks in images. In Aucsmith [9], pages 258–272. This volume.

[40] Mark Lomas, Bruno Crispo, Bruce Christianson, and Mike Roe, editors. *Security Protocols: Proceeding of the 5th International Workshop*, volume 1361 of *Lecture Notes in Computer Science*, École Normale Supérieure, Paris, France, April 1997. University of Cambridge, Isaac Newton Institute, Springer-Verlag, Berlin, Germany. ISBN 3-540-64040-1.

[41] Alpha Tec Ltd. Eikonamark. http://www.generation.net/~pitas/sign.html, October 1997.

[42] Maurice Maes. Twin peaks: The histogram attack on fixed depth image watermarks. In Aucsmith [9], pages 290–305. This volume.

[43] Kineo Matsui and Kiyoshi Tanaka. Video-steganography: How to secretly embed a signature in a picture. *Journal of the Interactive Multimedia Association Intellectual Property Project*, 1(1):187–205, January 1994.

[44] Norishige Morimoto and Daniel Sullivan. IBM DataHiding proposal. Technical report, IBM Corporation, September 1997. Response to call for proposal issued by the Data Hiding SubGroup.

[45] Peter Nancarrow. Digital technology – Bane or boon for copyright? Computer Laboratory Seminars, University of Cambridge, November 1997.

[46] Wayne Niblack and Ramesh C. Jain, editors. *Storage and Retrieval for Image and Video Database III*, volume 2420, San Jose, California, USA, February 1995. IS&T, The Society for Imaging Science and Technology and SPIE, The International Society for Optical Engineering, SPIE.

[47] J.J.K. Ó Ruanaidh, W.J. Dowling, and F.M. Boland. Watermarking digital images for copyright protection. *IEE Proceedings on Vision, Signal and Image Processing*, 143(4):250–256, August 1996.

[48] International Federation of the Phonographic Industry. Request for proposals – Embedded signalling systems issue 1.0. 54 Regent Street, London W1R 5PJ, June 1997.

[49] Alan V. Oppenheim and Ronald W. Schafer. *Discrete-Time Signal Processing*, chapter 12, pages 768–834. Prentice-Hall International, Inc., Englewood Cliffs, NJ, USA, international edition, 1989. ISBN 0-13-216771-9.

[50] Adrian Perrig. A copyright protection environment for digital images. Diploma dissertation, École Polytechnique Fédérale de Lausanne, Lausanne, Switzerland, February 1997.

[51] Fabien A.P. Petitcolas. Weakness of existing watermarking schemes. http://www.cl.cam.ac.uk/~fapp2/watermarking/image_watermarking/, October 1997.

[52] Birgit Pfitzmann. Information hiding terminology. In Anderson [2], pages 347–350. Results of an informal plenary meeting and additional proposals.

[53] I. Pitas. A method for signature casting on digital images. In *International Conference on Image Processing*, volume 3, pages 215–218, September 1996.

[54] Geoffrey B. Rhoads. Steganography methods employing embedded calibration data. US Patent 5,636,292, June 1997.

[55] Joseph J.K. Ó Ruanaidh and Shelby Pereira. A secure robust digital image watermark. In *International Symposium on Advanced Imaging and Network Technologies – Conference on Electronic Imaging: Processing, Printing and Publishing in Colour*, Europto, Zürich, Switzerland, May 1998. International Society for Optical Engineering, European Optical Society, Commission of the European Union, Directorate General XII.

[56] Pamela Samuelson. Copyright and digital libraries. *Communications of the ACM*, 38(4):15–21, 110, April 1995.

[57] Ronald W. Schafer. Echo removal by discrete generalized linear filtering. Technical Report 466, Massachusetts Institute of Technology, February 1969.

[58] Bruce Schneier. Protocol interactions and the chosen protocol attack. In Lomas et al. [40], pages 91–104. ISBN 3-540-64040-1.

[59] Robert A. Scholtz. The origins of spread-spectrum communications. *IEEE Transactions on Communications*, 30(5):822–853, May 1982.

[60] Ishwar K. Sethin and Ramesh C. Jain, editors. *Storage and Retrieval for Image and Video Database V*, volume 3022, San Jose, CA, USA, February 1997. IS&T, The Society for Imaging Science and Technology and SPIE, The International Society for Optical Engineering, SPIE.

[61] Signum Technologies – SureSign digital fingerprinting. http://www.signumtech.com/, October 1997.

[62] Mitchell D. Swanson, Bin Zhu, and Ahmed H. Tewfik. Robust data hiding for images. In *7th Digital Signal Processing Workshop (DSP 96)*, pages 37–40, Loen, Norway, September 1996. IEEE.

[63] Mitchell D. Swanson, Bin Zhu, and Ahmed H. Tewfik. Transparent robust image watermarking. In *International Conference on Image Processing*, volume III, pages 211–214. IEEE, 1996.

[64] A.Z. Tirkel, G.A. Rankin, R.M. van Schyndel, W.J. Ho, N.R.A. Mee, and C.F. Osborne. Electronic watermark. In *Digital Image Computing, Technology and Applications – DICTA '93*, pages 666–673, Macquarie University, Sidney, 1993.

[65] R.G. van Schyndel, A.Z. Tirkel, and C.F. Osborne. A digital watermark. In *International Conference on Image Processing*, volume 2, pages 86–90, Austin, Texas, USA, 1994. IEEE.

[66] Georges Van Slype. Natural language version of the generic CITED model – ECMS (Electronic Copyright Management System) design for computer based applications. Report 2, European Commission, ESPRIT II Project, Bureau Vam Dijk, Brussel, Belgium, May 1995.

[67] Georges Van Slype. Natural language version of the generic CITED model – Presentation of the generic model. Report 1, European Commission, ESPRIT II Project, Bureau Vam Dijk, Brussel, Belgium, May 1995.

[68] A. Werner, J. Oomen, Marc E. Groenewegen, Robbert G. van der Waal, and Raymond N.J. Veldhuis. A variable-bit-rate buried-data channel for compact disc. *Journal of the Audio Engineering Society*, 43(1/2):23–28, January/February 1995.

[69] The Working Group on Intellectual Property Rights is part of the US Information Infrastructure Task Force, formed in February 1993.

[70] Raymond B. Wolfgang and Edward J. Delp. A watermark for digital images. In *International Conference on Images Processing*, pages 219–222, Lausanne, Switzerland, September 1996. IEEE.

[71] Raymond B. Wolfgang and Edward J. Delp. A watermarking technique for digital imagery: further studies. In *International Conference on Imaging, Systems, and Technology*, pages 279–287, Las Vegas, NV, USA, June 30–July 3 1997. IEEE.

[72] J. Zhao and E. Koch. Embedding robust labels into images for copyright protection. In *International Congress on Intellectual Property Rights for Specialised Information, Knowledge and New Technologies*, Vienna, Austria, August 1995.

[73] Jian Zhao. A WWW service to embed and prove digital copyright watermarks. In *European Conference on Multimedia Applications, Services and Techniques*, pages 695–710, Louvain-la-Neuve, Belgium, May 1996

[74] Jian Zhao.   The   syscop   home   page.   http://syscop.igd.fhg.de/   or http://www.crcg.edu/syscop/, February 1997.

Testing Digital Watermark Resistance to Destruction

Sabrina Sowers and Abdou Youssef[†]

The George Washington University
Department of Electrical Engineering and Computer Science
Washington, DC USA 20052
{sowers,youssef}@seas.gwu.edu

Abstract. Digital watermarking is the steganographic technique used to discourage the unauthorized distribution of digital media such as text, audio, still images, and video. Artists, publishers and any other individual or business that has a commercial interest in preventing illegal copies of their work are in need of a way to achieve this. There are commercial techniques available on the Internet (like Steganos) and other techniques that are being researched. A desirable watermark is undetectable and can always be recovered. The ability to be recoverable is of concern, since if the watermark is easily destroyed it is useless. This paper investigates three known steganographic algorithms with respect to their robustness against four image processing operations: filtering, bit-plane removal, DCT compression, and quantization. It is found that those steganographic algorithms often fail to recover the watermarks after the four image processing operations are performed.

1 Introduction

The information market wishes to efficiently distribute intellectual and artistic property over networks securely with minimum risk of copyright infringement. With the Internet becoming the marketplace of the present and the future, there is a need to protect digital merchandise from unauthorized distribution [19]. An area of research that tries to address this issue is *steganography*. Steganography is the study of concealing the existence of information [3, 16]. It is different from cryptography in that encryption hides the content of information in order to keep a person who may intercept the information (cryptanalyst) from understanding what he or she is seeing. The goal of steganography is that certain parts of the information not be readily detected by an unauthorized person who intercepts it (stegoanalyst). In [3], classical steganography is defined as the set of techniques that hides some information within digital media like text, images, audio or video. The process of embedding the information and detecting or extracting the embedded information sometimes involves symmetric key generation.

When dealing with digital media that is to be distributed on the Internet, the concern is to be able to authenticate ownership and identify unauthorized copies of digital media. The steganographic technique used to achieve this is *digital watermarking*.

[†] David Balenson is also acknowledged for his support of this work.

David Aucsmith (Ed.): Information Hiding 1998, LNCS 1525, pp. 239-257, 1998.
© Springer-Verlag Berlin Heidelberg 1998

Watermarking has its origins in papermaking, where papermakers marked their stock with insignias to identify their workmanship and distinguish their work from fraudulent imitations [19, 25]. A perfect modern example is official transcripts administered by colleges and universities. Many official transcripts are usually printed on thick paper stock and have a raised seal that identifies the corresponding college or university. Upon opening the envelope, the raised seal is a visual mark that testifies to its origins. If a person copies the transcript using some copy machine, the result is a not-so-clear document that has the word "COPY" replicated all over it. Thus, signaling to the viewer that it is a copy and could be doctored in some manner. So, how is this applied to digital media?

The general digital watermarking procedure is illustrated in Fig. 1. The watermarking technique embeds the watermark into the source data and a watermarked version results. The owner has a choice of compressing the original data before applying the watermark, after applying the watermark or both. This is heavily dependent on the nature of the technique. If the watermark is destroyed before the data is sent out onto the network, the watermark is useless.

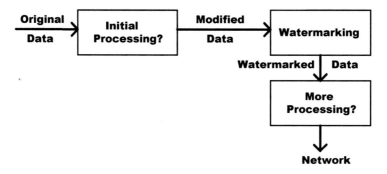

Fig. 1. General digital watermarking procedure

When there is a dispute as to whether or not data is authentic or has been corrupted, the owner applies his or her watermarking extraction/verification algorithm to the data. This algorithm depends on the technique used to embed the watermark. A possible extraction/verification procedure is shown in Fig. 2. The data under verification may need to go through some processing like decompression or change of format depending on the requirements of the extraction algorithm. This in itself can signify that the data has been modified. The extraction algorithm is applied to the test data and the result is the suspect watermark. The suspect watermark is compared to the original. In this procedure, the owner has a pre-determined threshold that will let him or her verify whether or not the test watermark is acceptable.

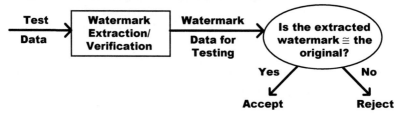

Fig. 2. Possible watermark extraction/verification procedure

It must be understood that the extraction method does not *prove* ownership unless there are laws governing the insertion and extraction of watermarks. The watermarks themselves are really useful to verify the source of a copy of data [17]. The original owner of a particular datum may have a database of all the recipients of that datum and can say whether or not the copy is an authorized distribution [21]. For the purposes of this paper, the digital medium of focus is images.

Returning to the official transcript example, it demonstrates two types of digital watermarking. If there is to be network distribution of official digital image transcripts, there needs to be a digital form of the raised seal and of the hidden replicating "COPY" for detection of copies. The digital raised seal is an example of a *visible digital watermark*. The digital version of the replicating "COPY" is an example of an *invisible digital watermark*. The invisible watermark is not revealed until some action is taken upon the source to uncover it.

The visible watermark's purpose is to discourage unauthorized distribution of digital images. By seeing the watermark, a person is less likely to copy or distribute the image without permission. It is desirable for a visible watermark inserted into an image to have several properties [17]:

- Obvious to the casual observer
- Requires automated insertion, where human involvement is minimized
- Covers a large area of the image
- Impossible to remove or render undetectable
- Maintains the quality of the image
- Identifies the owner or source of the image

A desirable invisible watermark has the same properties as the visible watermark except:

- It is undetectable to the casual observer
- There is a low probability that the watermark will be falsely detected when it does not exist
- It is placed in a "perceptually significant region of the data despite risk of distortion" [7]
- Localization–changes made to a section of an image affects the watermark in that section only

Though all of these properties are necessary, one major property, which is the focus of this paper's experimentation, is whether or not the watermark is able to resist destruction. A schematic diagram for testing watermark resistance is shown in Fig. 3. The original data is watermarked by some technique. The watermarked data is then subjected to some attack in order to try to destroy or distort the watermark. The extraction/verification technique associated with the watermarking algorithm is applied to the modified data that results from the attack. If the watermark is present (i.e., the extraction/verification algorithm is able to recognize the watermark), then the watermark is resistant to the attack. Otherwise, the watermark is not resistant.

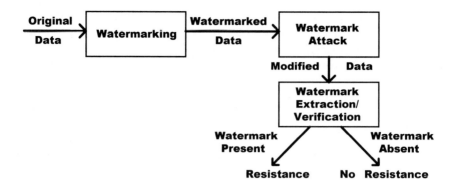

Fig. 3. Testing Watermark Resistance

The owner of an image may encourage users of his or her work to make alterations to suit their purposes like imploding, swirling, embossing, resizing, etc. But regardless of that, the source of the image has to remain verifiable. So, what is the watermark most vulnerable too? Knowing this can help the user determine whether or not a particular product suits his or her purposes. There are several steganographic algorithms available on the Internet[1] as well as published watermarking techniques for images [2, 4–9, 11, 13, 14] and video [10, 12]. In this paper, three digital image watermarking algorithms are tested for their robustness against watermark destruction. For more information on the advantages and disadvantages of some of the watermarking algorithms that have been developed, see [1]. There are also several web sites where further information can be found on steganography and digital watermarking.[2]

2   Watermarking Algorithms Under Consideration

In this section a review of three digital watermarking algorithms will be addressed. The first two are available on the Internet and can easily be implemented on a PC. The third is implemented using MATLAB®.

---

[1] Steganography Info and Archive. http:// members.iquest.net/~mrmil/stego.html
WWW References on Watermarking Techniques for Multimedia. http://www-nt.e-technik.uni-erlangen.de/~hartung/watermarkinglinks.html

[2] Steganography.   http://patriot.net/~johnson/Steganography/   and   http://www.cl.cam.ac.uk/~fapp2/steganography/
Data Embedding. http://www.lanl.gov/users/u078743/embed1.htm
WWW   Watermarking   Links   http://ltswww.epfl.ch/home-cgi-bin/format-page.cgi?watermarking/refs.html|refs
Papermaking, Watermarks http://www.ipst.edu/amp/watermk.html

2.1   HideSeek Version 5.0[3]

This is a DOS software package that is used to conceal information within GIF (Graphical Image Format) images. According to its creator, the algorithm takes the low order bit of each pixel and uses it to encode 1 bit. A pseudo-random number generator (PRNG) is used to distribute the information to be concealed randomly across the image. The concealed data is purported to be undetectable in greyscale images, but is noticeable in color images. HideSeek requires knowing the file size and the seed value to the PRNG. This information is encrypted in the GIF header to prevent easy extraction of the information using the International Data Encryption Algorithm (IDEA™) which is a conventional block cipher[4]. There is a restriction on the amount of information that can be concealed. It can be no larger than the size of the host image.

2.2   White Noise Storm (WNSTORM) © [5]

This is a DOS and UNIX software package developed by Ray "Arsen" Arachelian. The basic idea behind White Noise Storm is to conceal non-encrypted or encrypted messages within random data. This technique is useful for people who wish to send secure messages within PCX (Zsoft Paint Format) or BMP (Microsoft Windows Bitmap) images. It provides the algorithm for encrypting the message (WNSTORM) and for concealing the information in an image (WNINJECT). It is preferable, for extra security, to encrypt the information before it is concealed in the least significant bits of the image. Both parties must know the key in which the message was encrypted. This may not seem like a watermarking algorithm, since its intent is to send hidden messages. But the watermark is a hidden message that should not be uncovered unless the proper decryption scheme is used.

2.3   Simplified Version of Basic M-Sequence Approach

This technique is based on the algorithms described in [2] and the Constant Two-Dimensional Watermark algorithm discussed in [11, 14] where the advantages and disadvantages of the algorithm are also mentioned. A simplified version of the algorithms is presented below. In the simplified version, a static bipolar matrix[6], (which consists of only −1 and 1) such as the Walsh-Hadamard matrix will be used. After creating the watermark $W(x, y)$, it is added to blocks of corresponding size in the image $I(x, y)$. The pseudocode of the algorithm is as follows:

---

[3] HideSeek is freeware.

[4] IDEA™ is a trademark of Ascom-Tech AG and is freeware for non-commercial usage. Under European patent number: PCT/CH91/00117. For commercial use, obtain licensing details from Dieter Profos, Ascom Tech AG, Solothurn Lab, Postfach 151, 4502 Solothurn, Switzerland. Telephone: +41 65 242885, Fax: +41 65 235761.

[5] White Noise Storm is copyrighted freeware and cannot be exported outside of the United States.

[6] Will assume square matrices or images for simplicity.

Watermarking Algorithm

Given the original image $I(x, y)$ and the watermark $W(x, y)$

Repeat

       Extract an $N \times N$ block I' from $I(x, y)$

       $J' = I' + W$ where J' is the corresponding $N \times N$ watermarked block of the watermarked image J being created.

until no more disjoint $N \times N$ blocks of $I(x, y)$ to watermark

In the verification algorithm presented below a *matching by correlation* is used. The correlation between 2 images Z and W is defined as follows:

$$C_{ZW}(\sigma, \tau) = \sum_x \sum_y Z(x, y)\, W(x - \sigma, y - \tau) \qquad (1)$$

where $\sigma, \tau = 0, 1, \ldots N - 1$.

Verification Algorithm

Given a test image $Z(x, y)$ and the original watermark $W(x, y)$

Repeat

       Extract an $N \times N$ block Z' from $Z(x, y)$

       $\delta = c_{J'W}(0, 0) - c_{Z'W}(0, 0)$ where J' is the original watermarked image

       if $|\delta| <$ tolerance, then Z' is legitimate

until no more disjoint $N \times N$ blocks of $Z(x, y)$ to check

These algorithms will be applied to test images and then subjected to image processing techniques to test watermark resistance to destruction.

3   Techniques Used to Test Watermark Resistance to Destruction

There are many image processing techniques that can be used to attempt watermark destruction. If the watermark is not designed to withstand them, several techniques can have an effect on the watermark. When applying an image processing technique, the intention is to enhance some detail or remove some detail. By doing so, if there is information hidden within the image it can possibly be destroyed. Those computational techniques mentioned in this section are implemented using MATLAB®.

3.1   Filters

Filters are used for image enhancement and restoration. The filters used here are (1) standard gradient, (2) 3×3 high-pass, and (3) Gaussian filters. The gradient, high-pass and Gaussian filters are used for sharpening and highlighting edges or details in an image.

3.2   Bit-Plane Decomposition and Removal

An n-bit greyscale image can be decomposed into n 1-bit-planes. By removing some combination of the planes, compression can be achieved without noticeably distorting the image. Each plane can be characterized by 2^x, where $x \in \{0, 1, 2, ..., n-1\}$; the most significant bit-plane is at $x = n - 1$. The question is whether this bit-plane removal cause the watermarking algorithm to fail to recover the concealed data.

3.3   Discrete Cosine Transform (DCT) Compression

DCT [20, 23, 24] is the transform most commonly chosen for lossy data compression systems because it achieves a higher level of compression at better visual quality of images than those that result from other transforms. DCT is the international standard for transform coding systems. The DCT transform coding system used here is a JPEG-like system. Since in lossy compression the data that is removed is unrecoverable, the question is whether applying DCT compression to a watermarked image affects the watermark.

3.4   Optimal Non-Uniform Max-Lloyd Quantization

Quantization is a method used to reduce the representation size of data elements. It is used in transform coding, or as a standalone system applied to images directly to reduce their dynamic range (i.e., number of bits per pixel). A simple k-level scalar quantizer is defined as follows

1. $k+1$ decision levels $d_1, d_2, d_3, d_4, ..., d_{k+1}$
2. k reconstruction values $r_1, r_2, r_3, r_4, ..., r_k$,
3. Each decision interval $[d_i, d_{i+1})$ is called a *bin*. There are k bins. Depending on the type of quantizer, the bins can be equal or non-equal in size.
4. Each $r_i \in [d_i, d_{i+1})$.

There are two broad types of quantizers: *uniform* and *non-uniform*. A uniform quantizer is one where all decision intervals are of equal size and the reconstruction values are the middles of their corresponding intervals. Non-uniform quantizers, most notably Max-Lloyd quantizers, have varying length intervals to minimize distortions in the image [20, 23]. In order to quantize an image, for every x in the image find the bin that contains x and then replace x by the bin index. To dequantize (reconstruct the image), replace each bin index i by r_i. The Max-Lloyd algorithm for computing the optimal values for the d_i's and r_i's can be found in [20, 23].

In this paper, Max-Lloyd is applied to images directly to test the resistance of the various watermarking techniques against quantization.

4   Experimentation

Fig. 4 depicts the color GIF image used for testing HideSeek and Fig. 5 shows the greyscale BMP image used for testing WNSTORM and Simplified M-sequence.

Fig. 4. 260×361 color GIF image.   **Fig. 5.** 64×64 greyscale BMP image[7]

4.1   Performance of HideSeek Version 5.0

Fig. 6 depicts the stegoimage that is the result of concealing the watermark depicted in Fig. 7 within Fig. 4 using HideSeek. The dimensions of the stegoimage in Fig. 6 are greater than the original image, because the graphics toolbox that HideSeek uses to display GIF images has a default display size of 320×480. Therefore, the resulting stegoimage will have dimensions of 320×480. One disadvantage of HideSeek is that the stegoimage must maintain its dimensions. If the image is resized, then the watermark will be lost. The developer of this algorithm states that if the original image is a color image, the watermark will be visible. This is an obvious disadvantage, in that if the watermark is meant to be hidden, it limits the types of images to only greyscale.

---

[7] gvpmisc.bmp from Ghostview for Windows 3.1

Fig. 6. 320×480 color GIF Stegoimage.

Fig. 7. 32×32 greyscale GIF image (watermark) embedded in Fig. 5.

HideSeek vs. Filtering

The watermarking resistance testing procedure of Fig. 3 on HideSeek where the watermark attack is filtering. The modified images resulting from filtering the images of Fig. 6 are shown in Fig. 8–10. HideSeek failed to recover the watermark for all cases of the filters.

HideSeek vs. Bit-Plane Decomposition and Removal

As stated earlier, each pixel in a 8 bit greyscale image is represented by an 8 bit value and can be decomposed into 8 bit-planes. The GIF images of the greyscale bit-planes that resulted are depicted in Fig. 11 through Fig. 18.

Fig. 8. Result of gradient filter.

Fig. 9. Result of high-pass filter.

Fig. 10. Results of Gaussian filter.

Fig. 11. Plane 7.

Fig. 12. Plane 6.

Fig. 13. Plane 5.

Fig. 14. Plane 4.

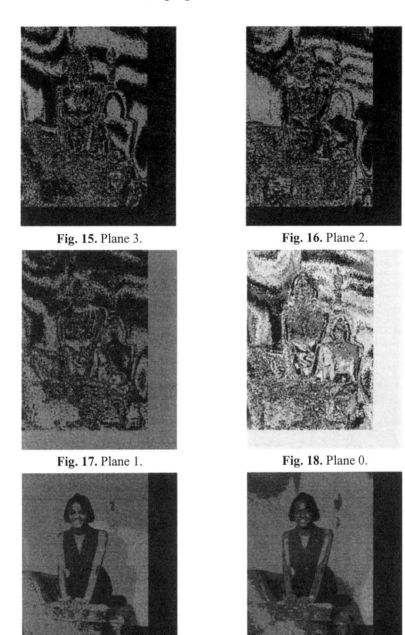

Fig. 15. Plane 3.

Fig. 16. Plane 2.

Fig. 17. Plane 1.

Fig. 18. Plane 0.

Fig. 19. Planes 7 through 5.

Fig. 20. Planes 7 through 4.

Fig. 21. Planes 7 through 3.

Fig. 22. Planes 7 through 2.

Fig. 23. Planes 7 through 1.

Fig. 24. Reconstructed stegoimage using DCT.

After decomposing the greyscale version of the stegoimage into its planes, the resulting GIF images of several combinations are shown in Fig. 19 through Fig. 23. HideSeek failed to recover the watermark from any of the images in Fig. 19 through Fig. 23.

HideSeek vs. DCT Compression
HideSeek failed on the image shown in Fig. 24 also. The watermark is not noticeable (if still present).

HideSeek vs. Max-Lloyd Quantization
The watermark data is noticeable in both the two- and four-level Max-Lloyd quantized images (Fig. 25 and Fig. 26). The effects of the quantization also caused HideSeek to fail to recover the watermark.

4.2   Performance of WNSTORM

The following message (more specifically, the characters):
    <return character>"Those who say it cannot be done, should not*<return char-acter>*interfere with the one who is doing it."*<return character><return char-acter><tab><tab><tab>*-Unknown
represents the watermark added to Fig. 27a using WNSTORM; and the result of concealing the watermark is shown in Fig. 27b. The developer of WNSTORM stated that error-free transmission is required for the hidden information to remain intact. In all the following cases, WNSTORM only recovered garbage data.

WNSTORM vs. Filtering
WNSTORM unsurprisingly failed to recover the watermark from the images in Fig. 28. The filters' job is to enhance pixels. Therefore, the changes caused by the filters are likely to affect the watermark.

WNSTORM vs. Bit-Plane Decomposition and Removal
Concealing the watermark in the least significant bits is an obvious disadvantage of the algorithm, since the removal of that plane will undoubtedly damage the watermark. A person may not be able to extract the watermark, but can destroy it and prevent the desired recipient from getting the correct image. The watermark was not recovered from any single bit-plane or combination of bit-planes.

Fig. 25. Reconstructed stegoimage using two-level Max-Lloyd quantization

Fig. 26. Reconstructed stegoimage using Four-level Max-Lloyd quantization.

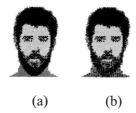

(a)   (b)

Fig. 27. (a) Original (b) BMP stegoimage: the hidden information is clustered around the chin.

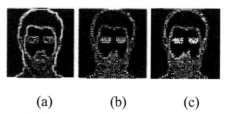

(a)   (b)   (c)

Fig. 28. Results of Filtering. (a) gradient (b) high-pass (c) Gaussian.

Fig. 29. These are the consecutive bit-planes from most significant to least significant.

One thing to note is that the decomposition of Fig. 27b depicted in Fig. 29 shows where the watermark is located in the image. The stegoanalyst now knows that the watermark exists. And, the visual results of the bit-plane combinations (Fig. 30) suggest that image tampering can occur.

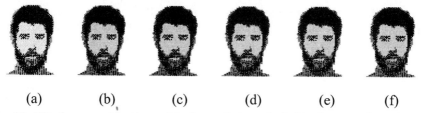

(a)   (b)   (c)   (d)   (e)   (f)

Fig. 30. Bit-plane combinations: (a) planes 7 through 5 (b) planes 7 through 4 (c) planes 7 through 3 (d) planes 7 through 2 (e) planes 7 through 1 (f) all planes.

Visually, Fig. 30b through Fig. 30f all resemble the stegoimage in Fig. 27b. Fig. 30a is lighter in the face, but the recipient will not know this characteristic beforehand. It is therefore possible to keep the rightful recipient from receiving the correct image by sending a tampered copy of the image.

Performance of Simplified M-Sequence Approach
Fig. 31 shows the images that resulted from applying Walsh-Hadamard matrices as the watermark to the image in Fig. 27a. The blocking effect is a result of applying the watermark to disjoint square blocks in the images as the algorithm describes. This can be a tell-tale sign that something has been applied.

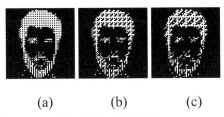

(a)   (b)   (c)

Fig. 31. Images: (a) Outcome of 2×2 Simplified M-sequence watermark (b) 4×4 watermark (c) 8×8 watermark

The results of filtering are depicted in Fig. 32. The images in (a)–(c) are the results of applying the gradient filter to the images in Fig. 31 respectively. The high-pass filter results are shown in (d)–(f) and the Gaussian results in (g)–(i). Fig. 33 shows the most significant bit-planes for each image. Fig. 34 is the result after applying DCT compression and the results of the two-level Max-Lloyd quantization is shown in Fig. 35. The images in Fig. 33 and Fig. 35 are quite similar.

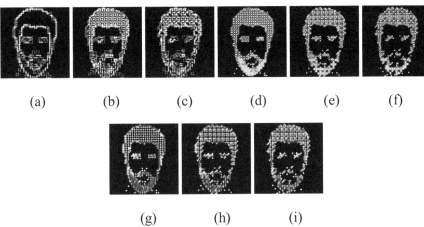

(a)   (b)   (c)   (d)   (e)   (f)

(g)   (h)   (i)

Fig. 32. Results of Filtering. (a–c) gradient (d–f) high-pass (g–i) Gaussian.

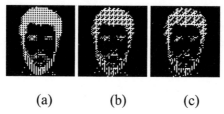

(a)   (b)   (c)

Fig. 33. Bit-planes: (a) 2×2 watermark (b) 4×4 watermark (c) 8×8 watermark [8].

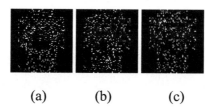

(a)   (b)   (c)

Fig. 34. Resulting images after DCT compression.

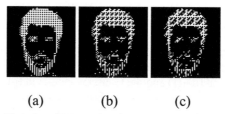

(a)   (b)   (c)

Fig. 35. Results using Two-level Max-Lloyd quantization. Did not affect the image because pixel values are between 0 and 1.

In Table 1 are the highest correlation values of all the blocks for each of the stegoimages shown in Fig. 31. Table 2 is the percentage of blocks whose correlation values agreed exactly after the image processing operation was applied. All the other blocks had values less than their corresponding correlation value of the original. Fig. 31a had 1094 blocks to check. Fig. 31b had 256 blocks to check and Fig. 31c had 64 blocks to check. The watermarks were distorted when the filters were applied to the stegoimages. DCT compression destroyed the watermarks for each of the stegoimages. The bit-plane decomposition/removal and the 2-level Max-Lloyd resulted in perfect correlation because the pixel values were not affected. Table 3 summarizes the results of all the watermarking techniques and their performance.

Table 1. The maximum matching by correlation values for the stegoimages and their corresponding watermark.

	Fig. 31a	Fig. 31b	Fig. 31c
Maximum Matching Correlation	6.5020	21.5020	76.9961

---

[8] The bit-planes for each image are visually similar. Only the most significant plane is shown here.

Table 2. The percentage of blocks whose correlation values agreed exactly.

	Fig. 31a	Fig. 31b	Fig. 31c
Gradient Filter	53.4 %	44.9 %	34.4 %
High-Pass Filter	55.2 %	45.7 %	34.4 %
Gaussian Filter	26.6 %	23.8 %	15.6 %
Bit-Planes	100 %	100 %	100 %
DCT	0 %	0 %	0 %
2-level Max-Lloyd	100 %	100 %	100 %

5   Summary of Results

Table 3. Was the watermark destroyed or distorted?

	HideSeek	WNSTORM	2 × 2 M-Sequence	4 × 4 M-Sequence	8 × 8 M-Sequence
Gradient Filter	Yes	Yes	Yes	Yes	Yes
High-Pass Filter	Yes	Yes	Yes	Yes	Yes
Gaussian Filter	Yes	Yes	Yes	Yes	Yes
Bit-Plane De-composition	Yes	Yes	No	No	No
Bit-Plane Com-binations	Yes	Yes	No	No	No
DCT	Yes	Yes	Yes	Yes	Yes
2-level ML	Yes	Yes	No	No	No
4-level ML	Yes	Yes			

6   Conclusions and Future Work

The hope is that there will be a digital watermarking algorithm that will be able to withstand any image processing technique used as an attack. Therefore, the only person able to recover the hidden information is the one who put it there and those authorized to do so. There are many software implementations and techniques available on the Internet. Users should choose the ones that best suit their purposes for digital watermarking.

HideSeek and WNSTORM are algorithms designed to send hidden information from one person to another. HideSeek is limited in that it only has undetectable hidden information for greyscale images. If it is expanded to handle color images and the data is not hidden in the least significant part of the image, but rather in the more perceptible regions, then it may perform better. It may be interesting to see how to augment HideSeek for this purpose. WNSTORM's main drawback is its requirement for error-free transmission. Error-free transmission is for the perfect world. The success of digital watermarking and other steganographic algorithms is dependent on the errors that occur [3, 16]. The source code for WNSTORM is provided with the executable. It is also a potential area of research to improve this drawback.

There has been study on a way to forge digital watermarks so that the actual source cannot be determined [25]. This places a limit on digital watermarking as a foolproof method. There is still more research to be done. And finally, two other broad areas are worth pursuing: Examination of other watermarking techniques and testing watermark resistance to other image processing operations.

References

1. Raymond B. Wolfgang and Edward J. Delp. "Overview of image security techniques with applications in multimedia systems". http://dynamo.ecn.purdue.edu/~ace/water/digwmk.html
2. R. G. van Schyndel, A. Z. Tirkel, C. F. Osborne. "A Digital Watermark", *Proceedings of the International Conference on Image Processing*, November, 1994, Austin, Texas, vol. 2, pp. 86–90.
3. Ross Anderson and Fabien Petitcolas. "On the Limits of Steganography". *IEEE Journal on Selected Areas in Communications (J-SAC), Special Issue on Copyright & Privacy Protection*, vol. 16 no. 4, pp 474–481, May 1998. http://www.cl.cam.ac.uk/~fapp2/papers/jsac98-limsteg/
4. Walter Bender, Daniel Gruhl and Norishige Morimoto. "Techniques for Data Hiding". *Proceedings of the SPIE*, volume 2420, February 1995, p. 40.
5. E. Koch and Z. Zhao. "Towards Robust and Hidden Image Copyright Labeling". *Proceedings of the 1995 IEEE Workshop on Non-Linear Signal and Image Processing*, June 1995.
6. I. Pitas. "A Method for Signature Casting on Digital Images". *1996 IEEE Proceedings of the International Conferences on Image Processing*, pp. 215–218.
7. I. J. Cox, J. Kilian, T. Leighton, and T. Shamoon. "Secure Spread Spectrum Watermarking for Images, Audio, and Video". *1996 IEEE Proceedings of the International Conferences on Image Processing*, pp. 243–246.
8. J. J. K. Ó. Ruanaidh, W. J. Dowling, and F. M. Boland. "Phase Watermarking of Digital Images". *1996 IEEE Proceedings of the International Conferences on Image Processing*, pp. 239–242.
9. Christine Podilchuk and Wenjun Zeng. "Perceptual Watermarking of Still Images". *Proceedings of the IEEE MMSP Workshop*, Princeton, June 1997, pp. 363–368.
10. Christine Podilchuk and Wenjun Zeng. "Watermarking of the JPEG Bitstream". *Proceedings of the International Conference on Imaging Science, Systems , and Technology*. CISST '97 International Conference, pp. 253–260.
11. Raymond B. Wolfgang and Edward J. Delp. "A Watermarking Technique for Digital Imagery: Further Studies". *Proceedings of the International Conference on Imaging Science, System, and Technology*. CISST '97 International Conference, pp. 279–284.

12. Tsung-Li Wu and S. Felix Wu. "Selective Encryption and Watermarking of MPEG Video". *Proceedings of the International Conference on Imaging Science, Systems , and Technology*. CISST '97 International Conference, pp. 261- 269.
13. Dave Benham, Nasir Memon, et. al. "Fast Watermarking of DCT-based Compressed Images". *Proceedings of the International Conference on Imaging Science, Systems , and Technology*. CISST '97 International Conference, pp. 243–252.
14. R. Wolfgang and E. Delp. "A Watermark for Digital Images". *Proceedings of the 1996 International Conference on Image Processing*, Lausanne, Switzerland, September 16–19, 1996, volume 3, pp. 219–222.
15. Birgit Pfitzmann. "Information Hiding Terminology". *Proceedings of Information Hiding*. Springer Lecture Notes in Computer Science, volume 1174 (1996), pp. 347–350.
16. Ross Anderson. "Stretching the Limits of Steganography". In *Proceedings of the First Workshop on Information Hiding*, 1996, pp. 39–48 http://www.cl.cam.ac.uk/ftp/users/rja14/stegan.ps.gz
17. M. Yeung and F. C. Mintzer. "Digital Watermarking for High Quality Images". *1997 IEEE Proceedings of the International Conferences on Image Processing*, pp. 357–362.
18. J. Brassil, S. Low, N. Maxemchuk, and L. O'Gorman. "Electronic Marking and Identification Techniques to Discourage Document Copying". *Proceedings of Infocom '94*, pp. 1278–1287, 1994.
19. Richard Wiggins. "Stop Those Copyright Claim Jumpers!: Corralling Your Content". *NewMedia*, newmedia.com, pp. 40–44, October 13, 1997.
20. R. Gonzalez and R. Woods. Digital Image Processing. Second Edition. Addison-Wesley Publishing, 1993.
21. Peter Wayner. Digital Copyright Protection. AP Professional, Chestnut Hill, Massachusetts, 1997.
22. M. Swanson, B. Zhu and A. Tewfik. "Transparent Robust Image Watermarking". *Proceedings of the 1996 International Conference on Image Processing*, Lausanne, Switzerland, September 16–19, 1996, volume 3, pp. 211–214.
23. Khalid Sayood. Introduction to Data Compression. Morgan Kaufman Publishers, Inc., San Francisco, California, 1996.
24. Majid Rabbani and Paul W. Jones. Digital Image Compression Techniques. SPIE Optical Engineering Press, Bellingham Washington, 1991.
25. Hal Berghel. "Watermarking Cyberspace". Communications of the ACM, November 1997, volume 40, No. 11, pp. 19–24.

Analysis of the Sensitivity Attack against Electronic Watermarks in Images

Jean-Paul M. G. Linnartz and Marten van Dijk

Eindhoven Philips Research Laboratories (Natlab),
Holstlaan 4, 5656 AA, Eindhoven, the Netherlands,
{linnartz, mvandijk}@natlab.research.philips.com

Abstract. In some applications of electronic watermarks, the device that detects whether content contains a watermark or not is in public domain. Attackers can misuse such detector as an oracle that reveals up to one bit of information about the watermark in each experiment. An information-theoretical analysis of the information leakage is provided, and a method is proposed to reduce the information leakage by orders of magnitude.

keywords: Cryptanalysis, Copy Protection, Electronic Watermarks

1   Introduction

It is an open problem whether reliable and secure *public watermarks* can exists. Such public watermarks allow anyone to detect electronic watermarks, while the security and robustness are not affected by this public knowledge. By *secure* we mean that knowledge about how to detect a watermark does not reveal how the watermark can be removed or altered. We call the watermarking scheme *reliable* if it is robust to typical transmission and storage imperfections (such as lossy compression, noise addition, format conversion, bit errors) and signal processing artefacts (noise reduction, filtering), whether intentional or not. Moreover, content that has not been watermarked may not trigger a detector, or at least this probability should be negligibly small. Typical requirements for watermarking methods are

1. The watermark should be secure. Erasing the watermark should be technically difficult.
2. The watermarking scheme should be reliable.
3. An original image and its marked version should be perceptually indistinguishable. After commonly accepted processing, e.g. MPEG lossy compression, the accumulated artifacts should not be visible.

Public watermarks are desirable for copy management and embedded signalling of author's and publisher's data within the content. In innovative copy protection schemes, as for instance intended for new generation (Digital Versatile Disc) DVD systems, a consumer device performs a watermark detection as

David Aucsmith (Ed.): Information Hiding 1998, LNCS 1525, pp. 258–272, 1998.
© Springer-Verlag Berlin Heidelberg 1998

part of its judgement whether the content is original, or a legal or illegal copy. Watermarked content on discs that do not have the correct physical identifiers of the original publisher will not be played. For all systems known to the authors, the watermark detection method, i.e., its algorithm and the "keys", have to be kept secret to avoid that copyright pirates can remove the watermark. It is often assumed that the watermark detector is therefore implemented as a tamperproof box such that the attacker can not reverse-engineer critical parameters or properties of the detector from the implementation. An important class of proposed detectors is covered in Section 2.

An attacker can nonetheless learn and erase the watermark by experimenting with the content that he inputs to the detector [1]. Unless special precautions are taken, the attacker gains one bit of information about the watermark in every attempt. This implies that the attack is linear with the number of pixels in the image. This is in sharp contrast with the common belief that an attacker must do order $O(exp(N))$ experiments to find a secret watermark in an image of N pixels. In Section 3 we describe the attack. An attacker is successful if he can modify a marked image such that the detector responds that it does not see a watermark, while the modifications to the image are invisible. We propose a countermeasure that increases the work load for an attacker by a several orders of magnitude in Sections 4-6.

2   Typical Watermarking Detector

Let us consider a rectangular image r of size N_1 by N_2 pixels. The coordinates of the pixels are denoted by $\boldsymbol{n} \in A = \{(n_1, n_2) : 0 \le n_1 \le N_1 - 1, 0 \le n_2 \le N_2 - 1\}$. The luminance of the pixel with coordinates $\boldsymbol{n}$ is denoted as $r(\boldsymbol{n})$. We represent the watermark as w or $w(\boldsymbol{n})$, which takes on a value in each pixel $\boldsymbol{n} \in A$. A watermark detector outputs $D = 1$ if it recognizes a watermark, otherwise $D = 0$.

The most commonly used watermark detector bases this decision on the correlation between the suspect image and (a possibly transformed version of) the watermark [2,3,4,5,6]. Although many authors do not explicitly mention a correlator as their detection method, many schemes published thus far are mathematically equivalent to detection by correlation, or extensions of this basic concept. Such detector, as for instance in Figure 1, extracts a decision variable y from the suspect image q through a correlation operation $R_w(q)$ with a locally stored copy of the watermark w;

$$y = R_w(q) = \sum_{\boldsymbol{n} \in A} w(\boldsymbol{n}) q(\boldsymbol{n}).$$

Then, if $y > y_{thr}$ with y_{thr} some threshold value, it decides that the watermark is present and it outputs $D = 1$, otherwise $D = 0$.

We refer to [4] for an evaluation of how a decision threshold y_{thr} relates to the probability of a missed detection (the watermark is present, but the detector thinks it is not) and the probability of a false alarm (no watermark is embedded,

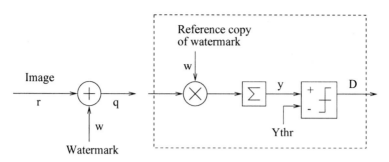

Fig. 1. *Correlator detector*

but the detector thinks one is). These probabilities measure the reliability of the watermarking scheme.

The output of the detector D can be seen as a random variable depending on y. In fact we have the Markov sequence

$$q \rightarrow y \rightarrow D,$$

where q, $y = R_w(q)$, and D are interpreted as random variables. I.e., the distribution function of random variable D, conditioned on the entire past, can be expressed exactly through conditioning only on the most recent random variable y.

Note that here we do not explicitly describe how an original image is watermarked in order to trigger a detector. In the standardization of watermarks for copy protection, it has become clear that only the detection algorithm needs to be prescribed, whereas the content owner can be given the freedom to use proprietary solutions for embedding the watermark. Particularly because of ongoing developments in perceptual modelling, such solutions tend to differ from implementation to implementation and to improve over time [7]. The reader may assume that the embedding method creates a new image q with $q = r + \eta * w$, where η is an appropriate embedding depth and $*$ is a pixelwise multiplication. The attack described in this paper is considered to be successful if the attacker manages to modify a watermark image in such a way that the detector will not be triggered. This neither implies that he recovered the original image precisely as it was before marking, nor that the new image is free of remnants from the watermark. However, one can use the r.m.s. modifications to the marked image as a first-order indication of the perceptual damage to the image.

In order to intuitively understand the concept of the attack and the countermeasures, we now present a geometrical interpretation of the correlator detector. This attack has been successfully executed against several more sophisticated watermarking methods [8].

Pictures are interpreted as vectors in an $N_1 N_2 = N$ dimensional vector space, see Figure 2. The vector space consists of three parts; $S_< = \{b : R_w(b) < y_{thr}\}$, $S_> = \{b : R_w(b) > y_{thr}\}$, and $S_= = \{b : R_w(b) = y_{thr}\}$. For pictures in $S_<$ the detector outputs 0. With probability close to one, a random unmarked image

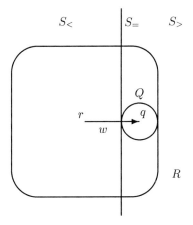

Fig. 2. *Geometrical Interpretation. Image r, Watermark w, Marked Image q*

$r \in S_<$. We will consider only those original images that do not raise a false alarm in a detector, that is we do not address the small fraction of those original images that by accident are within $S_>$. For marked pictures, which are in $S_>$ the detector outputs 1. On the separating surface $S_=$, the watermark detector also outputs $D = 0$. Area R contains all pictures which are perceptually indistinguishable from r. According to requirement 3 we have that $q \in R$.

Area Q contains modifications of q caused by typical transmission and storage imperfections and signal processing artefacts. According to requirement 3 such pictures should be perceptually indistinguishable from r as well, thus $Q \subseteq R$. The watermarking scheme should be reliable, see requirement 2, hence, $Q \subseteq S_>$. Summarizing, we have that $r \in R$, and $q \in Q \subseteq R \cap S_>$, and we assume that a watermarking method exists that allows q to be created.

The attacker's task is to find a point in $S_<$, preferably as close as possible to r. In practice, he will be satisfied with $\hat{r} \in S_<$ close to q and he hopes that $\hat{r} \in R$. We conclude this section by noting that in Figure 2 the geometrical shape of the areas are idealized.

3   The Attack

The attacker is assumed to have a marked image q (from which he attempts to remove the watermark) and to have access to the input and output of a watermark detector. This detector can for instance be in a tamperproof box, or it can be a remote server algorithm on a network that allows users to submit random images for watermarks detection.

In abstract terms, the attacker operates as follows [1]:

[Select random point in $S_<$, near $S_=$] He initially searches for a random point $q_0 \in S_<$ as close as practically possible to $S_=$. At this point it does not matter whether the resulting image resembles the original or not. The only criterion is that some minor modifications to the test image cause the detector to respond with $D = 1$ while other modifications result in $D = 0$. One method is to gradually replace more and more pixels in the image by neutral grey.

[Find tangent e_l] He then estimates the tangent e_l to the surface $S_=$ by taking a random vector t_j and searches the scalar values γ_j for which $q_l + \gamma_j t_j$ changes the decision of the detector. Typically, one only needs a single small positive or negative value for γ_j, e.g. $\gamma_j \in \{-1, +1\}$. A useful choice for t_j is zero for all pixels except for a single pixel n_j. That is, $q_l + \gamma_j t_j$ slightly increases or decreases the luminance of that pixel just enough to ensure to trigger the detector ($q_l + \gamma_j t_j \in S_>$). This provides the insight of whether $w(n_j) > 0$ or < 0. In a more sophisticated version, one can also estimate the value of $w(n_j)$.

This test is repeated for a complete set of independent vectors t_j, $j = 0$, 1, ..., $N - 1$. At the end the attacker has gained knowledge about w and, hence, about the shape of the surface $S_=$ near q_l. Using this knowledge he estimates the tangent e_l to the surface $S_=$ near q_l.

[Create a point q_{l+1} in $S_<$ near $S_=$] Combining the knowledge on how sensitive the detector is to a modification of each pixel, the attacker estimates a combination of pixel values that has the largest (expected) influence on the detector decision variable. The attacker uses the original marked image q (or q_l) and subtracts $\lambda_l * e_l$ resulting in a new point q_{l+1} in $S_<$ near $S_=$, such that the detector reports that no watermark is present. Parameter e_l is the tangent vector constructed in the previous step. Parameter λ_l may be found experimentally, such that λ_l may have the smallest perceptual effect on the image. A sophisticated attacker also exploits a perceptual model that makes the value of λ_l dependent on the pixel location. This is the final step for watermarking schemes with a simple correlator. If the surface $S_=$ is not a hyper plane, e.g., if the threshold value depends on the variance in the image, or if the surface is a collection of parts of hyperplanes, the attacker may iterate.

[Iterate] If the attacker is dissatisfied with the perceptual damage to the image, he may treat this image q_{l+1} again as a test image to estimate the local sensitivities. That is, he repeats the procedure for $l + 1$ (find tangent e_{l+1} and create a point q_{l+2} in $S_<$ on or very close to the separating surface $S_=$) until he finds a point q_n appropriately close to q.

If the surface $S_=$ in not a perfect plane, he may need to invoke more sophisticated searching algorithms, possibly including simulated annealing. However, for most correlator-based detection methods the attack only needs a single round of the above iterative process. For intuitive understanding we analyse the attack against a simple correlator/threshold detector with an idealised perceptual model. In this case a single round of iteration is sufficient. For ease of analysis we focus on the special case $w(n) \in \{-k, k\}$ where $k > 0$, i.e. similar to proposals as in for instance in [2,5].

4   Countermeasure

It appears possible to make the watermark detector substantially less vulnerable to the attack by randomizing the transition point y_{thr} of the detector. If the transition area $S_=$ is not a perfect plane, but a fuzzy area with random decisions by the detector if $y \approx y_{thr}$, an attacker will get much less information from each experiment performed in Step 2. If the randomization only occurs in a limited range of the decision value, the effect on the reliability is small.

For instance, instead of using one threshold y_{thr}, the detector uses two thresholds y_1 and y_2 with $y_2 > y_1$. If $y < y_1$, $D = 0$ and if $y > y_2$, $D = 1$. In the range $y_1 < y < y_2$, the detector chooses $D - 1$ with probability $p(y)$, where $p(y)$ is smoothly increasing in y.

4.1   Reliability

For reliability reasons the detector must respond $D = 0$ with very high probability for unmarked images and with $D = 1$ for marked images. Random responses are acceptable only in a transition range: y_1 is taken large enough such that the probability for a random, unmarked image not to generate $D = 0$ is small enough (probability of a false alarm). Similarly, y_2 is taken small enough such that the probability for a watermarked image not to generate $D = 1$ is small enough (probability of a missed detection). To satisfy the reliability requirements, the system designer should select the decision interval $[y_1, y_2]$ small enough such that the reliability of the detector stays within acceptable range. On the other hand, the length of the transition interval $[y_1, y_2]$ is taken large enough to ensure that for small changes to the image (resulting in small changes to y), the gradient of the decision probability $p(y)$ is only noticeable to an attacker after taking many samples and statistically processing these. It has been shown that the decision variable is a Gaussian random variable [9]. Its mean value corresponds to the energy in the watermark, defined as $E_w = \sum_{n \in A} w(n)^2$. The variance is determined by the variance of pixel luminance values, thus $\sigma^2 = Er^2 - E^2 r$ and other parameters. Erroneous detections occur with a probability that is determined by the energy in the watermark, the threshold setting and the variance of the random cross correlation between the original image and the reference watermark. If, in a detector without a countermeasure, a threshold of y_{thr} would be chosen, one could include the countermeasure by taking $y_1 = y_{thr}$ and $y_2 = \Gamma y_{thr}$. This would require the watermark to be embedded with a slight increase in energy, determined by Γ. This increase can be limited to a few dB, however, an detailed evaluation is outside the scope of this paper.

4.2   Sophisticating the Attack

Despite the random responses, an attacker can nonetheless extract information if he manages to estimate $p(q_0)$ and $p(q_0 + \gamma_j t_j)$. He could estimate these probabilities by repeated trials. Particularly, if $p(y)$ has a pronounced discontinuity at y_d, he could launch the attack near y_d. If for instance the detector would flip an unbiased coin when $y_1 < y < y_2$, the attacker launches the attack either at $y \approx y_1$ or $y \approx y_2$. In a few attempts he will learn whether the probability is 0, 0.5 or 1 for each $q_0 + \gamma_j t_j$.

There appears to be an optimum shape for $p(y)$ which minimizes the leakage of information, independent of the value of $R_w(q_0)$ at which the attack is executed. In the coming sections we will construct, study, and analyse this optimal shape.

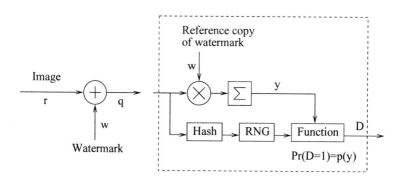

Fig. 3. *Improved detector using countermeasure*

Figure 3 gives an example of a possible implementation. For $y_1 < y < y_2$, the behavior is determined by the cryptographic Hash value generator, the Random Number generator and the Function. We notice that the implementation of Figure 3 results in a deterministic machine. That is if a fixed image q is input in the detector then either it always detects the watermark or it never detects the watermark. This avoids that an attacker estimates $p(y)$ by inputting the same image q in the detector over and over.

To the attacker not aware of the internal behaviour of the hash and random function generator,

$$Pr(D(q) = 1 | R_w(q) = y) = p(y).$$

Let us consider an attacker eager to find $p(y)$, who therefore manages to find small modifications $q + \epsilon$ to the image q, where $y = R_w(q) = R_w(q + \epsilon)$ ($R_w(\epsilon) = 0$ if the detector is a linear correlator). The output of the Random Number generator for these modifications $q + \epsilon$ differ in an unpredictable manner. Hence, for a fraction $p(y)$ of all small modifications $q + \epsilon$ we have $D(q + \epsilon) = 1$. Thus by interpreting q as a fixed picture and ϵ as a uniformly distributed random variable representing small modifications with $R_w(q) = R_w(q + \epsilon)$,

$$Pr(D(q + \epsilon) = 1 | R(q) = y) = p(y). \tag{1}$$

5   Probabilistic Behavior

As we argued before, preferably $p(y)$ is a smooth function. The attacker can still estimate the sensitivity of $p(y)$ to his intentional modifications $\gamma_j t_j$ of the image. Hence he will learn the relation between y and $\gamma_j t_j$. We will determine the optimum relation between $p(y)$ and y to protect against this attack.

Assume that the pirate has created a test image q_l in step 3 or initially in step 1 of the attack. In the following analysis we focus on step 2 (estimating the tangent). More specifically we investigate how the attacker can find $p(q_l + \gamma_j t_j)$ by making second-oder small modifications ϵ_i [1].

Let $R_w(q_l) = y$. For small modifications $q_l + \epsilon, |\epsilon| << |\gamma_j t_j|$ to the original image q_l approximation

$$y = R(q_l) \approx R(q_l + \epsilon)$$

holds. Thus the detector returns $D = 1$ with probability $p(y)$ for these small modifications, see (1). Henceforward, through many experiments with different ϵ_i's the attacker is able to estimate the value of $p(y) = p(R_w(q_l))$.

Let $q_{l,j,i} = q_l + \gamma_j t_j + \epsilon_i$ such that

$$R_w(q_{l,j,i}) \approx R_w(q_l + \gamma_j t_j).$$

For ease of notation we write q_i instead of $q_{l,j,i}$. Image $\gamma_j t_j$ is a bias, which we interpret as a test image which is non-zero only in one pixel n_j. For ease of notation we write t instead of $\gamma_j t_j$ and n instead of n_j. Let $t(n) = \alpha > 0$ and $\delta = \alpha k$. Then the effect Δy that t has on the decision variable is

$$\Delta y = R_w(t) = \alpha \cdot w(n) \in \{-\alpha k, +\alpha k\} = \{-\delta, +\delta\}.$$

Since R_w is (at least in a first order approximation) a linear function we have that

$$R_w(q_i) \approx R_w(q_l + t) = R_w(q_l) + R_w(t) = y + \Delta y$$

and if $p(y)$ is a smooth (differentiable) function

$$p(R_w(q_i)) \approx p(y + \Delta y) \approx p(y) + \Delta y \cdot p'(y),$$

where $p'(y)$ denotes the derivative of function p evaluated in y. Thus the detector returns output $D_i = 1$ with probability $p(y) + \Delta y \cdot p'(y)$ for image q_i, that is

$$Pr(D_i = 1|w(n) = +k) \approx p(y) + \delta \cdot p'(y),$$
$$Pr(D_i = 1|w(n) = -k) \approx p(y) - \delta \cdot p'(y). \tag{2}$$

Henceforward, through many experiments with different q_i's the attacker is able to estimate the value of $p(y) + \Delta y \cdot p'(y)$. If this value is more than $p(y)$ the

---

[1] Here q_l is the zero-order attempt, $\gamma_j t_j$'s describe first-order sensitivity measurements, and ϵ_i's describes second-order randomizations used by the attacker to measure statistical averages.

attacker concludes that $\Delta y = +\delta$ and $w(n) = +k$. If it is less than $p(y)$ the attacker concludes that $\Delta y = -\delta$ and $w(n) = -k$.

The idea is that the attacker gathers information about the polarity of the watermark in the pixel $w(n)$ through the series of test images q_i. This results in a sequence of outputs of the detector $D_1, D_2, \ldots, D_i, \ldots$. In the remainder we denote $D_1, \ldots, D_i$ by D^i. The average amount of bits needed to describe a realization of D^i is measured by the uncertainty about D^i, denoted by the entropy function $H(D^i)$. The average amount of bits needed to describe D^i given the knowledge of $w(n)$ is measured by the conditional uncertainty about D^i given $w(n)$, denoted by the conditional entropy function $H(D^i|w(n))$. The mutual information $I(D^i; w(n)) = H(D^i) - H(D^i|w(n))$ between D^i and $w(n)$ measures the amount of information D^i and $w(n)$ have in common. Hence, $I(D^i; w(n))$ measures the amount of information that the observation D^i reveals about the unknown $w(n)$. We notice that $w(n)$ takes on values $-k$ and $+k$ with equal probability, hence $H(w(n)) = 1$ bit. The entropy function h is defined as $h(x) = -x \log x - (1-x) \log(1-x)$ where the logarithm is of base 2. We notice that $h'(x) = \log((1-x)/x)$ and that the second derivative $h^{(2)}(x) = -1/(x(1-x) \ln 2)$. For a thorough treatment in information theory we refer to Cover and Thomas [10].

To defend the confidentiality of the watermark, the system designer of the copy protection scheme keeps the information that D^i reveals about the watermark as small as possible. He designs function p such that $I(D^i; w(n))$ is small enough. Let us analyse this mutual information. Let us consider the special case $i = 1$. From approximations (2) and the definition of entropy we infer that

$$H(D_1|w(n) = +k) \approx h(p(y) + \delta p'(y)),$$
$$H(D_1|w(n) = -k) \approx h(p(y) - \delta p'(y)),$$
$$H(D_1|w(n)) \approx (h(p(y) + \delta p'(y)) + h(p(y) - \delta p'(y)))/2,$$

and $Pr(D_1 = 1) = ((p(y) + \delta p'(y)) + (p(y) - \delta p'(y)))/2 = p(y)$, hence

$$H(D_1) = h(p(y)).$$

We conclude that

$$
\begin{aligned}
I(D^1; w(n)) &= H(D_1) - H(D_1|w(n)) \\
&\approx h(p(y)) - \frac{1}{2}[h(p(y) + \delta p'(y)) + h(p(y) - \delta p'(y))] \quad (3) \\
&\approx -\frac{(\delta p'(y))^2}{2} h^{(2)}(p(y)) \\
&= \frac{(\delta p'(y))^2}{2} \frac{1}{p(y)(1 - p(y)) \ln 2}. \quad (4)
\end{aligned}
$$

Let us consider the more general case $i \geq 1$. Let

$$F_s(x) = (p(y) + x)^s (1 - p(y) - x)^{i-s},$$
$$B(x) = -\sum_{0 \leq s \leq i} \binom{i}{s} F_s(x) \log \left(1 + \frac{F_s(-x)}{F_s(x)}\right),$$

and let its Taylor sequence be

$$B(x) = \sum_{j \geq 0} B^{(j)}(0) \frac{x^j}{j!}.$$

Then the following theorem holds. For its proof we refer to Appendix A.

Theorem 1. *Assuming that equalities hold in (2) we have*

$$I(D^i; w(\boldsymbol{n})) = \sum_{j \geq 1} B^{(2j)}(0) \frac{(\delta p'(y))^{2j}}{(2j)!},$$

where

$$B^{(2)}(0) = \frac{i}{p(y)(1 - p(y)) \ln 2}.$$

Hence,

$$I(D^i; w(\boldsymbol{n})) = i \cdot I(D^1; w(\boldsymbol{n})) + \sum_{j \geq 2} B^{(2j)}(0) \frac{(\delta p'(y))^j}{(2j)!}.$$

The system designer of the copy protection scheme wants to design $p(y)$ such that $I(D^i; w(\boldsymbol{n}))$ is as small as possible given that $p(y) = 0$ for $y \leq y_1$ and $p(y) = 1$ for $y \geq y_2$. We notice that the size of interval $[y_1, y_2]$ is related to the reliability of the detector, the smaller the interval the better the reliability. So, in practise the system designer chooses firstly the size of this interval such that the reliability of the detector will be in a reasonable range. Secondly, the system designer constructs an optimal function $p(y)$ (optimal in the sense that $I(D^i; w(\boldsymbol{n}))$ is as small as possible).

We notice that for a fixed function $p(.)$, $I(D^i; w(\boldsymbol{n}))$ solely depends on the value y. Therefore we define

$$I_i(y) = I(D^i; w(\boldsymbol{n}))$$

and we infer from Theorem 1 and (4) that a first order approximation gives

$$I_i(y) \approx \frac{2i\delta^2}{\ln 2} \left\{ \frac{(p'(y))^2}{1 - (2p(y) - 1)^2} \right\}.$$

By substituting

$$p(y) = \frac{1}{2} - \frac{1}{2} \cos(r(y)) \tag{5}$$

with $r(y) = 0$ for $y \leq y_1$ and $r(y) = \pi$ for $y \geq y_2$ we obtain

$$I_i(y) \approx \frac{2i\delta^2}{\ln 2} \frac{(r'(y))^2}{4}.$$

Hence,

$$|r'(y)| \approx \frac{\sqrt{2 \ln 2 I_i(y)/i}}{\delta}, \tag{6}$$

where $I_i(y)/i$ is the information leakage expressed in watermark bits per experiment. The system designer wants to have

$$\sup_y I_i(y)/i$$

as small as possible. The requirement that $\sup_y I_i(y)/i$ is as small as possible is equivalent to the requirement that $\sup_y |r'(y)|$ is as small as possible, see (6). We conclude that $r(y)$ linearly increases in the interval $[y_1, y_2]$. Thus

$$r(y) = \pi \frac{y - y_1}{y_2 - y_1} \tag{7}$$

and $\pi/(y_2 - y_1) \approx (\sqrt{2 \ln 2 I_i(y)/i})/\delta$, that is

$$I_i(y)/i \approx \frac{\pi^2}{2 \ln 2} \left\{ \frac{\delta}{y_2 - y_1} \right\}^2 \tag{8}$$

is the information leakage expressed in watermark bits per experiment. We have constructed the optimal shape of $p(y)$ and we conclude that the information leakage, expressed in watermark bits per experiment, decreases quadratically in the size of the decision interval. We notice that the reliability of the watermarking scheme gets worse (higher probabilities of missed detection and false alarm) if the size of the decision interval increases.

We have analysed a first order approximation of an optimal shape for $p(y)$. This means that (8) gives a first order approximation of the information leakage. A better approximation (actually an upper bound) is given by the next theorem. Its proof is presented in Appendix B.

Theorem 2. *Assuming that equalities hold in (2) and that $p(y)$ is defined by equations (5) and (7) we have that*

$$I(D^i; w(\boldsymbol{n})) \leq i \cdot I$$

with

$$I = 1 - h\left(\frac{1}{2} - \frac{\delta\pi}{2(y_2 - y_1)} \right) \approx \frac{\pi^2}{2 \ln 2} \left\{ \frac{\delta}{y_2 - y_1} \right\}^2 \approx I(D^1; w(\boldsymbol{n}))$$

if $\delta/(y_2 - y_1) < 1/\pi$, and $I = 1$ if $\delta/(y_2 - y_1) \geq 1/\pi$. Here $y_2 - y_1$ is the transition width of the decision interval and $\Delta y \in \{+\delta, -\delta\}$ is the effect that modifying one pixel has on the decision variable. Parameter I expresses the information leakage in watermark bits per experiment. The reliability of the watermarking scheme gets worse if the size of the decision interval increases.

6   Discussion

Example 1. Let us consider a digitized representation of a television frame in the NTSC standard, having $N = N_1 \times N_2 = 480$ by 720 pixels, with $w(\boldsymbol{n}) = \pm 1$. Then $R_w(w) = 345600$. A useful choice of detection thresholds can be $y_1 =$

115200 and $y_2 = 230400$. If the luminance is quantized into 8 bits $(0, \ldots, 255)$ one pixel test t can influence the decision variable y by at most $\delta = 255$ but a more realistic value is $\delta \approx 100$ relative to mid grey. In such case, $I = 5.4 \cdot 10^{-6}$ bits per test. So recovering the full watermark is 186000 times more difficult than without the randomized decision threshold.

In an attempt to increase δ the attacker may use a different base $\{t_0, t_1, \ldots, t_{N-1}\}$ (in the previous example and in Section 5 $t_j(\boldsymbol{n_j}) = \alpha$ and $t_j(\boldsymbol{n_m}) = 0$ for $m \neq j$). The effect of t_j on the decision variable is $R_w(t_j) = \sum_{\boldsymbol{n} \in A} w(\boldsymbol{n}) t_j(\boldsymbol{n})$. Notice that $w = \{w(\boldsymbol{n})\}_{\boldsymbol{n} \in A}$ is a random variable to the attacker and that the expected effect of t_j on the decision variable is $\mathrm{E}[R_w(t_j)] = 0$. For a spectrally white watermark [9], i.e., if $\mathrm{E}[w(\boldsymbol{n})w(\boldsymbol{n} + \Delta)] = 0$ for $\Delta \neq 0$, we find the second moment

$$\mathrm{E}[R_w(t_j)^2] = \sum_{\boldsymbol{n} \in A} \sum_{\boldsymbol{n} + \Delta \in A} \mathrm{E}[w(\boldsymbol{n})w(\boldsymbol{n} + \Delta)] t_j(\boldsymbol{n}) t_j(\boldsymbol{n} + \Delta)$$
$$= k^2 \sum_{\boldsymbol{n} \in A} t_j(\boldsymbol{n})^2 = k^2 E_{t_j}, \tag{9}$$

where $E_{t_j} = \sum_{\boldsymbol{n} \in A} t_j(\boldsymbol{n})^2$ is the energy in the test image t_j. Experiments with test image t_j reveal information about the value of $R_w(t_j)$ which gives us a linear relationship between the values of $w(\boldsymbol{n})$, $\boldsymbol{n} \in A$. We define the expected information leakage $I_i(y)$ in i experiments expressed in watermark bits by $I_i(y) = I(D^i; w) \approx i \cdot I(D^1; w) = i \cdot (H(D_1) - H(D_1|w))$ (notice that $I(D^i; w) = I(D^i; w(\boldsymbol{n_j}))$ if t_j is non-zero only in one pixel $\boldsymbol{n_j}$). See (2),

$$p(R_w(q_i)) \approx p(y) + R_w(t_j)p'(y). \tag{10}$$

Hence, $H(D_1) = h(\mathrm{E}[p(y) + R_w(t_j)p'(y)]) = h(p(y))$ and

$$H(D_1|w) = \sum_{\hat{w}} Pr(w = \hat{w})H(D_1|w = \hat{w}) = \sum_{\hat{w}} Pr(w = \hat{w})h(p(y) + R_w(t_j)p'(y))$$
$$= \mathrm{E}[h(p(y) + R_w(t_j)p'(y))]$$
$$= (\mathrm{E}[h(p(y) + R_w(t_j)p'(y))] + \mathrm{E}[h(p(y) - R_w(t_j)p'(y))])/2.$$

We obtain that the information leakage expressed in watermark bits per experiment equals

$$I_i(y)/i \approx \mathrm{E}[h(p(y)) - (h(p(y) + R_w(t_j)p'(y)) + h(p(y) - R_w(t_j)p'(y)))/2]$$
$$\approx \mathrm{E}[\pi^2 R_w(t_j)^2/(2 \ln 2(y_2 - y_1)^2)], \text{ see (4)},$$
$$= \frac{\pi^2}{2 \ln 2} \left\{ \frac{k\sqrt{E_{t_j}}}{y_2 - y_1} \right\}^2, \text{ see (9)}.$$

We have generalized (8) towards this new setting. Notice that for large E_{t_j} approximation (10), and hence the generalized formula, is not accurate anymore.

We conclude that for large E_{t_j} the attacker gains substantial information. However, large E_{t_j} is not suitable for watermark detection methods where $S_=$ is not a perfect hyperplane. Then $q_l + t_j$ would be influenced too much by t_j because of its large energy E_{t_j}.

7   Concluding Remarks

Electronic watermarks are a useful technical mechanism to protect Intellectual Property Rights. The use of watermarks in copy control for consumer electronic products, however, is not yet fully understood. We have investigated the sensitivity attack. The proposed countermeasure increases the workload by orders of magnitude, but the workload remains linear in the number of pixels.

In [1] a sensitivity attack is described that shows that if a watermark detection algorithm could be placed in a perfectly tamperproof box, this does not necessarily imply that the attacker cannot find a method to remove the watermark. This result questions the possibility to build perfect "public" watermarking schemes in which that attacker knows how to detect a watermark, but despite this knowledge he cannot remove or alter the watermark. A necessary condition for such system to be secure is that it should withstand the attack described here. Knowledge of the detection algorithm implies that the attacker can use the detector as an oracle to gain information about the watermark. As the attack proves, this is often sufficient to remove the watermark pixel by pixel. If the attack, or a more sophisticated elaboration of it, is successful against a black-box watermark detector, it would certainly be able to remove a watermark for which the attacker has the full details of the detection algorithm. All watermarking methods known to the authors are of the secret-key type, i.e., the watermark detector contains secret information, which could be exploited by an attacker to remove the watermark.

Acknowledgement

For helpful, interesting, and stimulating discussions we thank Ton Kalker, William Rey, Maurice Maes, and Geert Depovere.

A   Proof of Theorem 1

Assuming that equalities hold in (2) we will prove

$$I(D^i; w(n)) = \sum_{j \geq 1} B^{(2j)}(0) \frac{(\delta p'(y))^j}{(2j)!}.$$

For realizations $d^i = (d_1, \ldots, d_i)$ with $s(d^i) = |\{l : d_l = 1\}|$ we have that

$$Pr(D^i = d^i | w(n) = +k) = F_{s(d^i)}(+\delta p'(y)),$$
$$Pr(D^i = d^i | w(n) = -k) = F_{s(d^i)}(-\delta p'(y)),$$
$$Pr(D^i = d^i) = (F_{s(d^i)}(+\delta p'(y)) + F_{s(d^i)}(-\delta p'(y)))/2.$$

By definition of entropy and conditional entropy

$$H(D^i) = -\sum_{d^i} Pr(D^i = d^i) \log Pr(D^i = d^i),$$

$$H(D^i|w(\boldsymbol{n})) = (H(D^i|w(\boldsymbol{n}) = +k) + H(D^i|w(\boldsymbol{n}) = -k)/2$$
$$= -\frac{1}{2}\sum_{d^i} Pr(D^i = d^i|w(\boldsymbol{n}) = +k)\log Pr(D^i = d^i|w(\boldsymbol{n}) = +k) +$$
$$-\frac{1}{2}\sum_{d^i} Pr(D^i = d^i|w(\boldsymbol{n}) = -k)\log Pr(D^i = d^i|w(\boldsymbol{n}) = -k).$$

By combining all equations and noticing that $B(0) = -1$ we obtain

$$I(D^i; w(\boldsymbol{n})) = -\frac{1}{2}\sum_{d^i} F_{s(d^i)}(+\delta p'(y))\log\frac{1}{2}\left(1 + \frac{F_{s(d^i)}(-\delta p'(y))}{F_{s(d^i)}(+\delta p'(y))}\right) +$$
$$-\frac{1}{2}\sum_{d^i} F_{s(d^i)}(-\delta p'(y))\log\frac{1}{2}\left(1 + \frac{F_{s(d^i)}(+\delta p'(y))}{F_{s(d^i)}(-\delta p'(y))}\right)$$
$$= -[B(0) - \frac{1}{2}\{B(+\delta p'(y)) + B(-\delta p'(y))\}] = \sum_{j\geq 1} B^{(2j)}(0)\frac{(\delta p'(y))^{2j}}{(2j)!}.$$

Straightforward, but lengthy, computations give the desired expression for $B^{(2)}(0)$.

B   Proof of Theorem 2

We notice that $D_l \leftarrow w(\boldsymbol{n}) \rightarrow D^{l-1}$ is a Markov sequence since D_l and D^{l-1} only depend on each other because of their relation towards $w(\boldsymbol{n})$. Therefore we may conclude that

$$I(D_l; w(\boldsymbol{n})|D^{l-1}) = H(D_l|D^{l-1}) - H(D_l|w(\boldsymbol{n})D^{l-1})$$
$$= H(D_l|D^{l-1}) - H(D_l|w(\boldsymbol{n}))$$
$$\leq H(D_l) - H(D_l|w(\boldsymbol{n})) = I(D_l; w(\boldsymbol{n})).$$

Hence, by using (3)

$$I(D^i; w(\boldsymbol{n})) = \sum_{l=1}^{i} I(D_l; w(\boldsymbol{n})|D^{l-1}) \leq \sum_{l=1}^{i} I(D_l; w(\boldsymbol{n})) = ig(p(y), \delta p'(y)),$$

where for $0 \leq z \leq x \leq 1 - z \leq 1$

$$g(x, z) = h(x) - \frac{1}{2}[h(x + z) + h(x - z)].$$

Let us do some function research for $g(x, z)$ seen as function of x in the by us considered interval $[z, 1 - z]$. We notice that

$$\frac{d}{dx}g(x, z) = h'(x) - \frac{1}{2}[h'(x + z) + h'(x - z)],$$

thus $\frac{d}{dx}g(x,z)|_{x=1/2} = 0$. Further $\frac{d}{dx}g(x,z)|_{x=z} = h'(z) - h'(2z)/2 = \log((1-z)/z)-\log((1-2z)/2z)=\log((2-2z/(1-2z))>0$ and similarly $\frac{d}{dx}g(x,z)|_{x=1-z}<0$. For function $\frac{d}{dx}g(x,z)$ we compute

$$\ln 2 \frac{d^2}{dx^2}g(x,z) = \frac{-1}{x(1-x)} + \frac{1}{2}\left[\frac{1}{(x+z)(1-x-z)} + \frac{1}{(x-z)(1-x+z)}\right]$$

$$= \frac{-1}{x(1-x)} + \frac{x(1-x)+z^2}{(x^2-z^2)((1-x)^2-z^2)}.$$

This appears to be ≤ 0 iff $1/2 - \sqrt{z^2-3/4} \leq x \leq 1/2 + \sqrt{z^2-3/4}$. We conclude that $\frac{d}{dx}g(x,z) > 0$ if $x < 1/2$, $\frac{d}{dx}g(x,z) = 0$ if $x = 1/2$, and $\frac{d}{dx}g(x,z) > 0$ if $x > 1/2$. Hence, we have that $g(x,z)$ is maximal for $x = 1/2$.

We notice that

$$\frac{d}{dz}g(1/2,z) = \log\frac{1/2+z}{1/2-z} > 0.$$

Hence, $g(1/2,z)$ is increasing in z. We have that $p((y_2 - y_1)/2) = 1/2$ and $\delta p'(y) \leq \delta p'((y_2 - y_1)/2) = \delta\pi/(2(y_2 - y_1))$. Hence, $g(p(y),\delta p'(y))$ is maximal for $y = (y_2 - y_1)/2$ and we have that

$$g(p(y),\delta p'(y)) \leq 1 - h(1/2 - \delta\pi/(2(y_2 - y_1))).$$

References

1. I.J. Cox and J.M.P.G. Linnartz. "Public watermarks and resistance to tampering". ICIP 97.
2. W. Bender, D. Gruhl, N. Morimoto, and A. Lu. "Techniques for data hiding". *IBM Systems Journal*, Vol. 35.(3/4), 1996.
3. I.J. Cox, J. Kilian, F.T. Leighton and T. Shamoon. "A secure, robust watermark for multimedia". In *Information Hiding: First Int. Workshop Proc., Lecture Notes in Computer Science*, volume 1174, R. Anderson, ed., Springer-Verlag, pages 185–206, 1996.
4. J.P.M.G. Linnartz, A.C.C. Kalker, G.F. Depovere, and R. Beuker. "A reliability model for detection of electronic watermarks in digital images". In *Proc. Benelux Symposium on Communication Theory, Enschede, October*, pages 202–208, 1997.
5. I. Pitas and T.H. Kaskalis. "Signature casting on digital images". In *Proc. IEEE Workshop on Nonlinear Signal and Image Processing, Neos Marmaras, June*, 1995.
6. J.R. Smith and B.O. Comiskey. "Modulation and information hiding in images". In *Information Hiding: First Int. Workshop Proc., Lecture Notes in Computer Science*, volume 1174, R. Anderson, ed., Springer-Verlag, pages 207–226, 1996.
7. A.B. Watson. *"Digital Images and Human Vision"*. The MIT Press, 1993.
8. T. Kalker. "Watermark estimation through detector observations". In *Proceedings of the IEEE Benelux Signal Processing Symposium, Leuven, March*, pages 119–122, 1995.
9. J.-P. Linnartz, T. Kalker, G. Depovere. "Modelling the false alarm and missed detection rate for electronic watermarks". In *Proceedings of this Workshop*.
10. T.M. Cover and J.A. Thomas. *"Elements of Information Theory"*. John Wiley and Sons, Inc., 1991.

Steganalysis of Images Created Using Current Steganography Software

Neil F. Johnson and Sushil Jajodia

Center for Secure Information Systems
George Mason University
Fairfax, Virginia 22030-4444
http://isse.gmu.edu/~csis/
{njohnson,jajodia}@gmu.edu

Abstract. Steganography is the art of passing information in a manner that the very existence of the message is unknown. The goal of steganography is to avoid drawing suspicion to the transmission of a hidden message. If suspicion is raised, then this goal is defeated. Steganalysis is the art of discovering and rendering useless such covert messages. In this paper, we identify characteristics in current steganography software that direct the steganalyst to the existence of a hidden message and introduce the ground work of a tool for automatically detecting the existence of hidden messages in images.

1   Introduction

Steganography encompasses methods of transmitting secret messages through innocuous cover carriers in such a manner that the very existence of the embedded messages is undetectable. Creative methods have been devised in the hiding process to reduce the visible detection of the embedded messages. An overview of current steganography software and methods applied to digital images is examined in [14].

Hiding information, where electronic media are used as such carriers, requires alterations of the media properties which may introduce some form of degradation. If applied to images that degradation, at times, may be visible to the human eye [17] and point to signatures of the steganographic methods and tools used. These signatures may actually broadcast the existence of the embedded message, thus defeating the purpose of steganography, which is hiding the existence of a message.

Two aspects of attacks on steganography are detection and destruction of the embedded message.[1] Any image can be manipulated with the intent of destroying some

---

[1] The authors of [9] identify a watermark attack as an illicit watermark that forges or counterfeits a valid watermark. This form of attack is not investigated in this paper. However, counterfeited watermarks are vulnerable to the detection and destruction techniques identified in this paper.

David Aucsmith (Ed.): Information Hiding 1998, LNCS 1525, pp. 273–289, 1998.

hidden information whether an embedded message exists or not.[2] Detecting the existence of a hidden message will save time in the message elimination phase by processing only those images that contain hidden information. Detecting an embedded message also defeats the primary goal of steganography, that of concealing the vary existence of a hidden message. Our goal is not to advocate the removal or disabling of valid copyright information from watermarked images, but to point out the vulnerabilities of such approaches, as they are not as robust as is claimed.

In this paper we will look at steganography and watermarking techniques with equal interest. The difference between invisible digital watermarking (or imperceptible to the human eye) and digital steganography is based primarily on intent. Steganography conceals a message where that hidden message is the object of the communication. For example, sending a satellite photograph hidden in another image. Digital watermarks extend some information that may be considered attributes of the cover such as copyright. In the case of digital watermarks, the cover is the object of communication. Sometimes the methods used to embed a watermark and steganography messages are the same. Many digital watermarks are invisible to the human eye, but they may also be known. Watermarking techniques are more robust to attacks such as compression, cropping, and some image processing where the least significant bits are changed. For this reason, digital watermarks are used to embed copyright, ownership, and license information.

Invisible watermarking is treated as a subset of steganography though some aspects discussed are unique to tools identified as digital watermarking or steganography tools. When analysis for detection and destruction are applied, the steganography and watermarking tools are treated equally. The intent of this paper is to describe some methods of detecting and destroying hidden messages within computer images. Experimental results are presented to support these claims and identify characteristics in existing steganography software. We will provide a review of various weaknesses in some tools and illustrate how these may be exploited in steganalysis.

The rest of the paper is organized as follows. Section 2 introduces new terminology for steganalysis. Section 3 briefly introduces various methods for embedding information in images and categorizes tools used in this paper. Section 4 introduces some detection methods and identifies unique signatures of steganography tools which reveal the existence of hidden messages. Detection defeats the goal of steganography which is to hide the existence of an embedded message. We will provide examples of some characteristics in a sample of tools and illustrate how these may be vulnerable and exploited in steganalysis. Detection is but one part of steganalysis. Section 5 reveals limitations in the survivability of hidden messages and identifies methods for the destruction of such messages. Destruction methods and examples will be identified. The paper concludes with comments on steganography, steganalysis and related work. A list of additional readings, software, and resources used in researching this topic and additional information on steganography is available at http://isse.gmu.edu/~njohnson/Steganography.

---

[2] In this paper destruction of watermarks includes rendering watermarks unreadable or disabling the detection of a watermark.

2   Terminology

Steganography literally means "covered writing" and is the art of hiding the very existence of a message. The possible cover carriers are innocent looking carriers (images, audio, video, text, or some other digitally representative code) which will hold the hidden information. A message is the information hidden and may be plaintext, ciphertext, images, or anything that can be embedded into a bit stream. Together the cover carrier and the embedded message create a stego-carrier. Hiding information may require a stegokey which is additional secret information, such as a password, required for embedding the information.[3] For example, when a secret message is hidden within a cover image, the resulting product is a stego-image. A possible formula of the process may be represented as:

$$Cover\ medium\ +\ embedded\ message\ +\ stegokey\ =\ stego\text{-}medium \qquad (1)$$

New terminology with respect to attacks and breaking steganography schemes is similar to cryptographic terminology; however, there are some significant differences. Just as a cryptanalyst applies cryptanalysis in an attempt to decode or crack encrypted messages, the *steganalyst* is one who applies steganalysis in an attempt to detect the existence of hidden information. With cryptography, comparison is made between portions of the plaintext (possibly none) and portions of the ciphertext. In steganography, comparisons may be made between the cover-media, the stego-media, and possible portions of the message. The end result in cryptography is the ciphertext, while the end result in steganography is the stego-media. The message in steganography may or may not be encrypted. If it is encrypted, then if the message is extracted, the cryptanalysis techniques may be applied.

In order to define attack techniques used for steganalysis, corresponding techniques are considered in cryptanalysis. Attacks available to the cryptanalyst are ciphertext-only, known plaintext, chosen plaintext, and chosen ciphertext. In *ciphertext-only* attacks, the cryptanalyst knows the ciphertext to be decoded. The cryptanalyst may have the encoded message and part of the decoded message which together may be used for a *known plaintext* attack. The *chosen plaintext attack* is the most favorable case for the cryptanalyst. In this case, the cryptanalyst has some ciphertext which corresponds to some selected plaintext. If the encryption algorithm and ciphertext are available, the cryptanalyst encrypts plaintext looking for matches in the ciphertext. This *chosen ciphertext attack* is used to deduce the sender's key. The challenge with cryptography is not in detecting that something has been encrypted, but decoding the encrypted message.

Somewhat parallel attacks are available to the steganalyst. These are *stego-only, known cover, known message, chosen stego,* and *chosen message. A stego-only attack*

---

[3] Terms used in this paper to describe the steganography process are those agreed upon at the First International Workshop on Information Hiding [19]. The term 'carrier' is substituted with the media-type of the cover. For example, if the cover is a text file, then it is referred to as the cover text resulting in stego-text when hidden information is applied.

is similar to the ciphertext only attack where only the stego-medium is available for analysis. If the "original" cover-media and stego-media are both available, then a *known cover attack* is available. The steganalysis may use a *known message attack* when the hidden message is revealed at some later date, an attacker may attempt to analyze the stego-media for future attacks. Even with the message, this may be very difficult and may even be considered equivalent to the stego-only attack. The *chosen stego attack* is one where the steganography tool (algorithm) and stego-media are known. A *chosen message attack* is one where the steganalyst generates stego-media from some steganography tool or algorithm from a known message. The goal in this attack is to determine corresponding patterns in the stego-media that may point to the use of specific steganography tools or algorithms.

3   Steganographic Methods

The Internet is a vast channel for the dissemination of information that includes publications and images to convey ideas for mass communication. Images provide excellent carriers for hidden information and many different techniques have been introduced [1, 4, 14]. A subset of steganography and digital watermarking tools is used in this paper to test detection properties and robustness to manipulations in efforts to destroy or disable the embedded message. These tools can be categorized into two groups: those in the *Image Domain* and those in the *Transform Domain*.

Image Domain tools encompass bit-wise methods that apply least significant bit (LSB) insertion and noise manipulation. These approaches are common to steganography and are characterized as "simple systems" in [2]. The tools used in this group include StegoDos [22], S-Tools [24], Mandelsteg [25], EzStego [26], Hide and Seek (versions 4.1 through 1.0 for Windows 95) [27], Hide4PGP [28], Jpeg-Jsteg [34], White Noise Storm [23], and Steganos [29]. The image formats typically used in such steganography methods are lossless and the data can be directly manipulated and recovered. Including additional components such as masks or image objects to watermark an image is an image domain approach that is somewhat independent of image format.

The *transform domain* grouping of tools include those that involve manipulation of algorithms and image transforms such as discrete cosine transformation (DCT) [7, 16] and wavelet transformation [21]. These methods hide messages in more significant areas of the cover and may manipulate image properties such as luminance. Watermarking tools typically fit this categorization and the subset used in this paper is PictureMarc [30], JK-PGS [31], SysCop[4] [32], and SureSign [33]. These techniques are typically far more robust than bit-wise techniques; however a tradeoff exists between the about of information added to the image and the robustness obtained [14]. Many transform domain methods are independent to image format and may survive conversion between lossless and lossly formats.

---

[4] Though SysCop is a digital watermarking tool, some characteristics are similar to steganography tools when marking 8-bit gray-scale images.

JPEG images use the Discrete Cosine Transform (DCT) to achieve image compression. The compressed data is stored as integers; however, the calculations for the quantization process require floating point calculations which are rounded. Errors introduced by rounding define the lossy characteristic of the JPEG compression method [5]. The tool Jpeg-Jsteg [34] is a steganography tool that hides information by manipulating the rounding values of the JPEG[5] DCT coefficients. Information is hidden in the JPEG image by modulating the rounding choices either up or down in the DCT coefficients. Detection of such an embedded message would seem to be quite difficult. (An advantage DCT has over other transforms is the ability to minimize the block-like appearance resulting when the boundaries between the 8×8 sub-images become visible (known as *blocking artifact*) [12].)

Some techniques share characteristics of both image and transform domain tools. These may employ patchwork, pattern block encoding [4], spread spectrum methods [6] and masking [14] which add redundancy to the hidden information. These approaches may help protect against some image processing such as cropping and rotating. The patchwork approach uses a pseudo-random technique to select multiple areas (or patches) of an image for marking. Each patch may contain the watermark, so if one is destroyed or cropped, the others may survive. Masks may fall under the image domain as being an added component or image object. However, a mask may be added to an image by adjusting image properties or transform thus adopting characteristics of transform domain tools.

4   Detecting Hidden Information

Steganography tools typically hide relatively large blocks of information where watermarking tools place less information in an image, but the watermark is distributed redundantly throughout the entire image [16]. In any case, these methods insert information and manipulate the images in ways as to remain invisible to the human eye. However, any manipulation to the image introduces some amount of distortion and degradation of some aspect in the "original" image's properties.[6] The tools vary in their approaches for hiding information. Without knowing which tool is used and which, if any, stegokey is used, detecting the hidden information may become quite complex. However, some of the tools produce stego-images with characteristics that act as signatures for the steganography method or tool used.

To begin evaluating images for additional, hidden information, the concept of defining a "normal" or average image was deemed desirable. Defining a normal image is somewhat difficult when considering the possibilities of digital photographs, paintings, drawings, and graphics. Only after evaluating many original images and

---

[5] Joint Photography Experts Group (JPG/JPEG) is a device-independent method for storing images and supports 24-bit formats.

[6] Note: some basic insertion techniques place information between headers or other "unused" areas that are ignored by image viewers. This avoids degradation to the image, but are detectable in bit analysis.

stego-images as to color composition, luminance, and pixel[7] relationship do anomalies point to characteristics that are not "normal" in other images. Several patterns became visible when evaluating many images used for applying steganography. The *chosen message* and *known cover* attacks were quite useful in detecting these patterns. In images that have color palettes or indexes, colors are typically ordered from the most used colors to the least used colors to reduce table lookup time. The changes between color values may change gradually but rarely, if ever, in one bit shifts. Gray-scale image color indexes do shift in 1-bit increments, but all the RGB values are the same. Applying a similar approach to monochromatic images other than gray-scale, normally two of the RGB values are the same with the third generally being a much stronger saturation of color. Some images such as hand drawings, fractals and clip art may shift greatly in the color values of adjacent pixels. However, having occurrences of single pixels outstanding may point to the existence of hidden information.

Added content to some images may be recognizable as exaggerated noise. This is a common characteristic for many bit-wise tools as applied to 8-bit images. Using 8-bit images without manipulating the palette will, in many cases, cause color shifts as the raster pointers are changed from one palette entry to another. If the adjacent palette colors are very similar, there may be little or no noticeable change. However, if adjacent palette entries are dissimilar, then the noise due to the manipulation of the LSBs is obvious [10]. For this reason that many authors of steganography software and some articles stress the use of gray-scale images (those with 256 shades of gray) [3]. Gray-scale images are special occurrences of 8-bit images and are very good covers because the shades gradually change from color entry to color entry in the palette.

Using images with vastly contrasting adjacent palette entries to foil steganography software so that small shifts to the LSBs of the raster data will cause radical color changes in the image that advertise the existence of a hidden message [10]. Without altering the 8-bit palette, changes to the LSBs in the raster data may show dramatic changes in the stego-image:

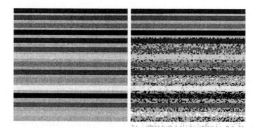

Fig. 1. Original 8-bit cover image (left), and the 8-bit
stego-image (right) created with *Hide and Seek*.

Some of the bit-wise tools attempt to reduce this affect by ordering the palette [26, 28]. Even with a few numbers of distinct colors, sorting the palette is may not be suf-

---

[7] A pixel is an instance of color. The dimension of an image is usually expressed in the number of pixels in width by the number of pixels in height. For example, a 10x10 image is one that is 10 pixels wide by 10 pixels in height.

ficient to keep from broadcasting the existence of an embedded message. Other bit-wise tools and a transform tool take it a step farther and create new palettes [24, 28[8], 32]. Converting an 8-bit image to 24-bit provides direct access to the color values for manipulation and any alteration will most likely be visually undetectable. The disadvantage is the resulting image is much larger in size and may be unsuitable for electronic transmission. A possible solution is to convert the image back to an 8-bit image after the information is hidden in the LSBs. Even if the colors in the image palette change radically, this method may still hide the fact that a message exists.

Word of caution: since 8-bit images are limited to 256 unique color entries in the image palette, consideration of the number of unique colors used by the image must be considered. For example, if an image contains 200 unique colors and steganography is applied then the number of unique colors could easily jump to 300 (assuming that LSB steganography alters on average 50% of the bits and the new colors are added). Reducing the image to 8-bit again will force the image into 256 colors. There is a high probability that some of the new colors created when modifying the LSBs will be lost.

One method around this is to decrease the number of colors to a value that will maintain good image quality and ensure that the number of colors will not increase beyond 256. This novel approach applies techniques described in [13, 20] and reduces the number of colors to no less than 32 unique colors. These 32 colors are "expanded" up to eight palette entries by adding adjacent colors in the palette that are very close to the original color [24]. This method produces a stego-image that is so close to the original cover image that virtually no visual differences are detected. However, this approach also creates a unique pattern which will be explored further in this paper.

4.1   Looking for Signatures

One method for detecting the existence of hidden messages in stego-images is to look for obvious and repetitive patterns which may point to the identification or signature of a steganography tool or hidden message. Distortions or patterns visible to the human eye are the easiest to detect. An approach used to identify such patterns is to compare the original cover-images with the stego-images and note visible differences (known-cover attack). Minute changes are readily noticeable when comparing the cover and stego-images. These subtle distortions may go unnoticed without the benefit of such a comparison. For example, distortion introduced into an image may resemble JPEG compression noise. This "noise" jumps out of the stego-images when compared with the original cover images. Without the benefit of using the cover image, such noise may pass for an integral part of the image and go unnoticed. In making these comparisons with numerous images, patterns begin emerge as possible signatures to steganography software. Some of these signatures may be exploited automatically to identify the existence of hidden messages and even the tools used in em-

---

[8] Hide4PGP provides command line options which gives the user flexibility in determining how image palettes are processed.

bedding the messages. With this knowledge-base, if the cover images are not available for comparison, the derived known signatures are enough to imply the existence of a message and identify the tool used to embed the message. However, in some cases recurring, predictable patterns are not readily apparent even if distortion between the cover and stego-images is noticeable.

One type of distortion is obvious corruption, as seen in Fig. 1 and discussed in [17]. A set of test images was created with contrasting adjacent palette entries as prescribed in [10]. Some of the tools, specifically those in the bit-wise set, produced severely distorted and noisy stego-images [26, 27, 29]. These distortions are severe color shifts that advertise the existence of a hidden message. Detecting this characteristic may be automated by investigating pixel "neighborhoods" and determining if an outstanding pixel is common to the image, follows a pattern, or resembles noise.

Not all of the bit-wise tools produce this type of image distortion. Several bit-wise programs and those in the transform set embedded information without visible distortion of the stego-image. Even though these tools pass this test, other patterns emerged that can be used to detect the possible existence of an embedded message.

8-bit color and gray-scale images which have color palettes or indexes are easier to analyze visually. Tools that provide good results "on paper" may have digital characteristics making the existence of a message detectable [22, 24, 25, 27, 32]. Unlike the obvious distortions mentioned in [17] or predicted in [10], some tools maintained remarkable image integrity and displayed almost no distortion when comparing the cover and stego-images on the screen or in print [14, 15]. The detectable patterns are exposed when the palettes of 8-bit and gray-scale images are investigated.

Detecting the existence of a hidden message is accomplished by creating an array of unique pixel values within the image. Then, sort by luminance calculated as follows [5]:

$$L = (0.299 \times Red) + (0.587 \times Green) + (0.114 \times Blue) \tag{2}$$

Investigation of image properties provides promising message detection techniques. Investigating known image characteristics for anomalies point out the possible existence of hidden information. Distortions or patterns visible to the human eye are the easiest to detect especially with the aid of comparing cover images with stego-images. In doing so, a knowledge-base of repetitive, predictable patterns can be established which identifies characteristics that assist in stego-only analysis. Such information assists in automating the detection processes. Such steganalysis tools can identify the existence of hidden messages and even the tools used to embed the messages [36]. Many bit-wise tools use LSB and similar approaches to hide data. Some times the data is encrypted and other times it is not.

4.2   Examples of Palette Signature

S-Tools

In an effort to keep the total number of unique colors less than 256, S-Tools reduces the number of colors of the cover image to a minimum of 32 colors. The new "base" colors are expanded over several palette entries. Sorting the palette by its luminance, blocks of colors appear to be the same, but actually have variances of 1 bit value. The approach is the same with 8-bit color and gray-scale images. When this method is applied to gray-scale cover images, the stego-image is no longer gray-scale as the RGB byte values within a pixel may vary by one bit. This is a good illustration of the limits of the human eye. However, the manner in which the pallet entries vary are uncommon except to a few steganographic techniques.

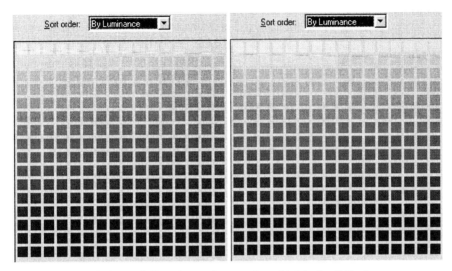

Fig. 2. Cover (left) and stego-image palette (right) after S-Tools.

Investigation of many images does not illustrate this pattern occurring "naturally." Gray-scale and other monochromatic images do not follow a similar pattern but the in each step in the palette entry all the RGB values are incremented the same so the pattern does not follow this example. Nor has it been found that images containing large areas of similar colors produce this pattern. Such images contain similar colors but the variance in colors is far greater than that represented by a stego-image produced by S-Tools. Other bit-wise and transform tools share similar characteristics to S-Tools [25, 28, 32].

SysCop

SysCop is the only transform tool that follows this pattern when manipulating 8-bit images. For example, adjacent pallet entries may be 00 00 00, 01 01 00, 01 00 01, etc. If an 8-bit cover image has near 256 colors, SysCop will reduce the number of colors, but not to the degree applied in S-Tools. Detecting a signature through the color variances in the palette for near 256 colors is more difficult than detecting such a pattern in S-Tools. SysCop does, however, typically buffer a number of pallet entries (32+) with black (00 00 00) before the raster data begins. A 256 color approximation of a photograph with black areas rarely has a large number of palette entries with values of (00 00 00). It is far more common for black areas to actually be a number of different colors near black.

Investigating SysCop's manipulation of gray-scale GIF[9] images requires a bit more than casual observation of the palette. In processing gray-scale images, SysCop generates the GIF87a formatted image but with an abbreviated palette table. For example, if the cover image is a GIF87a gray-scale image but only uses nine shades of gray, the image file still has a 256 color index in the file between offset values 0x0D through 0x30C ranging in values from 0 through 255. When SysCop processes the gray-scale files, the palette is reduced to the actual colors used in the stego-image. If nine colors are used in the stego-image, then only nine unique RGB triples are in the stego-image file's palette instead of the expected 256 color index.

Mandelsteg

Viewing the palette also points to the identification of fractal images generated using Mandelsteg. This tool is unique in that it does not manipulate any preexisting cover images, but generates Mandelbrot fractal graphics as cover images for hidden messages. If a file name is passed as a parameter to Mandelsteg, then the file is hidden in the Mandelbrot image. Depending upon the parameters, the image may vary in color and size. All Mandelsteg generated images have 256 palette entries in the color index and all have a detectable pattern in the image palette of 128 unique colors with two palette entries for each color.

Hide and Seek

Hide and Seek creates stego-images with different properties depending upon the version applied. Both versions 4.1 and 5.0 of Hide and Seek share a common characteristic in the palette entries of stego-image. Investigating the palettes of 265 color images, or viewing the histogram, shows that all the palette entries divisible by four for all bit values. This is a very unusual occurrence. Gray-scale images processed by version 4.1 and 5.0 have 256 triples as expected, but the range in sets of four triples from 0 to 252, with incremental steps of 4 (i.e. 0, 4, 8, ..., 248, 252). A key to detecting this when viewing images casually is that the "whitest" values in an image are 252 252 252. To date, this signature is unique to Hide and Seek. A typical gray-scale color index in a GIF image is from offset 0x0D through 0x30C ranges in triples (the three RGB entries are the same value) from 0 to 255.

In addition to recognizable patterns in the palette, Hide and Seek versions 4.1 and 5.0 have produced characteristics that point to the possible existence of a hidden message. In version 4.1 all files must be 320×480 pixels and contain 256 colors. If the image is smaller than the minimum, then the stego-image is padded with black space. If the cover image is larger, the stego-image is cropped to fit. Version 5.0 allows more sizes to be used for cover images, but the images are forced to fit an exact size. If the image is smaller than the minimum (320×200), then the stego-image is padded with black space. If any image is larger than the nearest allowable image size, then it is padded with black space to the next larger size. If any image exceeds 1024 pixels in width or 768 pixels in height, then an error message is returned. The padded areas are added prior to embedding the message and are thus used in hiding the message. If the

---

[9] Graphic Interchange Format developed by Compuserve to be a device-independent method of storing images.

padded area is removed from an image, then the message cannot be recovered. Images are forced into sizes 320×200, 320×400, 320×480, 640×400, and 1024×768. StegoDos produces a similar effect as it only works with 256 color, 320×200 images. If images are not this exact size, they are cropped to fit or padded with black space.

In Hide and Seek 1.0 for Windows 95 the image size restrictions are no longer an issue; however, the cover images are still limited to 256 colors or gray-scale. In previous version of Hide and Seek GIF images were used as covers. In the Windows 95 version, BMP[10] images are used due to licensing issues with GIF image compression. No longer do the stego-image palettes produce predictable patterns as in versions 4.1 and 5.0.

Hide4PGP

Hide4PGP uses 8-bit and 24-bit BMP images as cover images and provides a number of options for selecting how the 8-bit palettes are handled or at what bit levels the data is hidden. The default storage area for hidden information is in the LSB of 8-bit images and in the fourth LSB (that is the fourth bit from the right) in 24-bit images. BMP files have a 54 byte header. The raster data in 24-bit images follow this header. Since, 8-bit images require a palette (or color index), the 1024 bytes following header are used for the palette. Hiding plaintext and using the default settings in Hide4PGP, extracting the fourth LSB starting at the 54th byte for 24-bit BMP files and extracting the LSB starting at byte 1078 reveals the hidden plaintext message. If it so happens that the embedded message is encrypted, then cryptanalysis techniques can be applied in attempts to crack the encryption routine.

The options for selecting the bit level to hide information are: *1* for the LSB, *2* for the second LSB, *4* for the fourth LSB, and *8* for the eighth bit. Any of these options produce visible noise in many 8-bit images, so options to manipulate the image palette were added. These greatly improve the look of the resulting cover image but add properties that are unique to steganography and point the viewer to the possibility of a hidden message. Two options allow duplicating palette entries of colors that are more often used and ordering the palette entries to like colors. The number of duplicate entries is always an even number. This is characteristic that can be employed as at signature (similar to [24] and [32]). By ordering the palette, Hide4PGP, pairs similar colors together similar to the approach of [26].

Jsteg-Jpeg

In plotting the coefficients using the IDCT formula of JPEG images, the expected result is a relatively smooth graph for values of not equal to zero. However, plotting the coefficients of images created with Jpeg-Jsteg produce more erratic graphs and show steps resulting from duplicate coefficient values due to exaggerated rounding errors caused by storing the hidden information. This distortion is more noticeable for coefficient values less than zero [8].

---

[10] Windows and OS/2 bitmap picture file.

5   Destroying Steganography and Watermarks

Detecting the existence of hidden information defeats the goal of imperceptibility. Tools in the transform set are far more difficult to detect without the original image for comparison. Knowledge of an existing watermark may be knows so detecting it is not always necessary. A successful attack on a watermark is to destroy or disable it [2]. With each of the image and transform domain tools, there is a trade off between the size of the payload (amount of hidden information) that can be embedded and the survivability or robustness of that information to manipulation of the images.

The methods devised by the authors for destruction are not intended to advocate the removal or disabling of valid copyright information from watermarked images, as an illicit behavior, but to evaluate the claims of watermarks and study the robustness of current methods.[11] Some methods of disabling hidden messages may require considerable alterations to the stego-image. Destruction of embedded messages is fairly easy in cases where bit-wise methods are used since these methods employ the LSBs of images which may be changed with compression of small image processes. More effort is required with transform set of data hiding tools since the hidden message is integrated more fully into the cover. A goal for many transform methods is to make the hidden information (the watermark) such an integral part of the image that the only way to remove or disable it is to destroy the stego-image. Doing so will render the image useless to the attacker.

We will illustrate techniques for testing digital watermarks which provide similar functionality to watermarking test tools [35, 37]. Such tools and techniques should be used by those considering making the investment of watermarking to provide a sense of security of copyright and licensing just as password cracking tools are used by system administrators to test the strength of user and system passwords. If the password fails, the administrator should notify the password owner that the password is not secure.

Bit-wise methods are vulnerable to small amounts of image processing. A quick way to destroy many messages hidden with these techniques is to convert the image to a lossy compression format such as JPEG. Recompressing JPEG images processed with Jpeg-Jsteg will destroy the message embedded in the DCT coefficients as they are recalculated. The transform set of techniques that may apply transformations, redundancy, and masking merge the hidden information with integral properties of the images. These methods are more robust than the bit-wise methods, but are still vulnerable to destruction.

Consider this simple formula. Assume a measurement of the threshold of human imperceptibility in an image (t) and the portion above this threshold as image part that contains visible distortion if altered (v). The equation of image (I) is:

$$I = v + t \tag{3}$$

The size of t is available to both the owner watermark and to the attacker. As long as t remains in the imperceptible region, there exists some t' use by the attacker where

---

[11] The authors of the watermark testing tools share this view [18, 35, 37].

$I' = v + t'$ and there is no perceptible difference between I and I'. This attack may be used to remove or replace the t region. A variation of this attack is explored in [9] to the aspect of counterfeiting watermarks. If information is added to some media such that the added information cannot be detected, then there exists some amount of additional information that may be added or removed within the same threshold which will overwrite or remove the embedded covert information.

A series of image processing tests were devised to evaluate the robustness threshold of the bit-wise and transform tools. These tests will eventually alter the hidden information to the point that it cannot be retrieved. This fact may be viewed as a weakness of the "reader" instead of the "writer" in some of these tools. The motivation behind these tests is to illustrate what the techniques will withstand and what are some common vulnerabilities. The method of testing and measuring each tool consisted of using existing images and creating new images for testing. The images include digital photographs, clip art, and digital art. The digital photographs are typically 24-bit with thousands of colors or 8-bit grayscale. JPEG and 24-bit BMP files make up the majority of the digital photographs. Clip art images have relatively few colors and are typically 8-bit GIF images in our experiment. Digital art images are not photographs, but may have thousands of colors. These images may be 24-bit (BMP or JPEG) or 8bit images (BMP or GIF). Where necessary, images were converted to other formats as specified by the steganography or watermarking tool requirements.

A number of images from each type were embedded with known messages or watermarks and the resulting stego-images were verified for the message contents. In the robustness testing, the stego-images are manipulated with a number of image processing techniques and checked for the message contents. The tests include: converting between lossless and lossy formats, converting between bit densities (24-bit, 8-bit, grayscale), blurring, smoothing, adding noise, removing noise, sharpening, edge enhancement, masking, rotating, scaling, resampling, warping, converting from digital to analog and back (printing and scanning), mirroring, flipping, adding bit-wise messages, adding transform messages, and applying the unZign and StirMark tools to test the robustness of watermarking software. A series of tests were also performed to determine the smallest images that can be used successfully to hide data for each tool.

Minor image processing or conversion to JPEG compressed images was sufficient to disable the bit-wise tools. The transform methods survived a few of the image processing tests. Many images were used for each test as results varied between the use of 8-bit, 24-bit, lossless and lossy image formats. All tests were conducted using *Paint Shop Pro* by JASC and the results were recorded on whether the hidden information was detected and recovered with each steganography and watermarking tool. PictureMarc was added to images via Adobe *Photoshop*®. SureSign was added to images using both *Paint Shop Pro* and *Photoshop*.

With any one of the tests, tools that rely on bit-wise methods to hide data failed to recover any messages. The transform tools such as survived many of these tests, but failed with combinations of these image processes. Existing tools were also applied to the stego-images to test robustness [35, 37]. The observed success in making the watermark unreadable is in introducing small geometric distortions to the image then resampling and smoothing. This combines the effects of slight blurring, edge enhancement, and asymmetric resizing (warping). These combinations are very effective in reducing the ability for watermarking tools to identify the embedded watermark. Companies such as Digimarc and Signum Technologies maintain that even with severe image manipulation, the watermark may be recovered if both the altered watermarked image and the original image can be used together to extract the partially destroyed watermark.

An attractive feature in the use of watermarking technology in the Internet is the ability to use a software robot (softbot or spider) that searches through web pages for watermarked images. If watermarks are found, the information can be used to identify copyright infringement [30]. An attack that illustrates the limitation of such a softbot takes advantage of the image size limitations of a readable watermark by splitting the watermarked image into sufficiently small pieces so the watermark reader cannot detect the watermark [18]. This method does not attack the processing of an image to embed or remove a mark, but illustrates a way to bypass detection.

6   Related Work

This paper provided an introduction to steganalysis and identified weaknesses and visible signs of steganography. This work is but a fraction of the steganalysis approach. To date a general detection technique as applied to digital image steganography has not been devised and methods beyond visual analysis are being explored. Too many images exist to be reviewed manually for hidden messages. We have introduced some weaknesses of steganographic software that point to the possible existence of hidden messages. Detection of these "signatures" can be automated into tools for detecting steganography [36]. *Stegodetect* takes advantage of palette patterns and the characteristics, and analyzes pixel "neighborhoods." Tools for detecting hidden information are promising for future work in steganalysis and for verifying watermarks.

Steganography pertains not only to digital images but also to other media, including voice, text and binary files, and communication channels. The ease in use and abundant availability of steganography tools has law enforcement concerned in trafficking of illicit material via web page images, audio, and other files being transmitted through the Internet. Methods of message detection and understanding the thresholds of current technology are necessary to uncover such activities. Ongoing work in the area of Internet steganography [11] investigates embedding, recovering, and detecting information in TCP/IP packet headers and other network transmissions.

Development in the area of covert communications and steganography will continue. Research in building more robust digital watermarks that can survive image manipulation and attacks continues to grow. The more information is placed in the public's reach on the Internet, the more owners of such information need to protect themselves from theft and false representation. Success in steganographic secrecy results from selecting the proper mechanisms. However, a stego-image which seems innocent enough may, upon further investigation, actually broadcast the existence of embedded information.

7   Comments and Conclusion

Steganography transmits secrets through apparently innocuous covers in an effort to conceal the existence of a secret. Digital image steganography and its derivatives are growing in use and application. In areas where cryptography and strong encryption are being outlawed, citizens are looking at steganography to circumvent such policies and pass messages covertly. Commercial applications of steganography in the form of digital watermarks and digital fingerprinting are currently being used to track the copyright and ownership of electronic media. Understanding and investigating the limitations of these applications helps to direct researchers to better, more robust solutions. Efforts in devising more robust watermarks are essential to ensure the survivability of embedded information such as copyright and licensing information. Tools that test the survivability of watermarks are essential for the evolution of stronger watermarking techniques. Using these tools and methods described in this paper, potential consumers of digital watermarking tools, can see how much (or how little) effort is required to make the watermark unreadable by the watermarking tools.

Perhaps an inherent weakness in many watermark approaches, is the advertisement that an invisible watermark exists in a file. With steganography, if the embedded message is not advertised, casual users will not know it even exists and therefore will not attempt to remove the mark. However, advertising the fact that some hidden information exists, is only an invitation to "crackers" as a challenge. Some watermarking tools are distributed with over-the-shelf software, such as Adobe Photoshop® [30]. A method was recently advertised over the Internet that such a tool has been "cracked" and showed how to watermark any image with the ID of someone else. Almost any information can be added which can even be used to overwrite valid watermarks with "forged" ones. If humanly imperceptible information is embedded within a cover, then humanly imperceptible alterations can be made to the cover which destroys the embedded information.

Acknowledgement

The authors would like to thank Eric Cole, Prof. Zoran Duric and others to their contribution in reviewing and commenting on this paper, and David Sanders for his preliminary work in developing a steganalysis tool.

References

1. Anderson, R., (ed.): Information hiding: first international workshop, Cambridge, UK. Lecture Notes in Computer Science, Vol. 1174. Springer-Verlag, Berlin Heidelberg New York (1996)
2. Anderson, R., Petitcolas, F.: On the Limits of Steganography, IEEE Journal on Selected Areas in Communications, Vol. 16, No. 4, May (1998) 474–481.
3. Aura, T.: Invisible Communication, EET 1995. Technical Report, Helsinki Univ. of Technology, Finland, November 1995, http://deadlock.hut.fi/ste/ste_html (1995)

4. Bender, W., Gruhl, D., Morimoto, N., Lu, A.: Techniques for Data Hiding. IBM Systems Journal Vol. 35, No. 3&4. MIT Media Lab (1996) 313–336.
5. Brown, W., Shepherd, B.J.: Graphics File Formats: Reference and Guide. Manning Publications, Greenwich, CT (1995)
6. Cox, I., Kilian, J., Leighton, T., Shamoon, T.: Secure Spread Spectrum Watermarking for Multimedia. Technical Report 95–10, NEC Research Institute (1995)
7. Cox, I., Kilian, J., Shamoon, T., Leighton, T.: A Secure, Robust Watermark for Multimedia. In: [1] (1996) 185–206
8. Cole, E.: Steganography. Information System Security paper, George Mason University. (1997)
9. Craver, S., Memon, N., Yeo, B., Yeung, N.M.: Resolving Rightful Ownerships with Invisible Watermarking Techniques. Research Report RC 20755 (91985), Computer Science/Mathematics, IBM Research Division (1997)
10. Cha, S.D., Park, G.H., Lee, H.K.: A Solution to the Image Downgrading Problem. ACSAC (1995) 108–112
11. Dunigan, T.: Work in progress on Internet steganography which involves hiding, recovering, and detecting info hidden in the TCP/IP packet headers. Oak Ridge National Laboratory, Oak Ridge, TN.
12. Gonzalez, R.C., Woods, R.E.: Digital Image Processing. Addison-Wesley. Reading, MA, (1992)
13. Heckbert, P.: Color Image Quantization for Frame Buffer Display. ACM Computer Graphics, vol. 16, no. 3. July (1982) 297–307.
14. Johnson, N.F., Jajodia, S.: Exploring Steganography: Seeing the Unseen. IEEE Computer. February (1998) 26–34
15. Johnson, N.F.: Steganography. Information System Security paper, George Mason University (1995) http://isse.gmu.edu/~njohnson/stegdoc/
16. Koch, E., Rindfrey, J., Zhao, J.: Copyright Protection for Multimedia Data. Proceedings of the International Conference on Digital Media and Electronic Publishing, December 1994. Leeds, UK (1994)
17. Kurak, C., McHugh, J.: A Cautionary Note On Image Downgrading. IEEE Eighth Annual Computer Security Applications Conference (1992) 153–159.
18. Petitcolas, F., Anderson, R., Kuhn, M.: Attacks on Copyright Marking Systems. Second Workshop on Information Hiding, Portland, Oregon, April. This proceedings (1998)
19. Pfitzman, B.: Information Hiding Terminology. In: [1] 347–350
20. Wayner, P.: Disappearing Cryptography. AP Professional, Chestnut Hill, MA (1996)
21. Xia, X, Boncelet, C.G., Arce, G.R.: A Multiresolution Watermark for Digital Images. IEEE International Conference on Image Processing, October 1997 (1997)

Steganography Software References

Many other software applications are available that provide steganographic results. The following list gives a sample of software available for the PC platform. Every effort is being made to credit the authors of the software reviewed in this paper. However, some authors wish to remain anonymous. Additional software sources are listed at http://isse.gmu.edu/~njohnson/Steganography.

Image Domain Tools

22. Anonymous, Author alias: Black Wolf.: *StegoDos – Black Wolf's Picture Encoder v0.90B*, Public Domain. ftp://ftp.csua.berkeley.edu/pub/cypherpunks/steganography/ stegodos.zip.

23. Arachelian, R.: *White Noise Storm™ (WNS)*, Shareware (1994) ftp://ftp.csua.berkeley.edu/pub/cypherpunks/steganography/wns210.zip.
24. Brown, A.: *S-Tools for Windows*, Shareware 1994. ftp://idea.sec.dsi.unimi.it/pub/security/crypt/code/s-tools3.zip (version 3), ftp://idea.sec.dsi.unimi.it/pub/security/crypt/code/s-tools4.zip (version 4)
25. Hastur, H: *Mandelsteg,* ftp://idea.sec.dsi.unimi.it/pub/security/crypt/code/
26. Machado, R.: *EzStego, Stego Online, Stego*, http://www.stego.com
27. Maroney, C.: *Hide and Seek*, Shareware. ftp://ftp.csua.berkeley.edu/pub/cypherpunks/steganography/hdsk41b.zip (version 4.1), http://www.rugeley.demon.co.uk/security/hdsk50.zip (version 5.0), http://www.cypher.net/products/ (version 1.0 for Windows 95)
28. Repp, H.: *Hide4PGP*, http://www.rugeley.demon.co.uk/security/hide4pgp.zip
29. Hansmann F.: *Steganos.* Deus Ex Machina Communications. http://www.steganography.com

Transform Domain Tools
30. Digimarc Corporation: *PictureMarc™, MarcSpider™,* http://www.digimarc.com
31. Kutter, M., Jordan, F.: *JK-PGS (Pretty Good Signature).* Signal Processing Laboratory at Swiss Federal Institute of Technology (EPFL). http://ltswww.epfl.ch/~kutter/watermarking/JK_PGS.html
32. MediaSec Technologies LLC.: *SysCop™*, http://www.mediasec.com/
33. Signum Technologies, *SureSign*, http://www.signumtech.com
34. Upham, D.: *Jpeg-Jsteg.* Modification of the Independent JPEG Group's JPEG software (release 4) for 1-bit steganography in JFIF output files. ftp://ftp.funet.fi/pub/crypt/steganography.

Watermark and Steganography Analysis and Testing Tools
35. Kuhn, M., Petitcolas F.: StirMark. http://www.cl.cam.ac.uk/~fapp2/watermarking/stirmark/ (1997)
36. Sanders, D.: Stegodetect. Steganography detection tool (1997)
37. Anonymous: unZign. Watermarking testing tool available at http://altern.org/watermark/ – the author may be contacted through unzign@hotmail.com (1997)

Twin Peaks: The Histogram Attack to Fixed Depth Image Watermarks

Maurice Maes

Philips Research Laboratories
Prof. Holstlaan 4, 5656 AA Eindhoven, The Netherlands

Abstract. In this paper we present an attack to fixed depth image watermarks. The attack is based on histogram analysis of a watermarked image. With this attack, the watermark can often be reconstructed from just a few images, without using the detector.

1 Introduction

Digital watermarking is a research area which aims at hiding secret information in digital multimedia content including images, audio, or video. It is mostly used to embed copyright information in such a way that it is imperceptible by humans, but easily detected by a computer. Watermarks should be difficult to remove, and robust to for instance image compression, noise, scaling, etc.

Many presently used techniques for watermarking of digital images boil down to adding a pseudo-noise pattern to the images. The detection of the watermark is then done by correlating the possibly watermarked image with the pseudo-noise sequence, which is generated by a secret key.

This paper deals with an attack to these watermark methods. In particular, it will be shown that if the added noise sequence does not depend on the original image, that is if it is a so-called 'fixed depth' watermark, then it is easily hacked by a malicious attacker. Fixed depth watermarks are for instance proposed in Bender *et al.* (1996) and Pitas *et al.* (1995-1996). The concepts of our attacks also apply to image dependent, 'variable depth' watermarks.

The contents of this paper is as follows. In Section 2, we present a convenient framework in which we define images and operations on images. Watermarks are being introduced in section 2.1. We discuss the basic requirements of watermarks, and the embedding and detection details of so-called 'fixed depth' watermarks. Section 3 discusses a method to remove the watermark from an image when only an (unknown) part of the watermark is estimated correctly. Section 4 then describes our method to obtain a good estimate from an analysis of the histogram of a watermarked image.

2 Definitions

In this paper, images are rectangular arrays of pixels. Pixels are seen as points, rather than squares, so they can be seen as a subset of $\mathbb{Z}^2$. A digital image is

David Aucsmith (Ed.): Information Hiding 1998, LNCS 1525, pp. 290–305, 1998.

obtained by assigning colors or gray values to pixels. Usually these colors or gray values are represented by bounded integers. For watermark patterns, negative values are also allowed, and even though in this case the 'image' has no meaning in a visual context, such a pattern will also be called an image.

Let m and n be positive integers, representing the *width* and *height* of an image. The total number of pixels will be denoted by N, so $N = mn$. Consider the lattice $P \subset \mathbb{Z}^2$, defined by

$$P := \{p_{ij} = (i, j) \in \mathbb{Z}^2 \mid 1 \le i \le m, 1 \le j \le n\}. \tag{1}$$

The elements p_{ij} of P will be called *pixels*.

Let k be a positive integer, representing the dimension of the color space. Usually, $k = 1$ (for gray value images) or $k = 3$ (for color images like YUV or RGB). An image I is defined as a mapping

$$I : P \to \mathbb{R}^k. \tag{2}$$

We will write $I_{ij} = I(p_{ij})$, and I_{ij} represents the *color* of pixel p_{ij}.

Linear combinations and inproducts of two images are defined in a straightforward way.

2.1   Watermarks

A *watermark method* consists of

1. a *watermark embedding* algorithm, which assigns to each image I an image I_W, and
2. a *watermark detection* algorithm, which assigns to each image J a probability p that J is of the form I_W for some image I.

If an image J is of the form I_W for some image I, with probability p, we will say that in J, *the watermark is present* with probability p. The detection algorithm often simply returns 1 or 0, meaning whether the watermark is present or not. For the watermark embedding algorithm, an important requirement is that the watermark is invisible. For the detection algorithm, important requirements include the following. The detection should not need the original image: to decide whether J is of the form I_W, no a priori knowledge about possible candidates for I should be required. Furthermore, probabilities of false alarms and missed detections should be small, while the method should be robust with respect to several sorts of operations on images that in a specific application are likely to occur. Examples of such operations are data compression, noise, format conversions, geometric transformations or dedicated transformations applied by attackers.

2.2   Fixed Depth Watermarks

The Embedding Method. A commonly used watermark embedding technique is that of adding a pseudo-noise pattern to a digital image. This pattern may or

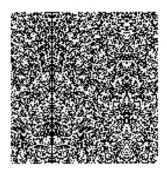

Fig. 1. An example of a watermark pattern

may not depend on the original image. A *fixed depth watermark* embedding method is a mapping which assigns to each image I an image I_W of the form

$$I_W = I + W, \tag{3}$$

where the *watermark pattern* W does not depend on I. The image W is said to be *of uniform depth d* if $|W_{ij}| = d$ for all i, j. The image W is called is called *DC-free* if $\sum_{i,j} W_{ij} = 0$.

For gray scale images, the watermark patterns of uniform depth d that we consider are of the form

$$W_{\text{gray}}(p_{ij}) = \pm d \tag{4}$$

for all i, j. The '+' or '−' sign is determined according to some 2-dimensional pseudo-random noise pattern. An example of such a pattern is shown in Fig. 1.

In this figure of size $m = n = 128$, white blocks correspond to pixels p_{ij} for which $W_{\text{gray}}(p_{ij}) = d$, and black blocks correspond to pixels with $W_{\text{gray}}(p_{ij}) = -d$. To actually watermark images that are not exactly 128 by 128 pixels, the basic pattern is tiled so as to obtain the correct dimensions.

For YUV images, the watermark pattern W_{yuv} is commonly defined such that it effects the luminance value y only:

$$W_{\text{yuv}}(p_{ij}) = (\pm d, 0, 0). \tag{5}$$

When the then obtained watermarked image is converted to an RGB image by the well-known rule

$$(r, g, b) = (y + v, y - \frac{1}{6}u - \frac{1}{2}v, y + u), \tag{6}$$

then the watermarking effect is equivalent to adding the pattern

$$W_{\text{rgb}}(p_{ij}) = \pm(d, d, d) \tag{7}$$

directly to the RGB image.

The Detection Method. The detection method in its basic form consists of taking the inner product of the image J with the pattern W, and this inner product is compared with some threshold value to decide whether J is watermarked or not. Consider the gray scale watermark embedding method described above. Let J be a gray scale image. Then we define the *correlation* $y_W(J)$ to be

$$y_W(J) = W.J. \tag{8}$$

This value $y_W(J)$ is then compared with a threshold value $y_{\text{thr}}(J)$, which depends on J, to decide whether J is watermarked or not. To see why this works, note that an 'arbitrary' image I is not correlated with W, so $W.I$ is small. Now if I is watermarked and we consider $J = I_W$, then the inner product becomes

$$y_W(J) = W.J = W.(I + W) = W.I + W.W = W.I + d^2N.$$

Now d^2N will generally be large compared to $W.I$, and this enables detection of the watermark W. Of course, statistical analysis supports detection decisions.

3 Misleading the Detector

The purpose of a malicious attacker may be to obtain *full knowledge* of the watermark method, or just to *remove* the watermark from an image by *misleading the detector*.

When discussing vulnerability to malicious attackers, one should always have in mind the specific circumstances of an application. The attacker may have some knowledge of the watermark method. For instance, he may know or suspect that it is a fixed depth method. The attacker may or may not have the disposal of a detector. If he does, we assume the detector is a 'black box' to the attacker: it just says 'yes' or 'no', and no quantitative info is given. The attacker may have one or many watermarked images (with the same watermark) at his disposal.

In section 4, we will see that incautious application of fixed depth watermarks in some cases can enable an attacker to obtain complete knowledge of the method, using just a few watermarked images! For this he doesn't even need the detector.

However, when he is not that successful, he can still exploit a partial guess by misleading the detector: he can 'remove' the watermark by subtracting an estimated watermark from the watermarked image. To illustrate this, let us assume that detection is done as described in section 2.2. So we have

$$y_W(J) = W.I + W.W,$$

where, in general, we will have $W.I \ll y_{\text{thr}}(J)$ and $W.W > y_{\text{thr}}(J)$. Now suppose that an attacker has in some way estimated the watermark to be an image $\tilde{W}$. Let $\rho > 0$ be defined by

$$\rho = \frac{W.\tilde{W}}{W.W}. \tag{9}$$

In that case we will say that the attacker has *estimated* $\rho \cdot 100\%$ of the watermark. Now the watermark can be 'removed' from J, by subtracting $\rho^{-1}\tilde{W}$ from J. Let

$$\tilde{J} = J - \rho^{-1}\tilde{W}. \tag{10}$$

Then we have

$$
\begin{aligned}
y_W(\tilde{J}) &= y_W(J - \rho^{-1}\tilde{W}) \\
&= W.(I + W - \rho^{-1}\tilde{W}) \\
&= W.I + W.W - \rho^{-1}W.\tilde{W} \\
&= W.I,
\end{aligned}
$$

and this will generally be less than the threshold, so the watermark will not be detected in $\tilde{J}$. Let us consider the example of a uniform depth watermark.

Example 1. Suppose we have a watermark W of uniform depth $d = 1$. So $W.W = N$. Now suppose an attacker has estimated the sign of the watermark correctly for 75% of the pixels, while he has estimated it falsely for 25% of the pixels. Let $\tilde{W}$ be the estimated watermark, where $\tilde{W}_{ij} = \pm 1$ for all i and j. Then we have

$$W.\tilde{W} = \frac{3}{4}N - \frac{1}{4}N = \frac{1}{2}N,$$

so $\rho = \frac{1}{2}$, and we say that the attacker has estimated 50% of the watermark. From the above discussion, it follows that from a watermarked image J, the watermark can be removed by subtracting $2\tilde{W}$. Then, in pixels p_{ij} where the sign was estimated falsely, we have $|\tilde{J}_{ij} - I_{ij}| = 3$.

More generally, if $p\%$ of the pixels is estimated correctly, with $p > 50$, then

$$\rho = \frac{p - 50}{50},$$

so in a falsely estimated pixel, we have a maximum possible difference

$$|\tilde{J}_{ij} - I_{ij}| = 1 + \left\lceil \frac{50}{p - 50} \right\rceil.$$

Here $\lceil x \rceil$ denotes the smallest integer larger than or equal to x. Note that if ρ^{-1} is not an integer, then we cannot simply subtract $\rho^{-1}\tilde{W}$, because projection onto the color map then includes rounding for many pixels, and that can not be ignored. To circumvent this, we apply a dithering technique. Write $\rho^{-1} = k + r$ for $k \in \mathbb{N}$ and $r \in [0, 1)$. Then we 'randomly' divide the pixels into two disjoint sets P_1 and P_2 of approximate sizes $(1 - r)N$ and rN, respectively. Then we let

$$\tilde{J}_{ij} = \begin{cases} J_{ij} - k\tilde{W}_{ij} & \text{if } p_{ij} \in P_1, \\ J_{ij} - (k+1)\tilde{W}_{ij} & \text{if } p_{ij} \in P_2. \end{cases}$$

Note that $k(1 - r) + (k + 1)r = k + r = \rho^{-1}$, so the average difference between pixels values in $\tilde{J}$ and J is ρ^{-1}.

The above example shows that the quality of the image $\tilde{J}$ depends on how well the watermark is estimated. It also illustrates how to subtract $\rho^{-1}\tilde{W}$ in the case that ρ^{-1} is not an integer. The remaining question is how to determine ρ. An attacker can find out how good his estimate is, by replacing given percentages of the estimated watermark by random noise, and checking if the watermark is still detected. The same can be done for a watermarked image, and the noise percentages needed to remove the watermark in both the estimated watermark and the watermarked image can be compared.

4   Twin Peaks: The Histogram Attack

The histogram attack estimates a watermark by using only the histogram of an image. We first present some simple examples that illustrate this attack. We then introduce an operation called 'flattening' which may be applied to images to enhance the histogram attack. Next we present some experimental results, and then we discuss the method in some more detail. We conclude with a scenario how an attacker can exploit multiple images with the same watermark to come to a better estimate.

4.1   Examples

For the moment, let us assume we have gray scale images, and a uniform depth DC-free watermark of depth 1. Because the watermark pattern is DC-free, we know that 50% of the pixels will have their color decreased by 1, and 50% of the pixels will have their color increased by 1 (we ignore clipping at the values 0 and 255). Now suppose we have an original image in which an isolated color occurs. The histogram may for instance look like:

10	11	12	13	14	15	16
0	0	0	1200	0	0	0

So we have 1200 pixels with gray value 13 and neighboring colors do not occur. When this image I is watermarked, the histogram of J may look like:

10	11	12	13	14	15	16
0	0	573	0	627	0	0

For an attacker who suspects that the watermark is of depth 1 and DC-free, it is easily concluded that the 573 pixels having gray value 12, should all be pixels in which the watermark is -1. (If the watermark would have been $+1$, then the original gray value would have been 11, but in that case one would also expect pixels with gray value $11 - 1 = 10$ in the histogram of J). Similarly, the pixels with gray value 14 will all correspond to $+1$ watermark pixels with very high probability.

Isolated colors occur in images for instance when bits are suppressed or when the colors of an RGB are mapped to a limited smaller set of colors. The histogram attack is not limited to isolated colors however, but can also be applied to histograms with a 'peaky' look, or to histograms in which many short non-zero sequences, mutually separated by 3 or more zeros, occur. This will be illustrated in the following example, in which we examine part of the histogram of a watermarked image J, from which we reconstruct the histogram of the original image I. After we have done that, probabilities can be given for groups of pixels, depending on their gray value, whether they correspond to $+1$ or -1 watermark pixels. (In the remainder we will say that 'a pixel is a $+1$ or -1 pixel'.)

Example 2. The table below shows part of the histogram of the watermarked image J, and we will try to reconstruct the histogram of the original image I. We write I^k for the number of pixels in i with gray value k, and likewise for J.

	86	87	88	89	90	91	92	93	94	95	96	97	98
I	?	?	?	?	?	?	?	?	?	?	?	?	?
J	0	0	1320	1510	3756	2187	6824	4073	6234	3364	2074	0	0

Now note that the 1320 pixels with gray value 88 can only be -1 pixels, otherwise in I they would have had value 87, but then in the histogram of J, there would have been pixels with value 86 (all this, as well as the rest of the arguments in this example, is based on probabilities). So in I, there should have been a number of pixels with gray value 89, of which about 50% (the 1320 pixels) were -1 pixels. Also, about 50% would have been $+1$ pixels, so the total estimate of I^{89} is $2 \cdot 1320 = 2640$. A similar argument can be applied to the tail of the non-zero sequence, and we then obtain the following preliminary estimate for the histogram of I, where from the histogram of J, the $2640 + 4148$ pixels that have been reconstructed, are removed (so e.g. $J^{90} = 3756 - 1320 = 2436$). We obtain:

	86	87	88	89	90	91	92	93	94	95	96	97	98
I	0	0	0	2640	?	?	?	?	?	4148	0	0	0
J	0	0	0	1510	2436	2187	6824	4073	4160	3364	0	0	0

where the added 0's in the estimate for I are obvious. We can now repeat the above step to the extreme values in the remaining non-zero sequence in the histogram of J, and obtain

	86	87	88	89	90	91	92	93	94	95	96	97	98
I	0	0	0	2640	3020	?	?	?	6728	4148	0	0	0
J	0	0	0	0	2436	677	6824	709	4160	0	0	0	0

and next

	86	87	88	89	90	91	92	93	94	95	96	97	98
I	0	0	0	2640	3020	4872	?	8320	6728	4148	0	0	0
J	0	0	0	0	0	677	228	709	0	0	0	0	0

Finally, we add $677 + 677$ to obtain the estimate for I^{92}, and we get

	86	87	88	89	90	91	92	93	94	95	96	97	98
I	0	0	0	2640	3020	4872	1354	8320	6728	4148	0	0	0
J	0	0	0	0	0	0	228	32	0	0	0	0	0

We do not bother about the remaining $228 + 32 = 260$ pixels which are less than 1% of all the pixels. It should be noted that the above method of reconstructing the histogram of I is certainly not the theoretically optimal way to reconstruct it. We will return to the reconstruction method later. Now, given the estimated histogram of I, we can compute for groups of pixels in J the probabilities that they are -1 or $+1$ pixels. This is illustrated in the following table:

	86	87	88	89	90	91	92	93	94	95	96	97	98
I est	0	0	0	2640	3020	4872	1354	8320	6728	4148	0	0	0
$p(-1)$	0	0	1	1	0.65	0.31	0.63	0.83	0.33	0	0	0	1
$p(+1)$	1	0	0	0	0.35	0.69	0.37	0.17	0.67	1	1	0	0

To explain these probabilities, note that, given the above estimate for (the histogram of) I, a pixel in J with gray value 88 can only be a -1 pixel, since in the estimate for I, there are no pixels with gray value 87. A pixel in J with gray value 91, can originate from the 3020 pixels in I with gray value 90 if it is a $+1$ pixel, or it can originate from the 1354 pixels with gray value 92 if it is a -1 pixel. The probabilities of either of these being the case are

$$\frac{3020}{3020 + 1354} = 0.69 \quad \text{and} \quad \frac{1354}{3020 + 1354} = 0.31,$$

respectively. All other probabilities are computed similarly.

For gray scale images, the eventual estimate for the watermark can be based on the above probabilities. The best we can do is guess that for instance *all* pixels in J with gray value 91 are $+1$ pixels, because $p(+1) > p(-1)$ for these pixels. Note that the exact probabilities tell us how good our estimate is! Indeed, 31% of the 2187 pixels with gray value 91 in J will be estimated falsely!

For RGB images, a similar analysis as above can be applied to all color components, so for each pixel, the eventual estimate can be based on 3 computed probabilities.

4.2 Flattening

In this section we will introduce 'flattened' images. For the histogram attack it is often advantageous to first filter the image J, e.g. with the filter

$$F = \begin{bmatrix} -1/9 & -1/9 & -1/9 \\ -1/9 & 8/9 & -1/9 \\ -1/9 & -1/9 & -1/9 \end{bmatrix}.$$

For more detailed information on filtering we refer to e.g. Van Den Enden and Verhoeckx (1989). The filtered image $\bar{J} = FJ$ will be called the *flattened* image.

Fig. 2. The flattened image of lenna. Apart from some edge locations, the flattened image looks like a flat grey image.

Fig. 2 illustrates the flattened image of lenna, where the gray value 127 is added to FJ to visualize the result. The flattening filter is chosen such that if J contains a watermark, then $\bar{J}$ also contains the watermark 'just as hard', but the color range of the flattened image is much smaller than that of the original.

4.3   Practical Results

Before we discuss the histogram attack any further, let us consider some results obtained with this attack. We applied the attack to 10 RGB test images shown in Fig. 6. Table 1 shows the estimated percentages of the watermark, where the images are all watermarked with uniform depth 1. The first column lists the results when the attack is directly applied to the images. The second column lists the results when it is applied to the flattened images.

It is obvious from this table that the results of this attack very much depend on the particular image. Images with smooth histograms are not very vulnerable, while images with a peaky histogram can be extremely vulnerable to this attack. We also see that flattening increases the result in most cases. Fig. 3 shows the

image	% for J	% for $\bar{J}$
airplane	5.4	30.4
baboon	1.0	7.1
clown	5.6	20.0
cornfield	3.8	17.4
lenna	1.0	26.2
mobcal	5.2	17.5
monarch	22.9	36.7
peppers	5.9	25.8
sail	20.5	10.3
tiffany	54.4	27.9

Table 1. The correctly estimated percentages for 10 test images watermarked with depth 1, when the histogram attack is applied to the original watermarked images, as well as to the flattened images.

histograms of the original and watermarked images of baboon and monarch. The histogram of monarch contains many isolated peaks, which after watermarking are replaced by twin peaks. The very smooth histogram of baboon is almost uneffected by watermarking.

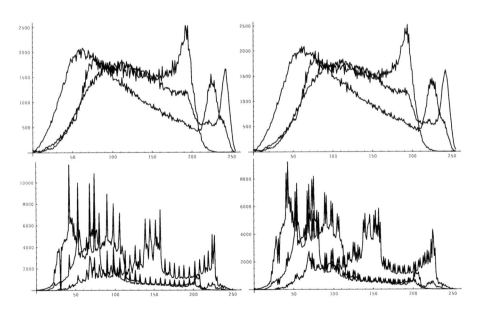

Fig. 3. The histograms of baboon (upper) and monarch (lower), of the original (left) and watermarked (right) images, respectively. All 3 color components are plotted within the same figure.

Histograms of flattened images usually consist of only one peak (ignoring small peaks at 0 and 255 caused by clipping). The width of the peak is related to the vulnerability to the histogram attack. Fig. 4 shows the histograms of the flattened watermarked images of baboon and monarch images. The narrower peak of monarch leads to a better estimate.

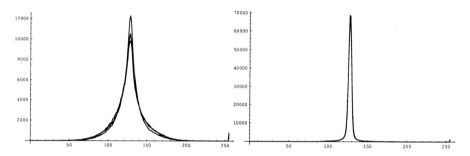

Fig. 4. The histograms of the flattened images of the watermarked baboon (left) and monarch (right). All 3 color components are plotted within the same figure.

4.4   Non-zero Length Sequences

As was illustrated by the influence of the width of the peaks of the flattened images, and as also illustrated by Example 2, the length of non-zero sequences in the histograms have an impact on the achieved estimate of the watermark. Short non-zero sequences yield high estimates. Note that 'non-zero' need not be taken literally: when large numbers are surrounded by relatively small numbers, our analysis applies as well. To illustrate the effect of the length of non-zero sequences, we consider images consisting of uniform noise within a given limited range. So each pixel in the image has any of colors within the range with equal probability. We say we have an image of non-zero length l. We can now compute the result of the histogram attack when it is applied to such an image.

Proposition 1. *Let l be an integer with $l \geq 3$ and let I be an image consisting of uniform noise of non-zero length l. Then the histogram attack applied to $J = I_W$ gives an expected estimate of*

$$\frac{2}{l} \cdot 100\%. \tag{11}$$

if I is a gray scale image. If I is an RGB image and the noise in all color components are independent, then the expected estimate is

$$\left[1 - \left(\frac{l-2}{l} \right)^3 \right] \cdot 100\%. \tag{12}$$

Proof. Let $x := N/l$. Consider the gray scale image first. Assume for convenience that the noise is in the range $\{101, 102, \ldots, 100 + l\}$. The expected numbers in the histograms of I and J are as follows. We have

	99	100	101	102	...	$100 + l - 1$	$100 + l$	$100 + l + 1$	$100 + l + 2$
I	0	0	x	x	...	x	x	0	0
J	0	$x/2$	$x/2$	x	...	x	$x/2$	$x/2$	0

From the histogram of J, we see that $J^{100} + J^{101} + J^{100+l} + J^{100+l+1} = 2x$ pixels are estimated correctly (either $p(-1) = 1$ or $p(+1) = 1$), while for the other pixels, no reasonable estimate can be done because $p(-1) = p(1) = \frac{1}{2}$. For the latter pixels, the expected contribution to the inner product $W.\tilde{W}$ is 0. The correctly estimated pixels contribute $2x$, which corresponds to a fraction $2x/N = 2/l$ of the total inner product. This proves (11).

To prove (12), note that a pixel is correctly estimated when it is among the $2x$ correctly estimated pixels in either of the 3 colors. The probability that a pixel is among the $N - 2x$ remaining pixels (that is the probability that it can *not* be estimated correctly) equals

$$\left(\frac{N - 2x}{N}\right)^3 = \left(\frac{l - 2}{l}\right)^3.$$

So the fraction of correctly estimated pixels equals $1 - \left(\frac{l-2}{l}\right)^3$.

4.5   The Algorithm

We will now sketch the basic algorithm of the histogram attack. We assume we have a fixed depth watermark applied to a gray scale image. Recall that for a DC-free uniform depth $d = 1$ watermark, a randomly chosen pixel is a $+1$ or -1 pixel, each with probability $p = 1/2$. We now consider more general watermarks, with possible depths $d_1 < d_2 < \ldots < d_k$ occurring with probabilities $p_1, p_2, \ldots, p_k$, where $0 < p_i < 1$ for all i, and where $\sum_{i=1}^k p_i = 1$. We will say that we have a

$$\{(d_1, p_1), (d_2, p_2), \ldots, (d_k, p_k)\} \tag{13}$$

watermark. So a DC-free uniform depth $d = 1$ watermark is a $\{(-1, 1/2), (1, 1/2)\}$ watermark, and the sum of two such statistically independent watermarks gives a $\{(-2, 1/4), (0, 1/2), (2, 1/4)\}$ watermark. Now consider what happens to the histogram of an image when it is watermarked with a watermark as given in (13). If a pixel in I has gray value h, then after watermarking it has value $h + d_i$ with probability p_i (we then say that the pixel is a d_i pixel). So, if I^h denotes the number of pixels with histogram value h, we find that the expected contribution of these pixels to J^{h+d_i} equals $p_i I^h$.

Note that in all this we ignore clipping effects at the values 0 and 255. Taking care of clipping in this model is not really difficult, but cumbersome to describe in detail. Let us now have a closer look at the steps in the main algorithm.

Step 1. From the histogram of the watermarked image J, a *most likely* histogram of an original, unwatermarked image I is computed.

In principle, from the statistics of the watermark model, the most likely histograms of I (it need not be unique!) can be determined. This however leads to very involved computations, and heuristic approaches as described in Example 2 seem to work well enough. In a greedy way, we determine a best approximation of the histogram of J, by 'building it up' from basic patterns that represent the distribution of the various depths in the watermark. The basic pattern should be proportional to

$$\{p_1 d_1, p_2 d_2, \ldots p_k d_k\}.$$

This pattern is fitted (e.g. from left to right) at the positions in the histogram of J. When it fits a number of times, then at the corresponding position in I, we get the estimate for the histogram of I. The histogram of J is adapted, and we proceed at the next position.

Step 2. From the histogram of I as computed in Step 1, probabilities of being d_k pixels are assigned to the values in the histogram of J.

Given a pixel in the histogram of J with gray value h, this pixel is a d_i pixel with probability

$$P(h, d_i) = \frac{p_i I^{h-d_i}}{\sum_{j=1}^{k} p_j I^{h-d_j}}. \tag{14}$$

Step 3. For each pixel in J, the watermark is estimated based on the probabilities computed in Step 2. If all probabilities p_i are equal to some probability p, then we simply estimate a pixel with gray value h to be a d_i pixel if $P(h, d_i)$ is maximum for this i. If J is really a watermarked image, then all estimated depths are equally likely to occur.

If however the probabilities p_i are not all equal, things are a bit more subtle. If $p_{\max}$ is the maximum of all p_i with corresponding depth $d_{\max}$, we should prevent that all pixels are estimated to be $d_{\max}$ pixels. This can be done by enforcing that the correct fraction of about $p_i N$ pixels, are estimated to be d_i pixels. One way to achieve this which works in practice is to use

$$\tilde{P}(h, d_i) = \frac{I^{h-d_i}}{\sum_{j=1}^{k} p_j I^{h-d_j}} \tag{15}$$

instead of (14. We have divided the right-hand side of (14) by p_i, and the probabilities in (15) should be normalized to speak of probabilities in a correct sense.

4.6   Attacks Using Many Images

The more watermarked images an attacker has at his disposal, the easier it will be to extract the watermark, provided that all images contain the same watermark. Assume we have k watermarked images $J_1, J_2, \ldots, J_k$, all of the same format and containing the same watermark. We then compute k watermark estimates $\tilde{W}_1, \tilde{W}_2, \ldots, \tilde{W}_k$, and we combine these to obtain a final estimate $\tilde{W}$. To illustrate this, consider the example of a uniform depth $d = 1$ watermark for which estimating the watermark boils down to determining the sign of the watermark in all images. So for each of the estimated watermarks $\tilde{W}_j$ with $1 \leq j \leq k$, pixels are estimated to be $+1$ or -1 pixels. A straightforward way of estimating $\tilde{W}$ is by doing a majority vote: a pixel in $\tilde{W}$ is estimated to be $+1$ if it is estimated $+1$ more often in $\tilde{W}_1, \tilde{W}_2, \ldots, \tilde{W}_k$ than it was estimated -1.

We can statistically analyse the effect of combining the estimates, provided that the probabilities of a pixel being estimated correctly in the k images are independent of each other. Suppose for convenience that k is odd, and that in each image, each pixel is estimated correctly with probability p. Then a pixel is estimated correctly in $\tilde{W}$ if it is correctly estimated in at least $(k+1)/2$ images. The probability $P(p, k)$ that this is the case equals

$$P(p, k) = \sum_{j=(k+1)/2}^{k} p^j (1 - p)^{k-j} \binom{k}{j}. \tag{16}$$

In Fig. 5, we have used (16) to compute the estimated percentages of $\tilde{W}$ as a function of k.

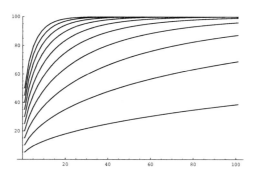

Fig. 5. The estimated percentages of $\tilde{W}$ when the watermark is estimated on the basis of k estimated watermarks with correctly estimated percentages of $5, 10, 15, \ldots, 50\%$. The horizontal axis represents the number k.

5   Conclusions

We have shown that fixed depth watermarks are easily hacked by attackers. Based on only a few images, and without the use of the detector, almost complete knowledge of the watermark can be obtained by the histogram attack. We have also shown how the detector can be misled in the case that only partial knowledge of the watermark can be obtained.

Fig. 6. The images: airplane, baboon, clown, cornfield, lenna, mobcal, monarch, peppers, sail and tiffany. The original sizes of these images are 512×512 or 720×576 pixels.

Variable, image dependent depth embedding is absolutely necessary to be more robust against hackers. Even then, some of the principles of the attack described here can be applied, and with enough watermarked images at the disposal of an attacker, good estimates can be obtained.

Histogram analysis may be required before embedding, in order to prevent the histogram attack. In the case of peaky histograms, noise should be added before or after embedding the watermark, or the histograms should be smoothed in other ways.

Some watermark methods are based on changes in the DCT coefficients of an image. Again, if these changes are not image-dependent, an analogous histogram attack in the DCT domain can be applied.

As a final remark, note that histogram analysis may also be used for watermark detection. There may exist applications in which one is not so much worried about malicious attackers, but where the watermark has to survive geometric transformations or cropping. Detection becomes a difficult task under these circumstances, and a layered approach seems to be a good option. Histogram analysis may then well be applied to give a first indication of whether a uniform depth watermark is present in such a transformed image. If the histogram indication is negative, further exhaustive searching is not needed. If the histogram indication is positive, then the analysis can be continued to search for the actual watermark.

References

1. Bender, W., Gruhl, D., Morimoto, N., Lu, A.: Techniques for data hiding, IBM Systems Journal **35** No. 3/4 (1996) 313–336
2. Nikolaidis, N., Pitas, I.: Copyright protection of images using robust digital signatures, IEEE Int. Conf. on Acoustics, Speech and Signal Processing (ICASSP-96) **4** (1996) 2168–2171
3. Pitas, I., Kaskalis, T.H.: Applying signatures on digital images, IEEE Workshop on Nonlinear Image and Signal Processing, Neos Marmaras, Greece (1995) 460–463

4. Pitas, I:.A method for signature casting on digital images, IEEE Int. Conf. Image Processing (ICIP'96), vol. III, Lausanne (1996) 215–218
5. Van Den Enden, A.W.M., Verhoeckx, N.A.M.: Discrete Time Signal Processing, Prentice-Hall (1989)
6. Voyatzis, G., I. Pitas, I.:. Chaotic mixing of digital images and applications to watermarking, European Conf. on Multimedia Applications, Services and Techniques (ECMAST'96) **2** Louvain-la-Neuve, Belgium, (1996) 687–695

An Information-Theoretic Model for Steganography

Christian Cachin *

MIT Laboratory for Computer Science
545 Technology Square
Cambridge, MA 02139, USA
cachin@acm.org

Abstract. An information-theoretic model for steganography with passive adversaries is proposed. The adversary's task of distinguishing between an innocent cover message C and a modified message S containing a secret part is interpreted as a hypothesis testing problem. The security of a steganographic system is quantified in terms of the relative entropy (or discrimination) between P_C and P_S. Several secure steganographic schemes are presented in this model; one of them is a universal information hiding scheme based on universal data compression techniques that requires no knowledge of the covertext statistics.

1 Introduction

Steganography is the art and science of hiding information such that its presence cannot be detected. Motivated by growing concern about the protection of intellectual property on the Internet and by the threat of a ban for encryption technology, the interest in techniques for information hiding has been increasing over the recent years [1]. Two general directions can be distinguished within information hiding scenarios: protection only against the detection of a message by a passive adversary and hiding a message such that not even an active adversary can remove it. A survey of current steganography can be found in [2].

Steganography with a passive adversary is perhaps best illustrated by Simmons' "Prisoners' Problem" [19]. Alice and Bob are in jail and wish to devise an escape plan. All their communication is observed by the adversary (the warden), who will thwart their plan by transferring them to a high-security prison as soon as he detects any sign of a hidden message. Alice and Bob succeed if Alice can send information to Bob such that Eve does not become suspicious.

Hiding information from active adversaries is a different problem since the existence of a hidden message is publicly known, such as in copyright protection schemes. Steganography with active adversaries can be divided into watermarking and fingerprinting. Watermarking supplies digital objects with an identification of origin; all objects are marked in the same way. Fingerprinting, conversely, attempts to identify individual copies of an object by means of

---

* Research supported by the Swiss National Science Foundation (SNF).

David Aucsmith (Ed.): Information Hiding 1998, LNCS 1525, pp. 306–318, 1998.
© Springer-Verlag Berlin Heidelberg 1998

embedding a unique marker in every copy that is distributed. If later an illegal copy is found, the copyright owner can identify the buyer by decoding the hidden information ("traitor tracing") [13,16,17].

Since most objects to be protected by watermarking or fingerprinting consist of audio or image data, these data types have received most attention so far. A number of generic hiding techniques have been developed whose effects are barely perceptible for humans but can withstand tampering by data transformations that essentially conserve its contents [4,8].

A common model and terminology for information hiding has been established at the 1996 Information Hiding Workshop [15]. An original, unaltered message is called covertext; the sender Alice tries to hide an embedded message by transforming the covertext using a secret key. The resulting message is called the stegotext and is sent to the receiver Bob. Similar to cryptography, it is assumed that the adversary Eve has complete information about the system except for a secret key shared by Alice and Bob that guarantees the security. However, the model does not include a formal notion of security.

In this paper, we introduce an information-theoretic model for steganography with a passive adversary. We propose a security notion that is based on *hypothesis testing*: Upon observing a message sent by Alice, the adversary has to decide whether it is an original covertext C or contains an embedded message and is a stegotext S. This is the problem of distinguishing two different explanations for the observed data that is investigated in statistics and in information theory as "hypothesis testing." We follow the information-theoretic (non-Bayesian) approach as presented by Blahut [6] using the relative entropy function as the basic measure of the information contained in an observation. Thus, we use the relative entropy $D(P_C \| P_S)$ between P_C and P_S to quantify the security of a steganographic system (or stegosystem for short) against passive attacks. If the covertext and stegotext distributions are equal and $D(P_C \| P_S) = 0$, the stegosystem is perfectly secure and the adversary can have no advantage over merely guessing without even observing a message.

However, some caution has to be exerted using this model: On the one hand, information-theoretic methods have been applied with great success to the problems of information encoding and transmission, starting with Shannon's pioneering work [18]. Messages to be transmitted are modeled as random processes and the systems developed in this model perform well in practice. For information hiding on the other hand, the relation between the model and its validity is more involved. A message encrypted under a one-time pad, for example, is indistinguishable from uniformly random bits and this method is perfectly secure according to our notion of security. But no warden would allow the prisoners to exchange random-looking messages! Thus, the crucial issue for the validity of a formal treatment of steganography is the accuracy of the model for real data.

Nevertheless, we believe that our model provides insight in steganography. We hope that it can serve also as a starting point for further work to formalize active adversaries or computational security. (A game-theoretic approach to information hiding with active adversaries is presented by Ettinger [10].) A first extension would be to model the covertext source as a stochastic process and consider statistical estimation and decision techniques. Another idea would be to value the possible decisions and use the methods of statistical decision theory [5].

Related to this work is a paper by Maurer [12] on unconditionally secure authentication [11,21]. It shows how Simmons' bound [20] and many other lower bounds in authentication theory can be derived and generalized using the hypothesis testing approach. Another information-theoretic approach to steganography is [24].

The paper is organized as follows. Hypothesis testing is presented in section 2 from an information-theoretic viewpoint. section 3 contains the formal description of the model and the security definition. In section 4, we provide some examples of unconditionally secure stegosystems and discuss the effects of data compression. A universal information hiding scheme that requires no knowledge of the covertext statistics is presented in section 5. It is based on a universal data compression algorithm, which is similar to the well-known Lempel-Ziv algorithms [3,23]. Some extensions and conclusions are given in section 6.

2   Review of Hypothesis Testing

We give a brief introduction to hypothesis testing and to information-theoretic notions (see [6,7]). Logarithms are to the base 2. The cardinality of a set S is denoted by $|S|$. The *entropy* of a random variable X with probability distribution P_X and alphabet $\mathcal{X}$ is defined as

$$H(X) = -\sum_{x \in \mathcal{X}} P_X(x) \log P_X(x).$$

The *conditional entropy* of X conditioned on a random variable Y is

$$H(X|Y) = \sum_{y \in \mathcal{Y}} P_Y(y) H(X|Y = y)$$

where $H(X|Y = y)$ denotes the entropy of the conditional probability distribution $P_{X|Y=y}$.

Hypothesis testing is the task of deciding which one of two hypotheses H_0 or H_1 is the true explanation for an observed measurement Q [6]. In other words, there are two possible probability distributions, denoted by P_{Q_0} and P_{Q_1}, over the space $\mathcal{Q}$ of possible measurements. If H_0 is true, then Q was generated according to P_{Q_0}, and if H_1 is true, then Q was generated according to P_{Q_1}. A *decision rule* is a binary partition of $\mathcal{Q}$ that assigns one of the two hypotheses to each possible measurement $q \in \mathcal{Q}$. The two possible errors that can be made in a decision are called a *type I error* for accepting hypothesis H_1 when H_0 is actually true and a *type II error* for accepting H_0 when H_1 is true. The probability of a type I error is denoted by α, the probability of a type II error by β.

A method for finding the optimum decision rule is given by the Neyman-Pearson theorem. The decision rule is specified in terms of a threshold parameter

T; α and β are then functions of T. The theorem states that for any given threshold $T \in \mathbb{R}$ and a given maximal tolerable probability β of type II error, α can be minimized by assuming hypothesis H_0 for an observation $q \in \mathcal{Q}$ if and only if

$$\log \frac{P_{Q_0}(q)}{P_{Q_1}(q)} \geq T. \tag{1}$$

In general, many values of T must be examined to find the optimal decision rule. The term on the left hand side in (1) is called the *log-likelihood ratio*.

The basic information measure of hypothesis testing is the *relative entropy* or *discrimination* between two probability distributions P_{Q_0} and P_{Q_1}, defined as

$$D(P_{Q_0} \| P_{Q_1}) = \sum_{q \in \mathcal{Q}} P_{Q_0}(q) \log \frac{P_{Q_0}(q)}{P_{Q_1}(q)}. \tag{2}$$

The relative entropy between two distributions is always nonnegative and is 0 if and only if the distributions are equal. Although relative entropy is not a true distance measure in the mathematical sense because it is not symmetric and does not satisfy the triangle inequality, it can be useful to think of it as a distance. The binary relative entropy $d(\alpha, \beta)$ is defined as

$$d(\alpha, \beta) = \alpha \log \frac{\alpha}{1 - \beta} + (1 - \alpha) \log \frac{1 - \alpha}{\beta}.$$

The following relation connects entropy, relative entropy, and the size of the alphabet for any random variable $X \in \mathcal{X}$: If P_U is the uniform distribution over $\mathcal{X}$, then

$$H(X) + D(P_X \| P_U) = \log |\mathcal{X}|. \tag{3}$$

Relative entropy and hypothesis testing are linked through the Neyman-Pearson theorem above: The expected value of the log-likelihood ratio in (1) with respect to P_{Q_0} is equal to the relative entropy $D(P_{Q_0} \| P_{Q_1})$ between P_{Q_0} and P_{Q_1}. The following standard result shows that deterministic processing cannot increase the relative entropy between two distributions.

Lemma 1. *Let P_{Q_0} and P_{Q_1} be probability distributions over $\mathcal{Q}$. For any function $f : \mathcal{Q} \to \mathcal{T}$, let $T_0 = f(Q_0)$ and $T_1 = f(Q_1)$. Then*

$$D(P_{T_0} \| P_{T_1}) \leq D(P_{Q_0} \| P_{Q_1}).$$

Because deciding between H_0 and H_1 is a special form of processing, the type I and type II error probabilities α and β satisfy

$$d(\alpha, \beta) \leq D(P_{Q_0} \| P_{Q_1}). \tag{4}$$

This bound is typically used as follows: Suppose that δ is an upper bound on $D(P_{Q_0} \| P_{Q_1})$ and that there is a given upper bound on the type I error probability α. Then (4) yields a lower bound on the type II error probability β. For example, $\alpha = 0$ implies that $\beta \geq 2^{-\delta}$.

A similar result holds for a generalized hypothesis testing scenario where the distributions P_{Q_0} and P_{Q_1} depend on knowledge of an additional random variable V. The probability distributions, the decision rule, and the error probabilities are now parameterized by V. In other words, the probability distributions are $P_{Q_0|V=v}$ and $P_{Q_1|V=v}$ for all $v \in \mathcal{V}$, the decision rule may depend on the value v of V, and the error probabilities are $\alpha(v)$ and $\beta(v)$ for each $v \in \mathcal{V}$. Let the average type I and type II errors be $\overline{\alpha} = \sum_{v \in \mathcal{V}} P_V(v)\alpha(v)$ and $\overline{\beta} = \sum_{v \in \mathcal{V}} P_V(v)\beta(v)$.

The *conditional relative entropy* between P_X and P_Y (over the same alphabet $\mathcal{X}$) conditioned on a random variable Z is defined as

$$D(P_{X|Z} \| P_{Y|Z}) = \sum_{z \in \mathcal{Z}} P_Z(z) \sum_{x \in \mathcal{X}} P_{X|Z=z}(x) \log \frac{P_{X|Z=z}(x)}{P_{Y|Z=z}(x)}. \tag{5}$$

It follows from the Jensen inequality and from (4) that

$$d(\overline{\alpha}, \overline{\beta}) \leq D(P_{Q_0|Z} \| P_{Q_1|Z}). \tag{6}$$

3   Model and Definition of Security

Fig. 1 shows our model of a stegosystem. Eve observes a message that is sent from Alice to Bob. She does not know whether Alice sends legitimate *covertext* C or *stegotext* S containing hidden information for Bob. We model this by letting Alice operate strictly in one of two modes: either she is active (and her output is S) or inactive (sending covertext C).

If Alice is active, she transforms C to contain an *embedded message* E using a *secret key* K. (Alternatively, Alice could also generate C herself.) Alice may use a *private random source* R for embedding. The output of the hiding process is the stegotext S. Bob must be able to recover E from his knowledge of the stegotext S and from the key K. Expressed in terms of entropy, the system satisfies:

1. $H(S|CEKR) = 0$. The stegotext is determined uniquely by Alice's inputs.
2. $H(E) > 0$. There is uncertainty about the embedded message.
3. $H(E|SK) = 0$. Bob must be able to decode the embedded message uniquely.

If Alice is inactive, she sends covertext C and no embedding takes place. The embedding mechanism, E, K, and R can be thought of as absent.

Repetition is not considered in this model; it encompasses everything sent from Alice to Bob. For example, if Alice sends multiple messages to Bob and at least one of them contains hidden information, she is considered active and S consists of the concatenation of all her messages.

The probability distributions are assumed to be known to all parties if not stated otherwise. In addition, Bob knows whether Alice is active or not.

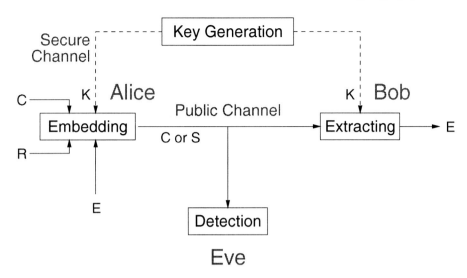

Fig. 1. The model of a secret-key stegosystem with passive adversary. It shows the embedded text E, the covertext C, the stegotext S, Alice's private random source R, and the secret key K shared by Alice and Bob. Alice is either sending covertext C or stegotext S.

Eve, upon observing the message sent by Alice, has to decide whether it was generated according to the distribution of the innocent covertext C or according to the modified distribution of the stegotext S, i.e., whether Alice is active. Since this task is a hypothesis testing problem, we quantify the security of a stegosystem in terms of the relative entropy distance between P_C and P_S.

Definition 1. *A stegosystem as defined above with covertext C and stegotext S is called ϵ-secure against passive adversaries if*

$$D(P_C \| P_S) \ \leq \ \epsilon.$$

If $\epsilon = 0$, the stegosystem is called perfectly secure.

Consider Eve's decision process for a particular decision rule, given by a binary partition $(\mathcal{C}_0, \mathcal{C}_1)$ of the set $\mathcal{C}$ of possible covertexts. She decides that Alice is active if and only if the observed message c is contained in $\mathcal{C}_1$. Ideally, she would always detect a hidden message. (But this occurs only if Alice chooses an encoding such that valid covertexts and stegotexts are disjoint.) If Eve fails to detect that she observed stegotext S, she makes a type II error. Its probability is denoted by β.

The opposite error, which usually receives less attention, is the type I error: Eve decides that Alice sent stegotext although it was a legitimate cover message C; this probability is denoted by α. As a special case, one can assume that Eve never makes a type I error and accuses Alice of sending hidden information when she is inactive ($\alpha = 0$). Such a restriction could be imposed on Eve by external mechanisms.

Lemma 1 imposes a bound on the achievable error probabilities by Eve. From (4) we obtain the following theorem.

Theorem 1. *In a stegosystem that is ϵ-secure against passive adversaries, the probability β that the adversary does not detect a hidden message and the probability α that the adversary falsely detects a hidden message satisfy*

$$d(\alpha, \beta) \leq \epsilon.$$

In particular, if $\alpha = 0$, then

$$\beta \geq 2^{-\epsilon}.$$

In a perfectly secure system we have $D(P_C \| P_S) = 0$ and therefore $P_C = P_S$; thus, Eve can obtain no information about whether Alice is active by observing the message.

As an example, suppose Alice is given a digital image m that she is permitted to send to Bob. Using a perceptional model, she has determined a set $\mathcal{M}$ of equivalent images that are visually indistinguishable from m. Regardless of whether Alice is active or not, she will send a randomly chosen element of $\mathcal{M}$ and this defines the probability space underlying C. Note that in our model, the adversary knows at least $\mathcal{M}$ and possibly also m. Alice can use the techniques described below for embedding information; however, to achieve robustness against active adversaries who modify the image, more sophisticated coding methods are necessary (see e.g. [8]).

It may be the case that external events influence the covertext distribution; for example, news reports or the local weather if we think of the prisoners' problem. This external information is denoted by Y and known all participants. Our model and the security definition above can be modified accordingly. The quantities involved will be conditioned on knowledge of Y and we consider the average error probabilities $\overline{\alpha} = \sum_{y \in \mathcal{Y}} P_Y(y)\alpha(y)$ for the type I error and $\overline{\beta} = \sum_{y \in \mathcal{Y}} P_Y(y)\beta(y)$ for the type II error, where $\alpha(y)$ and $\beta(y)$ denote the type I and type II error probabilities for $Y = y$, respectively.

The modified stegosystem with external information Y, covertext C, and stegotext S is called ϵ-secure against passive adversaries if

$$D(P_{C|Y} \| P_{S|Y}) \leq \epsilon.$$

It follows from (6) that the average error probabilities satisfy $d(\overline{\alpha}, \overline{\beta}) \leq \epsilon$, similar to Theorem 1.

In the next section, we show that perfectly secure stegosystems exist for particular sources of covertext. We start with especially simple (or unrealistic) covertext distributions and then consider arbitrary covertext statistics and the effects of data compression. A universal stegosystem that includes data compression and does not rely on knowledge of the covertext distribution is presented in section 5.

4   Unconditionally Secure Stegosystems

The above model tells us that we obtain a secure stegosystem whenever the stegotext distribution is close to the covertext distribution without knowledge of the key. The embedding function depends crucially on knowledge about the covertext source. We assume first that the covertext distribution is known and design corresponding embedding functions.

If the covertext consists of independent and uniformly random bits, then the one-time pad provides a perfectly secure stegosystem. For completeness, we briefly describe this system formally.

Assume the covertext C is a uniformly distributed n-bit string for some positive n. The key generator chooses the n-bit key K with uniform distribution and sends it to Alice and Bob. The embedding function (if Alice is active) consists of the bitwise XOR of the particular n-bit message e and K, thus $S = e \oplus K$, and Bob can decode by computing $e = S \oplus K$. The resulting stegotext S is uniformly distributed in the set of n-bit strings and therefore $D(P_C \| P_S) = 0$. Thus, the one-time pad provides perfect steganographic security if the covertext is uniformly random.

As a side remark, we note that this one-time pad system is equivalent to the basic scheme of visual cryptography [14]. This technique hides a monochrome picture by splitting it into two random layers of dots. When these are superimposed, the picture appears. It is also possible to produce two innocent looking pictures such that both of them together reveal an embedded message.

For general covertext distributions, we now describe a system that embeds a one-bit message in the stegotext. The extension to larger message spaces is straightforward. Let the covertext C with alphabet $\mathcal{C}$ have an arbitrary distribution P_C. Alice constructs the embedding function from a partition of $\mathcal{C}$ into two parts such that both parts are assigned approximately the same probability mass under C. In other words, let

$$\mathcal{C}_0 = \min_{\mathcal{C}' \subseteq \mathcal{C}} \left| \sum_{c \in \mathcal{C}'} P_C(c) - \sum_{c \notin \mathcal{C}'} P_C(c) \right| \quad \text{and} \quad \mathcal{C}_1 = \mathcal{C} \setminus \mathcal{C}_0.$$

Alice and Bob share a one-bit key $K \in \{0, 1\}$. Define C_0 to be the random variable with alphabet $\mathcal{C}_0$ and distribution P_{C_0} equal to the conditional distribution $P_{C|C \in \mathcal{C}_0}$ and define C_1 similarly over $\mathcal{C}_1$. Then Alice computes the stegotext to embed a message $e \in \{0, 1\}$ as

$$S = C_{e \oplus K}.$$

Bob can decode the message because he knows that $e = 0$ if and only if $S \in \mathcal{C}_K$.

Theorem 2. *The one-bit message stegosystem described above is*

$$\frac{1}{\ln 2} \left(\mathrm{P}[C \in \mathcal{C}_0] - \mathrm{P}[C \in \mathcal{C}_1] \right)^2$$

secure against passive adversaries.

Proof. Let $\delta = P[C \in \mathcal{C}_0] - P[C \in \mathcal{C}_1]$. We show only the case $\delta > 0$. It is straightforward to verify that

$$P_S(c) = \begin{cases} P_C(c)/(1+\delta) & \text{if } c \in \mathcal{C}_0, \\ P_C(c)/(1-\delta) & \text{if } c \in \mathcal{C}_1. \end{cases}$$

It follows that

$$\begin{aligned} D(P_C \| P_S) &= \sum_{c \in \mathcal{C}} P_C(c) \log \frac{P_C(c)}{P_S(c)} \\ &= \sum_{c \in \mathcal{C}_0} P_C(c) \log(1+\delta) + \sum_{c \in \mathcal{C}_1} P_C(c) \log(1-\delta) \\ &= \frac{1+\delta}{2} \cdot \log(1+\delta) + \frac{1-\delta}{2} \cdot \log(1-\delta) \\ &\leq \frac{1+\delta}{2} \cdot \frac{\delta}{\ln 2} + \frac{1-\delta}{2} \cdot \frac{-\delta}{\ln 2} \\ &= \delta^2 / \ln 2 \end{aligned}$$

using the fact that $\log(1 + x) \leq x/\ln 2$.

A word on data compression techniques. Suppose the embedding as described above takes place before compression is applied to S (or C). Data compression is a deterministic process. Therefore, Lemma 1 applies and shows that if we start with an ϵ-secure stegosystem, the security of the compressed system is also at most ϵ. To put it another way, data compression can never hurt the security of a stegosystem and make detection easier for the adversary.

5   Steganography with Universal Data Compression

The stegosystems described in section 4 assume that the covertext distribution is known to all parties. This seems not realistic for many applications. However, if we extend the model of a stegosystem to stochastic processes and consider the covertext as an ergodic source, its distribution can be estimated by observing the source output. This is precisely what universal data compression algorithms do for the purpose of source coding. We now show how they can be modified for information hiding.

Traditional data compression techniques, such as Huffman coding, require a priori knowledge about the distribution of the data to be compressed. Universal data compression algorithms treat the problem of source coding for applications where the source statistics are unknown a priori or vary with time. A universal data compression universal algorithm achieves asymptotically optimal performance on every source in some large class of possible sources. Essentially, this is accomplished by learning the statistics of the data during operation as more and more data is observed. The best known examples of universal data compression are the algorithms by Lempel and Ziv [3,23].

We describe a universal data compression algorithm based on the concept of repetition times due to Willems [22], which is related to Elias' interval length coding [9]. Then we modify the algorithm to illustrate that a stegosystem can be constructed without knowledge of the covertext distribution. The performance of Willems' algorithm is inferior to the Lempel-Ziv algorithms for most practical data but it is simpler to describe and to analyze. We assume that covertext and stegotext in the model according to ection 3 are stationary stochastic processes. This corresponds to the ergodicity assumptions that are made for many data compression algorithms.

The Repetition Times Compression Algorithm: The algorithm is described for binary sources but can easily be generalized to arbitrary alphabets. The parameters of the algorithm are the blocklength L and the delay D. Consider a stationary binary source X producing $\{X_t\} = X_1, X_2, \ldots$ with values in $\{0, 1\}$. The source output is divided into blocks $Y_1, Y_2, \ldots$ of length L bits each. Encoding of a block Y_t operates by considering its *repetition time*, the length of the interval since its last occurrence. Formally, the repetition time Δt_y of the block $Y_t = y$ satisfies $Y_j \neq Y_t$ for $1 \leq j < \Delta t_y$ and $Y_{t-\Delta t_y} = Y_t$. If $\Delta t_y < 2^D$, the encoder outputs $C(\Delta t_y)$, using a particular variable-length encoding C of Δt_y described below. If $\Delta t_y \geq 2^D$, however, the block y is retransmitted literally. The distinction between repetition time encoding and literal data is marked by a single bit in the output stream.

Repetition time is encoded using the following code for integers between 1 and $2^D - 1$. Let $B_l(k)$ denote binary representation of the integer k using l digits and let $d = \lceil \log D \rceil$. The encoding C is

$$C(t) = B_d(\lfloor \log t \rfloor) \parallel B_{\lfloor \log t \rfloor}\left(t - 2^{\lfloor \log t \rfloor}\right),$$

where $\parallel$ denotes the concatenation of the bit strings. Thus, $C(t)$ contains first the binary length of t encoded using fixed length d and then the remaining bits of t except for the most significant bit. For initialization, a block y that occurs for the first time is encoded as if it had occurred at time $t = -y$.

The encoder and decoder maintain a buffer of the last 2^D blocks of the source. In addition, the encoder maintains an array indexed by L-bit blocks y that contains the position t_y (modulo 2^D) where y last occurred (the time buffer). Encoding and decoding therefore take only a constant number of operations per block. The formal analysis of the scheme [22] using $D = L$ shows that for $L \to \infty$, the encoding rate (the average number of code bits per source word) converges to the entropy rate of the source X.

The Modification for Information Hiding: The stegosystem based on Willems' algorithm exploits the fact that the average repetition time of a block $Y_t = y$ yields an estimate of its probability since it will converge to $P_Y(y)^{-1}$. If the block y is replaced with another block y' close to y in average repetition time (and therefore in probability), the source statistics are only slightly altered. Information is only hidden in blocks with low probability, as determined by a stego rate parameter $\rho > 2^{-D}$. Alice and Bob share an m-bit secret key K and Alice wants to hide an m-bit message E.

Here, both the encoder and decoder maintain a time buffer indexed by blocks. In addition to the index t of the last occurrence of block y, each entry contains also its average repetition time $\overline{\Delta t}_y$ and the number of its occurrences so far, n_y. For each encoded block y with repetition time Δt_y, the average repetition time $\overline{\Delta t}_y$ is replaced by $(n_y \overline{\Delta t}_y + \Delta t_y)/(n_y + 1)$. In addition, n_y is increased, but never beyond 2^D. Let $r(y)$ denote the rank function of blocks that associates with a block y the rank of $\overline{\Delta t}_y$, considering the current values of the average repetition times.

Information hiding takes place if the encoder or the decoder encounters a block y such that $\overline{\Delta t}_y \geq \frac{1}{\rho}$ (before updating buffers). If this is the case, bit j of the message m is embedded in y' according to

$$y' = r^{-1}\big(r(y) + (m_j \oplus K_j)\big)$$

and encoding proceeds as before with y' replacing y. In other words, y' is either equal to y or to the block immediately following y in the average repetition time ranking, depending on the embedded bit. The decoder computes the average repetition times in the same way and can thus detect the symbols containing hidden information and decode E similarly.

Compared to data compression, the storage complexity of the encoding and decoding algorithms is increased by a constant factor, but their computational complexity grows by a factor of about L due to the maintenance of the ranking.

The resulting stegosystem achieves asymptotically perfect security since the distance between the probabilities of the exchanged blocks vanishes. The formal statement of this will be given in the full version of the paper.

6   Extensions

The presented information-theoretic model for steganography can be considered as one particular example of a statistical model. We propose to consider also other approaches from statistical decision theory. As noted before, an immediate extension would be to model the covertext source as a stochastic process.

Simmons' original scenario of the prisoners' problem includes authentication, that is, the secret key K shared by Alice and Bob can partially be used for authenticating Alice's messages. The reason for this is that Alice and Bob want to protect themselves (and are allowed to do so) from a malicious warden that tries to fool Bob into accepting fraudulent messages as originating from Alice. This implies some changes to the model. Denote the part of the key used for authentication by Z. Then, for every value z of Z, there is a different covertext distribution $P_{C|Z=z}$ induced by the authentication scheme in use. However, since the adversary Eve does not know Z, the covertext distribution to consider for detection is P_C, the marginal distribution of P_{CZ}. We note that this model differs from the general scenario with an active adversary; there, the adversary succeeds if she can destroy the embedded hidden information (as is the case in copyright protection applications, for example). Here, the prisoners are only concerned about hiding information in messages that may be authenticated to detect tampering.

As already mentioned in the Introduction, the assumption of a fixed covertext distribution seems to render our model somewhat unrealistic for the practical purposes of steganography. But what are the alternatives? Should we rather study the perception and detection capabilities of human cognition since most cover data (text, sound, images) is ultimately intended for human receivers? Viewed this way, steganography could fall entirely into the realms of image, audio, and speech processing or artificial intelligence. However, it seems that the information-theoretic model and other statistical approaches will ultimately be more useful for deriving statements about the security of information hiding schemes – and a formal security notion is one of the main reasons for introducing a mathematical model of steganography.

Acknowledgment

I am grateful to Victor Boyko, Mark Ettinger, Ron Rivest, and Michael Waidner for interesting discussions on this subject.

References

1. R. Anderson, ed., *Information Hiding*, vol. 1174 of *Lecture Notes in Computer Science*, Springer, 1996.
2. R. J. Anderson and F. A. Petitcolas, "On the limits of steganography," *IEEE Journal on Selected Areas in Communications*, vol. 16, May 1998.
3. T. C. Bell, J. G. Cleary, and I. H. Witten, *Text Compression.* Prentice Hall, 1990.
4. W. Bender, D. Gruhl, N. Morimoto, and A. Lu, "Techniques for data hiding," *IBM Systems Journal*, vol. 35, no. 3 & 4, 1996.
5. J. O. Berger, *Statistical Decision Theory and Bayesian Analysis.* Springer, 2. ed., 1985.
6. R. E. Blahut, *Principles and Practice of Information Theory.* Reading: Addison-Wesley, 1987.
7. T. M. Cover and J. A. Thomas, *Elements of Information Theory.* Wiley, 1991.
8. I. J. Cox, J. Kilian, T. Leighton, and T. Shamoon, "A secure, robust watermark for multimedia," in *Information Hiding* (R. Anderson, ed.), vol. 1174 of *Lecture Notes in Computer Science*, Springer, 1996.
9. P. Elias, "Interval and recency rank source coding: two on-line adaptive variable-length schemes," *IEEE Transactions on Information Theory*, vol. 33, pp. 3–10, Jan. 1987.
10. M. Ettinger, "Steganalysis and game equilibria," in *Proc. 2nd Workshop on Information Hiding* (D. Aucsmith, ed.), Lecture Notes in Computer Science, Springer-Verlag, 1998.
11. J. L. Massey, "Contemporary cryptography: An introduction," in *Contemporary Cryptology: The Science of Information Integrity* (G. J. Simmons, ed.), ch. 1, pp. 1–39, IEEE Press, 1991.

12. U. M. Maurer, "A unified and generalized treatment of authentication theory," in *Proc. 13th Annual Symposium on Theoretical Aspects of Computer Science (STACS)* (C. Puech and R. Reischuk, eds.), vol. 1046 of *Lecture Notes in Computer Science*, pp. 190–198, Springer, 1996.

13. M. Naor, A. Fiat, and B. Chor, "Tracing traitors," in *Advances in Cryptology: CRYPTO '94* (Y. G. Desmedt, ed.), vol. 839 of *Lecture Notes in Computer Science*, 1994.

14. M. Naor and A. Shamir, "Visual cryptography," in *Advances in Cryptology: EUROCRYPT '94* (A. De Santis, ed.), vol. 950 of *Lecture Notes in Computer Science*, pp. 1–12, Springer, 1995.

15. B. Pfitzmann, "Information hiding terminology," in *Information Hiding* (R. Anderson, ed.), vol. 1174 of *Lecture Notes in Computer Science*, Springer, 1996.

16. B. Pfitzmann and M. Schunter, "Asymmetric fingerprinting," in *Advances in Cryptology: EUROCRYPT '96* (U. Maurer, ed.), vol. 1233 of *Lecture Notes in Computer Science*, Springer, 1996.

17. B. Pfitzmann and M. Waidner, "Anonymous fingerprinting," in *Advances in Cryptology: EUROCRYPT '97* (W. Fumy, ed.), vol. 1070 of *Lecture Notes in Computer Science*, Springer, 1997.

18. C. E. Shannon, "A mathematical theory of communication," *Bell System Technical Journal*, vol. 27, pp. 379–423, 623–656, July, Oct. 1948.

19. G. J. Simmons, "The prisoners' problem and the subliminal channel," in *Advances in Cryptology: Proceedings of Crypto 83* (D. Chaum, ed.), pp. 51–67, Plenum Press, 1984.

20. G. J. Simmons, "Authentication theory/coding theory," in *Advances in Cryptology: Proceedings of CRYPTO 84* (G. R. Blakley and D. Chaum, eds.), vol. 196 of *Lecture Notes in Computer Science*, Springer, 1985.

21. G. J. Simmons, "An introduction to shared secret and/or shared control schemes and their application," in *Contemporary Cryptology: The Science of Information Integrity* (G. J. Simmons, ed.), pp. 441–497, IEEE Press, 1991.

22. F. M. Willems, "Universal data compression and repetition times," *IEEE Transactions on Information Theory*, vol. 35, pp. 54–58, Jan. 1989.

23. J. Ziv and A. Lempel, "A universal algorithm for sequential data compression," *IEEE Transactions on Information Theory*, vol. 23, pp. 337–343, May 1977.

24. J. Zöllner, H. Federrath, H. Klimant, A. Pfitzmann, R. Piotraschke, A. Westfeld, G. Wicke, and G. Wolf, "Modeling the security of steganographic systems," in *Proc. 2nd Workshop on Information Hiding* (D. Aucsmith, ed.), Lecture Notes in Computer Science, Springer-Verlag, 1998.

Steganalysis and Game Equilibria

J. Mark Ettinger

Los Alamos National Laboratory
Mail Stop B-230
Los Alamos, NM 87545
505-665-4789
ettinger@lanl.gov

Abstract. Steganography is the study of methods of concealing data in the noise of another data set. Steganalysis is the field of discovering hidden data and disrupting covert channels. We introduce a two-player, zero-sum, matrix game for the purpose of modeling the contest between a data-hider and a data-attacker. We then solve the game for equilibria, demonstrating that the form of the solution depends on whether the permitted distortion is less than or greater than d_c, the critical distortion. This critical point is a simple function of several parameters which define the game. We then solve two example cases to demonstrate the ideas presented in the general solution. The value of the game is the amount of information that may be reliably stored in the data set.

Keywords. Steganalysis, Cryptanalysis, Equilibria, Shannon Entropy, Binary Symmetric Channel, Active Warden Attack.

1 Introduction

Recently techniques in steganography have received a great deal of attention [1,6], mostly from members of the signal processing and cryptological communities. Steganography concerns techniques for concealing data in the noise of other data. Primary applications include digital watermarking for copyright protection of digital data and covert communications. Many methods for hiding data have been proposed [2,3,7] but to this point there have been no quantitative methods developed for assessing the security of any of these methods.

Steganography is related to, though distinct from, cryptography. The goal of a secure cryptographic method is to prevent an interceptor from gaining any information about the plaintext from the intercepted ciphertext. The goal of a secure steganographic method is to prevent an observant intermediary from even obtaining knowledge of the mere presence of the secret data. In most applications the embedded message will be encrypted before hiding. Otherwise the natural language structure in the message will be statistically detectable. Also, we are primarily interested in the case where digital data is hidden in a digital data set. Therefore we assume that the hidden message is a pseudorandom bit sequence.

In cryptology, the complementary endeavor to finding secure encryption methods is called cryptanalysis and is concerned with discovering techniques for

David Aucsmith (Ed.): Information Hiding 1998, LNCS 1525, pp. 319–328, 1998.
© Springer-Verlag Berlin Heidelberg 1998

breaking cryptographic schemes. To this point in time the analogous field of *steganalysis* remains almost completely mathematically undeveloped. In order to begin to remedy this it is important to utilize the proper notion of breaking a steganographic system. The purpose of steganography is to hide data and therefore the primary counterobjectives are to *discover* the presence of hidden data (perhaps in a probabilistic setting) and/or to reduce the channel capacity of the covert channels. The first type of attack is sometimes called a *passive warden attack* and the second type an *active warden attack*. Notice that we do not demand that the hidden message is recovered for a steganalytic attack to be successful, though the question of to what degree this may be accomplished is certainly of interest. The question of then decrypting the recovered message is a classical cryptanalytic question and lies outside the interests of steganalysis proper.

Cryptology has emerged over the years from a collection of ad hoc techniques into a sophisticated discipline utilizing ideas from many areas of mathematics and contributing to the development of mathematics. We believe that steganology holds a similar promise of deep connections with and potential contributions to various branches of mathematics and applied mathematics, especially pattern recognition. With the hope of leveraging some of the success of cryptanalysis, in this paper we borrow several operating assumptions on our way to a mathematical assessment of the security of steganographic algorithms. In particular, we assume that all algorithms are public knowledge and that the security of the system resides in a *secret key*. This assumption, basic to cryptology, will manifest in the formulation of the matrix games that we use to model covert channels.

As we mentioned, there are two different types of attacks on steganographic systems. The first of the two attacks is detecting the presence of the hidden information and the second is interruption of communication by overwriting the hidden information. In this paper we introduce a game-theoretic model of the second type of attack. The data Hider chooses a distribution of locations to hide data in the data set subject to a limit on the amount of distortion he may introduce into the data set. This distortion parameter is thus an measure of the noise in the data set. The Attacker also chooses a distribution of locations to hide pseudorandom noise in an attempt to overwrite the hidden data. In this paper the Attacker is subject to the same distortion limit as the Hider. Associated to any pair of strategies there is an associated payoff which measures the amount of data that is communicated. The Hider desires a strategy which maximizes this payoff whereas the Attacker desires to minimize this payoff. We therefore have a two-player, zero-sum game and we then proceed to solve this game for optimal strategies and payoffs.

This paper is organized as follows. In the next section we review the basic concepts of game theory that we require for our analysis. In section 3 we define the particular game that models the steganographic scenario. In section 4 we solve the game for optimal strategies and associated payoffs. In section 5 we give two examples of the solutions deduced in section 4 and we conclude in section 6 with a brief discussion of future research directions.

2   Review of Matrix Games

We now briefly summarize the main ideas and results we will need from the classical theory of games. For further explanation, consult the excellent reference [5]. A *real-valued, two-player, zero-sum game* consists of two sets of pure strategies S^1, S^2 and two payoff functions $P^1 : S^1 \times S^2 \to \mathbf{R}$, $P^2 : S^1 \times S^2 \to \mathbf{R}$ such that $P^1(s,t) = -P^2(s,t)$ where $s \in S^1$ and $t \in S^2$. We will refer to player 1's payoff simply as *the payoff function* and denote it by P with the understanding that the game under consideration is zero-sum. Without loss of generality assume that Player 1 is trying to maximize the payoff and Player 2 is trying to minimize the payoff. In all of the games studied here the sets of pure strategies will be finite. A *mixed strategy* is a probability distribution over the set of pure strategies. A pure strategy is therefore a mixed strategy with a point mass as the distribution. When the pure strategy sets are finite a mixed strategy may be written as a vector $\mathbf{x} = (x_1, \ldots, x_j)$ where $Prob(S = s_i) = x_i$. The payoff P' for a pair of mixed strategies extends the payoff function P and is defined to be the expected payoff:

$$P'(\mathbf{x}, \mathbf{y}) = \sum_{i,j} x_i y_j P(s_i, t_j). \tag{1}$$

Since $P' = P$ for pure strategies we will simply write P for both functions. An *equilibrium* for a game G is a pair of mixed strategies, $\mathbf{x}^*$ for Player 1 and $\mathbf{y}^*$ for Player 2, such that for all mixed strategies $\mathbf{x}, \mathbf{y}$ we have

$$P(\mathbf{x}, \mathbf{y}^*) \le P(\mathbf{x}^*, \mathbf{y}^*) \le P(\mathbf{x}^*, \mathbf{y}). \tag{2}$$

Equilibria strategies are the only correct strategies to play because they have the property that neither player may benefit by deviating from an equilibrium strategy. Equilibria strategies therefore represent the solution to the game-theoretic situation. The fundamental theorem of game theory (originally proved by Von Neumann and Morgenstern, [8]) states that every finite, zero-sum game has at least one equilibrium in mixed strategies and that the payoffs at each equilibria are the same. This number is called the *value* of the game.

3   A Steganological Game

Consider the following scenario. An individual wishes to covertly communicate by hiding messages in the noise of some data files. Suppose all data files sent by this individual, say Player 1, pass through some gateway, perhaps a computer server, which is under the control of Player 2. Player 2 wants to automatically introduce noise into *all* data files passing through the gateway in order to disrupt any such covert communication. Player 2 does not examine the files individually to try to find hidden information. Rather, the disruption is completely automatic.

We now introduce a game to model this steganographic scenario and in the next section we solve for the optimal mixed strategies. The scenario is as follows and utilizes the assumptions discussed above. The data is a pseudorandom sequence of bits and is to be hidden in an N-pixel, 2^l-level greyscale image. Both players will modify the values of bits throughout the image under the constraint that the total amount of distortion must remain less than some known constant, say d. The game could easily be modified to permit different levels of distortion for the Hider and Attacker. We use the most simple model of distortion possible in that changing the value of a least significant bit is 1 unit of distortion, modifying a next-to-least significant bit is 2 units of distortion, etc., until finally modifying a most significant bit is 2^{l-1} units of distortion. We emphasize that by using different distortion measures, more sophisticated models of the effects of modifying an image may be accommodated in this game-theoretic framework. See the section on further work for a discussion of variations on this measure.

Player 1 is the data Hider and seeks to maximize the amount of hidden data whereas Player 2 is the Attacker and seeks to minimize the amount of hidden data communicated by introducing noise. A pure strategy for Player 1 is an l-tuple of nonnegative real numbers $\mathbf{x} = (x_0, x_1, \ldots, x_{l-1})$ such that

$$\sum_{i=0}^{l-1} x_i 2^{i-1} \leq d. \tag{3}$$

Given a strategy $\mathbf{x}$, x_i is the number of bits that the Hider will store in the set of ith lowest order bits in the image. Note that x_i is allowed to be a noninteger, whereas in actual fact one must store an integer number of bits. We will see that in general we require nonintegers in order to obtain equilibria but that utilizing integer valued vectors in practical situations is an acceptable approximation. The locations of the hidden bits within a set are chosen pseudorandomly and are therefore uniformly distributed over all N bits in position i. Because half of the original bits will, on average, agree with the bits to be hidden, hiding x_0 bits in the low order bits will on average result in $x_0/2$ units of distortion. This observation gives rise to the distortion inequality. Similarly, a pure strategy for Player 2 is an l-tuple of nonnegative real numbers $(y_0, y_1, \ldots, y_{l-1})$ such that

$$\sum_{j=0}^{l-1} y_j 2^j \leq d. \tag{4}$$

The distortion here is different since Player 2 will flip all y_0 of the low order bits. Again the locations are chosen pseudorandomly and are uniformly distributed throughout all N possible choices. Conceptually what we now have are l independent *binary symmetric channels* [4] where the probability for a hidden bit to be flipped in channel C_i is y_i/N. Notice that both pure strategy sets are finite and therefore mixed strategies may be written as vectors, $\mathbf{X}, \mathbf{Y}$.

Let us now consider the construction of the payoff function for this game. Suppose Z is a discrete random variable that takes the value z_i with probability p_i, i.e. $P(Z = z_i) = p_i$. The Shannon entropy [4] of Z is given by:

$$H(Z) = \sum_i p_i \log \left(\frac{1}{p_i} \right). \tag{5}$$

If the log is taken base 2 than H has units of bits. If Z takes on only two possible values with probabilities p_1 and $1 - p_1$ then we abbreviate the entropy by writing

$$H(p_1) = -p_1 \log(p_1) - (1 - p_1) \log(1 - p_1). \tag{6}$$

The channel capacity for a binary symmetric channel with bit error probability p is $1 - H(p)$ [4]. The channel capacity is the asymptotic average number of bits communicated through the channel per bit sent through the channel and this limit is approached by using error-correcting codes. For each channel C_i, $0 \le i \le l - 1$, the Hider sends x_i bits and the probability for a bit error due to the noise introduction by the Attacker is y_i/N. Therefore the payoff function for the game is given by:

$$P(\mathbf{x}, \mathbf{y}) = \sum_{i=0}^{l-1} x_i \left[1 - H \left(\frac{y_i}{N} \right) \right]. \tag{7}$$

This represents the total number of bits that are communicated on average utilizing error correcting codes to compensate for the distortion introduced by the Attacker.

4   Equilibria for the Game

We now wish to solve the above game for equilibria. Recall that these are strategies such that assuming the other Player is playing his optimal strategy, the given strategy is optimal, i.e. no improvement is possible by deviating. Since a pure strategy is a tuple, $\mathbf{x} = (x_0, \ldots, x_{l-1})$, we will write mixed strategies, i.e. probability distributions over the set of pure strategies, as vectors with capital Latin letters, $\mathbf{X}$, and $P(\mathbf{X} = \mathbf{x}) = \mathbf{X}(\mathbf{x})$. It turns out that this game has an equilibrium in pure strategies. Therefore in the following derivation we proceed by assuming the equilibrium we seek consists of pure strategies and our subsequent calculations validate this assumption.

To solve for an equilibrium, recall the payoff function:

$$P(\mathbf{x}, \mathbf{y}) = \sum_{i=0}^{l-1} x_i \left[1 - H \left(\frac{y_i}{N} \right) \right]. \tag{8}$$

Let

$$M_i = 1 - H \left(\frac{y_i}{N} \right) \tag{9}$$

be the channel capacity for the ith channel. Using the fact that neither player desires to deviate from an equilibrium strategy let us solve for an optimal strategy for the Attacker, $\mathbf{y} = (y_0, y_1, \ldots, y_{l-1})$. Fix all components of $\mathbf{x}$ except for x_j and x_k where $0 \le j < k \le l - 1$ and consider distributing the remaining distortion

$$d_{jk} = d - \sum_{i \ne j, k} 2^{i-1} x_i \tag{10}$$

between these two components. We may now consider the *partial payoff function* P_{jk} which is the portion of the payoff function, Equation 8, concerning only the two channels C_j and C_k. Consider the following equation for the partial payoff function as a function of x_j:

$$P_{jk}(x_j) = x_j M_j + x_k M_k = x_j M_j + \frac{d_{jk} - 2^{j-1}x_j}{2^{k-1}} M_k. \tag{11}$$

In order to find an equilibrium we must insure that the Hider does not profit from readjusting x_j and x_k for a fixed $\mathbf{y}$. Therefore we have

$$\frac{dP_{jk}}{dx_j}(x_j^*) = M_j - 2^{j-k} M_k = 0 \tag{12}$$

for an equilibrium x_k^* and thus

$$M_j = 2^{j-k} M_k. \tag{13}$$

If there is enough total available distortion, and this point will become more clear below, then this equation must hold for all $0 \le j < k \le l - 1$ and so for any equilibrium strategy $\mathbf{y}$ we have

$$2^{k-j} \left[1 - H\left(\frac{y_j}{N}\right)\right] = 1 - H\left(\frac{y_k}{N}\right). \tag{14}$$

In particular if $k = j + 1$ then we have $2M_j = M_{j+1}$. For fixed d and N Equations 4 and 14 determine the equilibrium strategy $\mathbf{y}^*$ and this can be solved numerically.

We now sketch the form of these solutions. Notice that in order to satisfy $2M_k = M_{k+1}$ for all $0 \le k \le l - 2$ requires a critical amount of allowable distortion $d_c(l, N)$. For suppose that $M_{l-1} = 1$, i.e. the Attacker introduces no noise in channel C_{l-1}, the most expensive channel in which to introduce noise. Then the above channel capacity constraints reduce to $M_{l-2} = 1/2$, $M_{l-3} = 1/4, \ldots$, and in general

$$M_i = 2^{-(l-1-i)}. \tag{15}$$

Define a pseudoinverse to the binary symmetric channel capacity function $Cap(p) = 1 - H(p)$ as $Cap^{-1}(M) =$ unique p such that $Cap(p) = M$ and $0 \le p \le 1/2$. Then $Cap^{-1} : [0, 1] \to [0, 1/2]$ and we have

$$d_c(l, N) = \sum_{i=0}^{l-1} 2^i N Cap^{-1}\left(2^{-(l-1-i)}\right). \tag{16}$$

This is the minimal amount of distortion necessary in order for the Attacker to simultaneously satisfy Equation 14 for each i. If $d \ge d_c(l, N)$ then the Attacker's strategy is to distribute d among all channels subject to these constraints. As mentioned previously, these constraints determine the noise allocation subject to the distortion limitation. Notice also that

$$d_{total} = \sum_{i=0}^{l-1} 2^i N/2 \tag{17}$$

is the amount of distortion necessary to reduce all channels to zero capacity. This is equivalent to flipping each bit of each pixel with probability $1/2$, i.e. randomizing the image. Of course in a practical situation such extreme distortion would be prohibited.

Now what is the proper strategy if $d < d_c$? Since it costs twice as much for the Hider to place data in C_{i+1} as it does in C_i, there is an implicit reduction in the channel capacity of the higher order channels. Define a quantity called the *effective channel capacity*

$$M'_i = 2^{-i} M_i. \tag{18}$$

which is the reciprocal of the number of units of distortion required on average to communicate one logical bit of information in channel C_i. Notice that if $y_i = 0$ then $M'_i = 2^{-i}$. Also note that Equation 14 is equivalent to

$$M'_i = M'_j \tag{19}$$

for all i, j. If $d < d_c$ then the Attacker's optimal strategy consists of equalizing as many of the lowest order effective channel capacities as allowed by the distortion limit. In other words, the Attacker first introduces noise into C_0, reducing M'_0 until reaching the point $M'_0 = M'_1 = \frac{1}{2}$. If he has not reached the distortion limit then he continues to introduce noise into C_0 and now also C_1, maintaining the relation $M'_0 = M'_1$ until he reaches the point $M'_0 = M'_1 = M'_2 = \frac{1}{4}$ and so on until the limit d is reached.

Let us now solve for the Hider's optimal strategy. For a fixed $\mathbf{x}$ consider the partial payoff functions as functions of y_j:

$$P_{jk}(y_j) = x_j \left[1 - H\left(\frac{y_j}{N}\right) \right] + x_k \left[1 - H\left(\frac{d_{jk} - 2^j y_j}{2^k}\right) \right] \tag{20}$$

for $0 \leq j < k \leq l - 1$ where

$$d_{jk} = d - \sum_{i \neq j,k} 2^i y_i \tag{21}$$

is again a constant of remaining distortion. In order for $\mathbf{y}^*$ to be an equilibrium strategy it is necessary the Attacker does not profit from readjusting and therefore we have

$$\frac{dP_{jk}}{dy_j}(y_j^*) = 0. \tag{22}$$

Taking the derivative and carrying through the calculation yields:

$$\frac{x_j}{x_k} = \frac{2^{j-k} \log \frac{p_k^*}{1 - p_k^*}}{\log \frac{p_j^*}{1 - p_j^*}} \tag{23}$$

where $p_i^* = y_i^*/N$. For fixed N, d and from $\mathbf{y}^*$ derived above we can also solve this numerically. This process yields pure strategies $\mathbf{x}^*$ and $\mathbf{y}^*$ with nonnegative, possibly noninteger coordinates. The total number of logical bits communicated is given by

$$P(\mathbf{x}^*, \mathbf{y}^*) = \sum_{i=0}^{l-1} x_i^* \left[1 - H\left(\frac{y_i^*}{N}\right)\right]. \tag{24}$$

The fact that the components may not be integers requires comment. Recall that a pure strategy is an l-tuple of nonnegative *real* numbers, representing the number of bits to be stored in a particular channel. However a noninteger coordinate in a tuple would evidently have no practical interpretation. For example, for the strategy $(5, 10.5, \ldots, \pi)$ we have no way of actually storing 10.5 bits in the N next-to-least significant bits or π bits in the N most significant bits. In practice this issue is insignificant as the channel capacities are continuous functions of the strategy components. Therefore neither player can profit significantly from the other player's need to approximate a noninteger strategy with integer components. Asymptotically as N goes to infinity the difference in the payoffs resulting from using the exact equilibrium and an integer approximation goes to zero.

5   Two Numerical Examples

Let us consider two concrete examples of the preceding game. Numerical solutions to all sets of nonlinear equations were obtained by the use of simple Mathematica programs. In the first example we will have $d < d_c$ and in the second example we have $d > d_c$. Consider an 8-bit, 256 level greyscale image with 10^6 pixels. For the first example suppose we set the distortion to be equivalent to freely replacing the two least significant bits in each pixel. Then $d = 3 \times 10^6$. Solving Equation 16 yields $d_c(8, 10^6) \approx 2.4 \times 10^7$. Solving Equations 14 and 4 numerically yields the following solutions for the optimal Attacker strategy and is presented in Table 1. Solving Equations 23 and 4 numerically yields the following solutions for the optimal Hider strategy and is presented in Table 2. These solutions and Equation 24 give

$$P(\mathbf{x}^*, \mathbf{y}^*) = 346264. \tag{25}$$

Table 1. Optimal Strategy for Attacker ($d = 3 \times 10^6$, $N = 10^6$)

Channel	0	1	2	3	4	5	6	7
y_i	359526	302710	224980	123138	9376	0	0	0
p_i	.359	.303	.225	.123	.01	0	0	0
M_i	0.058	0.115	.231	.462	.923	1	1	1
M_i'	.058	.058	.058	.058	.058	$2^{-5} = .031$	2^{-6}	2^{-7}

Table 2. Optimal Strategy for Hider ($d = 3 \times 10^6$, $N = 10^6$)

Channel	0	1	2	3	4	5	6	7
x_i		97114	134406	181347	228526	192530	0	0	0

For the second example let $d = 5 \times 10^7$. This level of distortion corresponds to treating between 5 and 6 of the lowest bits in each byte as replaceable. Solving Equations 14 and 4 numerically yields the following solutions for the optimal Attacker strategy and is presented in Table 3. Solving Equations 23 and 4 numerically yields the solutions for the optimal Hider strategy and is presented in Table 4. These solutions and Equation 24 give

$$P(\mathbf{x}^*, \mathbf{y}^*) = 381120. \tag{26}$$

Table 3. Optimal Strategy for Attacker ($d = 5 \times 10^7$, $N = 10^6$)

Channel	0	1	2	3	4	5	6	7
y_i	463672	448647	427440	397568	355659	297361	217774	114101
p_i	.463	.449	.427	.398	.356	.297	.218	.114
M_i	.004	.008	.015	.030	.061	.122	.244	.488
M_i'	.004	.004	.004	.004	.004	.004	.004	.004

Table 4. Optimal Strategy for Hider ($d = 5 \times 10^7$, $N = 10^6$)

Channel	0	1	2	3	4	5	6	7
x_i		52624	74324	104830	147456	206254	285075	383418	478426

We now make a final interesting observation. Consider $P(x^*, y^*)$, the total amount of information communicated as a function of d. If $d = 0$ then clearly $P = 0$ because the Hider cannot alter any bits and if $d = d_{total}$ then $P = 0$ because the Attacker can randomize the data set. Numerical analysis suggests that P is concave, achieves a maximum at $d_{max} \approx 37N = 3.7 \times 10^7$ and $P(d_{max}) \approx .405N = 405000$.

6 Further Work

One may imagine many variations on the game formulation studied here. For a more general formulation of the problem see [6]. The game presented in the present work is a simultaneous move game and models the situation whereby the Attacker does not have the privilege of witnessing the Hider's move before deciding on a strategy. In a practical situation this may occur if, for example, the Attacker is in control of a server through which a large number of files with potential hidden data pass. The Attacker may set up an automated system to intentionally introduce noise into all data files to disrupt the covert channels. Another scenario occurs if the Attacker examines files individually and then introduces noise based on this analysis. Presumably this would decrease the channel capacity of the covert channels. This latter scenario would be modeled by a game in which the Attacker moves *after* the hider.

Another area which needs further consideration is the distortion measure. In fact, the actual distortion introduced by changing bits is a difficult problem, probably requiring consideration of the details of human vision. Large areas of uniform color are especially sensitive to even small local changes. Therefore our analysis is probably more relevant to images without these large uniformities. Quantitative analysis of these problems will be an important advance in steganalysis.

7   Acknowledgments

I would like to thank Mike Murphy, Mike Neergaard, Ted Handel, Brook Sandford, and the anonymous referees for their corrections and comments.

References

1. Ross Anderson editor. *Information Hiding. First International Workshop. Cambridge, U.K., May/June, 1996. Proceedings.* Lecture Notes In Computer Science Series Number 1174. Springer-Verlag, 1996.
2. W. Bender, D. Gruhl, N. Morimoto, A. Lu. "Techniques For Data Hiding." IBM Systems Journal Vol. 35, 1996, pp. 313–336.
3. I. Cox, J. Kilian, Tom Leighton, Talal Shamoon. "A Secure, Robust Watermark for Multimedia" in [1].
4. Robert J. McEliece. *The Theory of Information and Coding.* Addison-Wesley, 1977.
5. Guillermo Owen. *Game Theory.* Academic Press, 1995.
6. Joseph A. O'Sullivan, Pierre Moulin, J. Mark Ettinger. *Information Theoretic Analysis of Steganography.* 1998 IEEE International Symposium on Information Theory.
7. M. Sandford, J. Bradley, T. Handel. "The Data Embedding Method." Los Alamos Technical Report 9LA-95-2246UR.
8. J. Von Neumann and O. Morgenstern. *The Theory of Games and Economic Behavior.* Princeton University Press, 1944, 1947.

Modelling the False Alarm and Missed Detection Rate for Electronic Watermarks

Jean-Paul Linnartz, Ton Kalker, and Geert Depovere

Philips Research Laboratories
Prof. Holstlaan 4, WY8, 5656 AA Eindhoven, The Netherlands
{linnartz, kalker, depovere}@natlab.research.philips.com

Abstract. Theoretical modeling of watermarks allow prediction of the detector reliability and facilitates the development of more reliable systems. In particular, mathematical evaluation is relevant to estimate the rate at which "false alarms" occur. In this paper, the probability of incorrect detection (missed detection or false alarm) is expressed in terms of the watermark-energy-to-image-luminance-variance ratio. We present some counterintuitive results which show for instance that the reliability of detection significantly depends on spatial correlation in watermark. Moreover we find that a small but uncompensated random DC component in the watermark can have a significant effect on the reliability.

1 Background

New multi-media networks and services facilitate the dissemination of audio and video content, but at the same time make illegal copying and copyright piracy simple. This has created a need to embed copyright data in the content in an indelible way. Particularly if watermark detection is part of an active copy control concept on Consumer Electronics (CE) and PC platforms, typical requirements include [1,2,3,4,5,6].

1. Erasing or altering the watermark should be difficult.
2. The watermarking scheme should be robust against typical transmission and storage imperfections (such as lossy compression, noise addition, format conversion, bit errors) and signal processing artefacts (noise reduction, filtering), even if such operations are intended to erase the watermark.
3. It should be robust against typical attacks, e.g. those described in [5].
4. False alarms, i.e., positive responses for content that does not contain a watermark should not occur (orders of magnitude) more often than electronic or mechanical product failures. CE devices or PC-s should not fail to work due to an erroneously triggered watermark detector.
5. The watermark should be unobtrusive, and not be annoying to bona-fide users.

The "low false alarm" requirement appears to be too stringent to determine the error rates only by experiments. This has been our motivation to develop a mathematical model for the reliability of watermark detectors.

David Aucsmith (Ed.): Information Hiding 1998, LNCS 1525, pp. 329–343, 1998.

The aim of this paper is to contribute to the understanding and modelling of the reliability of watermark detectors. This involves the development of a mathematical framework and verification of critical assumptions.

The organization of the paper is as follows. Section 2 models the image (Sect. 2.1) and the watermark (Sect. 2.2–2.4). The analysis presented in this paper requires a detailed definition of the DC-component and the spatial correlation of the watermark, which we include in section 2.3 and 2.4, respectively. Section 3 discusses the detector. The reliability of a generic correlator is derived, and special cases are dealt with. A few counterintuitive results are obtained, discussed and verified. Numerical results are plotted in section 4, and verified by experiments. Section 5 concludes this paper.

2   Formulation of the Model

Our model extends previous work, such as [1,2,3,6] to regard the image as noise or interference during the detection of a weak wanted signal (namely the watermark). However, we consider spatial correlation properties of the image to be known to a large extent and we address (pseudo-) randomness in the watermark generation.

2.1   Image Model

We consider a rectangular image of size $N = N_1 N_2$ pixels. The (gray level or) luminance of the pixel with coordinates $\boldsymbol{n} = (n_1, n_2)$, $(0 \leq n_1 \leq N_1 - 1, 0 \leq n_2 \leq N_2 - 1)$ is denoted as $p(\boldsymbol{n})$. We denote $\boldsymbol{0} = (0,0)$, $\boldsymbol{e_1} = (1,0)$ and $\boldsymbol{e_2} = (0,1)$, so $\boldsymbol{n} = n_1 \boldsymbol{e_1} + n_2 \boldsymbol{e_2}$. The set of all pixel coordinates is denoted as A_N, where

$$A_N = \{\boldsymbol{n} : 0 \leq n_1 \leq N_1 - 1, 0 \leq n_2 \leq N_2 - 1\}.$$

In color pictures, $p(\boldsymbol{n})$ is a YUV or RGB vector, but for the sake of simplicity we restrict our discussion to the luminance of the image, in which $p(\boldsymbol{n})$ takes on real or integer values in a certain interval.

The k-th sample moment of the gray level of each pixel is denoted as $\mu_k = A[p^k(\boldsymbol{n})] = \frac{1}{N} \sum_{\boldsymbol{n} \in A_N} p^k(\boldsymbol{n})$, where A is a spatial averaging operator over area A_N. In particular, μ_1 represents the average value or "DC-component" in a pixel and $\mu_2 = A[p^2]$ represents the average power in a pixel and $E_p = N \mu_2$ is the total energy in an image. The sample variance is $\sigma^2 = A[p(\boldsymbol{n}) - \mu_1]^2 = \mu_2 - \mu_1^2$.

We assume that the image has homogeneous statistical properties (wide-sense spatial stationarity), so the spatial correlation only depends on the difference vector $\boldsymbol{\Delta}$. We define

$$\Gamma_{p,p}(\boldsymbol{\Delta}) = \frac{1}{N} \sum_{\boldsymbol{n} \in A_N} p(\boldsymbol{n})p(\boldsymbol{n} + \boldsymbol{\Delta}),$$

In order to make the evaluation of our examples tractable, we simplify the image model assuming the first-order separable autocorrelation function (acf) [10,7,8]

$$\Gamma_{p,p}(\Delta) = \mu_1^2 + \sigma^2 \alpha^{|\Delta|}$$

where we defined $|\Delta| = |\Delta_1| + |\Delta_2|$. Here α can be interpreted as a measure of the correlation between adjacent pixels in the image. Experiments, e.g. in [6] reveal that typically $\alpha \approx 0.9 \ldots 0.99$. We denote $\tilde{p}(\boldsymbol{n})$ as the non-DC components of the image, i.e., $p(\boldsymbol{n}) = \mu_1 + \tilde{p}(\boldsymbol{n})$, so $\Gamma_{\tilde{p},\tilde{p}} = \sigma^2 \alpha^{|\Delta|}$.

Some of the above assumptions seem a crude approximation of the typical properties of images. From experiments such as those to be reported in section 5, it will appear that estimates based on this simplification are nonetheless reasonably accurate for our purpose. The accuracy of the model will be verified by measuring μ, σ and α from images and using these parameters in a theoretical evaluation, which we compare with purely experimental results. These assumptions, however, exclude certain images, such as binary images, line art or computer-generated graphics with a limited number of grey levels.

2.2   Watermark Model

The watermark is represented by $w(\boldsymbol{n})$ which takes on real values in all pixels $\boldsymbol{n} \in A_N$. A watermark detector has to operate on the observed (marked or unmarked) image $q(\boldsymbol{n})$. We aim at detecting whether a particular watermark is present or not, based only on the knowledge of $w(\boldsymbol{n})$. In copy control applications, the unmarked original $p(\boldsymbol{n})$ is not available at the detector. Watermarked images have similar properties as unmarked images, except that perceptually invisible modifications have been made. We assume $q(\boldsymbol{n})$ to provide sufficiently reliable estimates of the properties (μ_k and $\Gamma_{p,p}$) of $p(\boldsymbol{n})$.

The watermark $w(\boldsymbol{n})$ is embedded in the image. Typically, $q(\boldsymbol{n}) = p(\boldsymbol{n}) + \theta(\boldsymbol{n})w(\boldsymbol{n})$, where we do not yet specify the embedding depth $\theta(\boldsymbol{n})$. In the analysis we will focus on detection, thus simplify the embedding process by taking $\theta(\boldsymbol{n}) \equiv 1$ for all $\boldsymbol{n} \in A_N$.

Our model implicitly assumes that no spatial transformation of the image (resizing, cropping, rotation, etc.) is conducted. Such transformation may require a search during detection, which is outside the scope of this analysis.

In the following, we will not consider a particular, fully described watermark but a class of watermarks having specific spatial properties. In practice, this could be the set of all watermarks that are generated by a certain algorithm, but with different seeds for the pseudo-random generator.

For two watermarks w_1 and w_2 out of such class, the (deterministic) spatial inner product is

$$\Gamma_{w_1,w_2}(\boldsymbol{\Delta}) = \frac{1}{N} \sum_{\boldsymbol{n} \in A_N} w_1(\boldsymbol{n}) w_2(\boldsymbol{n} + \boldsymbol{\Delta}),$$

where we assume for simplicity that $\boldsymbol{n} + \boldsymbol{\Delta}$ wraps around when it formally falls outside the set A_N. The total energy in the watermark equals

$$E_w = \sum_{\boldsymbol{n} \in A_N} w^2(\boldsymbol{n}) = N\Gamma_{w,w}(\boldsymbol{0}).$$

If we consider an ensemble of many watermarks generated by a particular watermark generation algorithm, the statistical correlation is defined as

$$R_{w_1,w_2}(\boldsymbol{\Delta}) = \mathrm{E}[w_1(\boldsymbol{n})w_2(\boldsymbol{n} + \boldsymbol{\Delta})]$$

For virtually all watermark generators that we are aware of, the expected value of a measured $\Gamma_{w,w}$ equals $R_{w,w}$ with negligible small deviations if the size of the watermark set A_N is sufficiently large.

Such a property does *not* hold for images, where due to the lack of ergodicity, it is unlikely that the spatial correlation $\Gamma_{p,p}$ of a particular image converges in mean-square to the statistical correlation $R_{p,p}$ over a collection of different images.

2.3   DC Components

The DC content of the watermark is defined as $D_0 = \mathrm{A}[w(n)] = \frac{1}{N}\sum_{\boldsymbol{n}\in A_N} w(\boldsymbol{n})$. An individual watermark is DC-free iff $D_0 = 0$. This cases has been addressed extensively by Pitas [1] and others.

For an arbitrary value of D_0, we observe that

$$N^2D_0^2 = \sum_{\boldsymbol{n}\in A_N}\sum_{\boldsymbol{k}\in A_N} w(\boldsymbol{n})w(\boldsymbol{k}) = E_w + \sum_{\boldsymbol{n}\in A_N}\sum_{\boldsymbol{k}\in A_N, \boldsymbol{k}\neq\boldsymbol{n}} w(\boldsymbol{n})w(\boldsymbol{k})$$
$$= E_w + \sum_{\boldsymbol{n}\in A_N}\sum_{\boldsymbol{\Delta}\neq\boldsymbol{0}} w(\boldsymbol{n})w(\boldsymbol{n}+\boldsymbol{\Delta}) = E_w + N\sum_{\boldsymbol{\Delta}\neq\boldsymbol{0}}\Gamma_{w,w}(\boldsymbol{\Delta}) \tag{1}$$

This implies that a designer who desires to choose D_0 and E_w must face restrictions on the spatial correlation $\Gamma_{w,w}$.

In practice, a watermark can for instance be created by randomly generating a $+k$ or $-k$ pixel value independently for each pixel $\boldsymbol{n}$. Then, D_0 is a random variable with zero-mean ($ED_0 = 0$) and positive variance. Thus, each individual watermark does not necessarily have a zero DC component. We call a *watermark generation process* or a set of watermarks to be "statistically DC-free" or "DC-free in the mean" iff $ED_0 = 0$. This is a necessary, but not a sufficient condition for all individual watermarks to be DC-free. When the generation process is DC-free with probability one, we call it absolutely DC-free, or adopting a term used in probability theory [15], we write "(almost) surely" (a.s.) DC-free.

2.4   Watermark Spectrum

Quasi-White Watermarks For a watermark with a given D_0, one can consider the class of (quasi-) white watermarks, which satisfy $\Gamma_{w,w}(\boldsymbol{\Delta_1}) = \Gamma_{w,w}(\boldsymbol{\Delta_2}) = \eta$ for $\boldsymbol{\Delta_1}, \boldsymbol{\Delta_2} \neq \boldsymbol{0}$, where η is some constant ($|\eta| << E_w/N$). In such case the spatial autocorrelation resembles a δ-function with a peak of amplitude E_w/N at $\boldsymbol{\Delta} = \boldsymbol{0}$. For $\boldsymbol{\Delta} \neq \boldsymbol{0}$,

$$\Gamma_{w,w}(\boldsymbol{\Delta}) = \eta = (N^2D_0^2 - E_w)/(N(N-1)) < 0.$$

It can be shown that the corresponding spectral energy density is flat, except for a DC-component.

In particular, we see that for a DC-free watermark ($D_0 = 0$) with non-zero energy ($E_w > 0$), the watermark values $w(\boldsymbol{n_i})$ and $w(\boldsymbol{n_j})$, $\boldsymbol{n_i} \neq \boldsymbol{n_j}$ cannot be statistically uncorrelated, because $\eta < 0$. *

We will call a watermark generation process "quasi white and DC-free a.s." if $D_0 = 0$ a.s. and its autocorrelation function is

$$\Gamma_{w,w}(\boldsymbol{\Delta}) = \begin{cases} E_w/N & \text{if } \boldsymbol{\Delta} = \boldsymbol{0} \\ \frac{N^2 D_0^2 - E_w}{N(N-1)} & \text{if } \boldsymbol{\Delta} \neq \boldsymbol{0} \end{cases}$$

In the performance analysis, we will mainly use the statistical correlation $R_{w,w}$ over the ensemble of watermarks rather than the deterministic $\Gamma_{w,w}$. The behavior of R can be shown to be similar to that of Γ.

Let's consider some pixel $\boldsymbol{n_0}$ with a non-zero watermark value $w(\boldsymbol{n_0}) = k_0$. This implies that the $N - 1$ other pixels in the image must compensate for this through

$$\sum_{n_i \in A_N \setminus \boldsymbol{n_0}} w(\boldsymbol{n_i}) = ND_0 - k_0$$

For a quasi-white watermark generation process, we define $R_{w,w}(\boldsymbol{\Delta_1}) = R_{w,w}(\boldsymbol{\Delta_2}) = \eta_R$ for $\boldsymbol{\Delta_1}, \boldsymbol{\Delta_2} \neq \boldsymbol{0}$. We find

$$E[w(\boldsymbol{n_i})|w(\boldsymbol{n_0}) = k_0] = (ND_0 - k_0)/(N - 1),$$

so, for $\boldsymbol{\Delta} \neq \boldsymbol{0}$,

$$R_{w,w}(\boldsymbol{\Delta}) = E[E[w(\boldsymbol{n_0})w(\boldsymbol{n_0} + \boldsymbol{\Delta})|[w(\boldsymbol{n_0})]] = E\left[w(\boldsymbol{n_0})[\frac{ND_0 - w(\boldsymbol{n_0})}{N - 1}]\right]$$

We get

$$R_{w,w}(\boldsymbol{\Delta}) = \begin{cases} \frac{E_w}{N} & \text{if } \boldsymbol{\Delta} = \boldsymbol{0} \\ N\frac{D_0^2}{N-1} - \frac{E_w}{N(N-1)} & \text{if } \boldsymbol{\Delta} \neq \boldsymbol{0} \end{cases}.$$

A "purely white" watermark generation process requires that the correlation equals exactly zero except at $\boldsymbol{\Delta} = \boldsymbol{0}$, where $R_{w,w}(\boldsymbol{0}) = E_w/N$. We have seen that purely white watermarks cannot be absolutely DC free, but have $D_0 = \sqrt{E_w}/N$

Low Pass Watermark As an other example, we will treat the case that the watermark has a low-pass spatial spectrum. This method has been advocated for instance by Cox et al. [4]. In such situation, a potential attacker can less easily tamper with the watermark by low-pass filtering. Moreover, JPEG compression

---

* A similar small negative correlation outside the origin ($\boldsymbol{\Delta} \neq \boldsymbol{0}$) is often ascribed to a peculiarity of maximum-length pseudo-random sequences, as generated by a Linear Feedback Shift Registers (LFSR). However, the above argument reveals that it is fundamentally related to the requirement of the DC value. See also [13,14].

typically removes or distorts high-frequency components. A low-pass watermark can be generated by spatially filtering a (quasi-)white watermark. Perceptually this appears as a smoothing. A first-order two dimensional IIR spatial smoothing filter computes [11]

$$w_2(\boldsymbol{n}) = (1 - \beta^2)^2 \left[w_1(\boldsymbol{n}) + \beta w_2(\boldsymbol{n} - \boldsymbol{e_1}) + \beta w_2(\boldsymbol{n} - \boldsymbol{e_2}) - \beta^2 w_2(\boldsymbol{n} - \boldsymbol{e_2} - \boldsymbol{e_2}) \right]$$

from an original w_1. It can be shown that in case of a purely white watermark w_1 at the input, such a first-order filter generates a new watermark w_2 with correlation function [11]

$$R_{w_2,w_2} = \frac{E_w}{N} \beta^{|\Delta|}$$

Another method of generating a low pass watermark is to use a pseudo random $\{-k, k\}$ generator which gives a statistically dependent output for neighboring pixels.

3   Correlator Detector

Correlation detectors are interesting to study, for several reasons. They are a mathematical generalization of the simple but nonetheless important scheme in which $w \in \{-1, 0, +1\}$. To discuss this subclass of correlators first, let's denote $A_- = \{\boldsymbol{n} : w(\boldsymbol{n}) = -1\}$ and $A_+ = \{\boldsymbol{n} : w(\boldsymbol{n}) = +1\}$. Watermarks are detected by computing the sum of all pixel luminances at locations where the watermark is negative, i.e., $s_- = \sum_{\boldsymbol{n} \in A_-} q(\boldsymbol{n})$ and the sum of all luminances where the watermark is positive, i.e., $s_+ = \sum_{\boldsymbol{n} \in A_+} q(\boldsymbol{n})$. Then, an expression such as $y = (s_+ - s_-)/N$ is used as a decision variable. See for instance [1,2] for schemes that are related or can be shown to be equivalent. From our more general results to follow it can be concluded that that two aspects have a significant effect on performance.

[Spatial Correlation] Spatial correlation occurs if the probability that $n_i \in A_-$ statistically depends on whether $n_j \in A_-$ for some pair of differing pixel locations $n_i \neq n_j$. We will see that high spatial correlation substantially reduces reliability.

[Compensation of DC components in the watermark] If the number of pixels in sets A_- and A_+ are generated as binomial random variables such that the *expected value* of the number of elements in both sets is identical ($ED_0 = 0$, but the variance of $D_0 = O(N^{-1})$), the performance is significantly worse than when the number of elements is always precisely the same ($D_0 = 0$ a.s.). This is in contrast to our intuition that if pixels are put in A_- and A_+ with probability $1/2$ and independently of each other, the statistical effect of a differing number of elements in each class would become negligibly small for increasing image sizes. Our theoretical and experimental results refute this belief.

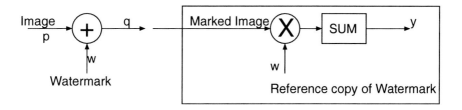

Fig. 1. Watermark Embedder and Correlation Detector

Another reason to address correlators (sometimes called "matched filters" [12]) is that these are known to be the *optimum* detector for a typical situation often encountered in radio communications, namely the Linear Time-Invariant (LTI), frequency non-dispersive, Additive Gaussian Noise (AWGN) channel, when the receiver has full knowledge about the alphabet of waveforms used to transmit a message. Less ideal situations often are addressed with appropriate modifications of the matched filter.

In a correlator detector, a decision variable y is extracted from the suspect image $q(\boldsymbol{n})$ according to correlation with a locally stored copy of the watermark $\hat{w}(\boldsymbol{n})$ typically with $\hat{w}(\boldsymbol{n}) = C_d w(\boldsymbol{n})$, where w.l.o.g. we assume the constant C_d to be unity. The decision variable is $y = \Gamma_{\hat{w},q}(\boldsymbol{0})$, with

$$\Gamma_{\hat{w},q}(\boldsymbol{\Delta}) = \frac{1}{N} \sum_{\boldsymbol{n} \in A_N} \hat{w}(\boldsymbol{n})q(\boldsymbol{n} + \boldsymbol{\Delta})$$

Fig. 1 illustrates this correlation detector. The model covers all detectors in which the decision variable is a linear combination of pixel luminance values in the image. Hence, it is a generalization of many detectors proposed previously. It covers a broader class of watermarks then the binary $(w(\boldsymbol{n}) \in \{-k, k\})$ or ternary $(w(\boldsymbol{n}) \in \{-k, 0, k\})$ watermarks. In particular, it also includes methods in which the detection in conducted by correlation in the domain of DCT coefficients.

For our analysis, we separate y into a deterministic contribution y_w from the watermark, plus filtered "noise" from the image y_p.

$$y_w = \frac{1}{N} \sum_{\boldsymbol{n} \in A_N} \hat{w}(\boldsymbol{n})\theta(\boldsymbol{n})w(\boldsymbol{n})$$

Taking a uniform embedding depth $\theta(n) \equiv 1$, we get $y_w = \Gamma_{w,w}(\boldsymbol{0}) = \frac{E_w}{N}$. Moreover,

$$y_p = \frac{1}{N} \sum_{\boldsymbol{n} \in A_N} \hat{w}(\boldsymbol{n})p(\boldsymbol{n})$$

Regarding y_p, the mean value is found as the product of the DC component in the watermark and the image, namely

$$\mathrm{E}y_p = \frac{1}{N}\mathrm{E} \sum_{\boldsymbol{n} \in A_N} \hat{w}(\boldsymbol{n})p(\boldsymbol{n}) = \frac{1}{N}\left[\mathrm{E}\hat{w}(\boldsymbol{n})\right] \sum_{\boldsymbol{n} \in A_N} p(\boldsymbol{n}) = \mu_1 \mathrm{E}\hat{D}_0$$

Note that for a particular watermark with known DC-component, $Ey_p|D_0 = \mu_1\hat{D}_0$. Up to this point, results are irrespective of the correlation in pixels. The second moment is found as

$$Ey_p^2 = E\left[\frac{1}{N}\sum_{n\in A_N}\hat{w}(n)p(n)\right]^2 = \tag{2}$$

$$\frac{1}{N^2}E\left[\sum_{n_i\in A_N}\sum_{n_j\in A_N}\hat{w}(n_i)p(n_i)\hat{w}(n_j)p(n_j)\right]$$

In the above expression it is tempting to assume that cross terms with $n_i \neq n_j$ all become zero or negligibly small for sufficiently large images. However, a DC component may be present. Furthermore, in the following sections we will show that for correlated pixels ($\alpha > 0$) and spectrally non-white watermarks (e.g., $\beta > 0$) , non-zero cross terms substantially affect the results, even if $D_0 = 0$. Therefore we will not make this assumption here.

Because of the Central Limit Theorem, y_p has a Gaussian distribution if N is sufficiently large and if the contributions in the sums are sufficiently independent. The Gaussian behaviour will be verified experimentally in section 4. If we apply a threshold y_{thr} to decide that the watermark is present if $y > y_{thr}$, the probability of a *missed detection* (the watermark is present in $q(n)$, but the detector thinks it is not; false negative) is

$$P_{md} = \frac{1}{2}\text{erfc}\frac{y_w - y_{thr} + Ey_p}{\sqrt{2}\sigma_{y_p}}$$

where σ_{y_p} is the standard deviation of y_p, with $\sigma_{y_p}^2 = Ey_p^2 - [Ey_p]^2$. We find

$$P_{md} = \frac{1}{2}\text{erfc}\frac{E_w + \mu_1 NE\hat{D}_0 - N_1 N_2 y_{thr}}{\sqrt{2}N\sigma_{y_p}}$$

The presence of D_0 and μ_1 in this expression suggest that either the DC-terms must be appropriately compensated in selecting y_{thr} or that the suspect image $q(n)$ must be preprocessed to subtract the DC-term μ_1.

Given that no watermark is embedded, a *false alarm* (false positive) occurs with probability

$$P_{fa} = \frac{1}{2}\text{erfc}\frac{y_{thr} - Ey_p}{\sqrt{2}\sigma_{y_p}}$$

3.1   Example 1: (Quasi-)White and DC-Free Watermark

The quasi-white and DC-free watermark reasonably models most of the early proposals for increasing and decreasing the pixel luminance according to a pseudo random process. Using $p(n) = \mu_1 + \tilde{p}(n)$, one can write

$$Ey_p^2 = \mu_1^2 D_0^2 + \frac{1}{N^2}\sum_{n\in A_N}\sum_{\Delta:n+\Delta\in A_N}E\left[\hat{w}(n)\hat{w}(n+\Delta)\tilde{p}(n)\tilde{p}(n+\Delta)\right]$$

For an a.s. DC-free watermark, the first term is zero. In the forthcoming evaluation, the image size N is considered to be large enough and α is assumed to be sufficiently smaller than unity to justify ignoring of boundary effects. To be more precise, we consider $R_{w,w}(\mathbf{\Delta})\Gamma_{\tilde{p},\tilde{p}}(\mathbf{\Delta})$ to vanish rapidly enough with increasing $\mathbf{\Delta}$ to allow the following approximation: we consider the sum over $\mathbf{\Delta}$ to cover the entire plane R^2 even though the size of the image is finite. This allows us to write

$$\sigma_{y_p}^2 = \mathrm{E}y_p^2 = \frac{1}{N} \sum_{\mathbf{\Delta} \in R^2} R_{w,w}(\mathbf{\Delta})\Gamma_{\tilde{p},\tilde{p}}(\mathbf{\Delta})$$

Thus

$$\mathrm{E}y_p^2 = \frac{E_w \sigma^2}{N^2} - \sum_{\mathbf{\Delta} \neq 0} \left[\frac{D_0^2}{N-1} - \frac{E_w}{N^2(N-1)} \right] [\sigma^2 \alpha^{|\mathbf{\Delta}|}]$$

We use $\sum_{\mathbf{\Delta} \neq 0} \alpha^{|\mathbf{\Delta}|} = [(1+\alpha)/(1-\alpha)]^2 - 1$ to express

$$\mathrm{E}y_p^2 = \frac{E_w \sigma^2}{N(N-1)} + \sigma^2 \left[\frac{N^2 D_0^2 - E_w}{N^2(N-1)} \right] \left[\frac{1+\alpha}{1-\alpha} \right]^2$$

The second term becomes negligible for large N. We see that the effect of pixel correlations is significant only if α is close to unity (little luminance changes) in a small-size image. If the image is large enough, that is, if $N >> [(1+\alpha)/(1-\alpha)]^2$, we may approximate

$$\mathrm{E}y_p^2 \approx \frac{E_w \sigma^2}{N^2}$$

Experiments of section 4 confirm that in practical situations this is a reasonable approximation, provided that the watermark is white. Inserting the value obtained for the standard deviation σ_{y_p}, the error probability becomes

$$P_{fa} = \frac{1}{2} \mathrm{erfc} \frac{N y_{thr}}{\sqrt{2E_w}\sigma}$$

In Fig. 2, we consider a DC-free watermark and $y_{thr} = \frac{E_w}{2N}$ which provides $P_{fa} = P_{md}$. In practice one would presumably like to improve P_{fa} at the cost of P_{md}, but this corresponds to a simple horizontal shift of the curve. We plot

$$P_{fa} = P_{md} = \frac{1}{2} \mathrm{erfc} \sqrt{\frac{E_w}{8\sigma^2}}$$

versus the watermark-energy-to-image-luminance-variance E_w/σ^2, expressed in dB i.e., $10 \log_{10}(E_w/\sigma^2)$.

Defining the watermark-energy-to-image-luminance-variance as E_w/σ^2, thus as a signal-to-noise ratio, ensures that the curves and mathematical expressions become independent of the image size, its average luminance and sample variance. Moreover it matches common practice in statistical communication theory where one uses E_b/N_0, where E_b is the average energy per bit, and N_0 is the spectral power density of the noise.

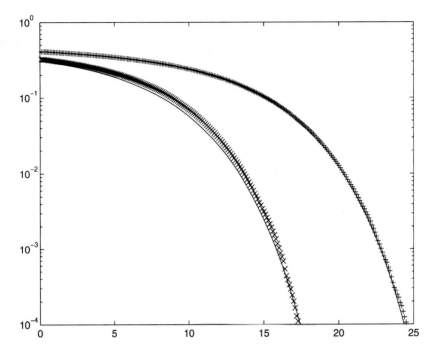

Fig. 2. Watermark detection error rates P_{fa} and P_{md} versus signal-to-noise ratio E_w/σ^2 for correlation detector. Experiments on "Lenna": "×": $D_0 = 0$ "+": random watermark, independent pixels, DC-free i.m. Solid lines: corresponding theoretical curves.

For reliable detection E_w/σ^2 is much larger than unity, but this does not imply that the watermark $w(n_i)$ in a particular pixel exceeds the luminance variance. This is similar to spread-spectrum radio where $E_b/N_0 \gg 1$ despite the fact that spectrally spoken the signal power is below the broadband noise [12].

It appears to be less relevant over how many pixels the watermark energy is spread as long as the total energy E_w and the image properties (σ in particular) are fixed. However, example 3.2.2 will show that if the watermark energy is not embedded by a spectrally white watermark, as assumed here, the results are different and do depend on the watermark "waveform" used. This is in contrast to spread-spectrum radio over AWGN channels.

3.2   Example 2: The Effect of a Non-zero DC Component

This section evaluates the method mentioned in sections 2.3, 2.4 and 3 to generate a watermark by randomly choosing $w(n) \in \{-k, +k\}$ with probability $1/2$ independently for every pixel. The resulting w may or may not be filtered by a two-dimensional first-order filter to created suitable low-pass spatial properties. Before any such filtering the number of elements in A_+ equals $N(1 + D_0)/2$, which is a binomial random variable with mean $N/2$ and variance $N/4$. Thus D_0 is zero-mean with variance $1/N$.

Intuitively one may believe that if N is large enough, setting a fixed detection threshold but without specifically compensating for a small random D_0 will not affect the performance of the detector significantly. Here we will prove different and show that the standard deviation of D_0 remains significant for large N and does not vanish rapidly enough to be negligible. **

We address the ensemble-mean behavior. Averaging over all possible watermarks generated this way, we get

$$\mathrm{E}y_p^2 = \frac{1}{N^2} \sum_{\boldsymbol{n} \in A_N} \sum_{\boldsymbol{\Delta}:\boldsymbol{n}+\boldsymbol{\Delta} \in A_N} [\mathrm{E}w(\boldsymbol{n})w(\boldsymbol{n}+\boldsymbol{\Delta})p(\boldsymbol{n})p(\boldsymbol{n}+\boldsymbol{\Delta})]$$

If we ignore boundary effects, i.e., summing over $\boldsymbol{\Delta} \in R^2$, we get

$$\mathrm{E}y_p^2 = \frac{1}{N_1 N_2} \sum_{\boldsymbol{\Delta} \in R^2} R_{w,w}(\boldsymbol{\Delta}) \Gamma_{p,p}(\boldsymbol{\Delta})$$

Inserting the previously discussed correlation functions of a low-pass image and a low-pass watermark, one sees that

$$\mathrm{E}y_p^2 = \sum_{\boldsymbol{\Delta} \in R^2} \frac{E_w}{N^2} \beta^{|\Delta|} [\mu_1^2 + \sigma^2 \alpha^{|\Delta|}]$$

$$\mathrm{E}y_p^2 = \frac{E_w \sigma^2}{N^2} \left[\frac{1+\alpha\beta}{1-\alpha\beta}\right]^2 + \frac{E_w \mu_1^2}{N^2} \left[\frac{1+\beta}{1-\beta}\right]^2$$

and, as we saw before $\mathrm{E}y_p = \mu_1 \mathrm{E}D_0$, so

$$\mathrm{E}\sigma_{y_p}^2 = \frac{E_w \sigma^2}{N^2} \left[\frac{1+\alpha\beta}{1-\alpha\beta}\right]^2 + \frac{E_w \mu_1^2}{N^2} \left[\frac{1+\beta}{1-\beta}\right]^2 - \mu_1^2 [\mathrm{E}D_0]^2$$

The two first terms are order $O(N^{-2})$. For large N, the second term (which accounts for variations in the DC offset) does *not* vanish compared to the first term. This result is somewhat counterintuitive as it shows that the effect of statistical fluctuations in D_0 does *not* vanish fast enough if the watermark is laid over more pixels.

In the special case of white watermarks, i.e., for $\beta \to 0$, one would expect $\sigma_{y_p}^2 = E_w \sigma^2 / N^2$. However, it tends to $E_w \mu_2 / N^2$ where $\mu_2 = \sigma^2 + \mu_1^2$. To illustrate the consequences of this result, we discuss two different watermark detectors.

3.2.1 The first system is designed around the observation that $\mathrm{E}(y_p|\text{watermark}) = E_w/N$ and $\mathrm{E}(y_p|\text{no watermark}) = 0$, where the expectation includes all

---

** A similar (but less significant) effect of random DC components occurs if a watermark is built by spatially repeating the same basic small pattern in a large size image and cutting the watermark near the image boundaries.

watermarks in the class. For a threshold half-way, i.e., $y_{thr} = E_w/(2N)$, the error rate goes into

$$P_{fa} = P_{md} = \frac{1}{2}\text{erfc}\sqrt{\frac{E_w}{8\left[\sigma^2\left[\frac{1+\alpha\beta}{1-\alpha\beta}\right]^2 + \mu_1^2\left[\frac{1+\beta}{1-\beta}\right]^2\right]}}$$

3.2.2 Alternatively, in the second system, the detection threshold is based on precise knowledge of the watermark including it DC component D_0. $E(y_p|$ watermark, $D_0) = E_w/N + \mu_1 D_0$ and $\mu_1 D_0$ otherwise. That is, the threshold is $y_{thr} = \mu_1 D_0 + E_w/(2N)$.

$$P_{fa} = P_{md} = \frac{1}{2}\text{erfc}\sqrt{\frac{E_w}{8\sigma^2}\left[\frac{1-\alpha\beta}{1+\alpha\beta}\right]^2}$$

The same performance can be achieved by $\tilde{q} = p - \mu_1$ instead of with q as input to the detector. This result reduces to the case of section 3.1 for white watermarks ($\beta = 0$).

We see that the second system outperforms the first one, In experiments, we found that typically μ_2 is about four times larger than σ^2. Hence, performance is better by about 5 to 10 dB. In Fig. 2 we took $\beta = 0$. For low-pass watermarks, the differences would be more pronounced.

4   Computational and Experimental Results

The use of randomly generated sequences provides watermarks that *on the average* may have the desired properties, but without a guarantee that individual watermarks also accurately possess the desired properties. This would lead to different results in our analysis and our experiments.

Therefore, in our experiments, we created quasi white and absolutely DC-free watermarks through appropriate pseudo-random sequences. An appropriate choice appeared to be binary watermarks, $w(n) \in \{-k, k\}$ with $\beta = 0$ generated by a 2-dimensional LFSR maximal length sequence [13,14] of length $2^{14} - 1 = (2^7 - 1)(2^7 + 1) = 127 \cdot 129$, with 127 and 129 being relatively prime. Such sequences have a negligibly small DC component: since $\sum_n w(n) = -1$, we get $D_0 = 1/(2^{14} - 1)$. Their spatial correlation function has the appropriate δ-function shape. Repetition of the 127 by 129 basic pattern leads to a periodic correlation function, but maintains virtually zero correlation outside the peaks. Experiments revealed that effects of cutting off this pattern at non-integer repetition numbers had negligible effect for the large images that we used $N_1 = 720, N_2 = 480$.

Fig. 2 compares the above theoretical results with measurements of the "Lenna" image. In the figure, we combined the results from one image and many watermarks. We computed the components of the decision variable and

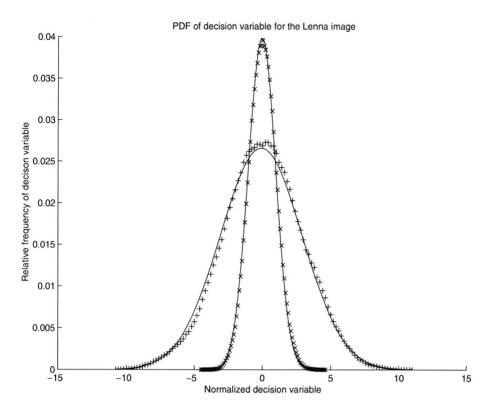

Fig. 3. Probability density of decision variable y_p for white and low-pass watermark on "Lenna". Theory: solid lines. Experiments: "$\times$" white ($\beta = 0$) and "$+$" low-pass ($\beta = 0.5$) watermark.

estimated which signal-to-noise ratio would be needed to achieve detection just above the threshold. Any particular image with a particular watermark gives a step-wise transition in the performance plot, at $y_w = 2y_p$. Combination of this step for many (more than 10^4) watermarks created the smooth curve.

We computed y_p by correlating with a normalized reference copy of the watermark $\hat{w} \in \{-1, +1\}$. In such case $y_w = k$, where k is the embedding depth of the watermark. We measured y_p from the image. To ensure correct detection for a particular watermark and image, the embedder must choose $k \geq 2y_p$, so $E_w = k^2 N_1 N_2 \geq 4y_p^2 N_1 N_2$. The shape of the curve confirms the (approximately) Gaussian behaviour of y_p. Other images produced the same curve.

To get consistent results, we had to generate a large set of watermarks fully independently. If one simply shifts the same watermark to create the set of test watermarks, correlation of pixels in the image leads to correlated decision variables. Moreover, shifting a single watermark can not simulate the effect of a random DC component. This would lead to a significant deviation from the theoretical curve and to a more stepwise (non-Gaussian) decrease of errors rates with increasing SNR. We noted that images with higher correlation are more sensitive to correlations among different watermarks during the experiments.

Fig. 3 compares white and low-pass watermarks. Both watermarks have been generated using a pseudo-random generator to create a white watermark. For the low-pass watermark, this was then filtered. The experiments confirm the Gaussian distribution. This result clearly shows that if the watermark is confined to low-pass components of the image, this significantly affects the reliability of detection. The standard deviation of the decision variable is larger. In this case, the random $+/-$ terms in y_p, which are due to multiplying the image p with the locally stored copy of the watermark $\hat{w}$, do not cancel as rapidly as these would vanish for a white watermark. If the watermark contains relatively strong low-frequency components (large β), the variance of y_p is stronger and the error rate is larger.

If the watermark contains relatively strong high-frequency components $\beta \approx 0$, the variance is weaker, so the watermark sees less interference from the image itself. However, such high-frequency watermark is more vulnerable to erasure by image processing, such as low-pass filtering (smoothing).

5   Conclusions

In this paper, we presented a mathematical framework to model the detection of electronic watermarks embedded in digital images, in particular for correlator detectors or matched filters. Several essential differences appear with the theory of (radio) transmission over a linear time-invariant channel with AWGN. Our model predicts reliability performance (missed detection and false alarms). In some special cases, particularly that of a white watermark, the signal-to-noise ratio (watermark-to-content-energy) appears the only factor to influence the reliability of detection. This leads to expressions for error probabilities similar to those experienced in radio communication (e.g. error function of square root of signal-to-noise ratio) However, the spectral properties of the watermark have a significant influence.

If a watermark detector is part of a standardized active copy control system, false alarms are a critical performance parameter. We believe that the analysis of this paper has provided enhanced insight in the rate at which these errors occur.

6   Acknowledgements

The authors greatly appreciated fruitful discussions with Joop Talstra and Jaap Haitsma.

References

1. I. Pitas, T. Kaskalis : "Signature Casting on Digital Images", Proceedings IEEE Workshop on Nonlinear Signal and Image Processing, Neos Marmaras, June 1995

2. W. Bender, D. Gruhl, N. Morimoto and A. Lu, "Techniques for data hiding", IBM Systems Journal, Vol. 35. No. 3/4 1996
3. J.R. Smith, B. O. Comiskey, "Modulation and Information Hiding in Images", in Proc. Workshop on Information Hiding, Univ. of Cambridge, U.K., May 30–June 1, 1996, pp. 191–201
4. I. Cox, J. Kilian, T. Leighton and T. Shamoon, "A secure, robust watermark for multimedia", in Proc. Workshop on Information Hiding, Univ. of Cambridge, U.K., May 30–June 1, 1996, pp. 175–190
5. I.J. Cox and J.P.M.G. Linnartz, "Public Watermarks and resistance to tampering", Presented at ICIP 97, Santa Barbara, CA, October 1997.
6. J.P.M.G. Linnartz, A.C.C. Kalker, G.F.G. Depovere and R. Beuker, "A reliability model for detection of electronic watermarks in digital images", Benelux Symposium on Communication Theory, Enschede, October 1997, pp. 202–208
7. Ton Kalker, "Watermark Estimation Through Detector Observations", in Proc. of the IEEE Benelux Signal Processing Symposium,1998, Leuven, Belgium, pp. 119–122.
8. Ton Kalker, Jean-Paul Linnartz and Geert Depovere, "On the Reliability of detecting Electronic Watermarks in Digital Images", acc. at Eusipco '98
9. I. J. Cox, M. L. Miller, "A review of watermarking and the importance of perceptual modeling", Proc. of Electronic Imaging 97, Feb. 1997.
10. N.S. Jayant and P. Noll., "Digital Coding of waveforms" Prentice Hall, 1984.
11. Ch. W. Therrien, "Discrete Random Signals and Statistical Signal Processing" Prentice Hall, 1992.
12. "Wireless Communication, The Interactive MultiMedia CD ROM", Baltzer Science Publishers, Amsterdam, 2nd Edition, 1997, http://www.baltzer.nl/wirelesscd
13. F.J. McWilliams and N.J.A. Sloane, "Pseudo-Random Sequences and arrays", Proc . of IEEE, Vol. 64, No.12, Dec. 1976, pp. 1715–1729
14. D. Lin and M. Liu, "Structure and Properies of Linear Recurring m-arrays", IEEE Tr. on Inf. Th., Vol. IT-39, No. 5, Sep. 1993, pp. 1758–1762
15. G.R. Grimmet and D.R. Stirzaker, "Probability and Random Processes", chapter on convergence of random variables, Oxford Science Publishers, 2nd Edition, 1992.

Modeling the Security of Steganographic Systems*

J.Zöllner*, H.Federrath**, H.Klimant**, A.Pfitzmann**, R.Piotraschke**,
A.Westfeld**, G.Wicke**, G.Wolf*

Dresden University of Technology, 01062 Dresden, Germany
*Institute for Operating Systems, Databases and Computer Networks
**Institute for Theoretical Computer Science
{zoellner, federrath, pfitza, westfeld, wicke, g.wolf}@inf.tu-dresden.de
{klimant, pi}@tcs.inf.tu-dresden.de

Abstract. We present a model of steganographic systems which allows to
evaluate their security. We especially want to establish an analogy to the
known-plaintext-attack which is commonly used to rate cryptographic systems.
This model's main statement is that the embedding operation of a
steganographic system should work **indeterministic** from the attacker's point of
view. This is proved by means of information theory.
Key words. Security and modeling of steganography, entropy, indeterminism,
secret communication, hidden communication

1   A Short Introduction to Steganography

Bruce Schneier characterizes steganography in the following way [1]: "Steganography
serves to hide secret messages in other messages, such that the secret's very existence
is concealed." He also states some historic examples, such as "…invisible inks, tiny
pin punctures on selected characters, minute differences between handwritten characters, pencil marks on typewritten characters, …".

These examples show that steganography itself is not a new technique. However, it
experiences a renaissance due to the ubiquitous use of computers and multimedia;
especially when graphical and audio data are involved. Consequently, most available
implementations of steganographic algorithms work on graphics or sound.

In Fig. 1 we illustrate the use of steganography on images.

* The work was sponsored by the German Ministry of Education, Science, Research and Technology and the Gottlieb-Daimler- and Karl-Benz-Foundation Ladenburg (Germany).

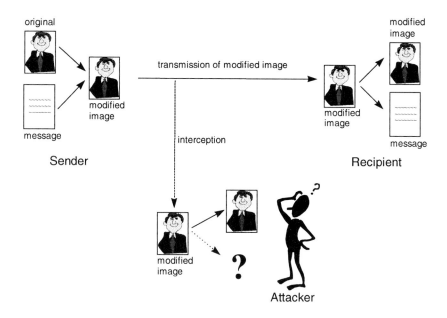

Fig. 1. Steganography with graphical data

On the left you can see the sender, who embeds the secret message into a graphic file (the "original"). She then transmits this modified file (here named "modified image") to the recipient shown on the right side. The attacker (at the bottom) intercepts this transmission. Only the recipient should be able to extract the message in the correct way. Of course this is possible only if there is a shared secret between the sender and the recipient. This could be for instance the algorithm for extraction itself or special parameters of the algorithm, e.g. keys.

2   Steganography vs. Cryptography

How do steganography and cryptography compare? The purpose of both is to provide secret communication. Cryptography hides the contents of a secret message from an attacker, whereas steganography even conceals the existence of this message. Therefore the definition of breaking the system is different. In cryptography, the system is broken when the attacker can read the secret message (for the point under discussion it does not matter how he does this).

Breaking a steganographic system has two stages:

1. The attacker can detect that steganography has been used.
2. Additionally, he is able to read the embedded message.

In our definition a steganographic system is insecure already if the detection of steganography is possible (first stage).

3   Related Work

3.1   The Basic Model of a Steganographic System

The model in Fig. 2 is based on the results of the discussions at the Information Hiding Workshop in Cambridge [2], which were continued in [3, 4]. We will call this model the Embedding Model.

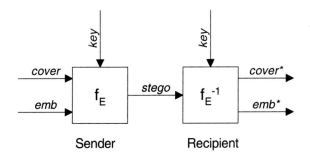

f_E:	steganographic function "embedding"
f_E^{-1}:	steganographic function "extracting"
cover:	coverdata in which *emb* will be hidden
emb:	message to be embedded
key:	parameter of f_E
stego:	coverdata with embedded message

Fig. 2. The Embedding Model

The input *cover* represents the untreated original data, *emb* the ones which will be embedded into *cover* by the function f_E. The resulting data called *stego* contain the message *emb*. The operation f_E^{-1} extracts the embedded data to *emb** and also produces an output *cover**. Naturally, *emb** should be equal to *emb* and in most cases *cover** is the same as *stego*. For concelation systems, *cover** is not of much interest anyway.

This model was not meant to be a model for evaluating the security of steganographic systems (or stegosystems for short) by the participants of the workshop. They merely tried – for a beginning – to put the ad-hoc knowledge of steganography into a more abstract form, for which purpose the figure shown serves quite well.

Therefore the above model is not of much use if you want to evaluate the security of a steganographic system. You can see the acting entities, the processing functions and their in- and output, as described in section 1. But there are no comments on the behavior of the function f_E and the knowledge and capabilities of possible attackers.

3.2   Information Theoretic Setting

In the following we will evaluate the model from section 3.1 by means of information theory. In "On the limits of steganography" [5] there is a section which addresses this approach. The authors argue with the entropy of *cover*, *emb* and *stego*, just like we will do, but don't go further into detail. They had a different goal with their paper: while we would like to present a commonly valid model for steganographic systems (and prove its validity by means of information theory), they do concentrate on the practical issues of steganography. Consequently the mentioned section is rather short and does not contain an actual proof for the (of course reasonable) statements which are made.

Another interesting approach to information theoretic evaluation of steganography can be found in [6].

4   Using Information Theory to Evaluate the Security of Steganographic Systems

Borrowing from cryptology, we introduce two forms of attacks on steganographic systems:
1. stego-only-attack: The attacker knows only *stego*.
2. stego-cover-attack: The attacker knows both *stego* and *cover*.

We will concentrate on the second attack in analogy to the known-plaintext-attack on cryptographic systems where the attacker is allowed to know every in- and output except the key and still should not be able to break the system. In addition, the first attack is a special case of the second and thus included in our further considerations.

It seems obvious that the attacker can detect differences between *cover* and *stego* if he gets to know both of them. If the differences are caused only by f_E he can break the system easily. To avoid this, the first solution is: The attacker must not know *cover*. This can be proved by means of information theory:

The embedding process can be described as the function
$$stego = f_E(cover, emb, key).$$
We assume a *cover* of m bits in which we want to "hide" n bits and the following notation:

C	the set of all bitstrings
cover	actual bitstring of length m ($cover \in C$)
E	the set of all bitstrings
emb	actual bitstring of length n ($emb \in E$)
K	the set of all keys
key	actual key ($key \in K$)
S	the set of all bitstrings ($S = C$)
stego	actual stego, i.e. bitstring that contains *emb* ($stego \in S$)

For a given alphabet X the entropy $H(X)$ describes the "uncertainty about X". That actually means the uncertainty about the occurrence of a certain element $x \in X$ [1]. The conditional entropy $H(X|Y)$ is the remaining uncertainty about X when knowing Y. The joint entropy $H(X,Y) = H(X) + H(Y|X)$ is the "union" of both entropies. The mutual information $I(X;Y)$ describes the amount of information about X you get if you know Y; $I(X;Y) = H(X) - H(X|Y)$ [7].

The attacker does
- suppose that some *emb* is hidden in *stego*,
- know the steganographic functions,
- have the knowledge and abilities to perform an attack on the stegosystem,
- have unlimited time and resources.

If in spite of all his efforts the attacker can not confirm his hypothesis that *emb* is hidden we will call the system "information theoretically secure".

4.1   Why Deterministic Steganography Can't Be Secure

The stegosystem is information theoretically secure if the attacker cannot gain any information about *emb* or E by examining *stego* and *cover* (or S and C, respectively). Thus, the mutual information is zero:

$$I(E;(S,C)) = H(E) - H(E|(S,C)) = 0. \tag{1}$$

That gives the fundamental security condition:

$$H(E|(S,C)) = H(E). \tag{2}$$

That means that the uncertainty about E – the entropy $H(E)$ – must not be decreased by the knowledge of S and C. Conclusion: E has to be **independent** from S and C.

Is it possible to meet this condition? It seems logical that – with the given assumptions – an attacker gains knowledge about a hidden *emb* just by comparing the corresponding *cover* and *stego*. We can assume that not only the alphabets S and C but also their entropies $H(S)$ and $H©$ are equal. There are differences in the conditional entropies, however:
- without embedded information: $H(S|C) = H(C|S) = 0,$
- with embedded information: $H(S|C) = H(C|S) > 0.$

The connection of uncertainty and information allows us to say: the uncertainty about S, if we know C (or vice versa) corresponds to the information about E that you can get by looking at S and C. Therefore, by embedding $emb \in E$ into $cover \in C$ we have a mutual information

$$I(E;(S,C)) = H(E) - H(E|(S,C)) > 0. \tag{3}$$

---

[1] Keep this relationship in mind when we partly look on only the alphabets in the following.

It follows:

$$H(E|(S,C)) < H(E). \tag{4}$$

This means that the security condition is not fulfilled. Therefore, the necessary and sufficient condition for secure steganography is:

$$H(S|C) = H(C|S) = 0. \tag{5}$$

This condition can be met only when

$$\forall i \in N, \, stego_i \in S, \, cover_i \in C : stego_i = cover_i.$$

Thus the steganography is reduced to a practically irrelevant special case[2]. If we exclude this case, it follows:

The security condition (2) can not be fulfilled under the given assumptions. This basically means that secure steganography is impossible when both *cover* and *stego* are known to the attacker.

4.2   Indeterminism and Steganography

An advanced solution to this problem is to have an indeterministic embedding operation. An indeterministic operation or process gives different results (within a certain range) every time it is computed. In other words, it contains randomness. Information theory supports this approach:

As stated above, it is impossible to provide information theoretically secure steganography if the attacker knows *cover* and *stego* (respectively C and S). Therefore we establish the following condition: When the attacker knows S, there remains an uncertainty about C, so that $H(C|S) > 0$. For that we introduce a new alphabet from which the actual *cover* is selected. We call this alphabet C_S or *Source*.

The effect of introducing C_S into the Embedding Model is shown in Fig. 3. We assume that f_E, C_S and S (or *stego*) are publicly known, whereas K and C (respectively *key* and *cover*) are unknown to attackers.

Since the actual cover is selected from C_S, we assume $C \subseteq C_S$. In addtion, we assume $H(C_S) \geq H\copyright$, which is both plausible for any selection and neccesary to achieve the intended indeterminism. It says that the uncertainty about the realisation of an actual *cover* from C_S must be greater than or equal to that about a realisation from C.

---

[2] This case is *cover* ≡ *stego*: You have to find a *cover* that already contains *emb*.

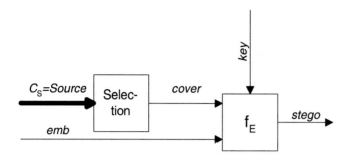

Selection: (random) selection of an actual cover from the source C_S

Fig. 3. Selection of covers from a source

The necessary uncertainty about C is then achieved by selecting every *cover* in a truly random process and keeping it secret afterwards. One example for such a process is the sampling of analog input, e.g. speech or images. The inaccuracy of the quantization provides the needed uncertainty. If the changes of *cover* during the embedding process remain within this range, the manipulations cannot be detected.

In analogy to the proof given before the fundamental security condition is:

$$H(E|(S,C_S)) = H(E), \tag{6}$$

what means that the uncertainty about E – the entropy $H(E)$ – must not be decreased by the knowledge of S and C_S, in other words: E has to be independent from S and C_S.

How can this condition be fulfilled? The attacker should not be able to detect changes in *cover* which are due to the embedding process by examining *stego*. Therefore we need a certain amount of uncertainty about *cover*, what means $H(C|S) > 0$. The necessary amount results from the relation between conditional entropy and mutual information:

$$H(C|S) \geq I(E;(S,C)) = H(E) - H(E|(S,C)). \tag{7}$$

If we assume the worst case that the attacker can determine E completely from S and C, we get:

$$H(E|(S,C)) = 0.$$

It follows that

$$H(C|S) \geq H(E). \tag{8}$$

This can be interpreted in the following way: Because the mutual information can be at most the size of $H(E)$, the necessary uncertainty about C must be at least the same size to make an attack on S impossible.

The same applies of course to attacks on C_S. Therefore we assume

$$H(C|C_S) = H(C|S) \tag{9}$$

and

$$H(C|C_S) \geq H(E). \tag{10}$$

With these conditions we need a joint entropy

$$H_O = H(C,C_S) = H© + H(C_S|C). \tag{11}$$

Because $C \subseteq C_S$ and $H(C_S) \geq H©$, it follows

$$H(C_S|C) \geq H(C|C_S).$$

When considering these relations we get a lower bound for the necessary joint entropy:

$$H_O \geq H© + H(C|C_S).$$

Using (10), we get

$$H_O \geq H© + H(E). \tag{12}$$

Since $H(C_S) \geq H©$, we assume $H(C_S,S) \geq H(C,S)$. From this follows:

$$H(C_S|S) \geq H(C|S). \tag{13}$$

According to Equation (8) it follows that the security-relevant bound

$$H(C_S|S) \geq H(E) \tag{14}$$

can be met. We may draw the following conclusion: When you observe the lower bounds for $H(C|S)$ (Equation (8)) and $H(C|C_S)$ (Equation (9)), attacks with knowledge of S and C_S (stego-source-attack) to prove the existence of E in S are not successful: The fundamental security condition (6) can be fulfilled.

Additionally we look at the conditions under which the stegosystem is secure when it is attacked via K. Therefore we require that an attacker (who knows S and C_S) can not obtain any information about (K, E)[3]. This can be expressed as follows:

$$I((K,E);(S,C_S)) = H(K,E) - H((K,E)|(S,C_S)) = 0 \tag{15}$$

$$= H(K,E) - H(K|(S,C_S)) - H(E|(S,C_S,K)) = 0.$$

When taking into account that $H(E|(S,C_S,K)) = 0$, we get:

$$H(K|(S,C_S)) = H(K,E)$$

or

$$H(K|(S,C_S)) = H(E) + H(K|E) \geq H(E), \tag{16}$$

respectively.

We can conclude from the proof above that cover must contain an uncertainty for the attacker to allow secure steganography between sender and recipient.

Furthermore the proof shows that information theoretically secure steganography is possible, if two conditions are met:

1. Knowledge of C_S and S must not decrease the uncertainty of an attacker about E and *emb* (see Equation (6)):
$$H(E|(S,C_S)) = H(E|S) = H(E).$$

---

[3] Although this requirement is actually too strong, it can be chosen for the theoretic approach, because we weaken it in the result (see Equation (14)).

To achieve this, the following constraints (compare Equations (12), (8) and (14)) apply:

$$H_O = H(C,C_S) \geq H© + H(E),$$
$$H(C|S) \geq H(E),$$
$$H(C_S|S) \geq H(E).$$

2. The conditional entropy of the key must be greater or equal to $H(E)$ to prevent an attack via K (see Equation (16)):

$$H(K|(S,C_S)) \geq H(E).$$

A third condition can be established (receiver condition): For the receiver (who knows $key \in K$) there must not be any uncertainty about $emb \in E$:

$$H(E|(S,C_S,K)) - H(E|(S,K)) = 0.$$

5   Introducing Indeterminism into the Steganographic Function

As we have seen in the previous section, the embedding has to be indeterministic to provide security against attackers who get to know the in- and output of the system.

The solution is to split the steganographic process "embedding" into an indeterministic and a deterministic part. These parts must not be distinguishable by the attacker and therefore have to take place in a trusted domain of the sender.

When, for example, the sender takes a digital image with an electronic camera, an attacker may know the scene which is depicted and the camera exactly. But the attacker – and even the sender – does not know the position of the camera and the direction it was pointed in a sufficiently exact manner (turning the camera even by a fraction of a degree results in a different image [8]). Thus, if the attacker gets hold of a digital image he is unable to decide whether the picture is an original one or has been treated by a steganographic system.

Another example is the sampling of analog data we already mentioned in section 4. When the sender takes samples of one analog waveform several times, he is extremely unlikely to get exactly the same digital data each time. This phenomenon is due to the inaccuracy of analog-digital-converters and the characteristics of quantization. If the function f_E mimics the process of sampling in a sufficiently exact manner, nobody without the key is able to decide whether a given digital sample contains steganographic data or not.

In both cases the **preprocessing** f_P (e.g. camera positioning, sampling) introduces randomness into the cover data. f_P can even be a product of multiple operations. The first of the above cases gives an example: It contains a sampling step, too.

The considerations so far lead us to a refined model of steganography which features a preprocessing f_P in addition to the embedding function f_E:

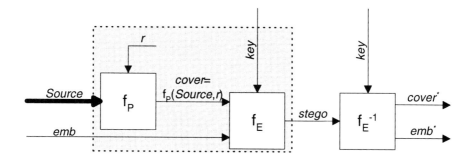

f$_P$:   preprocessing
r: random part of *cover* introduced by f$_P$ (may be parameter of f$_P$, but does not have to)

Fig. 4. Model with preprocessing

The difference to the Embedding Model shown in Fig. 2 is the enhanced view on steganography. We no longer concentrate on only the steganographic core function f$_E$ but look at the whole steganographic system. In the Embedding Model the attacker simply must not know *cover* for secure steganography. This is true for the model above as well, but with the parameter *Source* we model the uncertainty of the attacker about *cover*. This allows a more exact evaluation of steganographic systems.

The gray area in Fig. 4 marks a trusted domain which the attacker cannot intrude. You can see that he may know *Source* and *emb* and still should be unable to detect the steganography if he does not know *key*.

We would like to illustrate the concept of the trusted domain with an example: the ISDN telephony network. ISDN gives bit-transparent transport of digital data, which is crucial for secret communication with steganography. Imagine an ISDN telephone with analog-digital conversion and steganography integrated into one chip: Naturally the analog sound is *Source,* the digitized speech is *cover* and the voice-sampling is the preprocessing f$_P$. Whether the output of the integrated chip is *stego* or *cover* cannot be determined from the outside. An attacker may know *Source, emb* and even the characteristics of the sampling chip, but it does not help him to decide whether the output contains *emb* or not.

Now imagine the sampling and the steganography on different chips. If the attacker is able to eavesdrop the in- and output of the steganography chip alone, he is of course able to detect the use of steganography because he knows the actually used *cover*. Therefore, both chips have to be inside a trusted domain of the sender. In the first case the integrated chip serves as this trusted domain.

It seems obvious that the embedding function f$_E$ should be implemented according to the characteristics of the preprocessing. If, for instance, f$_P$ introduces white noise into the least significant bits of *cover* (as most analog-digital-converters do), then the embedding should spread *emb* over these bits of *cover* in a way that resembles white noise. Other processes may require completely different embedding techniques.

6   Conclusions

We can name two necessary conditions for secure steganography:
1. *Key* remains unknown to the attacker.
2. The attacker does not know the actual *cover*.

How can we guarantee this? The concealment of *key* corresponds to the one of symmetric cryptosystems. The second point is at first sight simply a condition to be met. As an alternative we can assume a set of input data named *Source*, from which the stegosystem chooses the actual *cover*. The attacker knows only *Source*. This model is well suited for the implementation of actual steganographic systems because the embedding can be tuned to f_P. The embedding exploits the randomness introduced by f_P and thus provides secure steganography. To implement a good steganographic function you naturally have to have as much knowledge about the preprocessing as possible.

References

1. B. Schneier, *Applied Cryptography*, 2nd ed. New York: John Wiley & Sons, 1996, p. 9.
2. B. Pfitzmann, "Information Hiding Terminology". In R. Anderson, *Information Hiding: first international workshop, Proceedings (Lecture notes in computer science; Vol. 1147)*, Berlin: Springer, 1996.
3. J. Zöllner, H. Federrath, A. Pfitzmann, A. Westfeld, G. Wicke, G. Wolf, "Über die Modellierung steganographischer Systeme". In G. Müller, K. Rannenberg, M. Reitenspieß, H. Stiegler, *Verläßliche IT-Systeme. Zwischen Key-Escrow und elektronischem Geld*, Friedr. Vieweg & Sohn Verlagsgesellschaft mbH, Braunschweig/Wiesbaden, 1997, pp. 211-223.
4. H. Klimant, R. Piotraschke, "Informationstheoretische Bewertung steganographischer Konzelationssysteme". In G. Müller, K. Rannenberg, M. Reitenspieß, H. Stiegler: *Verläßliche IT-Systeme. Zwischen Key-Escrow und elektronischem Geld*, Friedr. Vieweg & Sohn Verlagsgesellschaft mbH, Braunschweig/Wiesbaden, 1997, pp. 225-232.
5. R. Anderson, F. Petitcolas, "On the limits of steganography". To be published in *IEEE Journal on Selected Areas in Communications, Special Issue on copyright and privacy protection*. Available at: http://www.cl.cam.ac.uk/ftp/users/rja14/steganjsac2.ps.gz
6. C. Cachin, "An Information-Theoretic Model for Steganography". In *Information Hiding: second international workshop, Preproceedings*; 15-17 April 1998; Portland, Oregon.
7. R. G. Gallagher, *Information Theory and Reliable Communication*. John Wiley & Sons, 1968.
8. A. Westfeld, G. Wolf, "Steganography in a Video Conferencing System". In *Information Hiding: second international workshop, Preproceedings*; 15-17 April 1998; Portland, Oregon.

On Public-Key Steganography in the Presence of an Active Warden

Scott Craver

[1] Intel Corporation
Microcomputer Research Labs
2200 Mission College Blvd., Santa Clara, CA 95052-8119
[2] Department of Mathematical Sciences
Northern Illinois University
DeKalb, IL 60115

Abstract. The so-called **prisoners' problem,** in which two individuals attempt to communicate covertly without alerting a "warden" who controls the communications channel, has taken a number of forms, adorned with various assumptions or requirements which make the problem more or less difficult. One assumption which makes the problem considerably more managable is that the participants are allowed to share some secret information (such as an encryption key) prior to imprisonment. Another assumption, which makes the problem much more difficult, is that the warden be allowed to modify messages sent between the prisoners as well as read them. This paper describes techniques for *pure* steganography, in which no secret information needs to be shared before imprisonment. First, a modification of an existing protocol will be shown to admit pure steganography if the warden is not allowed to modify the contents of the channel. Then, a technique will be described that allows pure steganography between two prisoners in the presence in the presence of an *active* (content-modifying) warden.

This technique is possible through the use of two distinct channels rather than one: the subliminal channel for steganographic communication is augmented by a *supraliminal* channel, one in which information is not hidden from the warden but cannot be modified.

1 The Prisoners' Problem

The prisoners' problem was first posed by G.J. Simmons in 1983, and is generally considered to be the *de facto* model of covert communication. In this problem, two people, usually named Alice and Bob[1], are thrown in prison and intend to co-author an escape plan. The problem is that all communication between

---

[1] In the field of Cryptography, communications protocols usually involve two fictional characters named Alice and Bob. The standard convention is to name the participants in a protocol either alphabetically (Carol and Dave often succeed Alice and Bob in multi-person protocols), or with a name whose first letter matches the first letter of their role, such as Wendy the Warden, above.

David Aucsmith (Ed.): Information Hiding 1998, LNCS 1525, pp. 355–368, 1998.
© Springer-Verlag Berlin Heidelberg 1998

them is arbitrated by a warden, here named Wendy, who will place both parties in solitary confinement at the first sign of any suspicious communication. Alice and Bob must trade inconspicuous-seeming transmissions which contain hidden information that, they hope, Wendy will not notice.

Using terminology agreed upon in [6], the inconspicuous data that is used to hide the real message is usually referred to as cover-data or *cover-objects:* a letter is often called a cover-text, for instance, while an image may be called a cover-image. The hidden or *embedded* message is placed therein, turning the cover-object into a *stego-object.* Alice's and Bob's goal, then, is to trade stego-objects without Wendy realizing that they are in fact stego-objects.

Fig. 1. The prisoners' problem, illustrated

Further complications may hinder Alice's and Bob's escape. Wendy the warden may, in certain situations, be allowed to slightly modify messages as they are passed between the prisoners, to foil any hidden codes depending on the exact wording of the communication between them. In this case we call Wendy an *active* warden; without this ability she is considered a *passive* warden. One real-world example of an active warden is the censoring of telegrams by the United States government during World War II: the semantic content of telegrams could not be changed, but censors would slightly alter their exact wording, replacing words with close synonyms to foil possible secret codes [1].

It may be beneficial at this point to describe some common variations of the prisoners' problem. First, the warden's power to alter the transmissions between the prisoners affects the difficulty of the problem:

- A **passive warden** can do nothing but spy on the communications channel between the prisoners.
- An **active warden** is allowed to modify (slightly) the data being sent between the prisoners. Mild modification of text which does not alter its semantic content (say, replacing words with close synonyms) is an example of an active warden being active. The active warden must not modify data so much that innocent communication would be foiled.
- The case of a **malicious warden** is not often addressed. A malicious warden would be one who may alter the prisoners' messages with impunity, perhaps

composing entire messages for one prisoner while pretending to be the other. In this environment the prisoners can not hope to do much of anything! Fortunately, real-world situations prevent a warden from grossly altering the content of messages. Imagine the confusion if a large number of telegrams sent during World War II were altered in meaning, suppressed, or entirely fabricated by crafty censors on the lookout for spies!

As for the prisoners themselves, it should be pointed out that in the best case, they would not have to communicate prior to imprisonment, so as to (say) trade an encryption key. This best-case scenario, here called **pure steganography,** is very difficult to engineer. Current steganographic protocols generally assume that some information is shared between the prisoners prior to imprisonment. If this assumption was not allowed, little progress in information hiding could have been made to date.

The remainder of this paper is organized in the following fashion. In section 2 it will be shown how steganographers have managed to send information covertly in the presence of an active (and in some cases malicious) warden, provided that information such as secret and public keys can be traded beforehand. In section 3, we will see how a protocol, described by Ross Anderson in [1], allows steganography in the presence of a passive warden with only one prisoner knowing the other's public key. A modification of this protocol will be shown to admit *pure* steganography in the presence of a passive warden. Finally, section 4 will describe what are here called *supraliminal* channels, which allow pure steganography in the presence of an active warden. The paper will close with a discussion of the feasibility of supraliminal channels.

2   Private-Key Steganography

Let us assume that Alice and Bob are allowed to share a secret key prior to imprisonment, or even to trade public keys. This gives them the opportunity not only to communicate covertly, but to defeat an active warden. In the former case, steganography consists merely of encrypting a message in such a way that the ciphertext appears statistically random, and embedding the bits of the text in a known subliminal channel. The embedded information, of course, must be made to have the same distribution as the channel noise in order to foil statistical tests.

In the presence of an active warden, it is not enough to embed a message in a known place. If Alice can subtly alter the bits in an image, it follows that Wendy could scramble those same bits with as little impact, erasing whatever was being sent via the subliminal channel. In this case it is possible to use what is referred to in [1] as a "selection channel." Essentially, the secret information shared between Alice and Bob is used to determine *where* the message is hidden. A cryptographically secure pseudo-random generator, seeded by a secret key, can be used to pick a subset of pixels in an image, for instance, to be used to conceal the data. If Wendy attempts to make subtle changes to the image, she may only be able to scramble a small percentage of the actual channel bits, since she doesn't know exactly where they are. This scrambling can then be fixed using an error-correcting code.

The sharing of keys before imprisonment, however, is a requirement that we would ultimately like to see removed. It allows a great deal of freedom on the part of Alice and Bob – indeed, if they share public keys before imprisonment, they can even defeat a malicious warden by signing their secret messages to prevent impersonation – but it is not reassuring to think that if two people ever need to communicate covertly, they must know so far in advance that they can trade secret keys before a real-world "warden" starts listening in.

3   Public-Key Steganography

3.1   Boiling Out the Impurities

In public-key cryptography, it is not necessary for two people to share a secret key to establish a secure channel. One only needs to know the the other's public key. This suggests a possible approach to steganography in which a secret key does not have to be agreed upon by Alice and Bob prior to imprisonment. Some information must still be known *a priori* – one prisoner must know the other's public key – but from a practical perspective this is a much more reasonable requirement.

A protocol which allows public-key steganography in the presence of a passive warden is described by Ross Anderson in [1]. It relies on the fact that an encrypted message can be random enough to hide "in plain sight:"

1. Alice, knowing Bob's public key, encrypts her message with it to obtain an apparently meaningless ciphertext C.
2. Alice embeds C in a channel known to Bob (and, hence, to Wendy). The resulting stego-object is sent to Bob.
3. Bob has no idea if any message is hidden in the channel or not, but we can assume that the technique is standard enough that if he suspects a message, he will look for it. He retrieves a random-seeming string, attempts to decrypt it with his private key, and out pops Alice's message.

One problem with this approach is that Bob has no idea if anything is being sent: he may not even know Alice, and certainly does not know if she intends to use a steganographic channel. If the two traded a private key before imprisonment, at least Bob would know that some secret transmission was pending. In this case, Bob will just have to suspect that a hidden message might be present in any cover object he receives.

This is not too serious a problem, however: it is already assumed (as it usually is in cryptography) that the information-hiding technique used by Alice is known to all, and standard enough that Wendy would suspect its use. Certainly Bob can, too. As long as hidden content is suspected and can be easily extracted by a known method if it does exist, it is not unfair to assume that it will be discovered.

A more practical, related problem is that in a large group of possible recipients every single recipient must suspect hidden content in each object. Only the intended recipient will find it, of course; but in an environment such as a USENET newsgroup, where a large number of people may send stego-objects, each of which may be targeted toward an unspecified recipient, all the parties involved may spend the better part of each day looking inside every object. This is related to the previous problem, since it is the result of the message sender not being able to give the intended recipient any warning that a message is being sent.

3.2   Pure Steganography Using the Anderson Protocol

The assumption made above is not to be taken lightly, for it suggests that the protocol described in [1] is actually more powerful than may initially be suspected. If we can assume that Bob will attempt to decode what might or might not be a hidden message, then we can also assume (at least in the two-prisoner case) that Bob may attempt to participate in what might or might not be an ongoing steganography protocol. For example, suppose that Alice and Bob are astronomers residing on separate planets, each searching for signs of intelligent life in the universe. Bob receives from Alice's planet what might be a message, or what might be noise. He may decide to treat the signal as if it were a message, send one back in the same "language," and wait for a second signal to confirm his suspicion.

In the context of steganography, the situation is complicated by the fact that the signals being traded must be meaningless to everyone but Alice and Bob. We can imagine that if the search for extra-terrestrial Alice ends up beaming a meaningful signal to the nearby warlike Wendy, Bob may give away that his planet is inhabitable and ripe for colonization. On the other hand, the situation is made less complicated by the cryptologic assumption that whatever data-hiding or encryption algorithm is used is known to all.

In any case, the possibility that Bob may participate in a protocol on suspicion of a steganographic message suggests a method by which Alice may send Bob her public key while they are both imprisoned, *entirely eliminating the need for prior communication*. A passive warden is still required for this to happen, but this too can be relaxed, as will be demonstrated in the next section.

Protocol 1 *A modification of the protocol described in [1]*

This is essentially Anderson's protocol with an extra step at the beginning. It is assumed that a method of information-hiding is known to all, as well as a public-key encryption algorithm. Wendy is assumed to be passive.

1. Alice generates a random public key/private key pair.If she is using RSA, for instance, she could generate the large prime numbers used for the key by

picking cryptographically pseudo-random strings and testing for primality until one is found. She then selects another pseudo-random string for the public key. This is usually the way RSA keys are created.

2. Alice embeds the key in the subliminal channel, viewable by both Bob and Wendy, and sends the resultant stego-object to Bob. Neither Bob nor Wendy can determine if the channel contains noise or a key. If Wendy can only snoop, then Bob can attempt to communicate:

3. Bob suspects that the data in question is a public key, uses it to encrypt a short note of acknowledgement with a randomly chosen secret key for future covert transmissions, and sends this back to Alice embedded in a stego-object.

4. Alice suspects that the returned data is an encrypted key, decrypts it with her private key, and out pops a message from Bob. Now the two can communicate by an appropriate secret-key protocol.

At no point in the protocol does Wendy have any idea that the randomness means anything: Alice alone can deduce content from Bob's reply. As long as she is not allowed to insert her own information (and thus either foil the transmission or maliciously insert her own key to catch the two in the act), she can not conclude that communication has taken place.   □

If Wendy is capable of writing to the channel, then there is no way communication can take place: if Wendy does not utterly destroy the "in plain sight" bits, she can attempt a man-in-the-middle attack by overwriting Alice's key with her own. A more malicious warden could entirely spoof either Alice's or Bob's response. In that case, however, the original protocol would not work either, since in neither case would Bob have any way of identifying the author of the original message.

4   Public-Key Steganography in the Presence of an Active Warden

4.1   Cover-Plots and Supraliminal Channels

If we assume that the Warden can only make minor modifications to the possible stego-objects sent between Alice and Bob, then we can assume that there is some amount of *perceptually significant* information that the warden cannot change whatsoever. For instance, if Alice sends Bob a picture of a cow and Wendy can only modify 1 bit in every 100, we can assume that Wendy will not be able to turn the cow into a pig. In a novel, there could be explicit states of affairs or descriptions of characters so relevant to the plot that no information about those states can be changed without a significant rewrite of a number of portions of the book. If we develop some formal encoding of object and state-of-affairs descriptions, we have the makings for a channel through which Alice can send a small amount of information to Bob out in the open, but with high integrity. What we are describing here is a *supraliminal* channel rather than a *subliminal* one: information is hidden in plain sight, so obviously, in fact, that it is impossible to modify without gross modifications to the transmitted object.

Formally, we can define a *cover-plot* function $f : \mathbb{S} \to \{0,1\}^N$, where $\mathbb{S}$ is a set of possible encodings of state-of-affairs descriptions, or "cover-plots" – so called because they can be considered the plot, or content, of a cover-object. A cover-plot S is simply a formal description of content appropriate to the medium of the cover-object. Such a description could be used by an author or content-creator to compose a covertext C containing an *embedding* of S, and hence an embedding of the bit-string $f(S)$. The cover-plot function would have the following properties:

- The function would be known to both Bob and Alice (and hence we must assume that it is also known to Wendy).
- A member of the inverse image under f of any particular bitstring is feasible to compute, as is f itself.
- f is onto. It is not necessary for f to be one-to-one – indeed, if f is many-to-one Alice's job will be significantly easier, since she will have more freedom in choosing a cover-object which embeds a particular bit-string.
- A cover-object C can be created to contain a state-of-affairs description S such that an active warden cannot significantly change the encoding of S (that is, she cannot change S to S' such that $f(S) \neq f(S')$) without making unreasonable, wide-sweeping changes to the entire cover-object.
- A human being (or, ideally, a computer program) can deduce the exact state-of-affairs description embedded within a cover-object. The composer of the covertext can facilitate this deduction by making the embedding very clear, but this should not be so necessary that an object with an easy-to-interpret embedding is conspicuous.
- Clarifying the last property, an innocent cover-object without an explicitly embedded state-of-affairs description S can yet be interpreted as having one. That is, innocent cover-objects should have clearly deducible cover-plot descriptions (which map under f to random garbage) so that the presence of a clearly deducible cover-plot description is not indicative of a hidden message, unless the bit string $f(S)$ possesses some meaning.

This can be summarized as a channel that is **robust, blatant** and **inconspicuous.** Here, a **robust** channel is one whose content cannot be altered without making unreasonably drastic changes to the stego-object (i.e., requiring a malicious, instead of an active, warden). A **blatant** channel is one whose content is publicly accessible, a necessity if Alice is to send Bob information when no key is shared between them prior to transmission. For a channel to be **inconspicuous** as well as blatant may sound like a contradiction, but it is not: an inconspicuous channel is one whose existence alone is not indicative of a hidden message. A perfectly innocent image, containing no covert information, will seem to the warden to contain random cover-plot bits. If Alice sends Bob a cover-object with an obvious message in this supraliminal channel ("Bob: here is the secret plan to break of out of jail. Love, Alice") then Wendy can throw the two into solitary confinement. However, if Alice sends Bob apparently random cover-plot bits, perhaps a random session key to be used later, Wendy cannot conclude that the message is anything other than innocent, since innocent messages also contain random cover-plot bits. Only when that key is later used can Wendy know that covert communication is taking place.

One cannot help but notice the connection to digital watermarking, a form of information hiding in which the hidden data is required to be robust to significant modification of an image. In particular, a recent approach to watermarking, advocated by Ingemar Cox, *et al* in [3], has resulted in robust watermarking schemes using what largely resembles a subliminal channel with supraliminal aspirations. Cox, *ct al* emphasize the importance of hiding a watermark in *perceptually significant* components of an image, such as high-magnitude DCT matrix coefficients, so that an ownership label can survive a significant amount of abuse by a forger. Further, the watermark can still be made invisible, as the technique presented in [3] demonstrates. One may wonder if a similar scheme would allow the embedding of a supraliminal channel invisibly in an existing image, so that Alice and Bob need not compose a new image for each message for the explicit purpose of embedding a particular string of cover-plot bits.

Unfortunately, conceptual differences between robust watermarking and embedding bits in a supraliminal channel prevent the application of one to the other. In the former case, some sort of secret key is often used to embed a watermark, so that only those who know the key can detect or remove the watermark. A cover-plot, on the other hand, must be readable by all but removable by none. Also, the purpose of a supraliminal channel (and, indeed, steganography in general) is to hide a specific message of some meaning to the recipient; In the case of invisible watermarking, the embedded labels need not have any semantic content at all, or may be a function of the image. The scheme described in [3], for instance, embeds a vector of pseudo-random numbers picked from a normal distribution. In [4], it is discovered that in order for this scheme to become secure it may be necessary for the vector to be a function of a one-way hash of the image itself. In short, we have a difference of priorities: in watermarking, an ownership label can be meaningless, or picked to fit the cover-object, while the cover-object's content is given beforehand and is important. In steganography, the image can be meaningless, or picked to fit the embedded message, while the hidden message's content is given beforehand and is important.

Finally, if it was possible to embed a supraliminal channel in an existing image (for example) without significantly altering it, it would be equally possible for a warden to scramble the channel without significantly altering the image, since everybody knows where the information is and how to bury cover-plot bits inside. Hence the content of the cover-object should itself be a function of the information embedded within it. It may be hasty to declare it impossible for a supraliminal channel to be subliminal, but the two concepts seem to have irreconcilable differences.

Example 1. A rudimentary supraliminal channel for audio/video clips

In this example, the cover-object may be an audio-video clip in which people are speaking. The noise within the clip could be used to embed a subliminal channel. The set $\mathbb{S}$ of cover-plots is the set of all texts which can be spoken by Alice and unambiguously understood by Bob. The cover-plot function $f : \mathbb{S} \to \mathbb{N}$ is computed by hashing the text of each sufficiently long word, assigning each a numeric value.

For instance, suppose that each letter of the alphabet is assigned some agreed-upon numeric value. When an audio clip is received by Bob, he types into his computer all words of (say) at least six letters. For each word the computer calculates the product of the letters' numeric values, modulo some small prime p. These values can then be arranged left-to-right and treated as the base-p representation of an integer[2].

Alice must be able to compose a convincing body of text which hashes to a desired array of values. She has some flexibility in that smaller words can be used with impunity to generate a context for the larger words. She can then use a dictionary (or, more likely, a thesaurus) which can be searched by cover-plot values. Notice that the larger the number of values to which a word can hash (the larger the value of p in the above example), the harder Alice's job will be, and the more conspicuous a cover-plot might be given a small amount of time to create one. On the other hand, if the number of possible hash values is made small, the ease in composition on Alice's part is offset by a lower bandwidth.

Once this composition step is complete, Alice turns on a video camera and records herself (or other people) reciting the body of text she composed.

This channel is *blatant,* as long as the technique is made publicly available and the letters' numeric values are a known standard. The channel is *inconspicuous,* since every text document, innocent or not, has a cover-plot. Finally, the channel is *robust* unless Wendy is capable of seamlessly altering both the sound of Alice's voice and her lip movements so as to change the text of her speech. While this is possible with today's technology, there exist real-world domains where Wendy does not possess the time to do this (say, where she has to monitor hundreds of such transmissions per day or per hour), or where the cost in time and computation is too high to justify the altering of video clips on the mere suspicion that their text may have some future steganographic significance. Alternatively, she could completely re-record the message herself, hoping that Bob does not know what Alice looks or sounds like, but this would likely classify her as a malicious warden.   □

A formalized method for describing the plot, characters, etc. of a letter or book, or a describing the overall content of an image may also serve as good cover-plot functions; one could use details so central to a cover-object's content that to change them would require significant changes throughout the object. Perceptually significant components of certain transforms of the cover-object may also do the trick, provided one can feasibly compose a cover-object when given

---

[2] It would be necessary to keep in mind the frequency of letters and letter groups in the language used when deciding upon their numeric values (not to mention choosing values that are not multiples of p), so as to prevent patterns from showing up in the resulting array of hash values.

particular transform components that it must contain. This could make Alice's job much more difficult, but Bob's would be so simple that it could be completely automated. If a robust supraliminal channel can be entirely automated, requiring no (or negligible) human intervention in composing or interpreting a work, it could be quite a significant contribution to the field of steganography.

4.2   Public-Key Steganography with a Supraliminal Channel

Of course, a supraliminal channel is not appropriate for *subliminal* communication between Alice and Bob, for a number of reasons. First, the bandwidth will likely be very small, since the channel is engineered to be highly robust. The number of deducible states-of-affairs may be larger for a novel than for an image or video clip, but in either case it is unlikely that a single object could hold a reasonably sized message. A robust channel of this kind is more appropriate for transmission of a session key, as it will be used below.

Secondly, it is expected that Wendy also knows how to compute f, so any information passed through the channel is available to her. Unless the cover-plot bits have no apparent meaning, Alice and Bob are in serious trouble (or at least more serious than what previously got them thrown in prison).

With public-key cryptography, however, such a channel could be used to defeat an active warden. Usually it is assumed that Alice and Bob share a secret key. With a supraliminal channel, however, *a secret key can be exchanged covertly with no prior information,* right in front of an active warden. The protocol is described below and in figures 2 and 3.

Protocol 2 *Key exchange in the presence of an active warden*

In this protocol, Alice and Bob have no information prior to imprisonment. It is assumed that a public-domain cover-plot algorithm (as well as this protocol) is known to all, including Wendy. Alice and Bob perform the following steps:

1. Alice generates a random public key E and a private key D.
2. Alice then finds a cover-plot $S \in f^{-1}[E]$ within the inverse image of E.
3. Alice composes a cover-object C_1 containing an embedding of the cover-plot S, and sends this to Bob. At this point, Wendy can inspect the channel, and will find a random-looking string of cover-plot bits. There is no reason to expect anything unless the data is later used in some way, say as a session key. The cover-plot bits pass unmolested through the channel to Bob.
4. Bob extracts the cover-plot bits, suspecting that they represent a public key. He creates a pseudo-random secret key r, which he will later use to embed information in a subliminal channel, and encrypts it with the purported public key E to get a pseudo-random string $s = E(r, K_{\text{Alice}})^3$. He then finds a cover-plot $T \in f^{-1}[s]$, and creates a cover-object C_2 containing an embedding of T.

---

[3] He may also wish to append to r a note of acknowledgement before encrypting, so that Alice will know that the protocol is working.

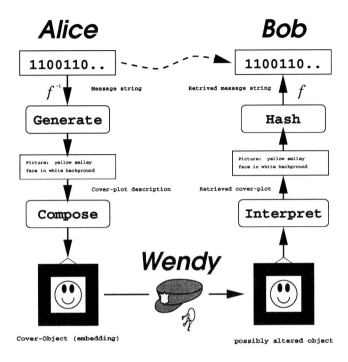

Fig. 2. How a cover-plot function is used to establish a supralminal channel.

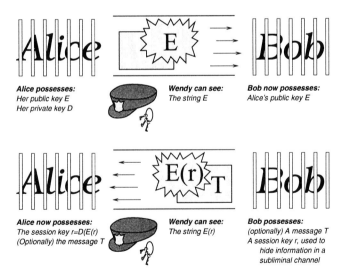

Fig. 3. Protocol using supraliminal and subliminal channels. Beneath each character is listed the information he or she knows once the illustrated step has taken place.

5. Bob now uses his secret key r to securely embed a message in the *subliminal* channel of the image, using an existing secret-key-based technique which the active warden cannot defeat. If the medium used to implement the supraliminal channel is not rich enough to support a subliminal channel, Alice and Bob can always postpone this step and embed their secret messages in the subliminal channels of subsequent cover-objects.

6. Bob sends C_2 to Alice. Now, Wendy can again snoop the channel, and now has (what she might suspect is) both E and $E(r)$. Even if she does suspect this, there is no indication that the strings are related in this way, and no way she can determine the value of r, and thus no way she can determine the existence of any subliminal message. Further, both strings are random-seeming enough that there is no indication that any covert communication is occurring. She sends the message through the channel to Alice.

7. Alice decrypts what she assumes to be $E(r)$ to get $r = D(E(r))$, and, optionally, snoops the subliminal channel using the secret key r to find a message.

8. Alice and Bob now communicate with impunity using a secure secret-key based scheme, with the random key r that they now both share. Wendy has no reason to suspect that a key exchange has occurred.

Statistical tests on the cover-plot bits may yield some deviation from what would be expected in an innocent object. However, the strings Alice and Bob share are already the product of cryptographically secure pseudo-random generators, and if the cover-plot bits of a certain medium typically fall into a non-uniform distribution, the bits can always be encoded in a manner that matches this distribution. Further, the strings transmitted via this channel are very short, and only two transmissions are needed to share a key. This may make statistical tests difficult.   □

5   Are Supraliminal Channels "Fair?"

There are a number of possible objections that may be made to the protocols presented here. First, just how fair is it to assume that the warden is not malicious? Why *not* impersonate Alice or Bob, or grossly modify their work for the purpose of foiling the possible covert communication? After all, Bob has no idea what cover-object to expect from Alice. He would not necessarily know if Wendy completely changed the transmitted object to something else.

The reason why Wendy can not be malicious in real-world situations is quite clear, but is sometimes forgotten when we focus entirely on the situation of two prisoners whose very names indicate that they intend to communicate covertly. A real-world warden, be she a postal censor or a system administrator, may deal with communications between a large number of people. At best she can suspect that trading of secret information is taking place, and may not be sure where or between whom. To significantly alter the meaning of large number of e-mail documents or telegrams is simply unacceptable behavior. Even if the recipients of those documents have no idea what content to expect, all subsequent communication would either give away the ruse or need to be intercepted and modified as well. David Kahn in [5] describes the concept of a "semagram," a secret communication not in written form:

> For example, during World War 2, censors intercepted a shipment of watches. Fearing that the position of the hands of the watches could be spelling out a secret message, they changed the position of the hands.

If no secret message existed in those watch-hands, the recipient would likely not care about the modification. On the other hand, if the recipient ultimately recieved a shipment of radial tires instead of watches, he or she would have legitimate reason to complain, as would everyone else who received a package subjected to a similar censoring methodology. Even if the recipient had no idea what content to expect, the resulting "thank you" note would be confusing indeed. Unless the United States could intercept all future transmissions from the recipient which allude to the shipment's content, the censorship will ultimately be discovered. In any case, such wide-scale modification of potentially innocent content is unreasonable. As Einstein may have put it, "Raffiniert ist der Gefängniswärter, aber boshaft ist er nicht."[4]

The big question-marks, however, regard the very feasibility of the supraliminal channel: can it be done efficiently? Further, is it fair to allow the cover-object to be a function of the information being sent? It is often assumed that the cover-object is given, and any message could be inserted therein. But the cover-object is assumed to be meaningless to Alice and Bob anyway, a mere front for the *real* message[5]; we might as well use the opportunity to hide actual content.

Efficiency is the real problem, in this author's opinion. Cover-plot functions mapping plot descriptions of stories or other high-level content would probably require a human being to perform both the composition and interpretation steps, and quite possibly the generation step as well (Fig. 2) One could develop a scheme which makes the interpretation step easy enough for a computer to manage, but in order to automate the entire process it may not help to turn a cryptographic problem into an artificial intelligence problem. If a supraliminal channel could be based on perceptually significant information that a computer is suited to both interpret and convincingly compose, this hurdle would seem much less daunting.

6   Conclusion

The prisoners' problem exists in many variations, often assuming that the prisoners share some information prior to imprisonment. *Pure* steganography, without any *a priori* secret knowledge between the communicating parties, is very difficult, but not necessarily impossible: a public-key steganography protocol has

---

[4] "Subtle is the warden but not malicious."

[5] One can imagine a sneaky warden successfully catching Bob by watching him pore over a 6 page cover-text for 2 hours and then quizzing him on its content.

been described in [1] which requires only that one party's public key be known to the other. Furthermore, certain assumptions allow this protocol to be modified so as to allow pure steganography in the presence of a passive warden. Finally, if a *supraliminal* channel as described in this paper can be feasibly implemented, secret key exchange and hence pure steganography can take place in the presence of an active warden.

References

[1] R.J. Anderson. Stretching the limits of steganography. In *Information Hiding*, volume Springer Lecture Notes in Computer Science v 1174, pages 39–48, May 1996.

[2] Ross J. Anderson, editor. *Information hiding: first international workshop*, volume 1174 of *Lecture Notes in Computer Science*, Isaac Newton Institute, Cambridge, UK, May 1996. Springer-Verlag, Berlin, Germany.

[3] I.J. Cox, J. Kilian, T. Leighton, and T. Shamoon. Secure spread spectrum watermarking for multimedia. Technical Report Technical Report 95-10, NEC Research Institute, 1995.

[4] S. Craver, N. Memon, B.L. Yeo, and M.M. Yeung. On the invertibility of invisible watermarking techniques. submitted to International Conference on Image Processing 1997, 1997.

[5] David Kahn. The history of steganography. In Anderson [2], pages 1–5.

[6] Birgit Pfitzmann. Information hiding terminology. In Anderson [2], pages 347–350.

Author Index

Springer
and the
environment

At Springer we firmly believe that an international science publisher has a special obligation to the environment, and our corporate policies consistently reflect this conviction.

We also expect our business partners – paper mills, printers, packaging manufacturers, etc. – to commit themselves to using materials and production processes that do not harm the environment. The paper in this book is made from low- or no-chlorine pulp and is acid free, in conformance with international standards for paper permanency.

Springer

Lecture Notes in Computer Science

For information about Vols. 1–1454
please contact your bookseller or Springer-Verlag

Vol. 1490: C. Palamidessi, H. Glaser, K. Meinke (Eds.), Principles of Declarative Programming. Proceedings, 1998. XI, 497 pages. 1998.

Vol. 1491: W. Reisig, G. Rozenberg (Eds.), Lectures on Petri Nets I: Basic Models. XII, 683 pages. 1998.

Vol. 1492: W. Reisig, G. Rozenberg (Eds.), Lectures on Petri Nets II: Applications. XII, 479 pages. 1998.

Vol. 1493: J.P. Bowen, A. Fett, M.G. Hinchey (Eds.), ZUM '98: The Z Formal Specification Notation. Proceedings, 1998. XV, 417 pages. 1998.

Vol. 1494: G. Rozenberg, F. Vaandrager (Eds.), Lectures on Embedded Systems. Proceedings, 1996. VIII, 423 pages. 1998.

Vol. 1495: T. Andreasen, H. Christiansen, H.L. Larsen (Eds.), Flexible Query Answering Systems. IX, 393 pages. 1998. (Subseries LNAI).

Vol. 1496: W.M. Wells, A. Colchester, S. Delp (Eds.), Medical Image Computing and Computer-Assisted Intervention – MICCAI'98. Proceedings, 1998. XXII, 1256 pages. 1998.

Vol. 1497: V. Alexandrov, J. Dongarra (Eds.), Recent Advances in Parallel Virtual Machine and Message Passing Interface. Proceedings, 1998. XII, 412 pages. 1998.

Vol. 1498: A.E. Eiben, T. Bäck, M. Schoenauer, H.-P. Schwefel (Eds.), Parallel Problem Solving from Nature – PPSN V. Proceedings, 1998. XXIII, 1041 pages. 1998.

Vol. 1499: S. Kutten (Ed.), Distributed Computing. Proceedings, 1998. XII, 419 pages. 1998.

Vol. 1501: M.M. Richter, C.H. Smith, R. Wiehagen, T. Zeugmann (Eds.), Algorithmic Learning Theory. Proceedings, 1998. XI, 439 pages. 1998. (Subseries LNAI).

Vol. 1502: G. Antoniou, J. Slaney (Eds.), Advanced Topics in Artificial Intelligence. Proceedings, 1998. XI, 333 pages. 1998. (Subseries LNAI).

Vol. 1503: G. Levi (Ed.), Static Analysis. Proceedings, 1998. IX, 383 pages. 1998.

Vol. 1504: O. Herzog, A. Günter (Eds.), KI-98: Advances in Artificial Intelligence. Proceedings, 1998. XI, 355 pages. 1998. (Subseries LNAI).

Vol. 1505: D. Caromel, R.R. Oldehoeft, M. Tholburn (Eds.), Computing in Object-Oriented Parallel Environments. Proceedings, 1998. XI, 243 pages. 1998.

Vol. 1506: R. Koch, L. Van Gool (Eds.), 3D Structure from Multiple Images of Large-Scale Environments. Proceedings, 1998. VIII, 347 pages. 1998.

Vol. 1507: T.W. Ling, S. Ram, M.L. Lee (Eds.), Conceptual Modeling – ER '98. Proceedings, 1998. XVI, 482 pages. 1998.

Vol. 1508: S. Jajodia, M.T. Özsu, A. Dogac (Eds.), Advances in Multimedia Information Systems. Proceedings, 1998. VIII, 207 pages. 1998.

Vol. 1510: J.M. Zytkow, M. Quafafou (Eds.), Principles of Data Mining and Knowledge Discovery. Proceedings, 1998. XI, 482 pages. 1998. (Subseries LNAI).

Vol. 1511: D. O'Hallaron (Ed.), Languages, Compilers, and Run-Time Systems for Scalable Computers. Proceedings, 1998. IX, 412 pages. 1998.

Vol. 1512: E. Giménez, C. Paulin-Mohring (Eds.), Types for Proofs and Programs. Proceedings, 1996. VIII, 373 pages. 1998.

Vol. 1513: C. Nikolaou, C. Stephanidis (Eds.), Research and Advanced Technology for Digital Libraries. Proceedings, 1998. XV, 912 pages. 1998.

Vol. 1514: K. Ohta, D. Pei (Eds.), Advances in Cryptology – ASIACRYPT'98. Proceedings, 1998. XII, 436 pages. 1998.

Vol. 1515: F. Moreira de Oliveira (Ed.), Advances in Artificial Intelligence. Proceedings, 1998. X, 259 pages. 1998. (Subseries LNAI).

Vol. 1516: W. Ehrenberger (Ed.), Computer Safety, Reliability and Security. Proceedings, 1998. XVI, 392 pages. 1998.

Vol. 1517: J. Hromkovič, O. Sýkora (Eds.), Graph-Theoretic Concepts in Computer Science. Proceedings, 1998. X, 385 pages. 1998.

Vol. 1518: M. Luby, J. Rolim, M. Serna (Eds.), Randomization and Approximation Techniques in Computer Science. Proceedings, 1998. IX, 385 pages. 1998.

Vol. 1520: M. Maher, J.-F. Puget (Eds.), Principles and Practice of Constraint Programming - CP98. Proceedings, 1998. XI, 482 pages. 1998.

Vol. 1521: B. Rovan (Ed.), SOFSEM'98: Theory and Practice of Informatics. Proceedings, 1998. XI, 453 pages. 1998.

Vol. 1522: G. Gopalakrishnan, P. Windley (Eds.), Formal Methods in Computer-Aided Design. Proceedings, 1998. IX, 529 pages. 1998.

Vol. 1524: G.B. Orr, K.-R. Müller (Eds.), Neural Networks: Tricks of the Trade. VI, 432 pages. 1998.

Vol. 1525: D. Aucsmith (Ed.), Information Hiding. Proceedings, 1998. IX, 369 pages. 1998.

Vol. 1526: M. Broy, B. Rumpe (Eds.), Requirements Targeting Software and Systems Engineering. Proceedings, 1997. VIII, 357 pages. 1998.

Vol. 1529: D. Farwell, L. Gerber, E. Hovy (Eds.), Machine Translation and the Information Soup. Proceedings, 1998. XIX, 532 pages. 1998. (Subseries LNAI).

Vol. 1530: V. Arvind, R. Ramanujam (Eds.), Foundations of Software Technology and Theoretical Computer Science. XII, 369 pages. 1998.

Vol. 1531: H.-Y. Lee, H. Motoda (Eds.), PRICAI'98: Topics in Artificial Intelligence. XIX, 646 pages. 1998. (Subseries LNAI).

Vol. 1096: T. Schael, Workflow Management Systems for Process Organisations. Second Edition. XII, 229 pages. 1998.

Vol. 1532: S. Arikawa, H. Motoda (Eds.), Discovery Science. Proceedings, 1998. XI, 456 pages. 1998. (Subseries LNAI).

Vol. 1533: K.-Y. Chwa, O.H. Ibarra (Eds.), Algorithms and Computation. Proceedings, 1998. XIII, 478 pages. 1998.

Vol. 1538: J. Hsiang, A. Ohori (Eds.), Advances in Computing Science – ASIAN'98. Proceedings, 1998. X, 305 pages. 1998.